COMPARATIVE POETICS

POÉTIQUE COMPARATIVE

VERGLEICHENDE POETIK

in honour of Jan Kamerbeek Jr.

edited by

D.W. Fokkema, Elrud Kunne-Ibsch
and A.J.A. van Zoest

© Editions Rodopi N.V., Amsterdam
Printed in The Netherlands
ISBN: 90-6203-279-6

Table des matières — Contents — Inhalt

* * *

JAN KAMERBEEK JR

Les études de Jan Kamerbeek Jr, on le sait, sont très appréciées des amateurs de musique et de poésie. Manifestement, la façon dont il fait de la littérature l'objet de ses analyses et de sa réflexion leur inspire un sentiment d'affinité et leur donne confiance dans ses occupations scientifiques avec la poésie et avec les poètes.

Souvent, quand il y a entre le théoricien et les amateurs de l'art une relation de cette nature, elle trouve son origine dans les qualités stylistiques de ses écrits. Le style peut, en effet, constituer un des mérites prépondérants des écrits théoriques, et il est juste qu'on l'admire. De plus, les beautés stylistiques garantissent, pour ainsi dire, au lecteur que l'auteur associe à sa recherche scientifique l'amour de l'art. Le pouvoir persuasif du style est légitime.

Cependant, le sentiment d'affinité que l'amateur de poésie et de musique éprouve en lisant les études de Kamerbeek n'est pas dû qu'à des qualités stylistiques. Certes, le lecteur en appréciera le style, mais il se rendra compte aussi que la méthode scientifique, en ce cas précis, empêche l'usage d'un style qui est raffiné d'un bout à l'autre. C'est qu'elle demande des citations, nombreuses et parfois longues. Dans la recherche théorique de la littérature, la citation n'a pas avant tout (comme c'est le cas dans l'oeuvre littéraire) une fonction de structuration; elle y est surtout d'ordre compositoire et démonstratif et s'y intègre, de façon prononcée, comme un argument ou comme une contre-épreuve. Du point de vue du style, la citation est une interruption frappante.

Si Kamerbeek réussit à captiver ses lecteurs, il y a donc plus que le style, il y a autre chose. Cet "autre chose" est, à mon opinion, le corollaire de quelques caractéristiques essentielles de son approche scientifique de la littérature. Voilà pourquoi j'ai voulu, dans mon introduction, partir des rapports que le lecteur qui aime la poésie et la musique entretient avec les écrits de Jan Kamerbeek Jr.

La circonspection avec laquelle le chercheur scientifique a l'habitude de formuler ses conclusions est très développée chez Kamerbeek. Lui aussi, comme tout chercheur, il sait que la vérité peut, en fin de compte, être différente de celle qu'il propose et qu'il est même probable qu'elle le sera, à l'avenir. "Je voudrais donc supposer", "ik zou willen veronderstellen", "was ich nun behaupten möchte", "het lijkt me onloochenbaar", "il me semble", "nu meen ik", "het lijkt me niet toevallig", "on peut", "man darf vermuten", "lässt sich sagen", "je veux tenter", "het is misschien niet toevallig", "men zou hier kunnen denken", "vielleicht", et cetera, voilà des tournures et expressions que, dans ses conclusions, Kamerbeek utilise abondamment. Cependant, il n'y a pas là que des réserves inspirées par la conviction qu'en science, comme ailleurs, une vérité n'est jamais définitive.

La possibilité d'être obligé de corriger ses conclusions est, d'une part, impliquée par la situation objective dans laquelle il fait son travail. D'autre part, son approche subjective de la littérature comporte un élément apparemment similaire mais qui est pourtant fondamentalement différent. Kamerbeek étudie les textes littéraires et scientifiques dont il fait l'objet de ses analyses avec une circonspection scrupuleuse non pas parce qu'il leur accorde, *a priori,* un statut d'objets privilégiés ou sacrosaints, mais parce qu'il est conscient de ce qu'ils peuvent contenir plus que le chercheur ne se croit en état de percevoir. D'une oreille attentive, Kamerbeek les ausculte et, grâce à une sensibilité longuement exercée, il y relève des particularités stylistiques, grammaticales, phonétiques et prosodiques subtiles, à peine perceptibles. Il *entend,* pour ainsi dire, les analogies et parallélismes sémantiques et syntaxiques, les similitudes et divergences d'intonation et de tonalité existant entre des textes différents. Et il n'ignore pas qu'il est possible d'entendre encore plus qu'il n'aperçoit en ce moment.

Cette approche de la littérature n'exclut pas la certitude concernant les résultats de la recherche. Ce que le texte lui permet d'entendre, de sentir et de ressentir trouve son appui et sa vérification dans ses connaissances étendues de la culture littéraire européenne. Kamerbeek n'est pas partisan d'une théorie de l'empathie. C'est avant tout son érudition qui lui offre la possibilité de s'assimiler les oeuvres et de les étudier. C'est elle qui nourrit sa faculté de faire des rapprochements intuitifs, d'établir des rapports inattendus; c'est elle qui dirige son dépistage des sources et qui arrange les données que lui propose l'expérience personnelle.

Si cette attitude envers la littérature préside à la méthodologie qu'adopte Kamerbeek dans ses recherches, elle détermine également l'optique par laquelle il présente ses sujets. Lorsqu'on célébrait à Groningue (1972) le centenaire de Johan Huizinga, Kamerbeek — qui, en 1929/1930, avait suivi à Bonn les cours de Curtius — prononçait une conférence intitulée "Johan Huizinga und Ernst Robert Curtius, Versuch einer vergleichenden Charakteristik". Parlant du travail philologique de Curtius, il signala "die gleiche Polarität von Makro- und Mikroskopie, die für Curtius' Arbeitsweise in zunehmenden Masse kennzeichnend war". Et il donna de l'auteur de *Europäische Literatur und Lateinisches Mittelalter* la citation suivante: "Eine Technik philologischen Mikroskopierens erlaubte uns, in Texten verschiedenster Herkunft Elemente von identischer Struktur aufzudecken, die wir als Ausdruckskonstanten der europäischen Literatur auffassen durften".

Ces paroles s'appliquent, toutes proportions gardées, parfaitement à la technique des recherches littéraires de Kamerbeek. C'est sa contribution à la théorie de la littérature que de découvrir, en repérant des éléments sémantiques identiques dans les textes de provenance différente, certaines traditions de la pensée dans la culture littéraire européenne — il l'a fait, par exemple, dans "Over het begrip "literaire generatie" " (1940), "Dilthey versus Nietzsche" (1950), "Legatum Velleianum" (1954), "Allard Pierson (1831-1896) en Wilhelm Dilthey (1833-1911)" (1957). C'est sa contribution aussi que de trouver, de la même manière, des notions-clés de mouvements littéraires internationaux — il l'a fait, par rapport au symbolisme littéraire et au néo-classicisme (en ce qui concerne ce dernier mouvement dans sa thèse *Albert Verwey en het nieuwe classicisme* (1966). Dans toutes ces études, la microscopie s'associe étroitement à la philologie macroscopique. Par l'observation scrupuleuse des plus petits éléments dans les textes qu'il sait rapprocher les uns des autres grâce à la coopération pertinente de son érudition avisée et des activités de sa sensibilité, les grandes lignes diachroniques et synchroniques se dessinent. Dans cette recherche sur les idées qui ont imprégné la culture littéraire et sur les mouvements littéraires, Kamerbeek attache une importance spéciale à ce qu'il appelle "l'intertextualité créatrice" et "l'émulation créatrice". Il est profondément convaincu que les textes ont une fonction créatrice, que leur production se fait en fonction d'une motivation par l'émulation agissant à l'intérieur des possibilités spécifiques de l'auteur. La tradition doit son existence à l'individu créateur utilisant le matériau traditionnel. S'appuyant

4

sur sa sensibilité développée et son sens aiguisé pour les éléments linguistiques qui, dans la relation intertextuelle, jouent un rôle dans la tradition, Kamerbeek a fait de cette efficacité du poète et de l'écrivain l'objet de ses études.

Ces éléments linguistiques peuvent être de nature générale ou de nature particulière; c'est dire qu'ils peuvent être opérants selon la tradition ou non. Kamerbeek a fait, et avec succès, de la sémantique historique, se concentrant sur des *loci,* des mots-clés, et sur des mots d'ordre littéraires spécifiques pour certains mouvements littéraires. Cette activité fait partie intégrante de presque toutes ses recherches, mais il l'a déployée également au sujet de concepts isolés, témoin " "La Dignité Humaine", esquisse d'une terminographie" (1957), "Tenants et aboutissants de la notion "couleur locale" " (1962).

Il y a une relation certaine entre les recherches lexicologiques qu'a faites Kamerbeek pour élucider "l'intertextualité créatrice" — que ce soit en fonction de l'étude des traditions ou non — et l'intérêt qu'il portera ultérieurement à l'iconicité des énoncés littéraires. Le dépistage des analogies sur le plan du vocabulaire, de la syntaxe, de la signification, de l'intonation et des formes prosodiques l'ont amené à concentrer son attention sur les rapports existant entre la position du mot ou du syntagme dans le texte, d'une part, et leur sens, d'autre part. Kamerbeek étudie l'intensification des valeurs verbales qui se présente là où la position particulière du mot ou du syntagme coïncide avec la fonction iconique de cette position au niveau du thème ou du motif. On trouve les résultats d'une telle recherche dans, par exemple, *De poëzie van J. C. Bloem in Europees perspectief* (1967) et dans sa conférence sur "Les poètes Jacques Bloem et Charles Baudelaire" (1974). Cette activité donne actuellement une impulsion nouvelle à sa recherche.

Formé à l'école de De Vooys, Walzel, Curtius, Baldensperger et Hazard, Kamerbeek est devenu un savant chez qui l'association de l'honnêteté intellectuelle et la sensibilité de la littérature va sans dire, ce qui la rend si remarquable. Armé de ces facultés précieuses, soutenu par son érudition, il a, dans des publications de grande qualité, élucidé sur certains points la structure de la littérature européenne; et il continue à le faire. C'est en reconnaissance de cette présence que des collègues lui dédient ce recueil, à l'occasion de son soixante-dixième anniversaire.

J. C. Brandt Corstius

NERVAL, GAUTIER, JEAN-PAUL
LE RÊVE D'UNE IDYLLE À LA FRANÇAISE

Claude Pichois (Paris et Vanderbilt University)

Dans le numéro spécial consacré en 1963 par la revue *Etudes germaniques* au "Bicentenaire de la naissance de Jean-Paul" nous avions reproduit un texte de Nerval intitulé: "*Le Bonheur de la maison* par Jean-Paul Richter. *Maria* — Fragment".[1] Ce texte avait été publié en 1831 dans *Le Mercure de France du XIXe siècle,*[2] où il était suivi de la mention: "(Traduit par Gérard)". Il présente la particularité bibliographique de n'avoir pas été recueilli en 1840 à la suite des deux *Faust,* contrairement à deux autres traductions de Jean-Paul par Nerval et de ne réapparaître que dans l'édition posthume des deux *Faust* en 1868.[3]

Le Bonheur de la maison, indiquions-nous en 1963, n'est pas une traduction de Jean-Paul: nous en avions reçu l'assurance d'Eduard Berend lui-même; ce n'est pas même la traduction d'un apocryphe allemand. Reste la possibilité que Nerval ait prêté à Jean-Paul — on ne prête qu'aux riches — un texte allemand dû à un auteur secondaire. Mais nous remarquions entre *Le Bonheur de la maison,* d'une part, et, d'autre part, des textes authentiquement nervaliens comme *Sylvie* des points de contact qui nous faisaient proposer cette hypothèse: *Le Bonheur de la maison* est une prose de Nerval, d'un Nerval qui déjà annonce le Nerval profond, secret, pudique des dernières années, d'un Nerval qui s'est masqué pour mieux s'exprimer.[4]

---

1. *Etudes germaniques,* janvier-mars 1963, p. 109-112.
2. T. XXXIII, p. 198-203.
3. [Faux titre:] *Oeuvres complètes de Gérard de Nerval — I — Les Deux Faust.* [Titre :] *Faust et le Second Faust de Goethe suivis d'un choix de ballades et de poésies de Goethe,* [. . .]*, Jean-Paul Richter,* [. . .]. Traduits par Gérard de Nerval, Paris, Michel Lévy frères, 1868, p. 414-419. Les deux autres morceaux ne sont pas des "ballades" ou des "poésies", mais des proses: les traductions de *Die Mondfinsternis* et de *Die Neujahrsnacht eines Unglücklichen.*
4. Le vrai Nerval, celui que voit le Révérend Père Jean Guillaume dont les

Depuis 1963, ni les germanistes, ni les nervaliens n'ont apporté aucun élément nouveau à cette hypothèse, silence qui tend à la transformer en certitude. Il faut dire que les groupements d'oeuvres de Nerval actuellement disponibles dans le commerce sont d'étranges rhapsodies ou résultent de tristes rapetassages.

Nous apportons maintenant un élément nouveau qui n'est pas de nature à simplifier le problème. Théophile Gautier a signé un texte intitulé de divers titres et qui présente avec celui de Nerval des similitudes évidentes. Voici les différentes publications de cette autre prose selon Spoelberch de Lovenjoul[5] :

— *L'Ame de la maison, ou la vie et la mort d'un grillon,* dans *Le Livre d'or,* keepsake hebdomadaire, 1839, n° 1. Il se peut que ce périodique soit mort peu après sa naissance. Le numéro 3 est introuvable, selon Spoelberch de Lovenjoul. Dans le numéro 1 la nouvelle est inachevée et ne se poursuit pas dans le numéro 2.

— *L'Ame de la maison,* dans *La Presse* des 13, 14 et 15 novembre 1839. La nouvelle, complète, est donnée comme une oeuvre inédite.

— *L'Ame de la maison,* dans *Le Fruit défendu,* recueil collectif, Paris, Desessarts, 1840.

— *La Maison de mon oncle,* dans *La Peau de tigre,* Paris, H. Souverain, t. III, 1852, in-8°.

— *L'Ame de la maison,* dans *La Peau de tigre,* Paris, Michel Lévy frères, 1866, éd. grand in-18. C'est le texte que nous citons.

— *L'Ame de la maison,* à la suite des *Jeunes-France,* dans la série des contes humoristiques qui terminent cette édition de l'ouvrage, Paris, Charpentier, 1873, in-18.

La nouvelle de Gautier, plusieurs fois publiée de son vivant, a été nécessairement plus remarquée que le texte de Nerval. Léon Cellier y voit un poème en prose qui serait à l'origine de *Ce que disaient les trois cigognes* (1858): "Pour qui [lit *L'Ame de la maison*] avec les yeux de Mallarmé, encore sous le coup de la mort de sa soeur Maria, le texte perd toute fadeur pour devenir bouleversant".[6] *Le Bonheur de la maison* avait-il eu Gautier pour premier lecteur?

éditions des *Chimères* et de *Pandora*, en attendant celle d'*Aurélia,* sont des modèles de science lucide et fervente. Nous tenons à le remercier d'avoir lu avec nous les deux textes que nous étudions ici.

5. *Histoire des oeuvres de Théophile Gautier,* Paris, G. Charpentier, t. I, 1887, p. 196, n° 434.

6. L. Cellier, "Deux Notes sur Mallarmé", *Mélanges de littérature française offerts à Monsieur René Pintard,* Strasbourg, 1975, p. 673-675.

Le texte de Nerval est plus proche du poème en prose que celui de Gautier, ne serait-ce que par sa longueur. Il commence par cinq points (nos trois points actuels) qui marquent bien le caractère de "Fragment" indiqué au titre. Le narrateur nervalien s'exprime à la première personne. Il est dans un "presbytère aux murailles blanches, aux contrevents verts" (souvenir de Rousseau qu'on retrouve dans *Sylvie*). L'oncle du narrateur qui vit dans ce presbytère depuis sa sortie du séminaire est obligé de faire un assez long voyage "pour recueillir les débris de sa fortune". Maria et le narrateur vont demeurer dans le presbytère après avoir éprouvé une grande tristesse au départ de l'oncle: ils ont l'impression qu'ils ne le reverront pas. Ils restent sous la garde de Berthe, la gouvernante de l'oncle, et de Jacobus Pragmater, ici simple silhouette. Le narrateur aime Maria de toutes ses forces: il pressent qu'il ne la reverra plus. Il est, en effet, envoyé au collège, à Paris.[7] Et Maria est mise en pension. Le narrateur évoque la triste vie de Maria dans sa pension. Puis, sans doute à l'occasion d'autres vacances, il se retrouve seul dans le "prieuré", devenu lugubre, parce que ce prieuré a perdu "l'âme de la maison". Tristesse, résignation.

Il nous semble être dans le Valois, chez l'oncle Boucher. Maria est la soeur d'Emerance, de Sidonie,[8] de Sylvie.

L'Ame de la maison (on a noté que ce titre se trouvait inclus dans *Le Bonheur de la maison*) contient beaucoup plus de détails et se présente d'abord comme une rétrospective. Le narrateur, qui au "souffle glacial du prosaïsme" a "perdu une à une toutes [ses] illusions", revoit sa jeunesse et s'exprime lui aussi à la première personne. Un souvenir particulièrement se détache, lié au prieuré de son oncle le chanoine, "à deux pas de la chapelle de Saint-Caribert". Gautier y va, bien entendu, d'une description de l'intérieur. On retrouve les mêmes personnages[9]: Maria, Berthe, Jacobus Pragmater, tous morts. Le portrait de celui-ci est buriné et justifie l'origine du

7. La phrase n'est par sur ce point d'une parfaite clarté: "Ce fut en effet vers ce temps que l'on jugea à propos de m'envoyer au collége pour terminer mon éducation ébauchée pas mon oncle, homme qui n'avait que du bon sens et qui n'était jamais allé à Paris."

8. Voir Nerval, *Oeuvres,* éd. A. Béguin et J. Richer, Bibliothèque de la Pléiade, t. I, 5e tirage, [1974], p. 462-463 et 465.

9. Gautier leur ajoute un chat, Tom. De plus, en un passage, il nomme le narrateur de son propre prénom.

nom: maître d'école, bedeau, chantre, sonneur, lecteur de Voltaire et de Rousseau (de Voltaire certainement plus que de Rousseau), esprit sec et étroit. Maria disparue est longuement évoquée par ce paragraphe, entre autres:

"L'herbe doit croitre bien haute sur ta fosse, car tu es morte là-bas, et personne n'y est allé: pas même moi, que tu préférais à tout autre, et que tu appelais ton petit mari.

Maria vivante est représentée avec le narrateur par un soir d'hiver, auprès de la cheminée dans laquelle s'engouffre le vent.[10] Scène d'idylle. Le grillon chante sa chanson. Jacobus Pragmater ne veut pas admettre que cet insecte est le porte-bonheur de la maison. Il donne un coup de pied violent du côté d'où provient le chant; quelques flocons de suie se détachent et avec eux la cellule du grillon. Jacobus Pragmater saisit celui-ci au moment où il allait entrer dans l'interstice de deux briques. Le grillon abandonne une de ses pattes et s'enfonce dans le trou. Berthe et les enfants sont pleins d'appréhension.

Quelques jours après, l'oncle reçoit une lettre: son banquier est en faillite. C'en est fini des beaux jours et des petits plats succulents. Au printemps, pour arranger ses affaires, l'oncle se décide à faire un voyage. Ici il convient de mettre en parallèle les deux textes:

NERVAL

[. . .] il le différa autant qu'il put, car il n'avait jamais quitté, depuis sa sortie du séminaire, son village enfoui au milieu des bois comme un nid d'oiseaux, et il lui en coûtait beaucoup pour se séparer de son presbytère aux murailles blanches, aux contrevens verts, où il avait caché sa vie aux yeux méchans des hommes. En partant, il remit entre les mains de Berthe, afin de subvenir à l'entretien de la maison pendant son absence, une petite bourse de cuir assez plate, et promit de revenir bientôt. Il n'y avait là rien que de très-

GAUTIER

[. . .] il le différa autant qu'il put; car il n'avait jamais quitté, depuis sa sortie du séminaire, son village, enfoui au milieu des bois comme un nid d'oiseau, et il lui en coûtait beaucoup pour se séparer de son presbytère aux murailles blanches, aux contrevents verts, où il avait si longtemps caché sa vie aux yeux méchants des hommes.

En partant, il remit entre les mains de Berthe une petite bourse assez plate pour subvenir aux besoins de la maison pendant son absence, et promit de revenir bientôt.

10. On remarquera le début: "Moi et Maria, nous étions seuls." Faute de goût?

naturel sans doute; pourtant, nous avions tous le coeur gros, et je ne sais pourquoi il nous semblait que nous ne le reverrions plus. Aussi, Marie [*sic*] et moi, nous l'accompagnâmes jusqu'au pied de la colline, trottant de toutes nos forces de chaque côté de son cheval, pour être plus longtemps avec lui. Quand nous fûmes las: Assez, mes chers petits, nous dit-il, je ne veux pas que vous alliez plus loin. Berthe serait inquiète de vous. Puis il nous haussa sur son étrier, nous donna à chacun un baiser, et piqua des deux.

Alors un frisson me prit, et des pleurs tombèrent de mes yeux, comme les gouttes d'une pluie d'orage; il me parut qu'on venait de fermer sur lui le couvercle du cercueil et d'y planter le dernier clou.

Oh! mon Dieu! dit Maria en laissant aller un soupir profond et comprimé, mon pauvre oncle, — il était si bon! — Et elle tourna vers moi ses yeux clairs nageant dans un fluide abondant et pur.

Il n'y avait là rien que de fort naturel sans doute; pourtant nous étions profondément émus, et je ne sais pourquoi il me semblait que nous ne le reverrions plus, et que c'était pour la dernière fois qu'il nous parlait. Aussi, Maria et moi, nous l'accompagnâmes jusqu'au pied de la colline, trottant, de toutes nos forces, de chaque côté de son cheval, pour être plus longtemps avec lui.

— Assez, mes petits, nous dit-il; je ne veux pas que vous alliez plus loin, Berthe serait inquiète de vous.

Puis il nous hissa sur son étrier, nous appuya un baiser bien tendre sur les joues, et piqua des deux: nous le suivîmes de l'oeil pendant quelques minutes.

Etant parvenu au haut de l'éminence, il retourna la tête pour voir encore une fois, avant qu'il s'enfonçât tout à fait sous l'horizon, le clocher de l'église paroissiale et le toit d'ardoise de sa petite maison.

Nous ayant aperçus à la même place, il nous fit un geste amical de la main, comme pour nous dire qu'il était content; puis il continua sa route.

Un angle du chemin l'eut bientôt dérobé à nos yeux.

Alors, un frisson me prit, et les pleurs tombèrent de mes yeux. Il me parut qu'on venait de fermer sur lui le couvercle de la bière, et d'y planter le dernier clou.

— Oh! mon Dieu! dit Maria avec un grand soupir, mon pauvre oncle! il était si bon!

Et elle tourna vers moi ses yeux purs nageant dans un fluide abondant et clair.

Là-dessus Gautier montre une pie aux cris moqueurs de laquelle le narrateur répond en jetant des pierres. Les adolescents rentrent au prieuré: "lui, naguère si gai, si vivant, il était silencieux et mort; l'âme de la maison était partie, ce n'était plus que le cadavre." Dans le texte de Nerval "l'âme de la maison" était Maria.

Gautier fait ensuite reparaître le grillon qui se chauffe à la flamme de l'âtre. Pragmater monte au grenier pour y chercher un livre. Un courant d'air souffle sa bougie. Dans l'obscurité il voit descendre sur un filet de lumière le fantôme de l'oncle, lequel se met à lire son exemplaire des oeuvres de saint Augustin. Pragmater s'évanouit. Il reverra le fantôme en plein jour dans le jardin. Les serviteurs, Maria et le narrateur ont la conviction que l'oncle est mort.

Un autre parallèle s'impose ici, de divergences surtout:

NERVAL	GAUTIER
[...] Maria était triste; et moi par conséquent, car je ne vivais que par elle et pour elle; ou si par hasard un sourire venait relever les coins de sa petite bouche et faire voir ses dents brillantes comme des gouttes de rosée au fond d'une fleur, c'était un de ces sourires vagues et mélancoliques qui remuent dans l'âme mille émotions confuses, mais poignantes, dont on ne saurait se rendre compte; quand elle souriait ainsi, l'expression de sa figure avait quelque chose de si sévère, un air de repos et de calme si profond, si harmonieusement mêlé à la grâce candide de ses traits enfantins, que toute pensée humaine s'effaçait à son aspect comme les étoiles au réveil de l'aube; le vide se faisait à l'entour, elle seule était tout. Moi, j'étais abîmé dans cette contemplation; car ce que je voyais, je ne l'avais pas encore vu. Une autre vie m'était ouverte; il y avait tant de promesses de bonheur dans ce regard doux comme un souvenir de paradis, tant de consolations sur ce front blanc et pur,	Maria dépérissait à vue d'oeil, et devenait d'une beauté étrange; ses yeux s'agrandissaient et s'illuminaient de l'aurore de la vie céleste; le ciel prochain y rayonnait déjà. Ils roulaient moelleusement sur leurs longues paupières comme deux globes d'argent bruni, avec des langueurs de clair de lune et des rayons d'un bleu velouté que nul peintre ne saurait rendre: les couleurs de ses joues, concentrées sur le haut des pommettes en petit nuage rose, ajoutaient encore à l'éclat divin de ces yeux surnaturels où se concentrait une vie près de s'envoler; les anges du ciel semblaient regarder la terre par ces yeux-là. A l'exception de ces deux taches vermeilles, elle était pâle comme de la cire vierge; ses tempes et ses mains transparentes laissaient voir un délicat lacis de veines azurées; ses lèvres décolorées s'exfoliaient en petites pellicules lamelleuses: elle était poitrinaire. Comme j'avais l'âge d'entrer au collége, mes parents me firent revenir à

dans ce sourire tant de morbidesse et de laisser aller! ... Aussi je compris que cela ne pourrait durer longtemps; je me mis à l'aimer de toutes mes forces, et à serrer ma vie afin de faire tenir une année en un jour.

la ville, d'autant plus qu'ils avaient appris la mort de mon oncle, qui avait fait une chute de cheval dans un chemin difficile, et s'était fendu la tête.

Un testament trouvé dans sa poche instituait Berthe et Pragmater ses uniques héritiers, à l'exception de sa bibliothèque, qui devait me revenir, et d'une bague en diamants de sa mère, destinée à Maria.

Mes adieux à Maria furent des plus tristes; nous sentions que nous ne nous reverrions plus. Elle m'embrassa sur le seuil de la porte, et me dit à l'oreille:

– C'est ce vilain Pragmater qui est cause de tout; il a voulu tuer le grillon. Nous nous reverrons chez le bon Dieu. Voilà une petite croix en perles de couleur que j'ai faite pour toi; garde-la toujours.

Un mois après, Maria s'éteignit. Le grillon ne chanta plus à dater de ce jour-là: l'âme de la maison s'en était allée. Berthe et Pragmater ne lui survécurent pas longtemps; Tom mourut, bientôt après, de langueur et d'ennui.

J'ai toujours la croix de perles de Maria. Par une délicatesse charmante dont je ne me suis aperçu que plus tard, elle avait mis quelques-uns de ses beaux cheveux blonds pour enfiler les grains de verre qui la composent; chaste amour enfantin si pur, qu'il pouvait confier son secret à une croix!

(O Gautier ! la croix de ta tendre amie semble empruntée aux héroïnes des mélodrames.)

Le narrateur revient ensuite au début du cercle qu'il avait commencé à parcourir. Il se retrouve à l'âge mûr ou blet. Il tisonne, comme Frédéric et Deslauriers, les cendres de son passé. Voici le dernier paragraphe:

> Mon âme ne s'éparpille pas au dehors, mes idées ne s'en vont pas à l'aventure parmi les choses du monde, sautant d'un objet à un autre; toute ma puissance d'animation, toute ma force intellectuelle se concentrent en moi; je fais des vers, excellente occupation d'oisif, ou je pense à la petite Maria, qui avait des taches roses sur les joues.

*

Si l'on s'en tient à la chronologie (Nerval, 1831; Gautier, 1839), il est évident que Gautier a lu et utilisé le texte de Nerval. Aux passages cités en parallèle on pourrait ajouter quelques détails. Celui-ci par exemple: "On ne saurait dire combien le prieuré devint triste quand Maria n'y fut plus; c'était comme si l'on eût éteint la paillette de lumière d'un tableau de Rembrandt" (Nerval); dans le prieuré de Gautier les vitraux de la fenêtre étroite "ne laissent passer qu'un demi-jour vague et mystérieux, digne d'un intérieur de Rembrandt". Le texte de Gautier contient des résonances nervaliennes: ainsi, le "petit mari" et Maria, qu'on a vus dans le paragraphe cité ci-dessus, évoquent le mariage de Sylvie et du narrateur enfants au chapitre VI de *Sylvie*. La perte des illusions mentionnée par Gautier au début de *L'Ame de la maison* constitue le thème du "Dernier Feuillet" de *Sylvie*.

Le problème est donc posé de deux textes étroitement apparentés par leur sujet et même par leur expression. Différentes solutions s'offrent. 1) Gautier a utilisé un texte de Nerval pour le développer. Mais alors comment expliquer que *Le Bonheur de la maison* figure en 1868 dans les *Oeuvres complètes* de Nerval, à la publication desquelles Gautier, qui en est le préfacier, a sans doute pris part, et tandis que *L'Ame de la maison* se lisait depuis 1866 dans *La Peau de tigre* publiée chez le même Michel Lévy? Et Gautier a assez d'imagination pour ne pas risquer de tomber sous le coup d'une accusation de plagiat. 2) Nerval et Gautier ont puisé à la même source. Mais alors comment expliquer la coïncidence presque littérale de deux passages? 3) Comme les poètes de la Renaissance Nerval et Gautier se sont exercés sur le même thème, peut-être parce qu'ils s'étaient associés pour écrire en collaboration un même ouvrage, de même qu'ils s'étaient associés pour écrire les *Confessions galantes de deux gentilshommes périgourdins*.

Cette dernière hypothèse a notre préférence dans l'état actuel de la documentation. Elle a l'avantage de rendre compte d'un dessein commun et de réalisations très différentes.

Le dessein commun est sans doute de doter la France d'un genre littéraire qui lui manque ou qui est fort peu représenté: l'idylle. C'est pourquoi le texte de Gérard de Nerval est placé sous le patronage de Jean-Paul, dont on connaît alors surtout des pensées détachées et des rêves et dont on sait qu'il a écrit des idylles. Précisément, en septembre 1830, la *Nouvelle Revue germanique* avait publié *Le Bonheur d'un pasteur suédois*.

A partir de ce dessein commun les voies divergent. Nerval qui, en 1831, n'a signé que des satires, des traductions, des anthologies, sent sourdre en lui le besoin d'une création plus personnelle. Avec *Le Bonheur de la maison* le voici déjà sur le chemin qui mène à *Sylvie,* oeuvre qui, par un de ses aspects importants au moins, est, au XIXe siècle, la seule idylle de la littérature française. Le thème, dès 1831, s'intériorise, même s'il est traité avec une abondance que ne connaîtront plus les oeuvres de la fin, si décantées.

Gautier, au contraire, s'abandonne à son goût du pittoresque, et même s'il révèle dans *L'Ame de la maison* sa hantise de la mort. Il est caractéristique à cet égard d'opposer une phrase de Nerval: "Le prieuré d'aujourd'hui est l'ancien, comme le cadavre est le corps, la bouteille vide, la bouteille pleine de vieux vin du Rhin; on a laissé le flacon ouvert, le parfum et la poésie se sont évaporés! ", phrase qui tend déjà vers Baudelaire et vers Proust, à cette phrase de Gautier relative à sa "pensée adolescente": "sa fleur, son velouté, son éclat, tout a disparu; comme l'aile de papillon qui laisse aux doigts une poussière d'or, d'azur et de carmin, elle a laissé son principe odorant sur l'index et le pouce de ceux qui voulaient la saisir dans son vol de sylphide."

Récupération par le pittoresque. Récupération aussi par le fantastique. Nous disions que, à l'exception du chat Tom, les personnages étaient les mêmes. En fait, le grillon apparaît chez Gautier comme un personnage principal.[11] Avec lui, petit dieu domestique, le fan-

11. La superstition attachée au grillon est bien attestée à l'époque. Le *Grand Dictionnaire universel du XIXe siècle* de Pierre Larousse, à l'article GRILLON (t. VIII), cite le *Dictionnaire raisonné universel d'histoire naturelle* de Valmont-Bomare (t. VI, 1800): "Il n'est pas rare de rencontrer des personnes, surtout

tastique, qui, durant ces années-là, domine la littérature d'imagination, se glisse dans le texte et autorise le fantôme de l'oncle à se
manifester dans le grenier ou le jardin.

Habent sua fata libelli... Les littératures nationales ont aussi leur
Fatum, qui asservit la poétique à des circonstances sociologiques
contraignantes. M. Robert Minder a bien montré que la littérature
allemande avait été marquée par les pasteurs, qu'elle s'était partielle-
ment écrite dans les presbytères.[12] La littérature française est plutôt,
par sa sociabilité même, une littérature de salon (ce qui n'a rien de
péjoratif). Il est beau que Nerval, en devinant Jean-Paul, lui ait apporté ce souffle pur de l'idylle.

parmi le vulgaire, qui ont du goût pour le chant des grillons, et qui croient même
que ces animaux portent bonheur à leur maison." A remarquer que *The Cricket
on the Hearth, A Fairy Tale of Home*, ne paraîtra en volume qu'en 1846
(première traduction française, 1847).

12. "Das Bild des Pfarrhauses in der deutschen Literatur von Jean Paul bis
Gottfried Benn", dans *Kultur und Literatur in Deutschland und Frankreich*,
Insel-Bücherei, n⁰ 771, 1962.

L'ICONICITE METAPHORIQUE

A. J. A. van Zoest (Utrecht)

1. On admet généralement que le signe iconique est le signe dont la relation entre le signe lui-même (le *representamen*) et le référent (l'objet dénoté) est une relation de ressemblance. On a pourtant compris aussi que cette définition du signe iconique pose le problème de savoir ce qu'il faut entendre par une relation de ressemblance. Ce problème a été signalé surtout par Eco (1968, 1972), qui cherche à le résoudre en renvoyant à une certaine identité des effets produits par le signe et par ses référents sur le plan de leur perception. Le désavantage d'une pareille solution, malgré tout ce qu'elle a de valable, est qu'elle déplace le problème de l'iconicité du domaine de la syntaxe sémiotique à celui de la pragmatique.

Il me semble qu'il est possible de rester à l'intérieur du domaine syntaxique (sémiotique), quand on définit le signe iconique d'après les descriptions verbales faites du signe et de son référent. On dira qu'il y a signe iconique si les descriptions verbales du signe et de son référent ont au moins un élément significatif en commun (le mot *significatif* a ici un sens, disons, statistique). Cette définition exige, bien entendu, l'établissement de quelques conditions concernant ces descriptions: elles doivent être plausibles, pertinentes et aussi simples que possible; elles doivent regarder les structures principales du signe décrit et ne pas être concentrées sur des détails accessoires, sur des futilités. Les descriptions doivent en outre — mais c'est là plutôt une exigence didactique — être fonctionnelles, dans ce sens qu'elles sont nécessairement faites au service de ce qu'elles veulent démontrer: la présence de quelque identité assurant le caractère iconique du signe en question.

Selon cette définition rajustée du signe iconique, l'iconicité qu'on constate dans un poème comme *La mandoline, l'oeillet et le bambou* d'Apollinaire se justifie par les descriptions suivantes: (a) la configuration du texte imprimé, considérée comme un signe, montre des structures géométriques bidimensionelles reconnaissables comme les contours d'une mandoline, d'un oeillet et d'un bambou; (b) la projection sur un plan des objets dénotés — donc après un passage du tridimensionnel au bidimensionnel — montre des contours identiques.

On constatera de même que plusieurs signes iconiques coïncident dans la formule *veni, vidi, vici* (exemple donné par Jakobson, 1966). L'ordre temporel des éléments syntaxiques y est identique à l'ordre temporel dénoté. L'ordre hiérarchique des éléments syntaxiques, groupés selon le principe de la gradation ascendante, est identique à la hiérarchie dénotée: le dernier événement dénoté est le plus important. La quasi-identité des trois éléments du signe (identités de phonèmes initiaux et finals, du nombre de phonèmes, de l'accentuation) correspond avec une quasi-identité sur le plan de la dénotation: arriver, voir et vaincre, c'était pour César presque une seule action. La rapidité de l'énonciation dénote la rapidité de la victoire remportée.

2. Tous les signes iconiques ne sont pas de la même nature. Celui qu'on trouve dans une poème concret, à composante visuelle évidente, tel *La mandoline, l'oeillet et le bambou,* est, comme dirait Peirce (2.277) une *image*. La polysémie de ce terme le rendant extrêmement inapproprié à un usage scientifique, il vaut mieux le remplacer par celui d' "icône topologique" (cf. Bense & Walther, 1973). Les signes iconiques qui se discernent dans *veni, vidi, vici* sont des *diagrams* dans la terminologie de Peirce. Disons que ce sont des "icônes diagrammatiques".

Dans l'icône topologique, la relation entre le signe et son référent est une relation simple: le signe représente les "simples qualités" du référent. Dans l'icône diagrammatique, cette relation est dyadique: la ressemblance entre le signe et son référent ne concerne que les relations entre leurs parties — elle est, pour ainsi dire, indirecte. Selon des exigences descriptives formulées ci-dessus, les deux classes d'icônes se définissent comme suit. Il y a icône topologique si, dans les descriptions du signe et du référent, une place significative est attribuée à un ou plusieurs mots appartenant au champ sémantique "spatialité" (ou: "configuration"). Il y a icône diagrammatique si, dans les descriptions du signe et du référent, une place significative est attribuée à un ou plusieurs mots appartenant au champ sémantique "relation" (ou: "proportion"; ou: "structure").

Les icônes diagrammatiques sont moins facilement reconnues que les icônes topologiques. Mais il est certain que les icônes diagrammatiques jouent un rôle considérable, dans le langage en général et plus particulièrement dans le langage poétique. Jakobson (1966) a insisté à juste titre sur ce rôle que l'iconicité diagrammatique joue dans le fonctionnement du langage, et il a sans doute vu plus clair que Chomsky, qui n'accorde à l'iconicité qu'un rôle tout accessoire.[1] C'est son grand mérite que d'avoir attiré l'attention sur la fonction fondamentale du signe iconique dans le langage (l'icône est, en effet, primaire dans la typologie des signes), d'avoir signalé l'intérêt de remonter aux réflexions sémiotiques de Peirce en général, d'avoir relevé l'importance du concept peircien de *diagram* en particulier (il a donné un grand nombre d'exemples d'iconicité diagrammatique, de nature surtout morphophonologique et syntaxique). Cependant, lorsqu'il suggère que Peirce "distinguait parmi les icônes deux sous-classes différentes" (Jakobson, 1966, p. 28), il se trompe. Peirce distinguait parmi les icônes trois sous-classes, la troisième étant celle des *metaphors*.

Ecoutons Peirce (2.277). "Hypoicons [= les signes à iconicité prédominante] may be roughly divided according to the mode of Firstness of which they partake. Those which partake of simple qualities, or First Firstnesses, are *images*; those which represent the relations, mainly dyadic, or so regarded, of the parts of one thing by analogous relations in their own parts, are *diagrams*; those which represent the representative character of a representamen by representing a parallelism in something else, are *metaphors*. "

Que Peirce fasse, dans la catégorie des icônes, une division en trois et non pas en deux, ne doit pas nous étonner. Toute sa typologie sémiotique se caractérise par une organisation trichotomique, ce qui est la conséquence de sa vision ontologique. Peirce distingue trois

---

1. Chomsky (1965), au lieu d'admettre que des exigences d'iconicité régissent, au fond, des contraintes syntaxiques, se sert de la notion d'"iconicité" pour expliquer pourqoi certaines phrases qui seraient correctes selon les règles grammaticales sont toutefois inacceptables ("unacceptable grammatical sentences"). C'est retourner la question, probablement pour sauver à tout prix un modèle descriptif. Peirce (2.280) avait écrit: "(. . .) icons of the algebraic kind (. . .) exist in all ordinary grammatical propositions (. . .)", et encore: "in the syntax of every language there are logical icons of the kind that are aided by conventional rules".

modes d'être: *First* ("Prime", le mode d'être de la possibilité), *Second* ("Second", le mode d'être de l'existence réelle), *Third* ("Tierce", le mode d'être de la généralité conventionnelle). Le Prime existe sans référence à rien d'autre; le Second dépend, pour son existence, de celle d'un Prime. Le Tierce, à son tour, implique l'existence d'un Second.[2]

Cette tripartition ontologique de Peirce explique ses tripartitions sémiotiques. Ainsi, le symbole (un Tierce), qui est le signe dont la relation entre signe et référent se fonde sur une "règle" (ou: "généralité"; ou: "convention") implique quelque indice (un Second), qui est le signe de la contiguïté existentielle. L'indice implique quelque icône (un Prime), le signe de la ressemblance et qui est signe, en principe, indépendamment de l'existence ou de l'inexistence d'un référent. De même, on est en droit de supposer qui Peirce admet que l'icône métaphorique est un Tierce, l'icône diagrammatique un Second, l'icône topologique un Prime.[3]

L'iconicité métaphorique a certainement sa place dans la théorie sémiotique de Peirce. Cependant, la notion n'a pas été élaborée par Peirce lui-même, ni — du moins à ce que je sache — après lui par quelque sémioticien acceptant les concepts peirciens comme points de départ de ses recherches. Cet oubli s'explique probablement par le fait qu'il est difficile de s'imaginer ce que serait une icône métaphorique, de concevoir ce qu'il faudrait entendre par le *parallelism in something else*. C'est le but de la présente étude que de s'attaquer à ce problème.

3. Je crois qu'on peut se faire une première idée de ce que c'est que l'iconicité métaphorique en pensant à K., le personnage principal du *Procès* de Kafka. Tout lecteur comprend que le roman ne raconte pas simplement l'histoire d'un arpenteur qui meurt finalement "comme

---

2. Pour une discussion de l'ontologie peircienne, voir Stearns (1952), et aussi Greenlee (1973).
3. Il est bon de se rendre compte du caractère relatif de cette assertion. Tout comme l'icône n'existe pas à l'état pur, il n'y a pas d'icône topologique pure; elle n'est jamais sans quelques aspects diagrammatiques et métaphoriques. Fondamentalement, tout signe est un Tierce; cf. Peirce (5.484): "(. . .) by "semiosis" I mean (. . .) an action, or influence, which is, or involves, a coöperation of *three* subjects, such as a sign, its object, and its interpretant, this tri-relative influence not being in any way resolvable into actions between pairs".

un chien", mais que son sujet fondamental est le mystère de la condition humaine. K. représente "métaphoriquement" l'homme en général.

On sait le succès de ce procédé littéraire. *En attendant Godot,* de Beckett, par exemple, est une pièce métaphysique, où les protagonistes, Vladimir et Estragon, "représentent l'humanité". Vladimir est explicite sur ce point, quand, au second acte, il fait des réflexions sur la situation où il se voit placé. Pozzo, devenu aveugle, s'est effondré à ses pieds, et Vladimir dit à Estragon: "Ne perdons pas notre temps en vains discours. (. . .) Faisons quelque chose, pendant que l'occasion se présente! Ce n'est pas tous les jours qu'on a besoin de nous. Non pas à vrai dire qu'on ait précisément besoin de nous. D'autres feraient aussi bien l'affaire, sinon mieux. L'appel que nous venons d'entendre, c'est plutôt à l'humanité entière qu'il s'adresse. *Mais à cet endroit, en ce moment, l'humanité c'est nous,* que ça nous plaise ou non. Profitons-en, avant qu'il soit trop tard. Représentons dignement pour une fois l'engeance où le malheur nous a fourrés. Qu'en dis-tu? (. . .) Il est vrai qu'en pesant, les bras croisés, le pour et le contre, nous faisons également honneur à notre condition."

Dans *L'étranger* et *La chute* de Camus, les protagonistes, Meursault et Clamence, sont plus que les héros d'un récit; ils réprésentent certains types d'homme. Le premier est l'homme authentique imprégné de l'absurde. Le second est l'homme avisé en lutte avec le problème de la justice.

Dans des textes de ce genre -- qui sont, pour ainsi dire, des paraboles ou des allégories --, les personnages, leurs attributs, leurs relations et les événements racontés ont une portée qui dépasse les significations littérales. Tous les éléments narratifs deviennent des "métaphores". La justification profonde de cet usage de la "métaphore" dans ces cas est peut-être la conception qui veut que la condition de l'homme, pour être rendue sensible, doit être racontée et non pas être expliquée, analysée, décrite ou illustrée.

L'usage "métaphorique" de la narrativité se justifie aussi, dans les pays totalitaires par exemple, par la situation politique, qui oblige l'auteur à voiler la portée littérale de son message essentiel. Au théâtre, on peut constater le phénomène dans *La punaise* de Maïakovski; c'est une pièce "métaphorique". Dans les pièces de Mrozek, une portée "métaphorique" de l'intrigue doit être devinée, et l'on peut hésiter si elle est de nature politique ou métaphysique. Probablement les deux s'y mélangent. Je me rappelle avoir vu à Prague une pièce assez fade où étaient ridiculisés des prêtres de l'inquisition espagnole. Quand je me plaignais du peu d'actualité de la pièce, on me répondit: "Mais c'est une métaphore". Les inquisiteurs représentaient les dirigeants du pays, aux yeux des spectateurs; la situation politique ne permettait pas de les ridiculiser autrement.

L'art cinématographique utilise parfois avec bonheur le procédé "métaphorique". La "métaphore" est d'ordre politique dans le film de Milos Forman *Hori, ma panenko* (*Le bal des pompiers*), où les pompiers représentaient les dirigeants communistes tchécoslovaques. La "métaphore" est d'ordre métaphysique dans *Profession: reporter* d'Antonioni. Les personnage principal y représente l'homme moderne en face d'une réalité qui est pour lui "un mystère massif" (cf. Visser, 1975).

Toutes ces "métaphores" narratives ne sont pas des métaphores au sens propre du mot; c'est pourquoi j'ai eu soin de mettre des guillemets en employant jusqu'ici les termes "métaphore", "métaphorique" et "métaphoriquement". La métaphore au sens propre du mot est un phénomène linguistique (rhétorique) dont la présence dans un texte linguistique se manifeste, sur le plan de la compétence, par la transgression de quelque règle de restriction sélective (cf. Matthews, 1971) et dont la signification doit être cherchée sur le plan de la performance par quelque opération d'ordre sémantique.

Les cas cités – chez Kafka, Beckett, Camus, Maïakovski, Mrozek, Forman, Antonioni – sont des cas d'iconicité métaphorique. Quand on parle de "métaphores" à leur sujet, on fait un emploi métaphorique du mot *métaphore*. On pourrait dire, en règle générale, qu'il y a iconicité métaphorique toutes les fois qu'on se sert métaphoriquement du mot *métaphore*.

4. Le sens métaphorique d'une narration, qu'elle soit cinématographique ou non, n'est pas toujours unanimement compris, comme une anecdote en rapport avec ce film le montre d'une façon amusante. Après la première du film en Tchécoslovaquie, 40.000 pompiers protestèrent et il fallut que le metteur-en-scène Forman leur explique qu'il s'agisse d'une "allégorie" (*Filmfacts*, 1968). Le critique du *Time* (12-6-1968) avait vu plus clair, en écrivant: "in an unfree society, there are no innocent words. Congeries of meanings attach themselves to every noun used in an effort to dodge censorship. A spade is not merely a spade when it is raised as a symbol of defiance. A story is no longer simply a story when it is also a parable of men oppressed".

La définition de l'icône métaphorique d'après sa description verbale serait donc la suivante: il y a icône métaphorique si dans les descriptions verbales du signe et de son référent entre nécessairement l'emploi d'une métaphore, au sens propre du mot.

Si, ainsi, l'icône métaphorique est définie d'après sa description verbale, le problème du fonctionnement de ce genre de signe iconique reste posé, et notamment celui de savoir ce qu'il faut entendre par le *parallelism in something else*, qui, aux dires de Peirce, en constitue la caractéristique essentielle.

4. Pour une compréhension de la notion de "parallélisme en quelque chose d'autre", l'analyse sémiotique qu'a faite Pelc (1971) du concept de "métaphore", au sens propre, peut rendre un service important. Pelc ne se fonde pas sur les concepts peirciens, mais ses points de départ théoriques pourraient être reformulés en termes peirciens, car il distingue avec bonheur, bien que de façon implicite, entre référent (*Object*) et interprétation (*Interpretant*). Ce n'est pas ici le lieu de résumer en détail l'analyse de Pelc, mais signalons qu'il considère que l'emploi métaphorique d'une expression fait entrer en ligne de compte trois expressions (dont deux sous-jacentes) composées des trois combinaisons possibles des deux référents et deux interprétations mis en oeuvre.

Donnons un exemple. Soit l'expression *un torrent de larmes,* dans laquelle le mot *torrent* est employé métaphoriquement. Dans cette expression, (E), le référent de ce mot est "torrent", son interprétation "abondance". Elle peut être remplacée par une expression *abondance de larmes*, (E$_2$), où le mot *abondance* a un référent et une interprétation indiqués par le même mot, "abondance". Cependant – et c'est là l'originalité des présupposés théoriques de Pelc –, ce remplacement ne se fait que grâce à l'existence supposée d'une troisième expression, (E$_1$), *torrent de larmes,* dans laquelle le mot *torrent* aurait tout simplement un référent "torrent" et également une interprétation littérale, "torrent".

C'est le rôle de cette dernière expression sous-jacente (E$_1$), sa relation avec les expressions E et E$_2$ (la métaphorique et sa "traduction littérale") qui nous intéresse ici, et encore exclusivement en ce qui concerne la nature des référents dans ces relations.

Pour ce qui est de la relation E-E$_1$ (ou E$_1$-E), Pelc pose comme condition, pour qu'il y ait métaphore, que "at least one designatum of the expression E_1 and every designatum of the expression E share the properties P_1, P_2, ..., P_n." Pour ce qui est de la relation E_1-E_2 (ou E_2-E_1), Pelc note: "The designata of the expressions E_1 and E_2 share the property P or the properties P_1, P_2, ..., P_n which is (are) the basis of comparison (*tertium comparationis*) "E_2 is like E_1". Thus, for instance, in the comparison "an eye like a star" the basis is the property of shining (P), and it can be shown to characterize each of the designata of the expressions E_2 ("a shining eye") and E_1 ("a star")." (L'expression métaphorique en question est "the stars of (her) eyes".)

Si l'on considère comme valides ces conditions posées à l'usage métaphorique d'un mot, il s'en suit que cet usage dépend d'une identité d'un ou plusieurs éléments (propriétés) dans deux référents différents — dont l'un serait celui de l'expression littérale, l'autre celui de l'expression métaphorique. L'expression métaphorique paraît donc faire entrer en ligne de compte deux référents différents, dans lesquels se manifeste nécessairement "quelque parallélisme".

Voilà un exemple de ce que pourrait être le *parallelism* dont parle Peirce, quand il caractérise l'icône métaphorique par un *parallelism in something else*. Ce *something else* est, par conséquent, un second référent — le même signe peut en avoir un nombre indéterminé — attribué au signe par l'un des locuteurs (ou les deux à la fois). Car, bien entendu, il appartient au destinateur et/ou au destinaire du signe de décider que le signe devra être pris dans un sens métaphorique ou non.

J'admets que ce qui vaut, selon Pelc, pour la métaphore au sens propre du mot, vaut également pour l'icône métaphorique. Les deux objets dénotés (référents) par le même signe *se ressemblent*. On peut faire de l'arpenteur K., du *Procès* de Kafka, une description verbale où entrent des éléments identiques à la description faite de l'homme en général: tous deux vivent sous le coup d'une accusation imprécise, tous deux meurent finalement "comme un chien". Vladimir, dans *En attendant Godot*, ressemble à l'homme en général, parce qu'on n'a pas besoin de lui, parce que, devant le malheur d'autrui, il a tendance à peser, les bras croisés, le pour et le contre d'une intervention personnelle. Et cetera. La ressemblance des relations entre l'élément textuel (signe) et leurs référents (littéral et "métaphorique") dépend d'une ressemblance globale entre le référent immédiatement dénoté et un autre référent, indirectement dénoté. C'est ce caractère médiat, indirect, de la dénotation "métaphorique" qui fait qu'elle se découvre plus difficilement que celle des autres icônes.

Dans les exemples cités, qui sont des exemples d'iconicité métaphorique au niveau macrostructural, la découverte de la "métaphore" peut sembler relativement aisée (pour ce qui est de son interprétation, c'est une autre histoire), mais il n'en est certainement pas de même des icônes métaphoriques du niveau microstructural. Cependant, elles existent, et je crois qu'une poétique comparative aura intérêt à les tracer, à les décrire et à en étudier le fonctionnement.

5. Pour se faire une idée de ce que c'est que l'iconicité métaphorique au niveau microstructural, on étudiera avec profit certaines observations très fines et perspicaces faites par le savant à qui le présent recueil est dédié, par J. Kamerbeek Jr. Avant de s'être familiarisé avec le concept d' "iconicité" — il s'en servira dans ses publications ultérieures —, il avait déjà repéré certains phénomènes poétiques, dont il avait souligné l'efficacité secrète, la séduction esthétique particulière.

Donnons un exemple, choisi parmi d'autres. Kamerbeek (1967,b) analyse les vers suivants du poète néerlandais J. C. Bloem, pris dans le poème *Ademen* (*Respirer*):

Vivre, c'est respirer, à peine plus.
Mais respirer, c'est, dans cette vallée,
S'approprier sa part d'infinité.[5]

Au sujet du deuxième vers cité, Kamerbeek écrit: "(...) quand on lit le vers à haute voix en se rendant compte de sa signification, on ne peut que descendre vers le mot *vallée*. Il est impossible — à moins d'adopter une intonation inadéquate (...) — de faire monter la mélodie. "Cette vallée" *est* une vallée, en vertu de la coopération des facteurs dont le poème se compose".[6] (Il faut se rendre compte, en

---

5. Texte original: *Leven is niet veel meer dan ademhalen.*/ *Maar dat is: in de diepten van dit dal*/ *De oneind'ge ruimte tot zich in te leiden.* Ce poème de Bloem comprend un grand nombre d'icônes, dont seulement celle qui sert mon argumentation est prise en considération ici.

6. Texte original: "(...) als men het vers hardop leest en zich van de betekenis van de woorden doordringt, kan men niet anders dan naar dit woord afdalen. Het is onmogelijk — op straffe van een inadequate (...) intonatie —, het op hoge toon uit te spreken. "Dit dal" *is* een dal, krachtens het samenspel der factoren waaruit het gedicht is opgebouwd."

lisant ces paroles, qu'en néerlandais l'intonation est plus libre qu'en français.)

A une autre occasion (Kamerbeek, 1974), un exemple comparable est donné. Il s'agit du deuxième vers de *Recueillement* de Baudelaire:

Tu réclamais le Soir; il descend; le voici:

au sujet duquel Kamerbeek note: "la descente du soir est admirablement rendue par la mélodie descendante de la phrase".

Dans les deux cas, chez Bloem et chez Baudelaire, on a affaire à l'iconicité métaphorique. Pourquoi? Expliquons-nous.

Il est évident que, lorsque le chercheur, *in casu* Kamerbeek, considère la mélodie d'un élément linguistique donné comme un phénomène significatif, il accorde à cet élément paralinguistique le statut de signe, notamment de signe esthétique. Ce signe est, en l'occurrence, une icône, puisqu'il se définit par la relation de ressemblance entre le signe lui-même (la mélodie descendante) et le référent (la vallée, le soir qui descend): le mot *vallée* "est" une vallée, la *descente du soir* "est" une descente. Cependant, cette description est métaphorique, car, bien entendu, le mot *vallée* n'est pas littéralement une vallée. Il ne peut être appelé ainsi que grâce au fait que l'usage nous permet de parler d'une mélodie qui monte et d'une mélodie qui descend. Qu'il s'agisse là de métaphores, a été souligné par Fonagy (1963).

Si les deux icônes que Kamerbeek a découvertes chez Bloem et chez Baudelaire sont des icônes métaphoriques selon le critère de la description verbale, la question se pose de savoir quel est ici le référent, absent à première vue (le *something else* de Peirce), dans lequel se manifeste l'identité partielle (le *parallelism* de Peirce, les propriétés communes de Pelc) avec le signe et son référent immédiat. Ce référent, cet objet indirectement dénoté, on doit le chercher dans les systèmes de représentation conventionnelle de la mélodie d'une phrase. Il existe, en effet, des systèmes sémiotiques conventionnels où la "descente" d'une mélodie (il est difficile sinon impossible de ne pas parler métaphoriquement des phénomènes phonétiques — ces métaphores sont des catachrèses) est représenté par une "descente" au niveau du signe: la tradition veut qu'une ligne descendante représente une mélodie "descendante", et cette "descente" est indiquée dans le "langage" gestuel par un mouvement descendant du bras et de la main.

Ce genre d'iconicité métaphorique, dont le *representamen* est la mélodie de la phrase ou d'une partie de la phrase, se présente sans doute fréquemment dans les textes poétiques. Voici encore quelques exemples.

Le premier est pris dans *Der römische Brunnen* de C. F. Meyer; la dénotation "monter" et "descendre" y coïncide avec une "ascension" et une "descente" au niveau du signe:

> *Aufsteigt der Strahl und fallend giesst*
> *Er voll die Marmorschale rund.*

Le deuxième, reposant sur le même principe, se trouve dans un célèbre distique de Schiller:

> *Im Pentameter steigt des Springquells flüssige Säule*
> *Im Hexameter drauf fällt sie melodisch herab.*[7]

De tels exemples ont encore l'intérêt de dissiper un malentendu assez courant, qui consiste à croire que l'iconicité est un phénomène exclusivement visuel. L'iconicité, ici, n'est reconnue que par la voie d'une perception auditive, qu'elle soit réelle ou mentale.

Un des plus beaux exemples d'une iconicité métaphorique se définissant par la descente mélodique se présente dans *Spousk pod vodou* (*Going under*) de Lidia Tchoukovskaïa. (Est-ce une coïncidence que ce titre − "métaphorique"! − nous parle déjà de descente?) L'auteur (le narrateur) y analyse les vers suivants:

> *Et sur la neige, en fête, splendide,*
> *Des traces de ski, comme un souvenir...*

Elle écrit: "Au mot *souvenir* la voix descend (russe: golos padaet), parce que, en se souvenant, le coeur "descend" (= le coeur se serre; russe: sertse padaet). Des traces dans l'âme, des traces dans la neige splendide." Certes, une telle observation nous conduit aux confins du vérifiable, puisque la description qui fait conclure à la présence de l'iconicité repose sur une métaphore psychologique et que l'attribution du référent psychologique est très personnelle. Cela n'empêche qu'on ne peut qu'admirer la finesse et la profondeur de l'observation ainsi que la netteté et le caractère adéquat de la description verbale

---

7. Ces deux passages m'ont été signalés par M. R. Wijbenga, de l'université de Groningue. Le poème de Schiller est riche en iconicité; ce distique a pour objet dénoté "le distique en général", et le pentamètre et l'hexamètre renvoient à des référents de ce nom. (Voir aussi Maatje, 1974, p. 206-207.)

au moyen de laquelle Lidia Tchoukovskaia nous fait entendre que nous avons affaire ici à un ressort secret et privilégié de la poésie.[8]

Ces icônes métaphoriques du niveau microstructural, dont le *representamen* est la mélodie d'une phrase ou d'une partie de la phrase, sont, de prime abord, bien différentes des "métaphores" globales citées au paragraphe 3. Soyons toutefois convaincus qu'elles sont de la même famille, que cette famille est nombreuse et qu'elle a des membres de toutes sortes.

Sur la diversité de l'iconicité métaphorique microstructurale d'autres remarques de Kamerbeek peuvent nous renseigner. Ainsi, il donne plusieurs exemples d'une iconicité métaphorique intervenant au niveau de la spatio-temporalité du texte. Je n'en citerai qu'un seul, parce qu'il est, plus que les autres de nature métaphorique, et parce que c'est un exemple cher à l'auteur, car il le cite dans deux publications différentes (1967 b, 1974). Il s'agit des célèbres vers de Malherbe (*Consolation à M. du Perrier*):

Et rose elle a vécu ce que vivent les roses
L'espace d'un matin.

En 1967, Kamerbeek écrit: "Le charme profond de ces vers ne s'explique pas tout simplement par la concision élégante de l'expression. Ce qui importe (. . .), c'est qu'ils parlent de "durée" en qu'en même temps ils ont une "durée". "L'espace d'un matin" s'intègre exactement dans l' "espace" du vers, entre les frontières duquel il est contenu".[9] En 1974, il cite les mêmes vers, et dit, pour expliquer ce qu'il appelle "le secret de ce groupe de mots": "Le dernier vers est une de ces réussites où le signifiant et le signifié sont identiques d'une manière absolue, les mots "l'espace d'un matin" occupant exactement "l'espace" du vers qui leur est réservé et réalisant par là ce que les

---

8. Voici le texte original de Tchoukovskaïa: "*I na pychnykh paradnykh snegakh/ lyjny sled, slovno pamiat o tom* . . . Na slove "pamiat" golos padaet, potomou chto sertse padaet, pripomniv. Sled v douche i sled na pychnykh snegakh." On imagine ce que la plume d'un L. Spitzer aurait fait d'un tel passage: il s'en serait servi comme point de départ d'une analyse stylistique qui aurait éclairci le message profond de ce beau livre.
9. Texte original: "De diepe bekoring van deze verzen valt niet zo maar te verklaren uit de elegante beknoptheid van zegging. Waar het (. . .) op aan komt, is dat ze over "duur" spreken en tegelijk "duur" hebben. "L'espace d'un matin" past precies in de "ruimte" van het vers tussen de grenzen waarvan het is vervat."

sémioticiens appellent une iconicité parfaite". Bien sûr, cette iconicité est métaphorique ou elle n'est pas.

Kamerbeek signale encore une troisième espèce d'iconicité métaphorique, peut-être plus secrète et plus raffinée encore que les préci-
tées. En analysant (1967,b) les vers finals du poème *Grafschrift*
(*Epitaphe*) de J. C. Bloem

> *Une pierre, fêlée par la verdure,*
> *Lettres et chiffres frustes, que la pluie remplit.*[10]

il note: "La pluie "remplit" les lettres et les chiffres frustes; elle achève
l'image du repos automnal, du transitoire de ce monde, en effaçant
presque ce qui n'etait déjà presque rien. Mais, en même temps, *remplit*
est le dernier mot du poème. En d'autres termes, le mot *remplit* "remplit" la place qui était encore ouverte avant qu'il soit là. Par sa position,
il est fidèle à sa signification, il en réalise la plénitude."[11]

Quand, dans une conversation privée, j'ai demandé à l'auteur
pourquoi il considère que le mot *remplit* "remplit" le poème, il a fait
la comparaison avec la dernière touche d'un peintre couvrant de
couleur, sur sa toile, le dernier endroit resté incolore. C'est donc
grâce à une pareille comparaison que l'élément textuel en question
reçoit son statut d'icône métaphorique: la relation entre le signe et
son référent est une relation de ressemblance en vertu de la ressemblance avec un référent mentalement ajouté, et sa description verbale
se fait par voie métaphorique (ce qui explique l'usage des guillemets,
lorsque Kamerbeek dit que le mot *remplit* "remplit" le poème).

Comme on pourrait soutenir que le mot *remplit* exécute lui-même
l'action qu'il dénote, la notion de "performativité", concept intro-
duit par Austin (1962), s'impose à l'esprit. Ce genre d'iconicité métaphorique pourrait être qualifiée d'iconicité performative. Kamerbeek
a associé les deux notions dans une boutade significative, en écrivant
(1973): "Innerhalb Wordsworth's Ouvertüre[12] wird die reinste
Ikonizität erreicht in dem Vers

10. Texte original: *Een steen, door 't groen gebarsten, en verweerde/ Letters
en cijfers, die de regen vult.*
11. Texte original: "De regen "vult" de verweerde letters en cijfers, en vol-
tooit het beeld van herfstelijke rust en vergankelijkheid door bijna uit te wissen
wat al bijna niets was. Maar tegelijk is "vult" het laatste woord van het gedicht,
"vult" het met andere woorden de plaats die open was voordat het er stond.
Door zijn plaatsing doet het zijn betekenis gestand, realiseert het de volheid van
zijn betekenis."
12. Il s'agit des vers introductoires du poème *The Prelude or Growth of a*

I cannot miss my way. I breathe again;

Ich behaupte das nicht, um die "natürliche" Bedeutung aus der Welt zu interpretieren. In dieser offenen Landschaft kann man atmen und es läuft da kein Weg, der über die anderen Wege zu bevorzugen wäre. Aber "I breathe again" bedeutet daneben auch: "Ich kann wieder dichten und füge dem Worte die Tat hinzu" (womit ein weitaus besseres Beispiel von "Performativität" gegeben ist als der bis zum Überdruss wiederholte Satz: "Ich erkläre den Krieg")."

Kamerbeek s'intéresse très particulièrement à ce genre d'iconicité, et depuis longtemps, comme on peut le constater en lisant le texte de son discours inaugural (1967,a). Si ses réflexions n'ont pas encore reçu l'attention qu'elles méritent, cela est peut-être dû au fait que, accumulant le métaphorique sur l'iconicité métaphorique, il considère certains mots comme plus spécialement appropriés à véhiculer l'expression d'une poétique immanente (au sens de "ars poetica"). Les mots *vent, respirer, voie* se rapportent, aux yeux de Kamerbeek, — et les passages cités de Bloem et de Wordsworth en sont des exemples — à la création poétique elle-même. Ce sont des "*ikonogene Wörter*". On comprend que ce mixage implicite des concepts d' "autoréférence", de "performativité" et d' "iconicité" en appelle fortement à la compréhension et au doigté analytique du lecteur.

Il s'agit de se rendre compte que l'iconicité métaphorique peut converger avec l'usage métaphorique — au sens propre — d'un mot. Tel est le cas des "mots iconogènes" de Kamerbeek. Ils sont des métaphores pour la création poétique elle-même, mais ils sont en même temps des icônes. Et, si l'on peut parfois parler de "performativité" à leur sujet, ce n'est que grâce à cet usage métaphorique.

Au chercheur s'intéressant à l'iconicité métaphorique d'un point de vue théorique, s'il est prêt à faire un travail attentif de triage et de démarcation, les études de Kamerbeek, où se manifeste une rare combinaison d'intuïtion et d'érudition, offrent un fonds extrêmement riche d'exemples.

Poet's Mind. Signalons — rien que pour relever une curieuse coïncidence (si c'en est une) — que, dès le début du poème, on trouve, aux vers 10-12, une "vallée" iconique: *What dwelling shall receive me? In what Vale/ Shall I take up my home and what sweet stream/ Shall with its murmur lull me to my rest?* Le vers que cite Kamerbeek est suivi de ceux-ci (vers 19-20): *Trances of thought and mountings of the mind/ Come fast upon me:* (...) La présence du mot *mountings* fait du mouvement ascendant de la mélodie encore une icône métaphorique.

6. Concluons. Il est certain que la notion d' "iconicité" est un instrument conceptuel efficace, sinon indispensable, dans l'étude sémiotique des systèmes (ou combinaisons de systèmes) de communication visuelle et/ou auditive, tels que l'art cinématographique, le théâtre, la danse, la musique, la peinture, l'architecture, etc. Elle aura également un rôle important à jouer dans l'étude de la langue (qui est d'ailleurs, elle aussi, un système de communication à perception visuelle et/ou auditive), vu le caractère absolument fondamental de l'iconicité dans *tout* système sémiotique (voir aussi Thom, 1973). Dans le langage poétique, l'iconicité doit son efficacité secrète mais pertinente sans doute aussi à cette circonstance spéciale caractérisant la communication par oeuvres littéraires (par des livres): elle se fait en l'absence physique directe du destinateur, de sorte que la fonction des signes par contiguïté (physique), c'est à dire des indices − qui sont, à mon sens, les signes à puissance impressive la plus forte − est pratiquement réduite à zéro. Cela vaut, bien entendu, pour toute oeuvre d'art; mais si cela est, des assertions comme celles de Lotman (1972) et de Greenlee (1973) que "tout art est iconique" se réfèrent également à l'art littéraire et aux langages qui utilisent des procédés poétiques.

Dans ces domaines, la notion d' "iconicité" est donc de même un outil conceptuel dont l'usage s'impose.

Cet usage a avant tout une grande valeur heuristique. Il en est de même de la distinction qu'on peut faire entre l'iconicité topologique, diagrammatique et métaphorique, et ce sera en fonction de sa valeur heuristique que cette distinction se fera et non pas dans un but exclusivement taxonomique. Cela est d'autant plus vrai, puisqu'elle n'est pas absolue, puisqu'elle dépend d'une prédominance, qui, à son tour, dépend de la perspective par laquelle on a choisi de considérer le signe étudié. Peirce a souligné ce fait en parlant de la distinction entre icônes, indices et symboles. Mayenowa (1973) a attiré l'attention sur l'absence de démarcation nette entre l'icône topologique et l'icône diagrammatique. De même, la démarcation entre l'icône métaphorique et les autres types d'iconicité est inévitablement floue; tout ce qu'on peut faire, c'est relever les traits prédominants dans la description verbale. D'une part, il est difficile d'éviter toute métaphore dans la description des icônes considérées comme non-métaphoriques. D'autre part, il est quasiment impossible − et indésirable! − de faire une description exclusivement métaphorique de l'icône métaphorique.

Donnons un exemple. Dans l'église de Broek-in-Waterland se trouve un vitrail, divisé en cinq sections représentant cinq phases de l'histoire de cette église. Le première montre la destruction de l'église par les Espagnols. La seconde représente l'église détruite et une église provisoire construite pour la remplacer temporairement. La troisième section montre la reconstruction de l'église originale, et on lit, dans le petit catalogue où le vitrail est décrit: "l'église provisoire passe à l'arrière-plan". En effet, l'église provisoire est représentée, dans la troisième section, plus en arrière que dans la deuxième. Ce passage à l'arrière-plan, sur le vitrail, est une icône, comme la description verbale nous le fait comprendre. Mais est-elle topologique, diagrammatique ou métaphorique? Il y a, sans doute, un peu des trois. Toute représentation picturale comporte des icônes topologiques et diagrammatiques. Cependant, la portée métaphorique de l'expression *passer à l'arrière-plan* (on comprend que l'église provisoire "devient moins importante") singularise ce fragment de la description du vitrail par rapport aux éléments textuels qui l'entourent; aussi est-on tenté de laisser prévaloir le caractère métaphorique de l'icône en question, contrairement aux autres icônes du vitrail, qui sont, elles, surtout de nature topologique.

Comparativement, on décidera de la même façon en classant les icônes poétiques.

Cela peut paraître d'une imprécision inadmissible, mais il n'en est rien. Le classement n'étant pas un but en soi, il ne demande pas plus de précision qu'il ne convienne à une bonne compréhension du phénomène étudié. Peirce lui-même, qu'on peut tout de même considérer comme le Linné de la sémiotique, a dit (2.265): "It is a nice problem to say to what class a given sign belongs; since all the circumstances of the case have to be considered. But it is seldom requisite to be very accurate; for if one does not locate the sign precisely, one will easily come near enough to its character for any purpose of logic" (rappelons que pour Peirce *sémiotique* était synonyme de *logique*).

Les icônes méritent donc d'être catégorisées, même imparfaitement. Que, parmi elles, il y ait des icônes métaphoriques de toutes sortes, j'espère l'avoir au moins rendu plausible par les exemples donnés. Je ne vois pas qu'il y ait quelque "modèle", quelque méthode ou procédure préétablie permettant de les découvrir dans les textes, surtout au niveau microstructural. L'important, pour le moment, c'est de savoir qu'on *peut* les trouver. Le chercheur se fiera à son intuition. Il peut, en cela, s'inspirer de l'exemple que Kamerbeek nous a donné.

Bibliographie

J. L. Austin, *How to do things with words,* Cambridge, Mass. 1962.
M. Bense & E. Walther, *Wörterbuch der Semiotik,* Köln, 1973.
N. Chomsky, *Aspects of the theory of syntax,* Cambridge, Mass. 1965.
U. Eco, *La struttura assente,* Milano, 1968.
U. Eco, "Introduction to a semiotics of iconic signs", in *Versus* 2/1, 1972, p. 1-15.
I. Fonagy, *Die Methaphern in der Phonetik,* Den Haag, 1963.
D. Greenlee, *Peirce's concept of sign,* Den Haag, 1973.
R. Jakobson, "A la recherche de l'essence du langage", in E. Benveniste, e.a., *Problèmes du langage,* Paris, 1966, p. 22-38.
J. Kamerbeek Jr , *Steeds gaat het vers zijn eigen weg,* Assen, 1967 (a).
J. Kamerbeek Jr , *De poëzie van J. C. Bloem in Europees perspectief,* Amsterdam, 1967 (b).
J. Kamerbeek Jr , "Über ikonogene Wörter", Amsterdam, 1973, texte polycopié.
J. Kamerbeek Jr , "Les poètes Jacques Bloem et Charles Baudelaire, un exemple d'intertextualité créatrice", texte d'une conférence prononcée le 21 novembre 1974 dans l'Institut Néerlandais à Paris, à paraître dans la *Revue de littérature comparée.*
Ju. M. Lotman, *Die Struktur literarischer Texte,* München, 1972.
F. C. Maatje, *Literatuurwetenschap,* Utrecht, 1974³.
R. J. Matthews, "Concerning a "linguistic theory" of metaphor", in *Foundations of language,* 7, 1971, p. 413-425.
M. R. Mayenowa, "An analysis of some visual signs; suggestions for discussion", in J. van der Eng & M. Grygar, eds., *Structure of texts and semiotics of culture,* Den Haag 1973, p. 197-208.
Ch. S. Peirce, *Collected papers,* vol. I-VI ed. by Ch. Hartshorne & P. Weiss, vol. VII-VIII ed. by A. W. Burks, Cambridge, Mass., 1931-1958.
J. Pelc, *Studies in functional logical semiotics of natural language,* Den Haag, 1971; chap. "Semiotic functions as applied to the analysis of the concept of metaphor": p. 142-194.
I. Stearns, "Firstness, Secondness and Thirdness", in Ph. P. Wiener & F. H. Young, eds., *Studies in the philosophy of Ch. S. Peirce,* Cambridge, Mass., 1952, p. 195-208.
R. Thom, "De l'icône au symbole; esquisse d'une théorie du symbolisme", in *Cahiers internationaux de symbolisme,* 22/23, 1973, p. 85-106.
H. S. Visser, " 't Vluchtige bestaan", in *Trouw,* 14-6-1975.

TOWARDS A COMPARATIST'S DEFINITION OF "DECADENCE"

C. de Deugd (Utrecht)

It is well-known that the contemporary Dutch author G. K. van het Reve[1] has at times called himself a decadent author, and at other times an author who stands "somewhere between Romanticism and Decadence". One of his earliest pronouncements on this theme can be taken from an interview in the middle sixties and, though relatively little known, I shall quote it here because of the interesting way in which Van het Reve himself links the character of his writings (which began to appear shortly after the second world war) with the decadent literature of the (post-)romantic era, that is, literature of the 19th century. Regrettably, scholars and critics have paid hardly any serious attention to his remarks.

Whether or not Van het Reve is really a decadent author depends, naturally, on the definition of Decadence in literature. However, there just does not exist an adequate, accepted definition of Decadence, at least I am not acquainted with one that satisfies the demands of scholarly research in its coverage of the facts. The following descriptive and interpretative approach is not intended to be more than a modest contribution to a definition of the concept of Decadence.

In the interview[2] Van het Reve says that he became aware of his own identity as a novelist by reading Mario Praz's *The Romantic Agony,* a study one may suppose to be generally known: "All of a sudden I saw that my writing about sex, drinking, death, the grave, cruelty and religion clearly carried on a venerable literary tradition of at least two centuries, that of Romanticism. I am to be located

---

1. Born in 1924. He has also published in English, and occasionally changed his name somewhat (change of first name — "Simon" —, leaving out "het", and the like.
2. *Elseviers Magazine*, August 20th 1966; he has repeated his statements on other occasions and his readers know that similar ideas have been printed on the covers of a few of his books.

somewhere between Romanticism and Decadence .... my aggressiveness derives from Romanticism, Decadence gave me my passive contemplation. The Ruthless Boy in *Nader tot U* (Nearer to Thee) is neither my ideal-ego as amateur psychologists have asserted, nor God — although he is surrounded by religious veneration and ecstasy — but very simply the homosexual pendant of *La Belle Dame Sans Merci*...[3]

I speak of Van het Reve not just to use him as a convenient point of departure, but because of the fact that decadent literature appears to him and many others not exclusively bound up with a specific *Zeitgeist* or with political, religious or, generally, social circumstances, *viz.* those of the second half of the 19th century. It means at the same time that an author, convinced of the decadent character of his oeuvre, does not make an attempt at defining or circumscribing the phenomenon "decadent literature" in order, subsequently, to try to decide whether his work fits this definition; but that he only advances a number of characteristics of what is more or less tacidly assumed to be decadent literature, points out that they are to be found in his works also, appeals to the well-known study of Praz (who does not give a definition either and does not even differentiate between Romanticism and Decadence) and . . . leaves it at that. If we would add a devout "amen" to it we would be faithfully conforming to Van het Reve's own style of writing but it would be somewhat paradoxical: we are here not at the end but at the very beginning of our problem.

To put the whole thing differently: Van het Reve implicitly posits anew two old questions, that have never been answered in a satisfactory way, *viz.* what *is* Decadence and by what *means* do we find out what it is.

Having stated the basic problem at hand, it would perhaps be

3. Translations are mine unless otherwise stated: "Maar toen kreeg ik toevallig het boek van Prof. Praz in handen, *The Romantic Agony,* en ging mij opeens een licht op. Ik zag opeens dat mijn geschrijf over sex, drank, dood, graf, wreedheid en religie prima aansloot op een eerbiedwaardige literaire traditie: die van de Romantiek. Ik sta ergens tussen de Romantiek en de Decadentie ... waarbij ik van de Romantiek de agressie heb en van de Decadentie de dadenloze bespiegeling. De figuur van Meedogenloze Jongen in *Nader tot U* . ... is niet mijn ideaal-ik, zoals amateurpsychologen wel hebben beweerd, en ook niet God — al wordt hij omgeven door religieuze vereering en vervoering — maar doodgewoon de homosexuele pendant van *La Belle Dame Sans Merci* .... *Loc. cit.*

helpful now to return briefly to the question of defining "the concept of decadence in literature". However, it would be incorrect not to mention first another aspect which many scholars are apt to accentuate: the relation between literature and society.

There certainly are "connecting lines" between the socio-economic developments in the 19th century on the one hand, and the literature of this period on the other. Much more than might appear at first sight is perhaps socio-economically determined. This, however, is a difficult and intricate problem. Even an avowed Neo-Marxist as Marcuse has pointed out that "the term 'decadent' far more often denounces the genuinely progressive traits of a dying culture than the real factors of decay".[4] This means, and I believe Marcuse is correct, that social decay and progressiveness are not necessarily mutually exclusive.

One thing stands out: the Marxist concept of alienation could not possibly be overlooked when probing the causes of the rise and decline of the aestheticist-decadent movement in the 19th century. But instead of probing these *causes* I should like to take a close look at the phenomena as such in order to attempt an answer to the questions which, as said before, are implicitly posited by Van het Reve's estimation of his own (contemporary!) writings.

Again coming back to the problem of defining Decadence, it is of course impossible, within the framework of an article of this length, to summarize the several discussions which can be found in the secondary literature. But it is possible to mention a number of references that enable the discriminating reader to judge for himself.[5]

4. Herbert Marcuse, *One Dimensional Man: The Ideology of Industrial Society* ("Sphere Book" Edition, London, 1968), p. 61.
5. Blok, W. *Verhaal en lezer: Een onderzoek naar enige structuuraspecten van "Van oude mensen de dingen die voorbijgaan" van Louis Couperus*, Groningen, 1960. Bourget, Paul, 'Théorie de la Décadence', in: *Essais de psychologie contemporaine, vol. I, Paris, 1899. Carter, A. E., The Idea of Decadence in French Literature 1830-1900*, Toronto, 1958. Cassagne, Albert, *La théorie de l'art pour l'art en France chez les derniers Romantiques et les premiers Réalistes*, Paris, 1906. David, Claude, *L'oeuvre poétique de Stefan George*. Abbeville, 1952. Drop, W. 'Verkenning van De Berg van Licht', in: *Handelingen van het zesentwintigste Nederlandse Filologencongres*, Groningen, 1960, pp. 162-165; 'Noodlot en romanstructuur bij Couperus' *Tijdschrift voor Nederlandse Taal- en Letterkunde* 79 (1963), pp. 288-305. Duthie, Enid Lowry, *L'Influence du Symbolisme français dans le renouveau poétique de l'Allemagne: Les Blätter für die Kunst de 1892 à 1900*, Paris, 1933. Elema, J., *De Tuin van Algabal*, Gronin-

Any attempt to formulate conclusions or ideas about Decadence (and its inseparable accompaniment Aestheticism) is beset with a methodological problem: how do we arrive at statements and conclusions that are verifiable and dependable? Not, in my opinion, by means of half-way a priori theories about decay, degeneration, artificiality, *fin-de-siècle* mood and so forth, and then applying these theories and considerations to a number of literary works of art. Although such methods may have their merits in certain sciences, the actual practice of literary scholarship has so clearly demonstrated their lack of reliability — leading to an accumulation of confusion — that one wonders why they have not long since been discredited as being inappropriate and inefficacious.

With no more pretention than the hope that it will turn out to be a workable method, I shall try to apply some sort of phenomenological approach which was introduced elsewhere, at the occasion

gen, etc., 1957. Farmer, Albert, J., *Le mouvement esthétique et "décadent" en Angleterre (1873-1900)*, Paris, 1931. Fischer, Ernst, "Zum Problem der Dekadenz", in: *Kunst und Koexistenz: Beitrag zu einer modernen marxistischen Ästhetik*, Reinbek bei Hamburg, 1966, pp. 155-179. Galle, Marc, *Couperus in de kritiek*, Amsterdam, 1963. Glur, Guido, *Kunstlehre und Kunstanschauung des Georgekreises und die Aesthetik Oscar Wildes*, Bern, 1957. Lachmann, Eduard, *Die ersten Bücher Stefan Georges: Annäherungen an das Werk*, Berlin, 1933. Lethève, Jacques, "Le thème de la décadence dans les lettres françaises à la fin du XIXe siècle", in: *Revue d'Histoire Litteraire de la France* 63 (1963), pp. 46-61. Linke, Hansjürgen, *Das Kultische in der Dichtung Stefan Georges und seiner Schule*, Köln, 1954. Livi, François, *J.-K. Huysmans. A rebours et l'esprit décadent*, Paris, 1972. Mattenklott, Gert, *Bilderdienst: Ästhetische Opposition bei Beardsley und George*. München, 1970. Poe, Edgar Allan, "The Poetic Principle", in: *The Works*, vol. V, London etc., 1895, pp. 101-124. Popma, K. J., *Beschouwingen over het Werk van Louis Couperus*, Amsterdam, 1968. Praz, Mario, *The Romantic Agony*, New York, 1956. Original title: *La carne, la morte e il diavolo nella letteratura romantica*. Richard, Noël, *Le mouvement décadent: Dandys, esthètes et quintessents*, Paris, 1968. Rosteutscher, Joachim, *Das ästhetischen Idol im Werke von Winkelmann, Novalis, Hoffmann, Goethe, George und Rilke*, Bern, 1956. Schaffner, Roland, *Die Salome-Dichtungen von Flaubert, Laforgue, Wilde und Mallarmé: Vergleichende Gestalt- und Stilanalyse*, Würzburg, 1956. Swart, Koenraad, W., *The Sense of Decadence in Nineteenth-Century France*, The Hague, 1964. Tricht, H. M. van, *Louis Couperus. Een Verkenning*, Den Haag, 1965[2]. Valkhoff, P., "Couperus en Lombard", in: *Ontmoetingen tussen Nederland en Frankrijk*, 's Gravenhage, 1943. Zagona, Helen Grace, *The Legend of Salome and the Principle of Art for Art's Sake*, Genève etc., 1960.

of which account was given of its scholarly legitimacy.[6] So I shall start from the fact that, despite the lack of satisfactory definitions of such conceptions as Aestheticism and Decadence and the numerous and sharply divergent ways in which they have been evaluated, there is the certainty that *by and large* we know what does and what does not belong in the aestheticist-decadent tradition. These phenomena can be gathered, organized and compared with one another and viewed more closely, and this will be done in the sense mentioned before: with all the phenomenological "Einklammerungen" etc. A description containing more nuances can, as I hope, be arrived at after we have enumerated and compared "the by and large cases" of the tradition under discussion. This paper will end with a suggestion as to how these (very many) nuances can perhaps be handled.

Working thus one discovers (as I hope can be substantiated in the following) an intricate relationship between decadent and aestheticist works. Decadence appears to be distinguishable but cannot be separated from Aestheticism: all decadent works are also to a certain extent aestheticist in character, but the thesis is not always reversible, that is, an aestheticist work is not necessarily decadent.

Against this background it becomes apparent that Aestheticism and Decadence can not but be discussed *together,* and that only in the course of this discussion it should be attempted to "crystallize" some distinctions between the two.

Surveying and comparing the data at hand one can distinguish, I believe, five main characteristics of aestheticist-decadent literature.

First of all: the basic and most salient feature of all Aestheticism and Decadence is the conviction that *beauty is the essence of art* and, accordingly, of all literature. Beauty is the first and last word with the esthetes and decadents, and with some of them this preoccupation has all the markings of a cult of beauty. One could say that the emphasis on beauty, stemming from Romanticism (one need but to think of Keats), becomes a glorification of beauty and with several of them it eventually grows into a kind of religious ecstasy and a veritable deification of the beautiful.

6. C. de Deugd, *Het metafysisch grondpatroon van het romantische literaire denken: De fenomenologie van een geestesgesteldheid*, Groningen, 2nd ed., 1972, Chapter 1.

It is superfluous to dwell upon this aspect for long. By way of general orientation it may suffice to mention a few of the most prominent names and titles in each country of Western Europe.

There were, for instance, in France writers like Flaubert, Théophile Gautier (his, still somewhat playful, *Préface to Mademoiselle de Maupin*), Baudelaire (his "Hymne à la Beauté" in *Les fleurs du mal*), Huysmans (particularly *À Rebours*); as concerns England, it is, of course the name of the author of *A Picture of Dorian Gray* that springs to mind, and not in the least part because of Wilde's famous (in his time many have said notorious) Foreword to his novel. Walter Pater, and especially *Marius the Epicurian* and the "Conclusion" to *The Renaissance* (which at one time was estimated by the author himself as being dangerous for "some of those young men into whose hands it might fall"[7]) should not be left unmentioned. In Flanders we may think of Pol de Mont. In the Netherlands one is inclined to refer to the Movement of the Eighties: to the young Albert Verwey, to Kloos, and particularly to Perk, whose attempt at applying the words of the Lord's Prayer to beauty (hallowed be thy name, etc.) is known to anyone with some acquaintance with Dutch literature. As for Germany, Stephan George stands out for his *Blätter für die Kunst* in general and his *Algabal* in particular.

The very heart of the matter has been so aptly expressed by Verwey: in 1905, looking back upon the Dutch Movement of the Eighties, and having in mind this deification of beauty, he wrote the memorable lines about the ideas and feelings of the men of the "eighties", comparing them to those of a devout person, worshipping his god. But the difference, according to Verwey, was that with them the god was poetry itself and the beauty of poetry.[8]

Naturally, when speaking of Dutch literature without extensively dealing with Louis Couperus one runs the risk of being reproached for omitting an important figure on the aestheticist-decadent scene. That reproach would be justified and in all likelihood even under-

7. Footnote to the third edition (1873); 1st Ed. 1868. For this reason he had omitted this piece in the second edition.
8. "Het gevoel waarin de poëzie die jongeren bracht of aantrof, was dat van den vrome die zijn god aanbidt; maar de god was de poëzie-zelf, beeld-geworden, de god was de Schoonheid". (*Inleiding tot de nieuwe Nederlandsche dichtkunst, 1880-1900,* Amsterdam 1905; Quoted from the 5th Edition, 1921, p. 12 (cf. p. 24).)

stated: Couperus is not just an important, but a most prominent figure in the present context; he is, to my mind, the only European author who wrote a thoroughly decadent novel, which by all standards is great literature, *viz. De berg van licht.* Since so annoyingly little has been written about him with regard to his decadence, a separate, far more extensive treatment than can be given here would be required in order to do him even partial justice.[9] Here just a cursory glance at the monumental work of Couperus has to suffice. In connection with this first and basic feature there are not only his pronouncements such as when he speaks of the "priest of beauty" (and as such undergoes a "consecration"),[10] but there are also major parts of his *Collected Works* that show that Couperus in every way imaginable was reponsive to beauty and, likewise, that he himself tried time and again to array each particular subject with the highest possible degree of literary beauty.

The way all this is carried into effect is not to each of us as interesting as it was to many who lived during the aestheticist-decadent period, just like it is impossible for the very majority of us to conceive of *beauty* as being of such essential and lofty significance. We are inclined, rather, to value literature for its interpretative task, its *Deutung des Daseins,* perhaps even more for its concrete social values and sometimes for what Jaeger says that the poems of Homer do, namely "present the structure of reality in its entirety".[11] Art for art's sake as much as beauty for the very sake of beauty seems alien to the majority of us, living in the second half of the 20th century.

However this may be, the glorification of beauty was an extremely weighty matter with aesthetes and decadents, and it would be next to impossible to interpret many of their works correctly if we did not continuously keep in mind this very basis of their literary theory and practice.

The *second* of the five main characteristics is the marked emphasis on all *matters of form.* We are here concerned with a

9. A comparative study, *Louis Couperus in the Aestheticist-Decadent Tradition,* is ready for publication.

10. Louis Couperus, *Verzamelde werken,* Amsterdam 1953-1957, IX, pp. 597-98.

11. Werner Jaeger, *Paideia; The Ideals of Greek Culture,* translated by Gilbert Highet (3rd English Edition, 3 vols., Oxford, 1946), Vol. I, p. 429, note 34.

phenomenon the first traces of which can be found with late romantic authors, men who are on, and often over, the borderline between Romanticism proper and everything which for the sake of convenience we might refer to as post-romantic — authors like Alfred de Vigny, Edgar Allan Poe and several others of comparable attitudes. Especially the latter (Poe) evinces many signs of affinity with post-romantic thought; he had a decisive influence on three generations of French authors, many of whom were absorbed in the aestheticist-decadent tradition, while others exhibited many signs of spiritual kinship with it.

In fact, some of the poems of Poe are nothing but experiments with the "formal possibilities" of poetry, as for example his *Ulalume* ("The skies they were ashen and sober" .... etc.).

In this context one is disposed to think of how much emphasis the Romantics placed on the contents ("message", "meaning", "matter") of literature; to Shelley, Hugo, Wordsworth, Brentano and to all the others the "meaning", the content, was of the greatest moment. As to *Ulalume,* unquestionably a post-romantic poem, it is, in the light of the preceding Romantic poetry, almost astonishing to see how extremely meagre the content actually is: in Poe's poem of 94 lines the poet just journeys with Psyche his soul till they encounter a "legended tomb". At that moment the poet realizes that exactly one year ago he had buried his beloved Ulalume there. Gerrit Achterberg — how striking is the resemblance of Poe's theme to that of the very majority of Achterberg's poems — Achterberg could have said the same in six lines, but then, such a comparison would be unfair to Poe as his intent was to experiment with what, in his days, were rather revolutionary poetic forms.

Here he endeavours, perhaps not consciously, to settle with Romanticism and actually inaugurated a new era, an era in which aesthetes and decadents were in their prime.

That they do occupy an imporant place ought to be ascribed in part to the careful attention they paid to the formal aspects of literature and their intense love for arduous attempts at perfection in the "realm of form".

Naturally, this reminds us of the Movement of the Eighties in the Netherlands. The men of the eighties, as is well-known, stubbornly emphasized the idea that form and content are united, are "one", while in the practice of their writings, and occasionally even in their theoretical pronouncements,[12] they did not hesitate to show that to them form was of decisive and *supreme* importance.[13]

It is an inconsistency which is not restricted to the Dutch; something similar took place, for example, in France with the Parnassiens.

It can hardly be seen as accidental that the "Eighties", this renaissance of Dutch poetry, was accompanied by a revival of the sonnet, traditionally known as the extreme example of strictness of form.

These ideas are practiced everywhere in those writings about which there is no disagreement as to their belonging to the aestheticist-decadent tradition. One of the first ones to speak on this subject, Théophile Gautier, who in his *Mademoiselle de Maupin* (in the thirties of the 19th century) "promulgates" the confession that "la correction de la forme est vertu",[14] is in substantial agreement with a writer contributing to one of the last aestheticist-decadent journals, *viz.* George's *Blätter für die Kunst*, who speaks of "die heilige kunst der linien und mit dem lichtglanz der gedanken die vollendung der form".[15] These two examples are separated in time by more than half a century, but very many homogeneous pronouncements, and very often the corresponding practice, can be found throughout those sixty years.

It is deplorable that so very few studies are at our disposal on this point with regard to Couperus. Some of what is available, however, studies like those of Blok[16] and Drop[17], discloses how great an artist Couperus is with respect to formal (structural) aspects and .... the relationship between form and matter; for with him the painstaking and detailed attention paid to form does not monopolize the work as a whole as with so many writers (and not only poets) of congenial spirit. One can but hope for more studies in this vein.

12. Cf. Frank van der Goes in *De Nieuwe Gids*, 4,2 (1890) p. 279.

13. Cf. C. de Deugd, "Art for Art's Sake and Form and Matter", in *Miscellania litteraria,* ed. W. A. P. Smit and H. Sparnaay, Groningen, 1959, pp. 41-52.

14. *Mademoiselle de Maupin,* ed. M. A. Gondry, Wien, n.d. [1836], p. 63.

15. Paul Gérady, "Geistige kunst", *Blätter für die Kunst,* II, 4 (1894-1895) p. 111.

16. W. Blok, *Verhaal en lezer: Een onderzoek naar enige structuuraspecten van Van oude mensen de dingen die voorbijgaan van Louis Couperus,* Groningen, 1960.

17. W. Drop, "Noodlot en romanstructuur bij Louis Couperus" in *Tijdschrift voor Nederlandse taal-en letterkunde,* LXXIX (1963)pp. 288-305;zie ook van Drop. "Verkenning van De berg van licht", in *Handelingen van het zevenentwintigste Nederlandse filologencongres,* Groningen 1960, pp. 162-5.

Glur, a Swiss who wrote a small but fine study about Oscar Wilde and the *Georgekreis* has expressed it in a very interesting and even peremptory way. Speaking of aesthetes and decadents he says: "Man betet die Schönheit an, aber nur die *geformte* Schönheit".[18]

Here we witness phenomena which present a kind of culmination of what finds its ultimate origin in the Romantic period. What has been said in the foregoing should of course be put in relation to the idea of *l'art pour l'art,* art for the sake of art only, and the total rejection of the idea of mimesis.

Nature as a norm and criterion for art in the classical and especially the neo-classical sense of imitation had been questioned long before the "official" romantic period (cf. Young, for instance, and many authors with cognate ideas, some of them even writing at an earlier date than he[19]) and was brusquely, if not often with great contempt, dismissed by the romantics. But this did not mean that many romantics had no harmonious and intimate relationship with Nature — Wordsworth is positively not an exception in this regard.

This relationship is for aesthetes and decadents either non-existent (cf. Wilde's well-known and extremist formulation of this position: "nature imitates art") or of secondary importance in the sense that to them the *artificial,* which usually comes down to artificial *beauty,* comes first.

Authors like Gautier, Wilde, George, Huysmans, Couperus, Flaubert (and others to a greater or lesser degree) often love to render the most elaborate, ostentatious descriptions of whatever is artificial: the apparently indiscriminate accumulations of gold and marble, of crimson and purple, of all that glitters and sparkles, the exuberance, the artificial splendour and opulence.

The problem, often referred to in 19th century literary studies, *viz.* that of differentiating between romantic and post-romantic literature, or more specifically: between literature un-questionably romantic in character and predominantly astheticist-decadent literature, does not seem to be a conundrum beyond solution. Even if Praz, repeatedly quoted on matters related to

18. G. Glur, *Kunstlehre und Kunstanschauung des Georgekreises und die Aesthetik Oscar Wildes,* Bern, 1957, p. 16. Italics mine.
19. Edward Young, *Conjectures on Original Composition,* 1759. For this development see: C. de Deugd, "Mimesis", *Nieuw Vlaams Tijdschrift,* 28, (1975) pp. 710-734

43

romantic and decadent literature, does not make a distinction between romanticism on the one hand, and aestheticism-decadence on the other, it is beyond question that there is at least one conspicuous difference: the craving for the artificial — an aspect of the decadent mind not confined to the life literary — and the corresponding practice as briefly described here, definitely separates the romantics from the aesthetes and decadents. The latter are not "The Last Romantics" as Hough has it;[20] they are, though "children of Romanticism," basically of a different frame of mind.

The *third* feature of the aestheticist-decadent "movement"[21] is something that at first reading may be thought to be the same as what is traditionally called "impressionism", but for which I prefer the term "sensitivism", because the phenomena which I am endeavouring to depict, imply far more than just impressionism in the usual, historic sense.

Speaking of sensitivism it should be evident that I neither think of a literary movement for, obviously, there never existed anything of the kind, nor a specific sort of poetry, although some of Gorter's poems, for instance, have been called "sensitivist".

The term is used here to chart an internationally traceable current *away from* ideas, "*Tendenz*", abstractions (generally speaking, "ideal content") and *towards* an increasingly greater stress on the task and the possibilities of the senses. And only one aspect of it comes to life in impressionistic writing and criticism. It seems not difficult to demonstrate that these two, impressionism and what I have termed "sensitivism", are not the same when one thinks of Rimbaud's well-known "dérèglement systématique de tous les sens". Everything Rimbaud tries to do in this respect is related to the possibilities "of the life of the senses" but one could certainly not assert it to be an impressionist experiment.

However this be, the phenomenon is a truly international one.

20. Graham Hough, *The Last Romantics,* London, 1949.
21. I use the word movement here and at other places only for want of a better. Those which we by and large know to be aestheticist-decadent authors do have the characteristics which I try to disclose in this article, but they do not constitute a coherent group, a genuine "movement". They may show naturalistic features (Couperus), they may be "classified" as symbolists (cf. Mallarmé whose love of artificiality is known) etc.

One may think of the much practiced synaesthesia, which in the long run goes so far as to create the hope, perhaps even the expectation, that once there will come into existence something like "total art", an art which could appeal to *all the senses* at the same time. Baudelaire speaks of this in *Les fleurs du mal*[22] but of course such a development was not possible, although many did what, as far as sensitivist practices were concerned, was feasible within the framework of a literary work: Mallarmé; Rimbaud's experiments with the vowels, to each of which he attributed a certain colour; Gorter in *Mei*, which has been described as an "explosion of the wonderful life of the senses",[23] and also in many of his shorter poems; as well as Van Deyssel in some of his prose fragments. Something of it comes to life in Netscher's *Herfst in het woud* and Van Looy's *De nachtcactus*.

Like in France and The Netherlands, one finds the same and similar instances in Germany and England, primarily in the works that shall be named when discussing the next, that is, the fourth characteristic of aestheticist-decadent literature.

It was Van Eeden who as it were summarized the tendency of the Movement of the Eighties and, as became apparent from the foregoing enumeration, a major tendency of the literary spirit in Western Europe, when he said: "we people of this time enjoy the life of the senses as no generation before us has ever done".[24]

As to experiencing the splendour of the life of the senses one realizes how much kinship there is between the authors named and Couperus; his is often such a luxuriantly sensuous prose – not to speak of themes, see the next (fourth) characteristic – that he ought to be studied on the same level, that is, in a comparative study with those who are generally acknowledged as the representatives and outstanding spokesmen of the aestheticist-decadent movement, men like Oscar Wilde, Stephan George, Huysmans, *et al.* However, as said before, a separate treatment has become a necessity in his case; at

22. Cf. The poem "Tout entière," in Baudelaire, *Oeuvres complètes,* ed. Y-G. le Dantec and Claude Pichois, Pléiade (Paris 1961), p. 40.

23. J. A. Rispens, *Richtingen en figuren in de Nederlandsche letterkunde na 1880,* Kampen, 1938, p. 40.

24. Frederik van Eeden in *De Nieuwe Gids,* 1888, pp. 508-9: "Wij menschen van dezen tijd genieten ons zinnelijk leven zoals geen menschengeslacht dat ooit gedaan heeft."

present he can, just like the others, only be mentioned in a general way.

Thus far I have spoken of the veneration for *beauty*; second of the specific preference for poetical *form*; and, third, of what has here been termed *sensitivism.*

That the latter two points, are intimately related to the first, the "basic" feature which proved to be a veritable *cult* of beauty, seems clear; for, as concerns poetical form, one notes the attempts at enrichment of beauty by means of a detailed attention paid to all matters of form and, as concerns sensitivism, there is the intense experience of beauty in the realm of the sensuous.

Now a similar relationship seems to exist between the veneration for beauty and the *fourth* point to be discussed here, which could perhaps be called the thematic or the "thematological" one, in other words, the particular, very specific choice of themes among those "by and large" designated as Aesthetes and Decadents. In many respects we now enter the immediate realm of Decadence proper, but about distinctions and borderlines I shall have occasion to speak later.

It is a remarkable feature of our subject that those authors described here have evidently been restlessly in search of *themes,* in order to bring about a kind of beauty that should be different from whatever had been known by man before, and to bring it about by means of a very specific way of stimulating the senses, or, to put it more generally, the (artistic) sensibility.

This, of course, concurs in some way with what I previously called sensitivism. On the other hand, there is a decidedly new element here which, I believe, is the cause of our entering, as said, in many respects the domain of Decadence proper. This will become clearer when we discuss the fifth and last characteristic of aestheticist-decadent literature.

In practice this "thematic aspect" means that the same or very cognate themes appear over and over again and that they all possess certain qualities. To understand something of this coherence, the very frequent appearances and these specific qualities, is of the greatest significance if one wishes to understand the aestheticist and decadent mind.

There is an extensive study about three of the most favourite themes of the period — "flesh", "death" and "devil" — by Mario Praz[25] and therefore I can be somewhat concise as far as this topic is concerned.

In naming "exoticism" as one of the main preoccupations of the time, one goes right to the heart of what is to be discussed when dealing with this fourth characteristic. Exoticism is the desire, the nostalgic yearning for what is far removed and unfamiliar, for what is strange and exotic; the Orient, the Near East, decadent Ancient Rome, and so forth. In the words of Praz, the exoticist "transports himself in imagination outside the actualities of time and space and thinks that he sees in whatever is past and remote from him the ideal atmosphere for the contentment of his own senses".[26]

The examples are numerous. Those who are familiar with Baudelaire's *Les fleurs du mal* will be reminded of several of the poems in this collection, "Parfum exotique", "L'invitation au voyage", "À une Malabaraise", and so on; one might think of Flaubert's novel *Salambô*, Gautier's *Une nuit de Cléopatre*, *De berg van licht*, *Xerxes* and *Iskander* by Couperus, Stephan George's *Algabal* and many more.

A further accumulation seems superfluous; the point I am trying to make is that study of this post-romantic exoticism reveals something of basic importance because it will turn up later on time and again, when discussing other themes: one observes a continuous search for new and different "forms" of beauty in order to intensify and to invigorate what we might call — using a somewhat unusual expression — the sense-consciousness, that is, the awareness that human life is fully determined by the senses, that, as a matter of fact, "life" is to a very great extent the equivalent of "the life of the senses". Here we also notice the close relation between sensitivism and the choice and exploration of themes.

There is a search for new possibilities, not afforded by the immediate environment, the culture and the everyday people one lives with, for new opportunities of satisfying and abating the longing for beauty and of titillating and exciting the senses to an ever increasing degree and, consequently, the sensuous life in its entirety.

There is, for instance, the theme of the "femme fatale", that we

25. *The Romantic Agony,* English translation by Angus Davidson ("Meridian Books" Edition) New York 1956. Originally published in Italian.
26. *Op. cit.,* p. 200.

come across throughout Western Europe, in Swinburne, Pater, Wilde, Gautier, Flaubert, Moreau, etc. Heliogabalus, the late Roman emperor whose life, full of aberrations, cruelty and sacrilege ends in an orgy of murder and mass hysteria – this Heliogabalus dwells everywhere and certainly not only with George, Couperus or Lombard. There is a widespread interest in vampirism, in such abnormal practices as sadism, masochism, flagellantism, and so on. There is, furthermore, a similar interest in themes which, though not perverse, clearly deviate from what is common, e.g. narcissism, bisexuality and homosexuality.

Closely allied to what has been described thus far are such themes as the life and fate of abnormal characters in a, we might say "psychiatric sense", for example neurasthenic, hypochondriac, heavily depressed, hysteric, in a word, psychopathological, figures. (One finds these themes also in The Netherlands and occasionally even with those not noted for their being aestheticist-decadent authors: with Van Deyssel, Emants, Van Oudshoorn, Couperus and others.)

These and several others are the themes the remarkable post-- romantic sensibility of aesthetes and decadents appeared to have craved for.

The *fifth* and last characteristic carries us still further into the problems of Aestheticism and Decadence. It is the principle, not so much of the autonomy of literature as that of the *sovereignty,* the complete supremacy of literature over human life and nature. In practice it meant that everything that has been discussed up till now reached a kind of culminating point in the attempt to completely "aestheticize" literature *and* life.

The autonomy of literature is, at least to my mind, a principle which has rightly gained recognition. Literature is autonomous alongside other realms of life that are also autonomous. Art (literature) is autonomous in its own domain; interference from the outside need not be tolerated; essentially non-artistic demands need not be complied with, etc. It is from this point of view that such well-known ideas as, among others, that of art for art's sake originate – matters which are familiar, though not necessarily agreeable, or acceptable, to all of us and need not detain us here.

However, for those who are of a fully consistent aestheticist-decadent mind this autonomy is not enough. To them literature has

48

become of such paramount and dominating importance that it is the full sovereignty of literature that they demand and that implies that literature is to *reign,* also in other areas of life. Liteature reigns unconditionally; and, accordingly, everything becomes what I have termed "aestheticized".

In using this unusual word I mean, first, that literally everything is used for experiments with regard to beautiful effects and, second, that everything is explored to stimulate and excite the senses, even those realms of life and those aspects of human existence which, though often described, previously had never been linked with the idea of *beauty.*

The Decadents carry their peculiar cravings for increasingly stronger stimuli from ever new experiments to the length of seeking and seeing beauty in pain, in death, in mental and bodily cruelty (several methods of torture, for instance) in all kinds of human misery, in the suffering borne by martyrs in history, in such aspects of religion as the suffering of Christ, and so forth.

How widespread and powerful these ideas must have been can be gathered from the fact that even such an intelligent and level-headed poet as was Albert Verwey, as a young man, came to some extent under its influence. We know that Verwey later on moves away from the aestheticist and decadent aspects of the Movement of the Eighties but, as a youth, he, too, said: "Make poetry out of sorrow"[27] and he himself tries to do so as we see from his "Christ-sonnets" in which we find such lines as "Beauty of Sorrow on this dark earth", and the like.[28]

Something similar we find with Oscar Wilde. To him the life of Christ was "a manifestation of the beauty of sorrow, it was an idyll, the most wonderful of poems".[29] Stephan George "thinks" "Ein *Schmerz* der sich . . . in Schönheit und verhaltener, klarer Form äussert".[30]

The same holds good with respect to beauty and evil. Wilde's Dorian Gray had learned "to look upon evil simply as a mode

27. *Oorspronkelijk dichtwerk,* Amsterdam-Santpoort, 1938, vol. I, p. 37. "Van de liefde die vriendschap heet": "maak poezie/ Van leed."
28. *Op. cit.,* p. 38: "Schoonheid van Smarten op deez, donkere aard."
29. *De Profundis,* in *The Works of Oscar Wilde,* ed. G. F. Maine, London and Glasgow, 1960, pp. 868-69.
30. As formulated by Glur,*op.cit.,* p. 26.

through which he could realize his conception of the beautiful".[31]
Elsewhere he expresses almost literally the same idea but there the
word "evil" has been replaced by "suffering and sorrow".[32]

There is little use in continuing to quote and to refer. Also the
Movement of the Eighties presents us with much more (than the few
lines quoted from Verwey) that has hitherto not been brought into
the framework of an internationally oriented study. But here we
need no more than a few clarifying examples.

Nearing the end of the discussion[33] the reader may be justified in
asking whether I have now given a definition of Decadence. The
answer depends largely on what one considers to be a definition
when it concerns the field of literary studies. I have been aware from
the beginning that defining could only be done in a limited and more
or less tentative way.

Having started from the premise that *by and large* we know what
works belong in the aestheticist-decadent tradition, it must be
apparent, after the fivefold dissection, that there is a rather great
variety and this seems to be a crucial point. I am inclined to see the
very heart of Decadence in the last two of the "five" (however, such
works invariably contain much of the first three) but even
then, there remains a problem: it is perhaps not so difficult to say
what a full-fledged decadent work is, but what to say of the many
borderline cases of even works that are plainly riddlesome as to any
classification at all? Not even for a beginning student would it be a
problem to see that Huysmans' *À Rebours* and Beardsley's *Under the
Hill* are thoroughly decadent works, but what about Couperus' *Eline
Vere* and *Antiek Toerisme,* Busken Huet's *Lidewyde,* much of the
work of Arthur Schnitzler, and so on, or — and this is the reason why
I commenced with briefly speaking about Van het Reve — what can
be said of an ostensibly romantic-decadent work like *Nader tot U* or
of *De taal der liefde* and others of his writings?

31. Wilde, *Works,* p. 115.
32. *Op. cit.,* p. 872.
33. The problem of the existence of a specific "decadent style" has been
insufficiently investigated in literary studies and thus far I have not been able to
verify whether or not it is inherent in all decadent literature, although the term
"decadent. style" has been in use for a long time. (Cf. J. Kamerbeek's erudite
article" 'Style de décadence': Généalogie d'une formule", *Revue de littérature
comparée,* 39 (1965) pp. 268-86).

Perhaps there is a possibility that this phenomenological approach serves as some kind of "guide line". If it would be workable at all, we could perhaps use such classifications as "largely an aestheticist work but with such and such (minor) decadent features"; "aestheticist novel without a trace of decadence"; "predominantly decadent and exposing an extraordinary sensitivist awareness"; "thematologically speaking a decadent work but never crossing the proper boundaries of literary autonomy"; "a characteristically 'exotist' poem but no trace of Decadence", and so forth and so on.

Working thus, the notion of knowing "by and large" which is so *very basic* to all that has been written here, is not likely to disappear altogether, but it could perhaps be brought back to, scholarly speaking, more satisfying and reliable proportions.

Would it be worth our while trying it out only once . . . . on Van het Reve?

INTERPLAY OF SEMANTICS,
SYNTAX AND RHYTHM IN FET'S POEM:
WHISPERS, TIMID BREATHING

Jan van der Eng (Amsterdam)

Šepot, robkoe dychan'e,
    Treli solov'ja,
Serebro i kolychan'e
    Sonnogo ruč'ja,

Svet nočnoj, nočnye teni,
    Teni bez konca,
Rjad volšebnych izmenenij
    Milogo lica,

V dymnych tučkach purpur rozy,
    Otblesk jantarja,
I lobzanija, i slezy,
    I zarja, zarja! . .

Whispers, timid breathing,
    A nightingale's trills,
Silver and swaying
    Of a sleepy brook,

Night light, night shadows,
    Shadows wihtout end,
A series of magical changes
    On a dear face,

In the misty clouds — purple of a rose,
    Glistening of amber,
And kisses, and tears,
    And the dawn, the dawn! . .*

---

*Translation in: Richard F. Gustafson, *The Imagination of Spring: The Poetry of Afanasy Fet* (New Haven, 1966), p. 161.

This poem is the poetic report of a rendezvous characterised by intimacy and beauty, and – at the end – strong emotionality. The intimacy is expressed most strongly in line 1, the beauty in ll. 2-8 in the subtle enumeration of the auditive and visual characteristics of the night, that also pertain to the delight of two people engrossed in one another. The emotionality in the poem coincides with the break of dawn which seems to disrupt the intimate closeness of the lovers (ll. 9-12).

How can it be that the poet in twelve lines manages to lay down an ecstatic picture of the night, while at the same time he uses this picture to bring the delight of being together with the beloved to its culminating point and with the evocation of dawn connects symptoms of a dramatic separation? In other words: how does he manage to amass such a compact quantity of data with increasing expressivity and a dramatic culmination in such a small number of words?

An important means in this poem to convey a great deal of information in a few words is its syntactical structure. A nominative compound sentence, its segments being mostly asyndetic gives the opportunity to express divergent information, based on a few elements characteristic of all the nominative segments: the unity of place and time of all the data expressed in the asyndetic segments. At the same time this syntactic structure enables the poet to add other common characteristics to the variety of lexical groups in the consecutive segments most effectively. In this poem this happens in various ways. The potential emotional significant element connected with "šepot" (whispers) is being actualised in the second nominative segment of line 1 as a result of the effect of the word "robkoe" (timid) in the combination "robkoe dychanie" (timid breathing). The auditive element in "šepot" and "dychanie" is brought to the fore by the third segment, that is line 2 of the poem, and especially by the word "treli" (trills) in the combination "treli solov'ja" (a nightingale's trills).

The emotionality in "šepot" (whispers) and "robkoe dychanie" (timid breathing) is given a fresh impulse by the word "treli" (trills) with which it is easy to connect an element of passion. The information given in the other segments of the first stanza reveals the poetic facts characteristic of the presence of two lovers: whispering, the nightingale's trills, the murmuring of waters. Compare f.i. the beginning of Byron's Parisina:

It is the hour when from the boughs
The nightingale's high note is heard;
It is the hour when lovers' vows
Seem sweet in every whispered word;
And gentle winds and water near,
Make music to the lonely ear.

All these details, connected with the musical, the ethereal, the subtle are being actualised as significant aspects in all the segments of the first stanza and it is they who give the lovers' meeting its magic character. Auditive and visual elements of the landscape are united in one subtle sensitivity which characterises the lovers' presence.

The expressive force with which the data in stanza one are represented, rests on specific semantic and rhythmical devices.

Semantically dominant is the contrast between lines one and two, a contrast that is both auditive and emotional; silence / noise, emotion restrained / emotion acknowledged. Effective too, is the contrast auditive / visual in the first and last lines of the stanza. It is only with the very last word (ruč'ja: brook) that the visual element is made concrete. This postponing of the basic element is an important means to hold the reader's attention, to surprise him. It is not until the end of the first stanza that the attributive function of "serebro" (= serebristoe: silver) becomes clear.

Rhythmically stanza 1 is fascinating because of the always varying bond between the trochaic metre and the different intonational aspects of the nominative segments: the way in which these segments are spread over the lines shows a great diversity. The first segment consists of one noun, the following segments are enlarged with an increasing number of adjuncts: attributive adjuncts, noun-adjuncts in the genitive. This, of course, results in a striking diversity as to dynamics, stops and (accelerating) tempo.[1] The graphical presence of

---

1. My conception of dynamics is this: the force of utterance of the word that has the principal or logical accent within the syntagm (the syntagm consisting of either one or more than one word). I refer to this accent as a syntagmatic accent, connected with the principal word in the syntagm structure. A syntagm may be described as a syntactically complete intonational-semantic unit. A syntagm may coincide with a sentence, but a sentence can consist of more than one syntagm. Tempo is closely connected with dynamics: when a syntagm consists of more than one word, the various words as it were cluster round the one that carries the syntagmatic accent and they are pronounced rapidly: the less words there are in a syntagm the more the tempo slows down; the more words, the more the

three and two words alternately in a line, makes the reader aware of two phases in the rhythmical movement: the first two and the last two lines. The existence of these two phases is emphasized by the number of syllables in a line (eight and five alternately), and the number of metrical feet (four and three alternately). The alternation of feminine rhyme in the longer and masculine rhyme in the shorter lines also contributes to these two rhythmical phases. Even more forceful in this respect is the semantic caesura between an auditive and a visual element. What makes the division into two phases a positive reality is the intonational unity in the last two lines which contain only one nominative segment. This way three nominative segments in the first two lines are placed opposite one nominative segment in the last two lines. This means that dynamically the first two lines contain three syntagmatic accents while the last two lines have only one — though there is a certain hesitation as to the syntagmatic accent — until the attributive function of "serebro" (silver) becomes clear and "kolychan'e" (swaying) finally takes the accent. In addition to that, the first two lines have three pauses, the last two flow into one another in an enjambment-like way, and the only pause falls after the very last word of the stanza.

All this clearly indicates the great shift of tempo in the two halves of the stanza. The difference between the two halves becomes even more striking as a result of the changes in tempo in the first three segments and because of the intensified dynamics in the third segment (line 2). Cf. the acceleration after "šepot" (whispers) in "robkoe dychanie" (timid breathing) where both šyntagmatic accent and rhyme accent coincide (dychanie) and the tension between the syntagmatic accent and the rhyme accent respectively on the first and last syllable in "treli solov'ja" (a nightingale's trills). The intensified dynamic force in this line is extremely functional both for the already mentioned contrasts with line 1, and for the caesura auditive / visual between both halves of the stanza.

* * *

The second stanza continues the pattern of the compound

tempo accelerates. Pauses may occur at the end of a sentence (after the last word-accent in it, sometimes called the phraseological accent) or at a certain moment (moments) within the sentence (after the last word-accent of the syntagm). Inherent to pauses is a change in pitch. Cf.: B. V. Tomaševskij, *Stich i jazyk* (Moskva-Leningrad, 1959), p. 16.

nominative sentence. The lexical supply to the nominative segments is not as heterogeneous as it was in stanza 1: there is no concretion of auditive instances as essentials of man and bird, nor is there a direct picture of a landscape such as the sleepy brook in stanza 1. All the words and word-groups in the first three lines denote visual elements, but it is not until the last word of the stanza that a definite object is mentioned. The word before last adds a significant element of intimate emotional quality. With the indefinite quality of the visual elements corresponds a repeated emphasis on the interchanging of light and darkness in the first line and on its infiniteness in the second (svet nočnoj, nočnye teni, teni bez konca: night light, night shadows, shadows without end).

Line 3 consists of three words, two of which as to their visual aspect depend wholly upon the preceding lines: the words "rjad" (a series) and "izmenenij" (of changes); "volšebnych" (of magical) too inasmuch as the meaning of magic beauty is related to the interchanging of light and darkness. As a new significant element this line adds the aspect of movement to the visual data, especially by the word "izmenenij" (of changes). Here, the reader's attention is implicitly focused upon rustling leaves; this association is stimulated of course by the poetic surroundings in which the lovers' meeting takes place, cf. the already given quotation from Parisina.

The concretion in the last line ultimately projects the whole play of light and dark in the night on the dear face. The intimate human element is now given the central position and with the magical changes physionomical and psychological aspects are implicitly connected.

The expressivity of the information given, is, of course, closely bound up with the compact dosage of elements that require a supply from the poetic tradition and whose most essential significant aspects come to the fore only in the last words of the stanza. This is one of the reasons for the expressivity showing an ascending line.

An identical effect of gradation crystallizes in the word "volšebnych" (of magical): on the one hand this word most strongly expresses the element of beauty, which was present already in the preceding "svet nočnoj" (night light), "teni" (shadows) and earlier even in "serebro" (silver), "treli solov'ja" (a nightingale's trills); on the other hand it connects the beauty exclusively with the face of the beloved.

Subtle semantic and syntactic devices heighten the expressivity and produce modulations in the rhythm, which in their turn once more intensify the expressivity. The first segment of this stanza combines the semantic device of the oxymoron with syntactic inversion: the first and second segment are related to one another by means of the syntactic devices of epanastrophe and chiasm; epanastrophe also marks the relation between the second and third segment. The repetition – in inverted word-order – that is characteristic of this figure of speech, underlines the semantic path of a perpetuum mobile of light and darkness, now light being dominant, then darkness. This action also includes the preceding lines: "serebro i kolychanie" (silver and swaying).

The rhythmical modulations in the first place are related to the shift of the syntagmatic accent, which is due to the inversion in the first segment "svet nočnoj" (night light). The combination of chiasm and epanastrophe constitutes, apart from the syntactic inversion, also a dynamic inversion because of the shift of the syntagmatic accent: "nočnye téni" (night shadows).

In the next segment again we find a shift of the dynamics to the first word, though the word that has the syntagmatic accent is the same: "teni" (shadows). A dynamic subtlety here is the tension between the syntagmatic and the rhyming accent.

A chain-like construction of repetitions and inversions arises, giving the illusion of an accelerated rhythm and being very suggestive not only of the varying play of light and darkness, but also of the projection of light into darkness and darkness into light. Thus, in the word "teni" (shadows) we see a maximal actualisation of the significant elements of a less lighted area as opposed to a more lighted area.

The rhythm accelerates even more in the next lines. They are emphatically linked with the preceding lines by means of the continuity in visual details and their concretion, while the first word "rjad" (a series) takes over the numerical aspect given in the last words of the preceding lines: bez konca. The acceleration of the tempo is furthered by the extension of one nominative segment over two lines, a thing which is also to be found in the second half of stanza 1. However, a dispute is possible as to the dynamics, because both "serebro" (silver) and "kolychanie" (swaying) seem to have a certain claim upon the syntagmatic accent; in the last lines of stanza two, on the other hand, the accelerating tempo meets with no hindrance whatsoever. "Volšebnych", (of magical) being the word with the greatest expressive force, takes the syntagmatic accent. There is no possible doubt as to the syntactic-semantic functions of the various parts of this segment, which is the only one that is being characterized by two genitive-adjuncts.

In spite of the differentiations in tempo and dynamics, the lines and groups of lines in the first two stanzas may be compared with one another on the ground of broad correspondances in syntactic and rhythmical structure and on the ground of semantic equivalences as for instance intimacy, beauty, sensitivity.

* * *

In stanza 3 the compound nominative sentence is being continued. In the beginning its asyndetic character is maintained. In the last two lines, however, three of the four nominative segments are introduced by the conjunction "i" (and). The semantic function of this conjunction is the inducement of subsequent phases in the basic elements; at the same time there seems to be a relation of cause and effect between the elements preceding and those following "i". The pattern of being together in a restricted period of time is now disrupted. The lexical supply too, hints at changes and variations. This happens already in the segments of the first two lines in which we still find the asyndetic construction. The nominative segment that embraces the whole of line 1 is filled up with words indicating the break between night and day: the clouds of night are driven away by daylight.[2]

The sentence segment in line 2 only contains essentials of the break of dawn (otblesk jantarja: glistening of amber). The sentence segments in line 3 consist — apart from the conjunctions — of words expressing a direct emotionality; in these words, though expressing the intimacy of the being together, preceding significant elements such as the subtle, the ethereal, the musical, seem to be absent. In preceding segments the emotionality was as it were hidden in sensory perceptions. Words openly and directly expressing emotion never

2. Gustafson remarks that the successive images contribute to the suggestion of a progression in time: silver, night, shadows, purple, amber, dawn. Cf.: Richard F. Gustafson, *The Imagination of Spring: the Poetry of Afanasy Fet* (New York-London, 1966), p. 162.

58

filled up the whole of a sentence segment, they served as defining elements in the relation to the sensory perceptions. In stanza 3 the sensory element is being overflowed by an emotional wave producing physical reactions and expressions (i lobzanija i slezy: and kisses, and tears). The last line of the stanza at first glance seems to contain elements of visual observation but the connection with the preceding line, effected by the conjunction "i" (and), fills the observations with emotionality: "zarja" (dawn) acquires the quality of an exclamation, which most of all seems to express the ending of the night and with it the ending of the being together. The emotional quality of this exclamation is brought out in full intonational relief by the interpunction: an exclamation mark followed by suspense dots suggesting unspoken words. The traditional narrative-poetic theme of a lovers' parting at the break of dawn gives a definite dramatic colouring to the stanza.[3]

In spite of the dominant change in the visual and emotional elements, in the symbiosis of man and nature, the aesthetic quality is maintained in the lexical selection; it is to be found in "purpur rozy" (purple of a rose), in "otblesk jantarja" (glistening of amber), in the poetic "lobzanija" (kisses), in "zarja" (dawn).[4]

Of course this stanza, too, has its specific rhythmical variations, heightening the expressivity. Different from the preceding stanzas the rhythmical structure is closely connected with another syntactic process as to the nominative segments. There is no acceleration in the last two lines, but a pronounced slowing down resulting from the division into four segments instead of only one in the preceding stanzas. The two segments in the last line but one have been placed in contrast-like opposition, intensifying the emotionality of the elements "lobzanija" (kisses), "slezy" (tears). In the last line the repetition of the segment in combination with the exclamatory intonational structure has resulted in a culmination of emotion. The rhythmical modulations are also striking in the first two lines of the

3. Gustafson classifies this poem under the category "Descriptive Lyric". Op. cit. pp. 119-65. At the same time he points out that the "catalogue of images" suggests not only progression in time, but also an underlying story. Op. cit., p. 162.
4. This stanza is reminiscent of the traditional symbolism connected with the image of a rose. On the significance hereof see: Erik Egeberg, "A. A. Fet: Šepot, robkoe dychan'e,. . .", in: Scando-Slavica, tomus XV, p. 32.

third stanza: the introductory line is remarkable for the strict equivalence in words and metrical feet and the subsequent rhythmical monotony, which is accentuated by the absence of a clearly tonic positive part of the segment. This is, of course, a more or less logical result of the fact that this segment is the only one that contains one line and the only one that opens with an adjunct, which gives the momentary impression of a new sentence being started. Thus the suggestion of a new phase, the break of light, is strengthened. The next line (otblesk jantarja) turns it into certainty and rhythmically draws attention to itself by the unusual accumulation of consonants, marking the connection of prefix and stem and lengthening the accented vowel in 'ot' (otblesk: glistening).

* * *

All three stanzas have certain characteristics of construction in common. The acceleration of tempo, combinations of one syntagmatic and one rhyming accent in more than one line, a division in shorter and longer lines, in groups of lines, repetitions of consonants in lines or parts of lines.[5] This enables the poet to intensify the expressivity of his poetic information by oppositions of groups of lines, single lines or parts of lines throughout the poem. We find an unmistakable equivalence in lines 2, 6 and 10, based upon the syntactical structure (nominative segment plus genitive or prepositional adjunct), the number of metrical feet, the shortened foot with masculine rhyme, the syntagmatic accent on the first syl-

---

5. In this analysis I have not discussed the effect of the recurrence of certain vowels and consonants in different lines. This constitutes relations between lines, not based upon (for instance) parallelisms in the intonational structure nor upon the regular occurrence of trochaic trimeter and pentameter alternately, etc. Ll. one and three of stanza one show a striking correspondance as to the accented vowels 'o' and 'a', the unaccented vowels 'o' and 'y' and the consonants 'b', 'r', 'k', 'ch'. Sometimes there even is a correspondance in the positions of vowels and combinations of vowels and consonants. Cf.:
 . . .robkoe dychan'e
 serebro i kolychan'e
Such correspondances in lines that contain divergent significant data function as connective elements. In the last stanza we find another instance of vowel- and consonant sounds connecting divergent data. The sound structure – 'z', 'r', 'à', 'a' in dominant positions: rozy, jantarja, lobzanija, slezy, zarja – supports the causal coherence between visual and emotional elements and the transformation of the visual 'zarja' into an emotional instance.

lable, the rhyme accent on the last one. In the reader's mind this actualises the difference between the sensory spheres (auditive and visual) and the contrast at one sensory level (dark and light). At the same time the aesthetic component is emphasised more than once.

Cf.:　　　2 – treli solov'ja　　: a nightingale's trills
　　　　　6 – teni bez konca　　: shadows without end
　　　　　10 – otblesk jantarja　: glistening of amber

Lines 1 and 2, 5 and 6, 9 and 10 form obvious equivalent pairs in more than one respect. Again, the effect is one of clearly setting off the various sensory spheres and the contrasts within the visual sphere. Moreover, the second line in each one of the pairs (lines 2, 6 and 10) functions as an expression of the most essential point in the preceding line: line 2 (treli solov'ja) sets off the emotional-auditive character of line 1, line 6 (teni bez konca) the endless play of light and dark in 5, line 10 (otblesk jantarja) the break of dawn in line 9. It is also possible to compare the second halves of both stanzas one and two. They contain a pair of lines consisting of one sentence segment, the last line as a defining element being subordinated to the preceding one, and both pairs being identical in syntactical, intonational and morphological construction, both pairs showing an acceleration of tempo.

The comparison of these two pairs places two visual moments into opposition to one another, the first one referring to a detail of the landscape beauty, the other referring to the face of the beloved full of magical changes. In the first case beauty is an implicit element (in "serebro i kolychan'e": silver and swaying), in the second it is stated explicitly in the emphasising "volšebnych izmenenij" (of magical changes). The opposition of these two pairs of lines makes the reader aware of the gradation in the expression of beauty and draws his attention to the poignant meaning of "izmenenij" (of changes) in relation to the human face; he may even think of physionomical-psychological changes.

The fact that both the first and the last two lines of stanzas one and two may be compared with one another, implies the comparableness of both stanzas as a whole. In the reader's mind this opposition produces an awareness of the fact that in the first stanza in the two groups of lines there is a shift from the auditive to the visual sphere, which is absent in the second stanza. At the same time the reader must perceive that in stanza 1 the details of the landscape are presented as elementary facts, whereas in stanza 2 their primary function is to set off the dear face and their concretion is only secondary, rustling leaves being an implicit element.

The compositional equivalence in the first two stanzas is disrupted in the third and last stanza. It is the last two lines in particular that contain the strongest syntactic and intonational modifications. Line 1 of stanza 3 already contains notable differentiations in the syntactic structure, intonational pattern and the way in which the metre is actualised. All these very marked differentiations contribute to the poignant presentation of the turns and changes at the semantic level: the retreat of night before day and the dramatic parting.

* * *

Summarizing I would like to point out that the expressive force of this poem rests largely upon the effective use of two systems: the metrical system and the syntactic system. Sometimes they are divergent, sometimes they converge, as in the division into corresponding lines and groups of lines (though this pattern is disrupted again in the last stanza).

The use of the syntactic system enables the poet to effect changes in the dynamics, the pauses and the tempo. In the first two stanzas these changes do not affect the correspondance between the intonational pattern and the metrical system: this correspondance results in the same division into groups of lines. Both stanzas have a slow beginning (the first two lines) and a more rapid conclusion (the final two lines), though in the second stanza the tempo from the beginning is higher than in stanza one.

In stanza 1 the lexical constituents of the segments are semantically heterogeneous and correspond with the changes in intonation. This is why each segment acquires its own suggestive phraseological character.

The acceleration in stanza 2 corresponds with the growing tension in the presentation of the different aspects of light and darkness. It is only in the very last words of the stanza that these aspects are given their final touch: the connection with the enchanting presence of the beloved.

Stanza 3 shows the strongest semantic and intonational turns and changes disturbing the pattern of the preceding stanzas. The last two lines consist of four segments instead of only one as in the preceding stanzas. This slows down the tempo considerably. Compared with stanzas one and two the tempo here is slower even in the first two lines, as a result of the gradual start in line 1 with its maximum metrical realization and the accumulation of consonants in line 2.

The use of the causal-temporal conjunction "i" is another deviation of the pattern laid by stanzas one and two: at the semantic level it introduces different phases in the visual changes and the corresponding emotional reaction. The interpunction underlines this effect once more. All this clearly shows that the phraseological identity of the segments in the third stanza is marked not only by differentiations within the stanza but just as much by the break in the strophic pattern.

The expressiveness of the poem would never have been so great if it would not have been moulded into a fresh poetic form. This form is to be found in the "avantguarde" syntactic structure and in the very subtly developed rhythmical movement. It is to be found in the use of the motifs of an old, well-known theme, this time told in a highly restricted number of words: a lovers' meeting in a dream-like setting and the subsequent lovers' parting.

The tension in the poem is the result of the combination of all this. The syntactic-rhythmical structure and the scarcity of the lexical constituents stimulate the reader to add his own extras to the poetic information. From tradition, from reality and experience he will fill the rather abstract, statistic enumeration with a dramatic notion.

NIJHOFF'S MODERNIST POETICS IN EUROPEAN PERSPECTIVE

D. W. Fokkema (Utrecht)

In spite of its apparent simplicity, the early work of the Dutch poet Martinus Nijhoff (1894-1953) cannot easily be interpreted. One is tempted to consult his literary criticism and reflections on the meaning and function of poetry in order to find clues for understanding his poems. Of course, the code of Nijhoff's literary criticism is not necessarily the same as that of his poetry. But the dominant principles of the literary criticism may serve as heuristic devices in the endeavour to describe the poetic code that underlies his poetry and can be reconstructed on the basis of the extant texts. Such a constructed sender's code may serve as a framework of reference in our interpretative efforts; it will help us to advance hypotheses about the meaning of the various poems, and to decide between two or more equally possible interpretations.

Unfortunately, the concept of literary or poetic code is not clear at all. Code can be defined as a system of signs used to convey information. It is based on a mechanism or convention that fits the signifiers to their respective significations.[1] One might argue (with Lotman[2]) that literary texts have been encoded several times by means of various codes and subcodes, among which first of all the linguistic code and the literary code can be distinguished. But if we view literature as a secondary modelling system, superimposed on the linguistic sign system or interfering with it, then it still remains unclear at what levels of the text we should look for the particular literary signs which make up the relevant literary code. The problem becomes even more evident if we restrict the concept of literary sign to those elements and devices that potentially have an aesthetic ef-

1. Cf. Doede Nauta, *The Meaning of Information,* Approaches to Semiotics, 20 (The Hague: Mouton, 1972), p. 132.
2. Jurij M. Lotman, *Die Struktur literarischer Texte,* transl. Rolf-Dietrich Keil (München: Fink, 1972).

fect, or in some way or another have contributed to literary realizations of the text. Do not all elements and devices of the text, either on their own account or as a result of their particular arrangement, *potentially* have an aesthetic effect?

For the purpose of this article we shall assume that all poems in Nijhoff's volumes *De wandelaar* (1916), *Vormen* (1924), and *Nieuwe gedichten* (1934),[3] have been received as literary texts. Moreover, we must assume that all elements and devices in this poetry which do not belong to "ordinary usage" in language or poetic tradition (and which, in fact, represent a particular selection from all extant linguistic and poetic material) belong to the particular literary code of these texts. It appears from the reference to "ordinary usage" that the literary code is a relative concept. Any code operates against the background of other codes. The linguistic code operates against the background of a code of social and cultural conventions. The literary code operates against the background of the linguistic and cultural codes; the literary period code against the background of previous period codes; the code of all literary texts of one author against the background of a *prevalent* period code.

The concept of literary code is truly a relative concept, because one may as well describe the code of a particular corpus of literary texts as distinct from a *preceding* period code. In this paper I shall make some observations on the code of Nijhoff's early poetry as an example of a Modernist code, that is, as distinct from preceding period codes (Symbolism, Neo-Classicism, Futurism, and Expressionism). This implies that Nijhoff's code, as we shall try to reconstruct it, will have many elements in common with the codes of other predominantly Modernist writers, such as Paul Valéry, Jean Cocteau, Marcel Proust, T. S. Eliot, Ezra Pound, James Joyce, Thomas Mann, and, perhaps surprisingly for Dutch readers, Menno ter Braak and E. du Perron, although we cannot enter into comparisons between the various shades of Modernism here.

The examination of period codes *avant la lettre* by Ju. Tynjanov, Jan Mukařovský, René Wellek and others has led to the conclusion that no movement or writer is completely original. Texts that strike

3. I shall refer to the edition in the collected works: Martinus Nijhoff, *Verzameld werk,* 3 vols. (The Hague: Daamen, and Amsterdam: Van Oorschot, 1954-61). Volume 2 consists of two bindings. References will be made in the text, indicating volume and page.

65

us as original are usually re-organized presentations of familiar material. This is in conformity with Huizinga's belief that the number of cultural forms is rather limited.[4] The major spokesmen of a new literary period introduce new material only to a limited extent, but they do introduce a new way of looking at things. Their world model is the result of a new hierarchy of selective and combinatory principles that is applied to the extremely large, but limited inventory of traditional elements. Accordingly, a literary code can be described as governed by a system of organizing principles, dominated by a primary organizing principle. Such a principle, too, need not be completely new. It may have had a subordinate function in another system. Similarly, the various subordinate organizing principles in one code may acquire a dominant position in other codes.

At present, there seems to be no way of describing a literary code in great detail. For the time being we must restrict ourselves to the description of the system of principles on which words are selected and combined. A few steps can also be made to describe the particular inventory of literary signs that is selected from traditional material and appears in the texts under examination. But it is not at all certain that a more exhaustive description of literary codes will ever be possible. An exhaustive description may be incompatible with the particular role expected from the reader of literary texts. Exhaustive knowledge of the sender's code appears to be in contradiction with the ambiguity or polyinterpretability of the text which correctly have been considered preconditions of its aesthetic reception. Within the realm of the "aesthetics of opposition"[5] it is impossible to design a literary code in explicit and exhaustive terms, even of *one* text, as the literary code in any modern text may change slightly in the course of that text. The author (sender) may design some of the organizing principles of the text while writing the text, and the reader (receiver) must discover them while reading the text. The exhaustive description of literary codes, if at all possible, would reduce the informational content of literature and, if one accepts Lotman's view, its aesthetic effect. The particularity of the literary

4. Quoted by Jan Kamerbeek Jr. in his *Albert Verwey en het Nieuwe Classicisme: "De richting van de hedendaagse poëzie" (1913) in zijn internationale context* (Groningen: Wolters, 1966), p. 36.
5. Lotman, *Die Struktur literarischer Texte,* pp. 412-413.

text seems to forbid the exact and complete description of the literary code. On the other hand, the accumulated experience of literature has led to increasingly complicated sender's codes, which necessitates our reconstruction of them as far as possible in order to support our attempts at interpretation and to improve the conditions for intersubjective checking.

As suggested above, Nijhoff's criticism may reveal some of the organizing principles of his poetic code. There are two recurrent and predominant themes in Nijhoff's criticism: "the self-propelled movement of the once evoked word-form" (2, p. 193) and that of "one form and two contents" (2, p. 338). Both concepts are related and were often expounded in combination. After brief hints at it in 1922 (2, pp. 166 and 176), "the self-propelled movement of the once evoked word-form" was first mentioned by Nijhoff in 1924 in a context that emphasized the difference between poetry and the representation of reality:

> "Although it may derive its impetus, motif and imagery from the world of reality, the world of poetry remains another world. It is even not a direct reflection of reality in eternity. It is a completely separate world, which is approached by a separate action of the human spirit, however motivated by natural life. As a body is extended in its shadow, or as a diagram can be extended by mathematical construction, so (to be short) life approaches poetry. This has been made possible by another faculty of man: the possibility to oversee life in a thought, and to extend this thought, if transposed into form, until it, released, through the process of its own activity arranges its realization in the word-form. Thus, three kinds of acts: first, the act of life to produce a thought; second, the poetical act of transposing it into form, with [third], as a link between the two, the self-propelled movement of the once evoked word-form" (2, pp. 192-193).

One year later, in 1925, Nijhoff elaborated on this trichotomy:

> "Great art, to put it roughly, actually has one form and two contents: an empirical content (lit.: life-content), a form to express it and a spiritual content again of that form; in other words: a reality, an imagination and an image; or again in other words, with reference to the novel: characters, composition and revelations of superhuman power; or with reference to poetry: human or natural feeling, expression in the word, divine indication. Reality, expression, creation. The voice becomes word, the word becomes song. It can be said in a thousand ways, — this peculiar threefold function of art, which perhaps represents the purest form of human labour, and which brings about that nature becomes conscious of itself and that this

consciousness — initially a means — becomes the material for the creation of the highest spiritual awareness at the same time" (2, pp. 338-339).

At first sight, Nijhoff's view of literature does not appear particularly revolutionary. The essence of his trichotomy is that a literary text may have an empirical meaning, as well as a symbolic or mythological one. The literary text can be decoded as referring to a particular social context, but it can also be decoded as conveying a certain spiritual order or internal logic which escapes empirical verification or falsification. But the distinction between empirical truth as conveyed by the historian, and poetical truth which establishes the relations between "things that might happen" goes back to Aristotle.[6] Nijhoff is unambiguous in his claim that poetry aims at a spiritual order that can not be checked empirically. He characterized poetry by his contemporaries as

> "cosmic, ecstatic, mystical, religious, speculative (if you can digest the worn-out adjectives), [. . .] its aim is the expression of a superreality (*bovenwer-kelijkheid*) [. . .]. Human naturalness may be alien to it [. . .]. It departs from the direct pouring out, the emotion, and what one calls life. It finds its joys elsewhere: the clarification of relations,[7] the conscious form of an awareness, a separateness and absolutism of its world" (2, p. 340).

It is clear that for Nijhoff the world of poetry is different from that of reality. The question remains, however, by what means this super-reality can be described. The mere reference to "the self-propelled movement of the once evoked word-form" does not provide a convincing explanation, since the phrase itself should be clarified. The distinction of a superreality should not mislead one to equate "the self-propelled movement of the once evoked word-form" with the Surrealist "écriture automatique": the former is based on the rules of language and originates outside the poet or writer, the latter is a direct outflow of the author's psyche.[8] Therefore, in 1945,

6. T. E. Dorsch, ed., *Classical Literary Criticism* (Harmondsworth: Penguin, 1965), p. 43.
7. "Relations" is a free translation of *gestalte,* which here should be translated with a rather abstract equivalent.
8. Cf. André Breton's definition of Surrealism as "automatisme psychique pur par lequel on se propose d'exprimer, soit verbalement, soit par écrit, soit de tout autre manière, le fonctionnement réel de la pensée. Dictée de la pensée, en l'absence de tout contrôle exercé par la raison, en dehors de toute préoccupation esthétique ou morale." See his *Manifestes du surréalisme* (W.p.: J.-J. Pauvert, 1962), p. 40.

68

Nijhoff could characterize André Breton as the "restless seeker of a paradise *within* himself" (2, p. 966; italics added). Nijhoff's concept of the self-propelled movement of the word can be explained in relation to the "theory of language" he expounded a few years earlier.

Thirteen years before Jan Mukařovský distinguished between the autonomous and the communicative function of the work of art in his well-known essay "L'art comme fait sémiologique" (1934)[9], Nijhoff observed that every word has a double function:

"The first function is transmissive: language is a bridge, a means of communication; the words convey thoughts from man to man. Here the word is subordinate, not more than a means, mouldable, fluid, an obedient instrument, liable to subjective emphasis; here the strains make the music. On the other hand, language is an independent thing; the word is a separate material in which one may objectify psychic conditions as in any other material, such as marble or sounds. The word is an object, something that is full-grown and fixed, something with an existence of its own, gradually shaped from thousand elements of age-old reminiscences, associations and names" (1921) (2, pp. 97-98).

One may observe that, with respect to the latter function of language, Nijhoff is hinting at a concept of the word as a more or less autonomous entity. In 1924 he referred to "the autonomy of the word-form" (2, p. 193). But, as appears from various passages in Nijhoff's criticism, the *autonomy* of the word must be taken literally: the arrangement of words is organized by laws or rules which belong to these words. Characteristically he compares the work of the poet to that of the scientist:

"As the mechanician constructs new instruments and forces according to the directions of the mathematician, who through theoretical conclusions found secret laws (similarly as one discovers and predicts the movements of invisible stars by means of figures and formulas), likewise in all of us, perhaps unconsciously, the belief exists that things which do not contradict the nature of language, must also exist in the nature of reality, although they have remained hidden so far. Who has command of the laws of the word is a poet, a *trouvère,* a 'finder'. This explains the authority of a poem. That which can be said in this way, must also be true. And if perhaps reality cannot imitate

9. More accessible in its German translation "Die Kunst als semiologisches Faktum," in Jan Mukařovský, *Kapitel aus der Ästhetik,* transl. Walter Schamschula (Frankfurt: Suhrkamp, 1970), pp. 138-146.

the wild and flexible leaps of the word, or even contradicts the many arbitrary and daring turns, then we say with Hegel 'Schade um die Tatsachen' and keep to our preference for this second nature which man believes to have discovered himself. What does it matter whether Hamlet and Don Quixote did not exist? We know Pierrot and Faust better than people whom we encounter everyday" (2, p. 98).

The latter part of this quotation refers to the idealist distinction between particular description and universal type. But the difference between idealist aesthetics and Nijhoff's poetics is that the latter does not consider intuition or a given idea as the primary force behind poetical truth. It is the command of the rules of language -- of a technique — that opens the way to "the secret of all poetic eternity" (2, p. 233). It is not a force emanating from the poet's genius, but the technical command of laws existing outside the poet's personality.

This points to one of the characteristic differences between Modernism (as defined by Harry Levin[10]) and Romanticism. But we may distinguish also between Modernism and Symbolism in terms of Nijhoff's philosophy of language. In an essay on Hendrik Marsman, first published in 1924, Nijhoff expounded the view that language has passed through three stages or eras. He hardly elaborates on the hypothetical, primary stage in which words were a cry or the direct expression of an emotion, "as great and as deep as ether itself" (2, p. 232). During the secondary stage of its development the word has become a material body, a distinct thing, which addesses itself to all senses and not merely to our linguistic faculty, as words usually do in the present, tertiary stage. In the secondary stage the auditory and visual qualities of the word were stressed. "Every poet will understand me, when I say that one can see a word, see it as an object" (2, p. 232). The whole significance of the Symbolists, says Nijhoff, consisted in an attempt to hark back to this secondary stage by emphasizing the word as a thing, as a separate entity. With respect to the concept of the visuality of words, Nijhoff refers to Rimbaud's theory of the relation between sound and colour.[11]

10. Harry Levin, "What Was Modernism," in his *Refractions: Essays in Comparative Literature* (New York: Oxford Univ. Press, 1966), pp. 271-296.
11. Nijhoff probably thinks of Rimbaud's sonnet "Voyelles" (1871), published in his *Oeuvres complètes*, ed. Rolland de Renéville et Jules Moquet, Pléiade, 68 (Paris: Gallimard, 1954), p. 103. In his analysis of the poem J. J. M.

But for Nijhoff, who had stressed the laws of linguistic construction, the emphasis on the word as a thing is not the highest aim in poetry. In the present tertiary stage, language has still one possibility of growth, that is, through "a finer and preciser application of the theory of its relations: syntax" (2, p. 231). In this he follows Mallarmé[12] and Van Doesburg[13], but as appears from his poetical practice, Nijhoff treats syntax in a more conventional sense. He writes in 1924:

> "Only the great poets – whose perfect and purposely controlled technique unveils language and evokes the original word-organisms [from the primary stage], and in whose works these organisms develop a force of independent activity, far transcending their [i.e. the poets'] personal and human faculties – resurrect the recollection of this [original] word, that hardly has become flesh and continually reascends to its divine nature" (2, p. 233).

This, then, is the creative function of the word, based on reminiscences of a primary stage, which will escape precise description but which may be hinted at through the constructive force of poetic technique, predominantly that which Nijhoff calls syntax. The religious connotations of the quotation are clear. The wording shows a striking parallel with that in Viktor Šklovskij's essay "The Resurrection of the Word" (1914), which emphasizes that as a result of habituation we do not *see* things, but only recognize them.[14] It is hardly conceivable that Nijhoff would have known Šklovskij's work

Plessen does not conclude a close relation between sound and colour, but emphasizes the possibility that Rimbaud tended to see words as things. See J. J. M. Plessen, *Promébade et poésie: L'expérience de la marche et du mouvement dans l'oeuvre de Rimbaud* (La Haye: Mouton, 1967), pp. 287-311.

12. Stéphane Mallarmé, "Le mystère dans les lettres" [1896], in *Oeuvres complètes*, ed. Henri Mondor et G. Jean-Aubry, Pléiade, 65 (Paris: Gallimard, 1945), pp. 382-388.

13. Theo van Doesburg, editor of *De stijl* (1917-31), is the pseudonym of Christian Küpper (1883-1931), who also used the pen-name I. K. Bonset. In a manifesto, *De stijl* mentioned "syntax, prosody, typography, arithmetic, orthography" as means "to give the word a new significance and a new expressiveness." Quoted by J. J. Oversteegen, *Vorm of vent: Opvattingen over de aard van het literaire werk in de Nederlandse kritiek tussen de twee wereldoorlogen* (Amsterdam: Athenaeum, 1970), p. 61.

14. Russian title: "Voskrešenie slova". Translated into German as "Die Auferweckung des Wortes," in Wolf-Dieter Stempel, ed., *Texte der Russischen Formalisten*, vol. 2 (München: Fink, 1972), pp. 3-18. Cf. also Jurij Striedter, ed., *Texte der Russichen Formalisten*, vol. 1 (München: Fink, 1969), p. 15.

at the time he was writing his critique of Marsman's poetry, and I do not mention the parallel idea in Šklovskij in order to suggest influence. The concept of seeing a word as a thing, as something strikingly new, may be seen throughout such disparate movements as Symbolism, Futurism and Modernism. In this respect one might also point to a passage in Jean Cocteau's "Le secret professionel" (1922):[15]

> "L'espace d'un éclair, nous *voyons* un chien, un fiacre, une maison *pour la première fois*. Tout ce qu'ils présentent de spécial, de fou, de ridicule, de beau nous accable. Immédiatement après, l'habitude frotte cette image puissante avec sa gomme. Nous caressons le chien, nous arrêtons le fiacre, nous habitons la maison. Nous ne les voyons plus.
> Voilà le role de la poésie. Elle dévoile[16], dans toute la force du terme."[17]

In spite of the obvious parallels, one should also note the dissimilarities. Although Nijhoff possibly knew Cocteau's criticism (he confesses to have admired his early verse (2, p. 1167), one should observe that Nijhoff speaks of the visualization of the word or signifier, whereas Cocteau refers to the visualization of the signified object. In fact, Šklovskij referred to both when he explained the artistic process "as the device of making *things* strange and the device of the impeded *form.*"[18]

The emphatic distinction between signifier and signified can be considered a characteristic of Modernism, in contradistinction to the concept of the unity of form and content which, following a suggestion of Kamerbeek, can be held to be one of the main distinctive features of Symbolism.[19] In fact, the distinction between signifier and signified plays an important role in a number of Modernist devices, such as the self-reflection of the narrator on his own methods in literary prose, including the discussion of narrated time and the time needed for narration. A similar kind of self-reflection on technique by the lyrical subject can be observed in Modernist poetry, such as that of T. S. Eliot, Jean Cocteau and Martinus

15. Jean Cocteau, *Poésie critique,* vol. 1 (Paris: Gallimard, 1959), pp. 15-67.
16. Cf. Nijhoff's term *ontsluiert* (2, p. 233), translated as *unveils* in my quotation above.
17. Cocteau, *Poésie critique,* vol. 1, p. 49.
18. Striedter, ed., *Texte der Russischen Formalisten*, vol. 1, p. 15. Italics added.
19. Kamerbeek, *Albert Verwey en het Nieuwe Classicisme*, p. 3.

Nijhoff. In 1921, in a discussion of Russian avant-garde poetry, Roman Jakobson accepted a clear distinction between signifier and signified when he defined poetry as "an utterance with a set towards the expression," and explained that in poetry "the communicative function which predominates in practical and emotional language is reduced to a minimum."[20] Almost as if he knew Jakobson's concept of poetry, as well as Šklovskij's explanation of "the device of the impeded form," Nijhoff, in 1922, observes that the prose of the contemporary novelist Van Oudshoorn "slows down reading by emphasizing again and again and focussing the attention on the wording itself" (*de formulering zelf*) (2, p. 152). When, finally, Nijhoff speaks of "one form and two contents," he obviously rejects the idea of the unity of form and content.

The distinction between signifier and signified is the result of a certain technique, which likewise is a characteristic of Modernism. It is through a "perfect and purposely controlled technique," including syntax, that the great poets may resurrect the recollection of words of the primary stage of language. The words used in poetry do not give access directly to the superreality the poet aims at, but the original, primary words may be recollected as a result of an ingenious technical construction, quite compatible with a conventional concept of syntax. This also seems to be practised by Nijhoff in his own poetry. Syntactical inconsistencies, exclamatory phrases, or mere juxtaposition of words, are rare in his poetry, in which the period is a dominant organizing principle, and in that respect his code differs from that of Symbolism, Futurism and Expressionism.

Kamerbeek has correctly observed that the period was already restored as a primary organizing principle by Neo-Classicist writers, shortly before World War I.[21] But the Neo-Classicists and the Modernists had quite different reasons for taking the same position in this respect. The Neo-Classicists seemed to expect that traditional forms, if ordered by the poet's mind, could provide a reliable world model. On the other hand, Nijhoff and other Modernists had less confidence in traditional form, as well as the ordering capacity of the poet's mind. Nijhoff hoped only that poetic technique would evoke a

20. Roman Jakobson, "Novejšaja russkaja poezija," translated into German as "Die neueste russische Poesie," in Stempel, ed., *Texte der Russischen Formalisten,* pp. 19-136. The quotation is from p. 31.
21. Kamerbeek, *Albert Verwey en het Nieuwe Classicisme,* pp. 57-62.

certain recollection of primary words, but he never came close to the view that the secret of poetry could be expressed in words. In fact, he confessed that great poetry "can exist only as the end of poetry" (2, p. 141). This is also what transpires from his many poems which convey an immanent poetics, such as "Het steenen kindje" (1, p. 132) and "Het lied der dwaze bijen" (1, pp. 200-201). He seems to see his own poems as so many attempts to condition the reader to recollect the "primary words" which never have been written down, as is strikingly apparent from "Het kind en ik" (1, p. 202). One may see here a certain affinity with Eliot's concept of the "objective correlative."[22] Nijhoff's poetry consists of the creation of possibilities and never pretends to offer more. He does not hint at any reliable world model, but only at possible worlds. It is the relative or provisional value he attributes to the period which enables him to write a poetry of periods. Similarly, he can write epic poetry since the related story creates merely a possible world. Poetry is accepted as a construction.[23]

In contradiction to Neo-Classicism, which highly valued the role of the poet's mind or *Geist,* Nijhoff and other Modernists distrust any definite world model. They raised Mallarmé's dictum that "dans une société sans stabilité, sans unité, il ne peut se créer d'art stable, d'art définitif" (1891)[24] to one of their primary principles. Valéry, whom Nijhoff considered "France's greatest living poet" (2, p. 296), seemed to express the Modernist position adequately when he

22. Most convincingly expressed in his essay "Hamlet and His Problems" (1919), where one reads: "The only way of expressing emotion in the form of art is by finding an 'objective correlative'; in other words, a set of objects, a situation, a chain of events which shall be the formula of that *particular* emotion; such that when the external facts, which must terminate in sensory experience, are given, the emotion is immediately evoked." Reprinted in T. S. Eliot, *The Sacred Wood: Essays on Poetry and Criticism* (London: Methuen, 7th ed, 1950), pp. 95-104. The quotation is from p. 100. The difference, of course, is that Eliot phrased the 'objective correlative' in terms of *events,* whereas Nijhoff thinks in terms of *words.* Later, in 1935, Nijhoff seems to have approached Eliot's principle of the 'objective correlative' (2, p. 1174).
23. In 1935 Nijhoff writes: Poetry has become "more objective". "No direct lyrical pouring out of emotion, but short pieces of objectified life, constructed, composed, more in the style in which in early times epic poems were written" (2, p. 1172).
24. Mallarmé, *Oeuvres complètes,* p. 866.

pointed to poetry as a construction of possibilities ("On *organise tout le possible* du langage" (1929)),[25] and implied that the possibilities of a poetic construction will never be fully exhausted ("Un poème n'est jamais achevé" (1929)).[26] If Nijhoff never said the same, he certainly acted accordingly. He repeatedly changed the texts of his poems, even after they had been printed.[27] Like "The Waste Land", Nijhoff's poetry is a challenge to the interpreter of variants.[28]

The belief that, in spite of the non-finality of the text, it is worthwhile to attempt again and again to construct possible world models has a corollary in the sphere of literary history. In 1922 Nijhoff views the development of literature in modern times as a succession of "-isms", in fact, period codes. He sees the relative value of Futurism, Cubism, and Expressionism (2, p. 141). He is fully aware of the transient nature even of such a phenomenon as the *esprit moderne* (2, p. 294) and concludes in a truly Modernist fashion:

> "And so we are at present, in a time of many unsuccessful beginnings, sceptical about any new beginning, looking forward to it and disappointed again. Time and again we see the beginning of poetry, whereas in fact great poetry, through its human-superhuman character, can exist only as the end of poetry" (2, p. 141).

In Holland, the idea of the insufficiency of language in transmitting poetry, which obviously derives from Nietzsche,[29] was elaborated by

25. Paul Valéry, *Oeuvres,* ed. Jean Hytier, 2 vols., Pléiade, 127 and 148 (Paris: Gallimard, 1957-60), vol. 1, p. 547.

26. Ibid., p. 553.

27. Cf. Vestdijk's observation in his review of Nijhoff's *Nieuwe gedichten,* "Aestheticisme en menselijkheid," reprinted in S. Vestdijk, *Muiterij tegen het etmaal,* vol. 2: *Poëzie en Essay,* 2nd ed. (Den Haag: Bakker, Daamen, 1966), pp. 70-75; in particular p. 70.

28. Cf. Harry Levin, *The Waste Land: From Ur to Echt* (W.p.: Ann & J. Laughlin and New Directions, 1972). This privately circulated booklet is a review of *The Waste Land: The Facsimile and Transcript of the Original Drafts, Including the Annotations by Ezra Pound,* ed. by Valerie Eliot (London: Faber and Faber; New York: Harcourt etc., 1971). Variants in *Het uur u* (1937), a long poem by Nijhoff, were studied by Francis Lulofs in his *Verkenning door varianten: De redacties van Het Uur U van M. Nijhoff stilistisch onderzocht* ('s-Gravenhage: Bakker, Daamen, 1955).

29. Elrud Kunne-Ibsch, *Die Stellung Nietzsches in der Entwicklung der modernen Literaturwissenschaft* (Assen: Van Gorcum, 1972), pp. 5-28.

Menno ter Braak in a book-length essay *Het carnaval der burgers* (1930).[30] But the awareness of the succession of literary systems is an international phenomenon, predominant in the Modernist code. In 1922, Jean Cocteau wrote:

> "Celui qui veut à tout prix le modernisme, qui étonne le public par une débauche de couleurs et de surprises sur la vieille étoffe, au lieu de tisser une trame nouvelle, le progrès lui fera perdre sa place.
>
> Tout se démode, me dites-vous. C'est une autre affaire. Un chef-d'oeuvre n'est pas appelé chef-d'oeuvre, mais il transforme tout. Il est mode profonde. Chacun suit sans le savoir. Nécessairement, il se démode. Il est démodé par un autre chef-d'oeuvre. A la longue, d'abord, il prend du pittoresque. Ensuite, il cesse d'être vieille robe. Il entre au musée du costume."[31]

On various occasions Valéry expressed himself on the problem, perhaps most clearly in a letter of 1932:

> *"Ce qui est probable* en ces matières, c'est qu'une époque littéraire est avant tout une réaction. Elle se dispose *contre* quelque autre qui la précède. Le Symbolisme est né *contre* le Parnasse et le Réalisme, eux-mêmes dressés *contre* le Romantisme, et d'une part, en matière de sujets, d'autre part, comme revendication de la forme."[32]

Like Cocteau, T. S. Eliot, whose poetry and later drama Nijhoff greatly admired,[33] defended the position that a new work of art transforms the existing order: "for order to persist after the supervention of novelty, the *whole* existing order must be, if ever so slightly, altered" (1919).[34] One could add, if one wished, similar quotations from the Russian Formalists, in particular from Jurij Tynjanov's "On Literary Evolution" (1927).[35]

30. English: *The Carnival of the Bourgeois.* Reprinted in Menno ter Braak, *Verzameld werk,* 7 vols. (Amsterdam: Van Oorschot, 1950), vol. 1, pp. 5-159.

31. Cocteau, *Poésie critique,* vol. 1, p. 24.

32. Valéry, *Oeuvres,* vol. 1, p. 1738.

33. Nijhoff translated the following poems by Eliot: "The Love Song of J. Alfred Prufrock," "The Hippopotamus," "Journey of the Magi," "Lines for Cuscuscaraway and Mirza Murad Ali Beg," (3, pp. 538-548). He also reviewed (2, pp. 1043-1045) and translated *The Cocktail Party* (3, pp. 245-411). In 1935, Nijhoff says to have been influenced by Eliot's poetry (2, p. 1167).

34. "Tradition and the Individual Talent," in Eliot, *The Sacred Wood,* pp. 47-60. The quotation is from p. 50.

35. Russian title: "O literaturnoj evoljucii." Translated into German as "Uber die literarische Evolution," in Striedter, *Texte der Russischen Formalisten,* vol. 1, pp. 433-462.

The Modernist writers untiringly designed their possible worlds by means of provisional, to some extent arbitrary devices. They produced texts, which might as well have been written differently[36] or remained fragmentary in appearance or in fact.[37] In short, they lacked the self-confidence that still can be found with Mallarmé who, in 1891, expressed the belief that "le monde est fait pour aboutir à un beau livre."[38] The Modernist must think in terms of continuous movement, a concept that from the very beginning was connected with the *esprit moderne.*

But what keeps the Modernist going? How can he acquiesce in the transient or insufficient nature of his work? If it is true that the Modernist approach is relative, provisional, hypothetical, replaceable, and perhaps arbitrary, what is the significance of such an approach? One of the major principles of Modernism is that it has given up relying exclusively on the mind of the poet to explain the world. No Modernist formulated this clearer than Eliot, when, in 1919, he introduced the concept of depersonalization:

> "What happens is a continual surrender of himself as he is at the moment to something which is more valuable. The progress of an artist is a continual self-sacrifice, a continual extinction of personality. There remains to define this process of depersonalization and its relation to the sense of tradition. It is in this depersonalization that art may be said to approach the condition of science."[39]

> "Poetry is not a turning loose of emotion, but an escape from emotion; it is not the expression of personality, but an escape from personality."[40]

Possibly unaware of Eliot's early criticism, Nijhoff expressed himself in a similar way in his important review of the stories of Van Oudshoorn (1922).[41] Obviously speaking of Van Oudshoorn, but implying a more general application, Nijhoff writes:

36. Elrud Kunne-Ibsch, "Erzählformen des Relativierens im Modernismus, dargestellt an Thomas Manns *Joseph und seine Brüder* und Robert Musils *Der Mann ohne Eigenschaften,"* in *Festschrift Herman Meyer,* ed. A. von Bormann, K. R. Mandelkow, and A. H. Touber (Tübingen: Niemeyer,1976).

37. Cf., for instance, Eliot's famous line: "These fragments I have shored against my ruins;" from "The Waste Land," in T. S. Eliot, *Collected Poems 1909-1962* (London: Faber and Faber, 1974). p. 79.

38. Mallarmé, *Oeuvres complètes,* p. 872.

39. Eliot, *The Sacred Wood,* pp. 52-53.

40. Ibid., p. 58.

41. Oversteegen touched on the problem of the relation between Eliot and

"The writer, in whom 'man dies in order that the artist live', has been subjected to the rather general phenomenon of duplication as a result of which man becomes the observer of himself, but also to a process which one could call 'depersonalization' (*depersonalisatie*). The connection between the 'ego' and the 'alter ego' has been disrupted; a strange impersonality appears in one who views his own acts and achievements as automatic, and, while it experiences the feelings, observations and notions of the alter ego, the ego is incapable of intervening or directing the latter.

The result is a kind of defencelessness of the spirit. Nature and reality approach and, as it were, penetrate into the inner life, more common and ordinary than ever before, but the less comprehensible and completely uncontrollable and mysterious" (2, p. 153-154).

The absence or presence of depersonalization is a crucial criterion in Nijhoff's literary judgement. He admires A. Roland Holst because his poetry transcends the "personal-descriptive" level (*het persoonlijk-descriptieve*) (2, p. 360). He deplores that Herman Gorter after the completion of his *Mei* never again found "a theme outside himself, subject-matter from reality" for a large poem (2, p. 1058). In 1928, he translates Gide's *Paludes* (1895), which characteristically is preceded by a short foreword indicating that a book may be valued higher as the role of the writer in it is less important.[42] In his retrospective lecture of 1935 Nijhoff attempts to justify his preference for Proust by pointing to the vagueness and fluidity of the narrator, who is completely open to record every movement from outside in an account that becomes more objective as it records events that are farther removed from the observer (2, p. 1169).

Depersonalization is related to the principle of detached observation.[43] The state of disengagement is the result of an intellectual

Nijhoff in his *Vorm of vent*, pp. 132 and 153. See also Dirk W. Dijkhuis, "Nijhoff en Eliot/Eliot en Nijhoff," *Merlyn* 2 (1963-64), No. 6, pp. 1-25.

42. André Gide, *Roman, récits et soties, oeuvres lyriques,* ed. Maurice Nadeau, Pléiade, 135 (Paris: Gallimard, 1958), p. 89: "tant plus le livre vaut-il, que plus la part du scribe y est petite [. . .]." A more modest role of the writer implies a larger role for the reader. The appeal on the idiosyncratic reader to write significant sentences from *Paludes* on the blank page 149 is a remarkable prefiguration of Ingarden's interest in *Unbestimmtheitsstellen.* See Roman Ingarden, *Das literarische Kunstwerk,* 2. Aufl. (Tübingen: Niemeyer, 1960); first edition 1930.

43. Cf. Nijhoff's comment on his epic poem *Awater* (2, p. 1166). An English translation of *Awater* by James S. Holmes was published under the same title in *Delta* 4 (1961), No. 2, pp. 23-31.

process, of an awareness of one's own position in a world that, after World War I, did not provide any ready-made solutions. Or, as Nijhoff observed in 1920, the war had produced "an increased awareness of questions which for some time had occupied our minds" (2, p. 62). All illusions had been shattered, except that of the intellect. Ter Braak, himself in many respects a Modernist, in 1934 praises Nijhoff for his "intellectual self-control", the control of "the fairy-tale told by his linguistic faculty."[44] In fact, Nijhoff's criticism heavily depends on the criterion of a conscious awareness (*bewustzijn*). In 1922, he acclaims Van Oudshoorn's prose in that it is "cold, intellectual, and of an extremely tense consciousness" (2, p. 152). It is conscious arrangement that "lends value and significance to the world" (2, p. 156). He greatly admires Paul van Ostaijen because the latter rejected all critical, selective observation, which would imply a restriction on absolute observation (*het absolute 'zien'*), "a narrowing of consciousness, a deliberate limitation of consciousness" (1929) (2, p. 625). Finally he emphasizes the role of consciousness in the novels of Virginia Woolf,

> "whose characters are constructions of consciousness rather than personalities [. . .]. Every book by Virginia Woolf, every chapter of Joyce's *Ulysses* has been written in a different style. Not only what happens is important, but, in the first place, the way it is seen and represented" (1935) (2, p. 1170).

The emphasis on conscious arrangement and intellectual comprehension is one of the most evident characteristics of international Modernism. Harry Levin provides an array of examples in this respect, drawn from the writings of Pound, Eliot, Joyce, Thomas Mann, Proust, Gide, Valéry.[45] Their positions could be summarized in the latter's dictum: "Un poème doit être une fête de l'Intellect" (1929).[46]

Detached observation and conscious control of observation are principal values in Nijhoff's poetics. They are the ultimate means of a "defenceless spirit", whose pretensions have been reduced to that of conscientious recording. But again the question must be asked: what makes the Modernist acquiesce in this apparently passive role of

44. Ter Braak, *Verzameld werk,* vol. 5, p. 374.
45. Harry Levin, *Refractions*, pp. 271-296.
46. Valéry, *Oeuvres,* vol. 2, p. 546. Other relevant quotations from Nijhoff have been given above.

unselective recording? It is not subject-matter, but rather the way of seeing and recording that matters.[47] It is only one step from here to believe that the way of recording has an intrinsic significance. In slight variation of Cocteau, even anarchy can be considered order.[48] Does not the structure of Pound's writings confirm that possibility? [49]

The intrinsic link or resemblance between form and meaning, or signifier and signified can be considered an iconic relationship, if we adopt the terminology of Charles Sanders Peirce which recently has entered into major contributions to the science of literature through the efforts of Roman Jakobson and Jurij Lotman. Indeed, Jakobson observes the iconic principle at all levels of linguistic behaviour,[50] and Lotman considers iconicity as one of the major characteristics of literature.[51] Iconic signs abound in all texts. Yet, the particular emphasis on iconic signs in Modernism, without using the term, is all too evident and, together with other characteristics of the Modernist code, is one of its distinctive features.

On various occasions Nijhoff explained the iconic principle, without naming it. In 1925, he protests against the unorthodox spelling of the Dutch word "cirkel" (*circle*) as *sirkel* in the title of a volume of poetry by Henri Bruning (2, p. 257). In using an *s* instead of a *c*, writes Nijhoff, the suggestion of roundness has been lost. To him, the link between the letter and the meaning of the word is not completely arbitrary. He confesses to regard a word as "a living organism, which moves and breathes, and which through its form suggests a hidden, intrinsic meaning of a higher order" (2, p. 257). Discussing the poetry of A. Roland Holst in the same year, he believes that the latter possesses the secret of "a peculiar chemistry

47. When, in 1925, Šklovskij impregnated literary scholarship with that view, he probably acted on impulses from contemporary creative literature. Cf. Viktor Šklovskij, *Theorie der Prosa*, ed. Gisela Drohla (Frankfurt: Fischer, 1966), p. 165. (Translation of *O teorii prozy*.)

48. Jean Cocteau, "D'un ordre considéré comme une anarchie" (1923), in *Poésie critique*, vol. 1, pp. 67-87.

49. Harry Levin, *Ezra Pound, T. S. Eliot, and the European Horizon*: The Taylorian Lecture for 1974 (Oxford: Clarendon Press, 1975). See, in particular, pp. 25-27.

50. Roman Jakobson, "Quest for the Essence of Language," *Diogenes*, No. 51 (1965), pp. 21-38.

51. Lotman, *Die Struktur literarischer Texte*, pp. 40, 224, 270.

of the word" which takes advantage of the fact that "the gist of a word is not its meaning, which always is metaphorical (*overdrachte-lijk*), but the word itself" (2, p. 360). Here, we may recall Nijhoff's theory of "one form and two contents," quoted above, which refers to an empirical and a spiritual content, the second being of a higher order. The form may "immediately coincide with what I would call the second content" (2, p. 339). He views form not as a transparent wrapping of emotion, "but as matter of a spiritual order" (2, p. 340). Through form, through "the self-propelled movement of the once evoked word-form," one may hint at a superreality which cannot be described in any other way. In this context also belongs his view that "that which can be said in this way, must also be true." Nijhoff may have been one of the most convinced protagonists of iconicity in the modern period, but he is not by far the only one.

The heavy emphasis on iconicity had adverse consequences for interpretation. Nijhoff shared Eliot's opinion that "the experience of poetry, like any other experience, is only partially translatable into words" (1932).[52] In this context Eliot quoted I. A. Richards as having said: "It is never what a poem *says* that matters, but what it *is.*"[53] In principle, the New Critics and the Russian Formalists all supported this view.

Like Eliot, Nijhoff attempted to reconcile man with the results of modern technique. Whereas Eliot (and Pound) struggled with the word *taxi*,[54] Nijhoff successfully incorporated such words as *parallelogram* or *locomotief* in his poetry (1, pp. 25 and 222). Cocteau shared the urge to reconcile technical progress and poetry as appears from his poem "Les hangars" ("où se construisent les aéro-planes").[55] In 1935, Nijhoff observed: "The human soul must be adjusted to that which human technique apparently guilelessly has accomplished. Art can play a great role in this process of adjust-ment" (2, p. 1162). There are Futurist overtones in his view that in our age the engine is the only invention that can be compared with the Parthenon (ibid.). He confessed almost as much admiration for

---

52. T. S. Eliot, *The Use of Poetry and the Use of Criticism: Studies in the Relation of Criticism to Poetry in England* (London: Faber and Faber, 1964), p. 17. Nijhoff expressed himself in a similar way in 1935 (2, pp. 1170-1171).
53. Eliot, *The Use of Poetry*, pp. 17-18.
54. Levin, *The Waste Land: From Ur to Echt*, pp. 22-23.
55. Jean Cocteau, *Poésie 1916-1923* (Paris: Gallimard, 1925), pp. 93-99.

81

the skyscrapers of New York as for the cathedral of Chartres (2, p. 1163), and accepted the idea that poetry should be written not for eternity, but for a future, which itself, of course, would be a transitory thing. But how could man be reconciled with modern technique and its effects upon civilization? Nijhoff believes he has found the answer in the acknowledgement of its existence.

> "The presence of a force of nature, or unconsciousness, or the masses, or an abstraction in a thing, in whatever thing, makes that thing vibrate, and this charge (*geladenheid*) makes the thing into animated material, that is, beauty" (1935) (2, p. 1166).

This passage is not very clear, but the reference to "vibration" may put us on the right track. Vibration can be observed only against a contrasting background. The basis of Nijhoff's technique seems to be the combination of things "more common and ordinary than ever before" (2. p. 154) or even "banal" (2, p. 1166) with their opposite. If juxtaposition of incompatible elements can lead to awareness of their presence, the result is beauty, or a new spiritual order. The idea is supported by the iconic principle, according to which that which can be juxtaposed must be compatible. If the products of modern civilization can be incorporated in poetry, they are, by that very act, related to the individual poet or reader.

The main principles of Nijhoff's Modernist poetics, as derived from his critical writings, can be summarized as follows:[56]

1. The primary organizing principle. The lyrical subject is aware of the provisional or hypothetical nature of his point of view and also acknowledges his incapacity to interfere in the substance of his experience of the world, but he may increase his awareness of the possibility of arranging his experiences in various ways. The various possible ways of ordering the material of his experiences lead to a

---

56. I follow a general subdivision in ten categories (in fact nine, as the primary organizing principle can be subsumed under one of the following categories), applicable to both prose and poetry, which I have also used on other occasions. The choices determining the code of a particular literary period and made within the framework of the given categories might be projected on a grid, that more or less arbitrarily could be narrowed. It appears, however, that the choices made within the ten categories yield enough distinctive features to set the code of a particular literary period off from other, contiguous codes. In order to distinguish the code of one writer from the codes of other writers of the same period one would need a much narrower grid.

reflection on the categories of time and space, the point of view of the lyrical subject, and the partly iconic, partly arbitrary nature of language. Any linguistic order appears to be significant but, in the last instance, also insufficient. No poem is definite. As a result of the iconic principle, successive poems suggest successive moments of poetic order, and as such the continual movement of life.

2. *Degree of generalization vs. specification and qualification.* As a result of his awareness of the temporal or hypothetical nature of his point of view, the lyrical subject avoids generalization to the point of appearing evasive. The poems deal with specific experiences and particular events, but seem often to be inconclusive.

3. *The role of the narrator or the lyrical subject.* Although it is conscious arrangement that "lends value and significance to the world," the lyrical subject is primarily an observer who more or less arbitrarily tries his hand at various ways of recording, each of them acquiring significance as a result of iconic principles. The role of the lyrical subject is usually subdued, and sometimes completely submerged in an "auctorial" presentation (Cf. also paragraph 1).

4. *Fabula and sjuzet* and 5. *Description of characters*: Since we are dealing with poetry, these categories are hardly applicable here.

6. *The thematic material.* Any data acquired through perception may serve as thematic material. Also other, quasi observational data (including those of dreams or imagination), if recordable in perceptual terms, can be dealt with. There is a strong preference for visual and audile perception. Intellectual considerations remain in the background of the structure of representation, which may consist of a somewhat arbitrarily selected myth or legend ("Satyr and Christofoor" (1, pp. 83-84)), historical figure or event ("Memlinc" (1, p. 88), "Het jaar 1572" (1, pp. 436-437)) or situation from daily life ("Impasse" (1, p. 208)). In general, all empirical or quasi-empirical material in the poems points to a superreality and therefore acquires a mysterious, sometimes mythological significance.

7. *Time.* The indication of time may be exact and refer to a relative concept as well. For instance, the meaning of "een minuut of tien" (about ten minutes) in "De moeder de vrouw" serves only to stress the absurdity of counting time against the background of eternity.[57] More attention is paid to the concept of time than to the

57. Cf.A.L.Sötemann, "M. Nijhoff's 'De moeder de vrouw': een analyse in twee

concept of space. See also "Na een jaar" (1, p. 11) and "Het souper" (1, p. 108).

8. Space. In comparison with time, spatial relations have a subordinate function, but when treated they may easily be transformed from empirical data into supernatural constructions ("Het steenen kindje" (1, p. 132), "Het lied der dwaze bijen" (1, pp. 220-201)).

9. The relation between the text and extra-literary reality. Throughout Nijhoff's poetics, "the world of poetry remains another world than that of reality." There is a purposive separation of the two worlds, which obliges the reader to look for a "superrealist" interpretation behind the often "realist" surface. Detached observation being an ideal in Nijhoff's early poetics, there is no social or religious commitment in his poetry up to and including *Nieuwe gedichten* (1934). His aim to come to terms with modernity (by means of words), is, however, a purely cultural commitment.

10. Language. There is a strong awareness of the distinction between signifier and signified behind the theory of "one form and two contents" as well as behind the idea of "the self-propelled movement of the once evoked word-form." Nijhoff's poetics emphasizes the laws of syntax even more than the visuality of words. His poetry is one of periods, rather than disrupted sentences or single words. With a preference for the unadorned sentence structure the use of (impressionist) adjectives is rejected (2, p. 626). This obviously is a result of the subdued role of the lyrical subject which should record rather than comment.

Now that the main selective and combinatory principles of Nijhoff's literary code have been mentioned, one may wonder whether any significant observations can be made on the inventory of literary signs draw up on the basis of the extant poetical texts. Such an inventory should take account of all levels which may carry literary signs, such as phonology (rhyme patterns), lexicon (words or semantic features), syntax (syntactical constructions), thematics (range of thematic material). Since one cannot take such an inventory without numerable references to the poems (which being in Dutch will probably be of little interest to the foreign reader), I shall restrict myself to a few remarks on the lexicon. First, the lexicon of

etappes," *De nieuwe taalgids: W. A. P. Smit-nummer* (Groningen: Wolters-Noordhoff, 1968), pp. 134-146, in particular p. 143.

a literary code cannot be equated with the lexicon of a linguistic code, although the lexical signs of the literary code will often coincide with or be incorporated in the words of the linguistic lexicon. Therefore, in looking for the literary lexicon one should not attach too much value to the *Wortlaut* of the words, but rather investigate the distribution of semantic features. Not all lexical signs of the literary code reveal themselves by way of frequent use, as frequent repetition of the same words has a negative effect on the amount of information in the literary text and will weaken its literary character (as defined by Lotman). In the case of Nijhoff's early poetry, the lexicon of the literary code appears to consist predominantly of words having the semantic features of *awareness, perception, detachment* or *non– commitment, transitoriness, specificity* (at the level of the "realist" interpretation), and *generality* (at the level of the "superrealist" interpretation). This list can of course be extended with more specific semantic features, such as *newness* (awareness + transitoriness + x), *coolness* (detachment + perception + x), *music* (perception + transitoriness + x), *child* (non-commitment + transitoriness + x). Obviously more research can be done in this field.

We have inserted a few references to Nijhoff's poetry, but it should be recalled that his poetic code sketched so far (except for our comments on the lexicon) has been derived from his critical writings and may serve only as a heuristic framework for the interpretation of his poetry. It is theoretically possible that Nijhoff in his critical work expounded a kind of poetics slightly different from what he practised in his poetry. (If so, I believe the difference will be very slight indeed, although, of course, it is always possible that certain principles presented in the criticism have not materialized in the poetic texts and therefore can not, on the basis of the poetic texts alone, be reconstructed as part of the sender's code. For instance, one may not always be able to perceive a "superrealist" meaning behind the "realist" meaning of a poem.)

My description of Nijhoff's poetics is neither definite, nor exhaustive. It still needs more testing. Knowledge of the organizing pinciples of Nijhoff's code may further the interpretation of his poems. Let me briefly add one example. Various interpretations[58] have been

58. Summarized by J. J. A. Mooij in his article "De filosofie van de litera-

given of "Het lied der dwaze bijen" ("The Song of the Foolish Bees"),[59] first published in 1926 and incorporated in his volume *Nieuwe gedichten*. One critic, L. Wenseleers, has suggested that the poem should be interpreted as an allegory of the adventure of modern poetry. J. J. A. Mooij holds that such an interpretation does not necessarily follow from the text.[60] But in view of Nijhoff's poetic code we believe that a search for both a "realist" and a "superrealist" interpretation is warranted. In fact, the very first line ("A scent of higher honey") can only be interpreted metaphorically. If "higher" is taken merely as an indication of place, this line, in the context of the poem, is absurd, as everyone knows that high in the air there is no honey. Moreover, it would be impossible to smell that higher honey on earth. The word "song" in the title, however, refers to the highest stage of poetry (cf. Nijhoff's pronouncement that "the voice becomes word, the word becomes song"[61], and this may lead us once more to consult his statements about the "world of poetry", which represents a superreality, a higher order, and can be hinted at through the efforts of great poets who, through their command of the technique of syntax and "the self-propelled movement of the once evoked word-form", enable us to recollect the "original wororganisms" of the primary stage. The abstract nature of what Nijhoff calls syntax, or "the theory of the relations" of words is further explained with reference to music.

"As Nietzsche says somewhere, Beethoven did not make music like Mozart, but music of music. No singing naturalness, but a song which itself is a separate nature, which continues itself in a self-created world. This is a deeper, creative meaning of *l'art pout l'art*, which is still too often misunderstood as an exclusive watchword of the anti-social artist. Unlike language, music is not a general means of communication, and perhaps for that reason the musician, more so than the poet, is allowed a world of sound of his own [. . .]." (1925) (2, pp. 312-313).

It is clear from this quotation that also the poet is entitled to "a

tuurwetenschap," in *Controversen in de taal- en literatuurwetenschap* (Wassenaar: Servire, 1974), pp. 58-85; in particular pp. 75-77.
59. English translation in *Delta* 3 (1960), No. 4, p. 68.
60. Mooij, *Controversen*, p. 76.
61. Quoted above. Cf. also the lines in "Tweeërlei dood" (1, p. 131): "[. . .] en mijn woorden, stijgend,/zingen zich los van hun beteekenissen" ("and my words, ascending,/ loosen themselves from their meanings through singing.").

world of sound of his own." If one looks at the original wording of
Nietzsche's judgement of Beethoven in *Menschliches, Allzumenschliches,* we seem to come closer to a convincing interpretation of "Het
lied der dwaze bijen."

> *"Beethoven* und *Mozart.* — Beethovens Musik erscheint häufig wie eine tief-
> bewegte *Betrachtung* beim unerwarteten Wiederhören eines längst verloren
> geglaubten Stückes 'Unschuld in Tonen': es ist Musik über Musik. Im Liede
> der Bettler und Kinder auf der Gasse, bei der eintönigen Weisen wandernder
> Italiener, beim Tanze in der Dorfschenke oder in den Nächten des Karnevals,
> — da entdeckt er seine 'Melodien': *er trägt sie wie eine Biene zusammen*[62]
> indem er bald hier bald dort einen Laut, eine kurze Folge erhascht. Es sind
> ihm verklärte *Erinnerungen* aus der 'besseren Welt': ähnlich wie Plato es sich
> von den Ideen dachte. — Mozart steht ganz anders zu seinen Melodien: er
> findet seine Inspirationen nicht beim Hören von Musik, sondern im Schauen
> des Lebens, des bewegtesten *südländischen* Lebens: er träumte immer von
> Italien, wenn er nicht dort war."[63]

Whether Nietzsche's observation on Beethoven is convincing or
not is not under discussion here. The reference to the bee, however,
is relevant with respect to the interpretation of Nijhoff's poem. The
foolish bees, having collected their earthly honey, look for a higher
honey which belongs to the non-empirical world, to a higher, abstract order of "repeatedly not-naming" ("een steeds herhaald niet-
noemen"). Naturally, they must die; in terms of the empirical world
they are frozen to death and tumble down. However, their *attempt*
to look for a higher honey, of which they vaguely were aware, is a
hint at its existence and constitutes the very song that is mentioned
in the title. Rather than the search for just "the ideal" in general (as
Vestdijk suggests[64]) or the adventure of modern poetry (Wenseleers), the poem presents an immanent poetics and the fulfillment of
its poetic programme at the same time. For great poetry "can exist
only as the end of poetry", as an "evasive sign" ("ontwijkend
teken").

When poets and writers around 1915 renounced all efforts to

62. Italics added.
63. Friedrich Nietzsche, *Werke,* ed. Karl Schlechta, 3 vols. (München: Carl
Hanser, 2nd ed., 1960), vol. 1, p. 935.
64. S. Vestdijk, *De glanzende kiemcel: Beschouwingen over poëzie* (Amsterdam: De Driehoek, 2nd ed., 1956), pp. 164-166.

explain the world on the basis of preconceived concepts, and could no longer rely on their own intuition or conviction, they threw themselves open to random experience of the outside world, rearranged in accordance with the laws of language. In a time when, as Nijhoff observed in 1921, the great philosophies and religions had disappeared and "it is art alone that showed a reality above this world and its daily nature" (2, p. 92), the significance of the whole literary undertaking seemed to lie in the arrangement of experiences − in a construction of relations −, not in the experiences themselves. Words and word order were invested with a particular meaning they only occasionally had had before, since *something* had to be invested with a meaning. But the principle of iconicity, which always had played a role in language and literature, was not maintained very long in this predominant position. The idea of the intrinsic significance of poetic form appeared to be exhausted by the mid-thirties. Coinciding with the threat of Nazism, the invention of Socialist Realism, reportage on the Spanish civil war, and resistance literature in occupied Europe, ideological and religious commitment became again the ultimate rationale of literature, − if one did not stop writing at all. In the case of both Nijhoff and Eliot one sees an intensified interest in religious themes. In 1927 Eliot became a member of the Anglican Church, shortly after Cocteau had exchanged his addiction to opium for Roman Catholicism. Pound turned to Fascism; Gide set his hopes on the Soviet Union. Finally the Second World War wiped out nearly all remnants of Modernism, which after all was something of a luxury, an intellectual tribute to hypothetical constructions by "defenceless" minds. Moreover, if one indeed had been convinced that the world could be explained by investing significance in narrative devices and poetic forms − if one really had believed in iconic values −, one also must have experienced the centrifugal nature of the principle of iconicity. The order of unequivocal iconicity is as disparate as there are possibilities, in language. It truly is "un ordre considéré comme une anarchie." And it could not take long to discover that.[65]

65. I wish to thank Mr. E. M. Peet for his bibliographical assistance and Mr. H. Schvej for his editorial comments.

ON THE 'FOREGROUNDING' OF
GRAPHIC ELEMENTS IN POETRY.

J. J. A. Mooij (Groningen)

I

For many centuries poets have presented their work to the public not by means of a recital but by means of a written (or printed) text.[1] Recently there has been a revival of poetry readings; and modern technical methods make it possible to record such recitals. On the whole, however, this development has not substantially changed the situation. The written or printed text still counts as authoritative, and making a poem still largely means: writing it down. Moreover, I believe that the external course of things has led to a certain 'internalization'. At least since the time of Hellenism poets have felt themselves writers, which has been testified by many of their poems.[2]

Now it is a well-known fact that aestheticians and literary theorists, however different their views, hardly ever oppose the idea that sound not only has a certain direct relevance to poetry but that it is even part and parcel of every poem. On the other hand, as long as

1. The present essay resumes and elaborates some ideas from my article "De Rol van het Schrift in de Poezie", *Forum der Letteren* vol. 8 (1967-1968) (A. W. Sijthoff's Uitgevers Maatschappij, Leiden), pp. 175-207. I have also used some material from my paper on "The Role of Writing in Poetry", read at the Annual Conference 1969 of the British Society of Aesthetics, 19-21 September 1969 (unpublished).
2. Some examples taken from modern Dutch poetry are: H. Marsman, "*Tempel en Kruis*" (section I); M. Nijhoff, "Het Kind en Ik" (in *Nieuwe Gedichten*); Gerrit Achterberg, "Verzoendag" (in *Sneeuwwitje*); and idem, "Stenografie" (in *Vergeetboek*). A well-known exception is L. Vroman's "Voor wie dit Leest" (in *Gedichten, vroegere en latere*), in the sense that it shows much uneasiness about the situation. For some relevant data on the remote past, see E. R. Curtius, *Europäische Literatur und lateinisches Mittelalter,* 3rd ed. (Bern -München 1961), pp. 310-311, 312-313 and 321.

poets do not make use of very special typographical devices, the significance of writing or printing (apart from their great practical importance for the preservation of poetry) is denied or neglected or only half-heartedly acknowledged. In view of the situation sketched above this is very surprising indeed: could it be that the role of writing and printing has remained merely a practical one?

Let me first briefly illustrate my bold statement as to the neglecting of this role in the theory of the art of literature.

In many works the question of the significance that writing has for poetry is hardly mentioned at all. Among them there are such important studies as *Das sprachliche Kunstwerk* (by Wolfgang Kayser), *Allgemeine Literaturwissenschaft* (by Max Wehrli), and *The Nature of Poetry* (by Donald A. Stauffer). I think that Max Wehrli clearly states the principle that is largely the cause of this negligent attitude: "Sprache wie Literatur sind lautliche Zeichensysteme"[3] (Language as well as literature are phonetic sign systems.). Waldemar Conrad, in his study *Der ästhetische Gegenstand,* does discuss the question, but only to conclude that written symbols do not belong to the essence of poetic works of art.[4] Roman Ingarden's opinion is essentially the same. His theory of stratifacation, as expounded in *Das literarische Kunstwerk,* does not leave room for written symbols; in the end these are considered to be only regulative signals informing the reader about the sounds he has to actualize (really or imaginatively), but they would form no part of the literary work.[5] Other twentieth-century aestheticians, like Croce and Mikel Dufrenne, in spite of many differences of opinion, agree in not attaching to writing any poetic significance either.[6] Recently, William Craig Forrest proposed a modification of Ingarden's analysis of the literary work of art, adding (among other things) a stratum of kinaesthetic feelings in the speech organs. But still no visual sensuousness is taken into account; according to Forrest the "direct sensuousness of literature is

3. Max Wehrli, *Allgemeine Literaturwissenschaft* (Bern 1952), p. 48.
4. Waldemar Conrad, "Der ästhetische Gegenstand. Eine phänomenologische Studie", *Zeitschrift für Ästhetik und allgemeine Kunstwissenschaft,* vol. 3 (1908), pp. 479-480. Conrad adds that the significance of written symbols lies only in their communicative function ("Mitteilungsfunktion"), p. 480 n. 2.
5. Roman Ingarden, *Das literarische Kunstwerk,* 2d ed. (Tübingen 1960), ch. 14, esp. p. 393. (But see also p. 31 n. 3).
6. Mikel Dufrenne, *Le Poétique* (Paris 1963), pp. 10-12.

twofold: the sound of language and the kinesthetic feel of the bodily movements that produce language".[7]

The situation is different in Wellek and Warren's *Theory of Literature*. In chapter 12 (Wellek's chapter on 'The Mode of Existence of a Literary Work of Art') the authors point out not only the great practical importance of writing and printing, but also the artistic meaning of certain graphic devices. They reject the opinion that these are only "comparatively rare extravaganzas", stating that "the line-ends of verses, the grouping into stanzas, the paragraphs of prose passages, eye-rhymes or puns which are comprehensible only through spelling, and many similar devices *must be considered integral factors of literary works of art*".[8] This seems to be an auspicious start, but we are soon disappointed. When the authors in the very same chapter try to explicate the idea of a literary work as a "stratified system of norms", they follow Ingarden and they do not mention a visual stratum next to (or under) the stratum of sound. The empirical part of the structure of a literary work is explicitly identified with the sound-system.[9]

Readers of Abercrombie's *The Theory of Poetry* meet with a similar disappointment. Abercrombie remarks "that the existence of language as printed words has had a profound influence on the art of poetry. (. . .) We read poetry to ourselves more often than hear it read aloud; and poets, consciously or not, have taken advantage of this".[10] Comparing Dante and Milton with Homer, Abercrombie writes: "Their art is certainly not greater than Homer's, but it has finer modulations of significance. The thing is, that Dante and Milton, like every other printed or written poet, take advantage of the eye-appeal without losing the ear-appeal".[11] But Abercrombie says that he does not intend to treat this question in any detail. In the peroration of his book the qualities of the language of poetry are attributed exclusively to "sense and sound".

7. William Craig Forrest, "Literature as Aesthetic Object: The Kinesthetic Stratum", *Journal of Aesthetics and Art Criticism* 27, 1968-69, p. 459 (n. 12) and p. 455.

8. R. Wellek & A. Warren, *Theory of Literature*, 3d ed. (A Harvest Book), p. 144. My italics.

9. *Op. cit.,* p. 154.

10. Lascelles Abercrombie, *The Theory of Poetry*, sec. impr. (London 1926), p. 152.

11. *Op. cit.,* p. 153.

Next I must mention *Gehalt und Gestalt im Kunstwerk des Dichters* by Oskar Walzel. Walzel vigorously defends the importance of "seeing" in literature, but it becomes apparent that he only means seeing (of compositional structures etc.) with an inner eye. More recently, Northrop Frye (in his *Anatomy of Criticism*) has done the same sort of thing. After commenting on the "marks on a page" he soon substitutes a figurative sense of seeing for the literal sense.[12]

To be sure, a qualification should be made. Most aestheticians and literary theorists are indeed willing to concede that writing in verse-lines is very important for the recognition of poetry as such. They sometimes add that our attitude in reading poetry may be modified by this general character of the visual presentation, and that the white margin on the right side of the poem may even have a certain influence on the particular system of punctuation.[13] But then there is also a tendency to underestimate the importance even of verse-lines. This may be illustrated by the work of the Dutch linguist and philosopher C. F. P. Stutterheim, who has written what up till now are perhaps the most useful analyses of the role of writing in poetry.[14] Stutterheim acknowledges the fact that visual symbols may be primary symbols in literature (rather than secondary symbols in the sense of symbols of acoustic symbols). Even he, however, holds the view that typographical lines can only be symbols of verses which must be present, in a natural way, as audible units in the language-utterance itself (apparently the corresponding spoken utterance).

One would expect that the rise of concrete poetry since about 1950, if not twentieth-century poetry in general, should have influenced the views on the significance of graphic devices for poetry. Moreover, it would seem a matter of course that the contribution of semiotics to the theory of literature should also focus attention on signs and texts as visually perceptible phenomena. But hardly any

12. Northrop Frye, *Anatomy of Criticism. Four Essays* (Princeton 1957), pp. 73-78.

13. W. Gs. Hellinga & H. van der Merwe Scholtz, *Kreatiewe Analise van Taalgebruik* (Amsterdam-Pretoria 1955), pp. 52 ff. Roswitha Geggus, *Die wit in die Poesie. 'n Ondersoek na die funksionaliteit van die wit in die visuele aanbod van hedendaagse poesie* (Amsterdam 1961).

14. See esp. C. F. P. Stutterheim, *Problemen der Literatuurwetenschap* (Antwerpen-Amsterdam 1953), ch. IV: "Lezen en Luisteren" (Reading and Listening).

trace of this can be found in Ju. M. Lotman's important book on the structure of literary texts,[15] nor in *Semiotik der Literatur* by Götz Wienold. As to Lotman, this is the more remarkable because his book does contain some ideas which would make it very easy to account for some integration of graphic aspects of the text into the literary work of art. I will come back to some of these ideas in order to show in what way they are relevant to the question at hand.[16]

Of course, I do not claim that these introductory remarks should be a complete description of the situation in aesthetics and the theory of literature with regard to the problem under discussion.[17] Even so, I think that they do not give an unfair idea of this situation. I do not want to suggest either that written signs can offer the poet as much as the associated sounds. Nevertheless, I think that the importance of graphic signs in poetry is greater than the theory of poetry generally allows. I shall try to justify this opinion in the rest of my paper.

II

In reading poetry one is often confronted with signs which are not capable of an adequate acoustical interpretation. Think of certain uses of punctuation marks or combinations thereof; of the use of capital letters instead of small letters, or the other way round; of the use of abbreviations in modern poetry, and the like. Often, what would be an adequate acoustical interpretation is an interpretation which would be *differentially* adequate; that is to say, that the relevant acoustical interpretation would be sufficiently different from the acoustical interpretation adequate to another visual sign

15. Jurij M. Lotman, *Die Struktur literaturischer Texte,* (translated by Rolf-Dietrich Keil from the Russian original *Struktura chudozestvennogo teksta,* 1970), Fink Verlag, München 1972. See, e.g., Lotman's statement that the frame ("Rahmen") of a literary work of art consists of only two elements, viz. beginning and end (pp. 305 and 309). Apparently, Lotman is of the opinion that the medium of literature is time, not space (cf. p. 85); space enters only on the level of meanings (pp. 311-329). But see also his remaks on written language *vs.* colloquial language, on pp. 149-151.

16. See section III, below.

17. See, e.g., Emery E. George, "On Seeing and Hearing the Poem: An Experiment with Trakl's 'Afra'", *Orbis Litterarum* vol. 21 (1966), PP. 202-221; and Gérard Genette, "La Litterature et l'Espace", in his book *Figures II* (Paris 1969), pp. 43-48, esp. 45-46.

instead of the used one. If, in such a case, one way of writing or printing is the normal or standard one, it is especially the non-standard deviations which lose their force in the acoustic rendering. For instance, when some modern German poets no longer used capital letters as the initials of nouns, the difference from traditional spelling could not be rendered acoustically.

Perhaps this did not matter because from the poetic point of view nothing is lost in such a case. This is not evident, though. For one could argue that such devices are not essentially different from the case of poetic "foregrounding" (aktualisace) discussed by Jan Mukařovský in some of his writings. To be sure, among the components of a poem which can be foregrounded he does not mention any visual aspect of the written text. But if "foregrounding is the opposite of automatization, that is, the de-automatization of an act"; and if, in poetic language, "(foregrounding) is not used in the service of communication, but in order to place in the foreground the act of expression, the act of speech itself",[18] then it seems that written poetry allows for devices of foregrounding not available to oral poetry, and that even the abolition of capital letters may be one of these devices.

There are strong reasons to explore further this possibility of graphic devices of foregrounding. For, as Abercrombie says (see my quotation above), poets have taken advantage of the eye-appeal. Generally, they are quite prepared to use graphic devices to serve their ends. Writing in verse-lines is already a case in point. Nor is this device only or mainly parasitic upon the ear-appeal. For one thing, it may lend a higher degree of prominence and conspicuousness to repetitive and contrastive patterns in a poem, and thus substantially influence the structure of foreground and background of the work. For another thing, especially modern poets have used verse-lines in quite new and surprising ways. Of course, these uses may be connected with rhythmic patterns (and in a sense they should be so), but only hearing such a poem is an experience essentially poorer than hearing *and* seeing it; examples can be found in the expressionist

18. Jan Mukařovský, "Standard Language and Poetic Language", in *A Prague School Reader on Esthetics, Literary Structure, and Style,* selected and translated by Paul L. Garvin (Washington, D.C., 1964), pp. 17-30, esp. p. 19. Cf. the remarks on "actualization" in Victor Erlich, *Russian Formalism: History-Doctrine* (The Hague, 1955), pp. 156 and 158.

poetry of the period around 1920 (e.g. in the work of the Dutch poet H. Marsman).

Next to the rise and the development of writing in verse-lines, the use of punctuation marks should also be mentioned in this connection. Many poets have used these marks in subtle ways; and some modern poets have made very surprising combinations of them.[19] On the other hand, the abolition of punctuation that other poets have preferred to its subtle exploitation is also to be seen as the outcome of taking the graphic notation of a poem seriously.

Thirdly, the existence of so-called eye-rhyme further corroborates the view that poets did not shun the eye-appeal. To a great extent cases of hidden ear-rhymes belong to the same kind of phenomenon. Rhyming at great intervals can often be seen only. Some theorists (Kayser among others) think that the use of prepositions, articles and conjunctions in rhyming, unless these words are immediately followed by a pause, must be considered cases of eye-rhyme because, as a matter of fact, they cannot be heard in a recital.[20]

Our conclusion must be that many poets, probably by far the greater part of them, have considered the written text as relevant to and even important for their art. Apparently, they use it as something that belongs. The idea that they have not, or at least that they should not have done so appears to stem from a strong prejudice. This is the notion (explicitly expressed by Max Wehrli in the above mentioned quotation) that language is essentially spoken language; that it is an acoustic system of communication. Written language, in this perspective, is only a secondary way of symbolizing the spoken utterance. Historically, this view lines up with the facts. But the modern use of language, in science, in advertising, in journalism as well as in poetry, cannot be adequately described on the basis of this view. Graphic devices are nowadays far too prominent a phenomenon in language not to make the above view rather artificial. Written language has emancipated from its poor origins; the view that it has not is an example of the genetic fallacy.

As to poetry this means that one should either enlarge one's view of language, or give up the idea that the poetic work of art is a "sprachliches Kunstwerk". The former possibility is the more reason-

19. For example, see the combinations. . ."--: and . . .? : used by the Dutch poet P. C. Boutens in *Tusschenspelen* (1942).
20. W. Kayser, *Kleine deutsche Versschule,* 6th ed. (München 1958), p. 94.

able one. Anyhow, one should seriously consider the possibility that the written form of a poem may be one of its essential aspects at the same time. This would leave room for the poetic foregrounding of graphic elements, too.

Let us have a look at some prominent and interesting cases. Specific phenomena of foregrounding have been analyzed by Mukařovský in order to define the character of a certain style or period. I wonder whether the foregrounding of graphic elements has ever been, or is even now, the distinguishing mark of a period or of its leading style. But this is certainly not the only case of foregrounding, for foregrounding may show a more or less general, more or less systematic, more or less incidental character.[21] Lack of generality still leaves room for a systematic exploitation, and *a fortiori* for incidental use.

a. As examples of such a systematic exploitation will come to mind in the first place the so-called "carmina figurata", "technopaignia", "Figurengedichte" or "pattern poems" by poets like Theokritus, Simmias and George Herbert. Modern variants are the Calligrammes by Apollinaire and some cognate poems by the Flemish poet Paul van Ostayen. In these poems the outward form of the typographical image has been used for purposes of representation, either by arranging horizontal verse-lines of different lengths or by using also non-horizontal ways of printing, different letter types, different colours, etc. This genre of poems has known a certain (though discontinuous) tradition, and especially during the baroque period it enjoyed considerable interest. Hence, though the device has never been a general one, characteristic of a certain style or period, there has been supra-individual systematization.

Recently the movement of concrete poetry has taken up the thread of the above tradition in highlighting the visual appearance. But using a contour (with or without colours) purely for the purpose of representing material objects is only one of its minor techniques. For one thing, its contours and other formal qualities have become much more abstract. In this, concrete poetry heavily leans on recent developments in the plastic arts. Moreover, it seems to me that in certain concrete poems the poet has succeeded in integrating the background

21. See J. Mukařovský, "Die Ästhetik der Sprache" (The Aesthetics of Language), in J. Mukařovský, *Studien zur strukturalistischen Ästhetik und Poetik* (München 1973), pp. 100-141.

components with the frame of the foregrounded visual appearance. For in many cases there is not only a background consisting of sound and meaning, but also a structure of mutual relations. By way of an example I refer to *Sole Solo* by Carlo Belloli (1967). In other cases, e.g. in "Dans le silence lance l'air" by Henri Chopin (1962), the acoustic values are specially emphasized next to the visual image, which has resulted in visual poems cognate with the musical poetry by artists like Verlaine. A combination of different devices is also present in a poem like "Pomander" by Edwin Morgan (1964).[22]

The above considerations may make it clear that the term "foregrounding" is justified.[23] Concrete poetry may be seen as the outcome of a tendency to "foreground" the visually perceptible part of poetry. At the same time this helps to answer the question whether concrete poetry is poetry at all. It is understandable that this question has arisen, since concrete poetry is certainly not a central movement in poetry. Moreover, its devices are manifold, so that it may not be possible to give a useful all-enclosing answer. But marginal phenomena (apart from being interesting phenomena in their own right) can also be of use to gain an insight into central phenomena. And if my above considerations are right, there would be no reason at all to banish concrete poetry from the area of poetry. Many of its products would belong to it, albeit in the margin. For in attracting attention to the printed page, without abolishing for that reason all other factors of language, it serves a *bona fide* poetic end.

b. Next to the systematic forms of foregrounding there are incidental

22. All my examples, together with many other interesting specimina, are to be found in *An Anthology of Concrete Poetry,* edited by Emmett Williams (Something Else Press, New York 1967). Representational features appear, e.g., in the poems "Apfel" by Reinhard Döhl, "X M Poem" by Ian Hamilton Finlay, and "Geranium" by Mary Ellen Solt. For some kind of survey, see e.g. "Foreword and Acknowledgments" of this book, and the article by G. Borgers, "Visie op Visuele Poezie", in *Jaarboek van de Maatschappij der Nederlandse Letterkunde te leiden, 1972-1973* (Leiden 1974), pp. 3-13. For theoretical statements, see T. Kopfermann (ed.), *Theoretische Positionen zur konkreten Poesie* (Tübingen 1974). -The most recent developments in visual poetry I have left out of consideration; for these, see e.g. *Visual Poetry Anthology,* ed. by G.J. de Rook (Bert Bakker, The Hague 1975).

23. For some observations about the relations between background and foreground, see J. Mukařovský in P. L. Garvin, *op. cit.,* p. 19-22.

cases. They are *ad hoc,* and probably they are often the result of chance: they may be accidental as well as incidental. They occur, for instance, when the position of a word in the poem as a visually perceptible text gets special emphasis. This emphasis may be the result of a certain paralellelism between the position of the word and its meaning, this being a visual counterpart of sound symbolism. Some examples of this phenomenon can be found in a short poem of 8 lines by the Dutch poet A. Roland Holst ("Haat maakt haar dor", from part II of *Een winter aan zee,* 1937). The end of the poem is:

.... . De wereld, ouder
wordend, drong haar aan kant.

(. . . . The world, growing older, pushed her aside.)

The last word of the poem, meaning "border" or "edge", constitutes a corner of the text. It is the last part of the text to be reached by the reader; and the moment the reading comes to an end there is no room left within the poem. In consequence, the movement of reading along the words in their configuration on the page can be experienced as analogous to the pushing away of the woman. This process involves a sharp realization of the import of "kant" including the position this word has in the poem.[24]

The same poem also contains some enjambments which should be mentioned in this connection, viz. ". . . maten/overliepen en brand/ uitsloeg. . ." (. . . measures/ran over and fire/broke out . . .). The transition from one line to another (which is largely a visual phenomenon here) corresponds to the meaning of some of the relevant words.

Some such ideas might also be developed with respect to a sonnet by W. H. Auden, *The Sphinx.*[25] In my comment I shall also indicate how visual symbolism (in the above sense) co-operates with other devices.[26]

24. W. C. Forrest claims that meanings in poetry are "most complex when emphasized, commented on, and nuanced by sensation". (*op. cit.,* p. 458). I agree, provided the sensation is also allowed to be visual.
25. W. H. Auden & Christopher Isherwood, *Journey to a War* (London 1939), p. 19 = *W. H. Auden, A Selection by the Author* (Penguin Books 1958), p. 58. My comments also apply to the version in *Collected Shorter Poems 1927-1957* (London 1966), p. 120.
26. Cf. the remarks by Michael Riffaterre on the notion of "convergence" in

Did it once issue from the carver's hand
Healthy? Even the earliest conquerors saw
The face of a sick ape, a bandaged paw,
A presence in the hot invaded land.

The lion of a tortured stubborn star,
It does not like the young, nor love, nor learning:
Time hurt it like a person: it lies, turning
A vast behind on shrill America,

And witnesses. The huge hurt face accuses,
And pardons nothing, least of all success.
The answers that it utters have no uses

To those who face akimbo its distress:
'Do people like me? ' No. The slave amuses
The lion: 'Am I to suffer always? ' Yes.

In the first sentence the word "Healthy" has been given prominence, not only by the word order, by alliteration, and by the
departure from the expected iambic feet, but also because it appears
isolated from the rest of the sentence. In addition, I suggest that the
spatial separation between "healthy" and the rest of the sentence may
be viewed as a symbolic rendering of the sculpture issuing from the
carver's hand.

In the second stanza many sound-effects are present. In connection with the enjambment "turning/A vast behind", however, a
visual aspect seems to be involved too. The turning in question is not,
I think, a merely figurative turning. This is so mainly because the
speaker, instead of using the stock expression ("turning/its back")
calls to mind the concreteness of what is turned. The literal meaning
of "turning" is, I submit, reinforced by a turn in the distribution of
stresses (the stresses on "lies" and "turning" following each other
immediately) *and* by a turn in the direction of looking (the reader's
look being directed backwards to the left side of the page). Sound
symbolism and visual symbolism cooperate in bringing home to the
reader the quasi-reality of the sphinx's movement.

I think that the transition from the second stanza to the third also
contributes to the structure of this poem. The sphinx's attitude of

his article "Criteria for Style Analysis", *Word* vol. 15 (1959), pp. 154-174, esp.
pp. 172-174. Graphic devices should be included in what may be involved in
cases of convergence.

100

aloofness from its visitors, its imagined endeavour to get rid of them, is symbolically rendered by the enjambment across the dividing space between the two stanzas. This results in an intensification of the idea that the sphinx has, in a way, freed itself and now witnesses the scene from a distance.

III

My remarks on Auden's sonnet and the poem by A. Roland Holst may not be convincing in all respects to all readers. Indeed, what I have said can be taken as an attempt to maximize the import of graphic elements in poetry and the scope of their foregrounding. Even apart from such a procedure, there evidently is a risk of making unwarranted claims when we try to analyze the role of the visual data in poetry. For the symbolic (and other) possibilities offered by the writing of poetry are not always used, no more than the symbolic (and other) possibilities of sounds. But then a symbolic reading of enjambments etc. is by no means always recommendable as this would often lead to unbalanced or even senseless results. Perhaps this partly explains the ambivalent attitude of some prominent literary theorists with regard to the artistic relevance of graphic elements. Nonetheless, I think it is uncontestable that the above possibilities should not escape our notice so that whenever they are realized we may integrate them in our understanding of the poem.[27]

Now the degree of the cogency of considerations like the above strongly depends on their being incorporated into a general theory of literature. This could be a theory with the notion of foregrounding as its backbone. As a matter of fact, this is one reason why I have discussed, in the second section, the role of graphic elements especially with a view to the notion of foregrounding. However, from my argument it has appeared that this notion could only be useful for the question at hand if it were coupled with a new analysis of the structure of literary works of art according to which the written text

27. See also the illuminating interpretative comments by J. Kamerbeek Jr. on some poems by J. C. Bloem in his book *De Poëzie van J. C. Bloem in Europees Perspectief* (Amsterdam 1967), esp. p. 47 (on "De Dapperstraat"), pp. 53-54 (on "Regen en Maanlicht") and p. 23 (on "Grafschrift"). Part of what Kamerbeek says on some graphic features of his examples is very much analogous to part of what I say on the poem by A. Roland Holst.

is a component or a stratum of the work of art. Since the development of such an analysis is still in its first stage, the support for my approach is not as strong as it otherwise might have been.

Therefore it is to be appreciated that the theory of literature as recently proposed by Jurij Lotman also leaves room for the artistic use of graphic elements. A summary of the relevant parts of Lotman's theory may be suitable to conclude this essay. According to Lotman, art is a secondary language presupposing the existence of natural language, and built in accordance with its structure.

A work of art is a text in such a language; and the language of literature is one form of such a secondary language. In this language of literature natural language is used as material. Now Lotman argues that certain elements of a text which are extra-semantical from the point of view of the primary language, may be "semantisized" in the secondary language. What is, on one level of a literary text, purely syntagmatic may be of a semantic character on another level.[28] Moreover, features that are accidental to begin with, may lose this accidental character if used in a literary text.[29] They may be creatively used. In such a way conventional signs may get representional qualities.[30] Even *"noise"* can be turned into information in an artistic context; that is to say that elements which are external to the system of communication at hand may be incorporated into the system after all.[31]

All this is clearly applicable to the artistic use of certain features of the written text like those discussed above. And especially notion of turning noise into information makes it all the easier to reckon with the contribution of writing and printing. For even if one is unwilling to grant that these aspects belong to the relevant system of linguistic communication, Lotman's approach makes it possible to acknowledge that they may become significant. Quasi-disturbing factors arising e.g. from the printing in verse-lines (as contrasted with the one-dimensional flow of spoken language) can in such a way become parts of the informational pattern.

Lotman argues that this informational pattern in art is complex anyhow. There are various sub-structures and, moreover, these may

28. Lotman, *op. cit.*, p. 40. See also pp. 46 and 50.
29. Lotman, *op. cit.*, p. 37.
30. Lotman, *op. cit.*, pp. 90-91.
31. Lotman *op. cit.*, pp. 118-121. See also p. 84.

overlap because certain elements may belong to different sub-structures at the same time. The existence of these overlappings, too, will naturally lead to the view that the visual appearance of the poem, dependent on the codes of writing in general and of writing poetry in particular, is involved in the artistic object.[32/33]

32. Lotman, *op. cit.*, e.g. pp. 86-87 and 110. Lotman remarks that literary texts consist of subtexts, and he mentions the phonological level and the grammatical level (p. 86). Here, too, the graphic level could be easily incorporated into the theory.

33. In connection with my remarks on Lotman's work, see also D. W. Fokkema, "Semiotiek en Structuralisme in de Sovjetunie", *Forum der Letteren,* vol. 15 (1974), pp. 138-156, esp. pp. 144-146 and 152-153.

SHELLEY'S ODE TO THE WEST WIND,
A CASE OF WHIG HISTORY

J. J. Oversteegen (Amsterdam)

I

It is only fair to warn the reader, without scaring him off I hope, that he is going to read not more than some notes for one chapter of a book in progress. The main purpose of that book is to prove that the sonnet does exist as a separate genre.

This is probably not a surprising statement to most readers, but the following one may be: there is *no permanent formal property or set of properties* which constitutes the sonnet as a genre. Not even the 14 lines for, as Mönch's study shows, there are cases, comparatively rare I admit, of poems carrying 13, 15, 26 or even 40 lines, which are called 'sonnets' by their creators. And how could we deny them that right? If we want to avoid a normative approach, which I think we should, though not many writers on the subject seem to be inclined to do so, we cannot but accept as a fact that sonnets in *most* cases contain 14 lines, but not in all. On the other hand, not all poems of 14 lines can automatically be considered to be 'sonnets', unless one prefers to extend the concept so far that its descriptive force is lost.[1] Concepts are a blessing but not if your daughter cannot use them.[2]

Then what makes the sonnet a genre which is permanently present in poetry from the 13th Century on, so much so that it seems impossible to imagine such a thing as 'European literature' without it. The answer is, a certain way of looking at reality, a specific *optique.* Formal (constitutive) properties exist but they are time-bound; and, though there will never be an absolute break with the

1. Though he looks at the whole problem from a somewhat different angle, John Fuller holds the same opinion so far.
2. Recent literary theory confronts us with an abundance of interesting but from a descriptive point of view hardly useful concepts.

immediately preceding formal conventions[3], shifts in the set of constitutive formal properties have regularly occurred. If we take a bird's-eye view of the 'corpus sonneticum', poems which have no formal properties in common may yet belong to the corpus, which means to the same genre.[4] These changing sets of formal properties present only one permanent trait; they function as a signal. Whenever the typographical presentation of a text makes it recognizable as a sonnet, the reader's attention is channelled towards a specific view of the world.

This means that the permanent properties of the sonnet are to be found in its specific content or rather type of *Weltanschauung*, and not primarily in its form. The first thing the reader of a text with the 'sonnet-signals' of a given epoch looks for, is: Where is the 'turn', which is a brief way of asking where the opposite parts of the content meet.

To summarize this specific 'sonnetic' view on life I propose the word 'dialectical' in a broad sense. Whenever the world is seen as a duality which on a 'higher' or 'deeper' level is overcome, we might speak of a dialectical way of seeing. Sometimes the ultimate unity will be established by some type of explicit reasoning, e.g. in comparisons, in other cases the poem itself represents the act of synthesizing.

Some instances of dialectical *Weltanschauungen*, in other respects often quite discrepant, are: (Neo)platonism, with its opposition between phenomenality and reality; one of its many derivatives which is usually characterized as the metaphysical philosophy of the 'great chain of being', with its emphasis on the common base of the microcosm of man and the macrocosm of the universe; Romanticism (links with idealistic philosophy) and its offspring, literary Symbolism; but not less Marxism. Did not Johannes Becher in his later years defend the sonnet? A surprising change in his views on poetry which he himself explained by his marxist philosophical position.

Of course formal qualities are not irrelevant; used as a signal they direct the reader in the most efficient way to a specific content.

Some consequences of these suppositions: In periods in which a

3. Readers would, in that case, not be able to perceive the poem as a sonnet.
4. The reader will easily recognize the 'dynamic' view of the Russian Formalists, combined with Wittgenstein's 'family resemblance', in this description of the sonnet as a genre.

'dialectical' view of the world dominates, the sonnet is an apt vehicle for the poetic expression of insight in aspects of the world which cannot be analyzed by science or summarized in philosophical or religious doctrine in an equally effective way.

Secondly, the dominant *optique* on human existence, as expressed in European poetry from the 13th Century on, is dialectical and, we may add, up to a hundred years ago mainly Platonic. This only could explain what often amounts to a hegemony of the sonnet.

Thirdly, whatever formal variation of the sonnet is adopted, it has to be able to convey the ruling opinion on what is basic in man's condition. This means that a shift in constitutive formal properties will probably be an indication of some change in the view on life of a poet and his generation.

II

By now even the most benevolent reader who accepted my sweeping statements as potential truths, will feel inclined to interrupt and ask where the *logical* link between those chameleonic formal properties and a dominantly 'dialectical' view of the world is to be found. And if there is no logical link, how did the sonnet ever acquire this privileged position among literary genres?

My answer is that it is a birth-right; the sonnet is a deliberate construction which was meant from the beginning to be exceptionally suitable for the expression of the current views on the *conditio humana*. Let us take a quick look at how it all began.

We do not know which poem could rightly claim to be the first genuine sonnet, and it does not matter much. What we do know is that the sonnet was from the start treated as a genre. The intellectual élite at the court of Frederic II invented the form (perhaps by combining a Sicilian *strambotto* with an Arabic 6-liner, but that too is of no importance) and at once started to play games with it.

Usually Jacopo da Lentino is considered to have been the protagonist in this non-professional circle of poets. So I shall take one of his best known poems, *Io m'aggio posto in core a Dio servire,* for a short demonstration of the formal adequacy of the sonnet from a philosophical point of view.[5]

5. The Rosetti version of this sonnet should not be used since it contains ar

106

Some analytical remarks[6], based on different aspects of the poem.

Rhyme: different rhymes in 'octave' and 'sextet' (segmentation 8:6).

Metre or metric substratum: iambic, in all lines a *caesura* after the third, or sometimes the second iambus.[7] Ratio 3:2 or 2:3.

Syntax: Lines 1, 5, 9 and 13 initiate the only principal sentences of the poem (segmentation according to the ratio 4:4:4:2).[8] Also, the last lines of octave. and sextet are syntactically symmetrical though contrasting in meaning (ratio 8:6).

Keywords[9]: The first 'quatrain' is dominated by religious terms (*Dio, paradiso, auto loco*); the second 'quatrain' deals with wordly love (*Madonna,* i.e. 'my beloved', *blonda testa, claro viso,* perhaps *gaudire); the next six lines contain a combination of both (peccato, bel portamento, bel viso, morbido sguardare, consolamento, mia donna, ghiora*). The last line is marked by the fact that it is the only one in which heaven and earth meet in an affirmative way. 'La mia donna' is pictured in 'a state of glory' and thus associated with the virgin Mary. (In the last line of the octave 'la mia donna' is also present, but heaven and earth are 'divided'.)

All this results in a clear thematic structure: 4 lines in a religious context; 4 lines on secular love; 4 lines on the irreconcilable opposition between the two (only the negative word *sin* refers to the religious field of meaning); 2 lines in which the two meet, by renouncing carnal love. The beloved can only be *looked at* (there is a striking emphasis on the

inept last line (*gioia* in stead of *ghiora*); Kay incorporated a better version in his easily accessible *Penguin Book of Italian Verse.* The present article was completed when my colleague P. W. M. de Meijer drew my attention to the study by Aldo Menichetti in *Strumenti Critici* IX, 1 (February 1975) which offers most interesting opinions on the problems raised here.

6. Of course a thorough analysis will be presented in one of the early chapters of the book with which I have already threatened the reader. From now on I will not apologize for shortcuts, since the reason is always the same, and a *captatio benevolentiae* should not be stressed too much.

7. Often the syntactic structure marks the *caesurae*. In other cases they are caused by the pause before or after sacral words, like *Dio, paradiso.*

8. Apparently, the 'English type' is not *quite* a new invention.

9. 'Keywords' is used here as an abbreviation for: words with an outspoken frame of reference.

feature 'seeing'). The very last line, *veggiendo la mia donna in ghiora stare,* makes the poem end with a blast of trumpets.[10]

Thus we get a thematic segmentation on the model: 4 (A): 4 (B): 4 (-A + B) : 2 (+A +B), but no less 13:1, because the whole poem leads to the *pointe* in the last line, and on the level of the meaning of single words the combination +A +B is only accomplished in the last line, though prepared by the word *consolamento.*

Concluding, we may say that the content of the poem is based on a confrontation of heaven and earth within the frame of the dualistic religious thinking of the period. They are reconcilable (and in fact reconciled here) only by an act of renunciation which leads to the glorious elevation of the beloved in the last line.

From the point of view of formal structure we get as a result: 14 lines, divided in two quatrains and a sextet, the latter being subdivided in a 'quatrain' and two lines (not a couplet in the proper sense since the lines do not rhyme). From a thematic point of view the main segmentation is 4-4-4-(1-1) or even 13-1.

Each line is divided in two parts on the ratio 3:2.

According to the introductory remarks I made, this formal structure should be particularly apt to transmit the *Weltanschauung* of the author and his contemporaries. In what respect?

I have already mentioned that Neoplatonic philosophy holds the opinion that art is particularly suited to make the divine laws apparent which govern the universe. If a poem adds to this higher power of art in general a *formal organization* which in itself mirrors directly those same divine laws, we may expect this form to be particularly welcome. Now is there some sort of philosophical theory which meets these requirements? Certainly. All philosophical systems which maintain that visible phenomena are ordered numerically according to divine laws (and this type of thinking is abundant at the court of Frederic II) offer the principles on which the formal organization of a work of art can be modelled.

10. The marking of the last line by way of a *pointe* is well-known. It is interesting to see composers use the foregrounding of the last line in their musical versions of sonnets. An outspoken example is Monteverdi's *A Dio, Florida Bella* (a sonnet by Marino; recorded in the series *Das Alte Werk,* No.SAWT 9438-A). The first quatrain is sung by a male voice, the second by a female one; the first tercet by the choir; the first two lines of the last tercet alternatingly by male and female voce, the very last line again by the choir.

One of the outstanding personalities with whom Lentino, Della Vigna, (Rinaldo) Aquino and the other creative politicians around Frederic II had daily contact in their discussions, is Leonardo da Pisa. He is the writer of the *Abacus,* most important among medieval treatises on mathematics; today he is mainly known as the 'inventor' of the Fibonacci-series, the arithmetic version of the Golden Section. This sequence of numbers runs 1, 2, 3, 5, 8, 13, 21 etc., each new number being the sum of the two preceding ones. The further the series is continued the closer the ratio of the subsequent numbers approaches the Golden Section. We all remember the approximation 3:5 from our schooldays.

If we now look again at the result of our brief formal analysis of Lentino's sonnet, we see that all the numbers of the Fibonacci-series up to 13 appear, either in the structure of the whole poem or in its separate lines.[11] This seems sufficiently striking to permit us to formulate a hypothesis: One of the formal structural principles of the Sicilian sonnet is the Golden Section. The consequence of this hypothesis would be that the poem is, in its outward appearance, (partly) based on the 'godly principle' which was supposed to be at the root of all things human and cosmic. What form could be better adapted to the task of reflecting God's Creation in art objects than this one? [12] A passion for this 'ideal form' can thus be explained by starting at the prevailing Christian view on human existence (life is characterized and frustrated by antagonistic tendencies). At the same time, an important current in philosophy saw art as one of the means to surmount man's shortcomings by laying bare the divine laws underlying all our experiences and thus making them meaningful. This 'action art' would be all the more successful if its expression could be entirely organized according to the structural laws which permeate all natural phenomena. So the ideal form is numerically organized on the basis of given 'laws', such as the Golden Section.

11. I could even mention the iambus, according to certain theories, but since I am sceptical about those theories myself, I prefer to leave the 'smallest units' alone.

12. Much more could be said about mathematical and arithmetical aspects of the (early) sonnet. The 'holy' numbers 3 and 7, with their multiples 6, 9, 14, 21 etc. were frequently discussed by contemporary authors. Much later Schlegel, who incidentally mentions the Golden Section, points at the combination of 2 and 3 (2^3 and 2x3), 'square' or even 'cube' and 'triangle' which again leads to 14.

For a long time to come no changes were necessary, since the picture of the world and man's position in it stayed much the same.

The Dolce Stil Nuovo poets did not add new aspects to the fundamental structure of the sonnet. And Petrarch who in most histories is far too much considered as the poet who *created* the privileged position of the sonnet, worked (miracles) at the surface, at stylistic devices and 'musical' effects. Indirect proof of this limited field in which Petrarch's renovations were established, is to be found in the fact that the anti-Petrarchists aim their arrows at these aspects (plus the thematic preoccupation with an inconquerable love) and not at the structural principles, which are in fact much more emphasized by the Sicilians (and by some of the anti-Petrarchists!) than by Petrarch.

III

The first fundamental shift in the formal structure of the sonnet appears halfway the Pléiade-movement. What happened? To put it short: Because the Golden Section gradually loses its privileged position as *the* divine principle of order in the visible universe, the iambic pentameter with a *caesura* based on the ratio 3:5, the thematic structure based on the ratio 8:5:1 and other constitutive properties become arbitrary and replaceable. The later Renaissance was indeed still aware of the principle of the Golden Section but it is outruled in those cases in which it clashes with the new (or renewed) principle of symmetry. In architecture, e.g., harmony is mainly to be found in symmetry, though windows, doors etc. may still be designed on the Golden Section ratio. Now, to divide 5 iambs into two equal halves, which permit intricate playing with parallelisms, antinomies, chiasms, within the scope of one line, seems rather a complicated job.[13] The hexameter and the alexandrine, however, present in this respect no problem. This may have been an important, if not the main, reason for the Pléiade poets to switch to the six feet line, a switch which puzzled many a historian (or, worse, was accepted by them with perfect equanimity). Similar explanations can be given for other for-

13. Not an impossible job. It can be easily proved that Shakespeare often put a stop after the first syllable of the third iamb. For reasons of economy I refer the reader to the Jakobson/Jones analysis of *Th'Expence of Spirit*.

mal properties which constitute the French type.[14] There is continuity, not on the level of detailed formal organization, but on a more complicated one: the sonnet still has the special function to express a divine harmony in the world, the human experience of which is based on dichotomies. This harmony being conceived in a new way, the formal organization of the sonnet has to be adapted to these changed conditions. I feel free to use the title of Spitzer's analysis of the 'sonnet de l'Idée' by Du Bellay as a *raccourci* to prove at least the continuity: 'The Poetic Treatment of a Platonic-Christian Theme'.

To finish this steeple-chase, I will say some words on the third famous (or should I say notorious?) fence: the 'Shakespearean type'. It is not really as different from the sicilian form as is often supposed, if one considers it as an elaboration (conventionalization) of one of the original variables. The 4-4-4-2 structure allows for a very explicit, and even moralizing, dialectical development, for instance of this type: thesis/antithesis/ synthesis/ generalization of the synthesis (or: transformation into a new thesis, on a more general level.)[15]

Would it be too bold to suggest that this segmentation is quite appropriate in an age, inclined to (moral) generalization? [16] Much could be said about 17th and 18th century sonneteers (for instance that the supposition that the latter hardly exist is not justified), but I have to shift to another gear if I want to reach Shelley whose *Ode* remains my target of the day.

14. An interesting aspect of this shift in the history of the sonnet (and the same goes for later shifts) is that on a certain level (the syntactic, or the thematic, – that depends) the former phase is still apparent as a kind of 'substratum'. This too contributes to the continuity in the history of the genre. The opposite may also be true: in the substratum an abortive renovation can be pointed out. In Renaissance sonnetry we meet with structural substrata, showing the symmetry principle; there may be e.g. a thematic break after the 7th line, which has a 7-7 composition as a result (see Jakobson/Jones; in my examples I stick to poems, analysed by others, without thereby accepting all their conclusions of course).
15. Of course the terminology I use here is quite anachronistic, but I suppose that the reader will have no problems in putting these terms back in their historical context.
16. It is amusing to see how easy it would be to make a tear-off calendar with Shakespeare couplets. Probably it has been done already.

IV

The era of Romanticism, with its frontal attack on normative poetics, would seem to have to result in a fatal blow to the sonnet. Yet, as everyone knows, the opposite is true. The genre has never known such a hectic and vivid development as just then.[17] To explain this astonishing situation (the strictest genre known[18] survives the massacre of genres!), we need only think of one fact: the dialectical pattern of thinking, however changed and varied, continues to be dominant. The 'heterocosmic analogue', which is based on a tension between a universe of the Idea and phenomenal reality, is often considered to be a typically Romantic concept. So, a type of poem which gives special support to this view may always count on a room of its own. The formal structure will be turned upside down, ripped apart and pasted together again, whole poems or separate lines may be put on a Procrustes bed[19], − all that is part of the attack on normative poetics. But the need of that one signal: this is a sonnet, a poem about controversial themes or aspects of the world[20], which hold each other in balance, that need is still there. In order to satisfy it, the poet can never go so far that his poem is not recognized as a sonnet anymore, and the title will not be fully sufficient if he wants to avoid the readers' reaction: this is no sonnet at all (and consequently it is a failure). Every new poem which pretends to be a

17. If one accepts the normative Mönch-Jost approach, the behaviour of the Romantic sonneteers has even been too hectic and vivid, so that the genuine brand, 'das sonettische Sonett', only lived a cumbersome life ever after, surrounded in its old age by 'unsonettische' bastards in stead of by legitimate offspring.

18. The fact that the formal prescriptions vary in consecutive periods does of course not make the formal structure of a specific moment less strict.

19. The curtail-sonnet, the 'sonnet à rebours', the 40-liner, the 13-liner (sometimes amalgamated with the rondel); the 3-feet liner, the 7-feet liner, the 3-5-7-feet liner, even the one-foot-liner, − one could probably compose vast anthologies of these 'monstruosities', a Bomarzo of the sonnet, in most languages.

20. If the reader wants to protest against this way of seeing the function of (conventional) form, I would like to point out that in many cases a poem would be read differently if the reader were not aware of a dichotomy of some kind. In many sonnets, the form is a functional aspect of the interpretation.

sonnet or, to put it differently, which functions as a signal for a specific type of content, will have to be linked by at least *one* obvious constitutive formal property to its predecessors.[21]

What can English Romantic poets do if they want to preserve the specific possibilities of the sonnet? They can turn, and often they did turn, to other conventional types, but if they stick to the 'English signal' then they cannot avoid the basic element of 12 lines plus a couplet. *Within* these 12 lines, they can tamper with rhyme, rhyme-scheme, length of lines etc., and they practically all do, Shelley as well as the others.

Now what is the position of the *Ode to the West Wind?*[22]

At this crucial point I am confronted with an awkward fact: one might well doubt if this series of five stanzas (as Shelley himself calls them) is in fact a cycle of sonnets. But Shelley has a strange way of using genre-titles, even in this very case (the *Ode* is not an ode, which means a poem consisting of stanzas of the type 'one quatrain plus two tercets'). He systematically calls those poems 'sonnets' which are not at first sight recognized as such and in the clear-cut cases he only uses titles, as a rule without indications of genre. This, by the way, is a small additional argument in favour of the signal-character of formal properties, at least in Shelley's oeuvre.

Though I personally think that the 12 lines plus couplet-signal is sufficient reason to consider the stanzas of the *Ode* as sonnets, I shall call other authors as witnesses. John Fuller states: 'Shelley produced a novel variety in "Ode to the West Wind" which should be printed (though it is not always so) as a sequence of five "sonnets" to the scheme ababcbcdcdedee, whose reliance on Italian *terza rima* seems appropriate and decorous.' (p.33) 'Decorous' the structure of the Ode may be, 'appropriate' it certainly is, as we shall see later.

Mönch also mentions the *Ode,* but his opinion about Shelley's sonnets is in general less favourable. 'Der Grösste unter den englischen Romantikern, Percy Bysshe Shelley, wurde vollends mit dem Sonett nicht fertig. Was er an Sonetten hinausschleudert, sind geballte Ideen, packend, aufrüttelnd, erregend – zweifellos den genialen Charakter verratend – aber die Form wird vom Gedanken zer-

21. Again the reader will be reminded of Wittgenstein's 'family resemblance', and possibly of Morris Weitz's book on *Hamlet*-criticism.

22. The edition used here is the easily available Oxford Paperback *Poetical Works,* ed. by Hutchinson and corrected by Matthews (1970), pp. 577-579.

brochen, oder aber der Gedanke zerbricht an der Form selbst und bleibt Torso' (p. 172; this pure poetry should not be translated). Supposing that the reader is now willing to read (or to accept a possible reading of) the *Ode* as a series of five sonnets, I can at last come to my comment on the poem itself.

The most obvious variation on the 3 times 4 segmentation in a 12 line total of 5-feet iambs, seems to be a 4 times 3, for instance on a *terza rima* model, which indeed Shelley chose to offer his readers. Was this choice arbitrary?

What are the specific potentials of the *terza rima* supposed to be? Gero von Wilpert (p. 624, i.v. Terzine): 'Der Kettenreim bricht die innere Geschlossenheit der Einzelstrophen und fügt sie zu einer durch Reim verzahnten Reihe 3-zeiliger Perioden aneinander. Die ununterbrochene und bis ins Unendliche fortsetzbare Reimverkettung begünstigt inhaltlich eine durchgängige Verknüpfung weltweiter Ideen, wirkt jedoch auch in kleineren lyrischen Stücken, besonders – wegen der versteckten, ungewöhnlichen Regel der Reimfolge – für mysteriöse Themen. Die Dreizahl der Zeilen begünstigt einen Aufbau nach dem Schema von Thesis, Antithesis und Synthesis, wobei letztere wiederum Ausgangspunkt neuer Entfaltung wird.'

I could use almost every word of this quotation but I will not do so, because normally I would have been tempted to make ironical comments on 'mysterious themes' and other untestable statements. So I will stick to the factual side of Wilpert's characterization: the *terza rima* scheme smooths the way for 'infinite concatenation' (in form and content) and it is favourable to a thesis-antithesis-synthesis structure. The latter is exactly what I have maintained for the sonnet from its earliest stages on. This could mean that Shelley tries to take a new step forward in the development of the sonnet without losing his grip on the traditional specific power of the form, or even by elaborating on tradition itself.

Only, one has to admit that what he wins on one side he loses on the other, if we put the merits of his rather unusual choice in such an abstract way. One of the most striking assets of the sonnet is its closed form, its inner balance, precisely because of the dialectical potentials of the poem as a whole. A poet may hint at a dialectical structure in the line-by-line construction by using the *terza rima* 'signal',[23] but if he really uses these dialectical implications to the full, the entire stanza would either suffer from it or become extremely complicated. Shelley does indeed not emphasize the dialectical structure on the linear level, though some of the tercets could be analyzed in this sense. In fact, the stanzas are filled with dialectical notions but these are not systematically linked with the tercet-segmentation.

So, what remains are the other specific advantages of the *terza rima* (continuity) which are contrary to the advantages of the traditional sonnet-form (closedness)? If we take a provisional look at the whole *Ode* this contradiction seems doubtful. It is the old problem of the cycle. There is a well-known tendency among sonneteers to write cycles, which seems, just like the *terza rima* scheme, to violate the closed structure of the single sonnet. Mönch even considers the cycle as an unnatural phenomenon if it tries to be more than a group of poems on a common theme.

This addiction to a division of poetry in 'pure' and 'impure' applications, I gladly leave to Mönch's responsibility. We should, I feel, start at the other end. It is a fact that, from Dante and Petrarch on, there are many cases of 'horizontal' relations within sonnet-cycles, and not just 'vertical' (thematic) ones. This implies that we should not make a dogma of the insularity of the single sonnet. Close analysis alone could help us to describe the effect in each separate case. The rest of this essay will be an abridged version of a 'defense of Shelley's *Ode'*, on the assumption that it exists and that no normative system could perform a vanishing trick on it. I shall first present a survey of the formal structure of the whole cycle, then try out a provisional interpretation of the first stanza, ending with an (also sketchy) interpretation of the whole *Ode*.

V

All five stanzas are built on the aba/bcb/cdc/ded/ee rhyme-scheme. The couplet presents an interruption of the rhymestream, which is

23. Von Wilpert's note seems to imply that the *terza rima* scheme points at dialectical processes, but I am not sure that we are allowed to accept this as a solid fact. That is why I prefer not to go any further then 'continuity' and a possible hint at dialectical content.

taken up again in the next stanza, but not with the same rhymes. It will strike every reader, however, that the couplets are not equally outspoken as landmarks of an overall segmentation. The first stanza ends on the rhyme (air-)-where-hear, the second on (sepulchre-) sphere-hear, the third on (wear-)fear-hear, the fourth on (cloud-) bowed-proud, the last one on (mankind-)Wind-behind.

Some observations on these rhymes: The first three stanzas end with (approximately) the same rhymes, and exactly the same word. The couplets of Stanzas I and II rhyme from an auditory point of view,[24] but not from a visual one; the couplet of stanza III from both an auditory and visual one. Conclusion: there *is* an interruption of the stream in each case, but only a sharp one at the end of stanza III. The lines of demarcation are weakened at the end of I and II. The close relation between the first three stanzas, on the other hand, is emphasized by the last word, and, one may add, by the apostrophal character of all of them, indicated by 'Thou' in the first lines.

Such a relation does not exist between IV and V, neither among themselves nor with I, II or III. The whole cycle, then, is structured 3:1:1, as far as the rhyme-schemes are concerned.

This structure is confirmed by 1) the fact that I, II and III each (and perhaps even together) consist of one long phrase, whereas IV and V are broken up in several full sentences, 2) the appearance, quite emphatically, of the words 'I', 'me', 'my' in stanza IV and V only. Together these observations result in an overall formal structure of the cycle which takes up, consciously or not, the 3:2 ratio which is typical for the sonnet in its initial presentation. It is legitimate to state that Shelley effects a segmentation of the whole cycle which is in harmony with a traditional type of sonnet. The same goes, as with most English sonneteers, for the *caesurae* (if present). They divide the lines into parts according to the ratio 3:2 or 2:3, which, incidentally, is not obligatory in *terza rima* poetry whereas the five foot line is.

24. Not being a native speaker I have to be very wary about problems of rhyme because of the well-known liberal attitude of English poets in this respect, and because of the historical difference in pronunciation. So I keep on the safe side by summing up some random examples (from Shelley, page-numbers refer to Hutchinson/Matthews) of comparable rhymes: there-fair-wear (151), appear-atmosphere-wear-near (49), air-bear-dare-wear (63), fear-ne'er-murderer (78), her-fear (417), mirror-wearer-error (618). I think that, in the light of these examples, my statements on the *Ode* are not too bold.

Let us now take a closer look at the first stanza. We may begin by adding some observations on formal aspects to the general ones above.

1) Sound repetitions are used frequently, to such an extent that one is reminded of Petrarch: alliteration e.g. in line 1 (Wild-West-Wind, breath-being); assonance in line 12 (with-living-hill); both in line 9 (sister-Spring) etc.; even chiastic repetition can be pointed out, in line 7 (*cold-low*).

2) Personification, often on the basis of a classical or biblical allusion, strikes the modern reader: Autumn, Spring, the West-Wind, its azure sister; biblical allusion without personification is to be found in the resurrection from death at the blowing of a clarion.

3) Rhetorical figures of all sorts abundant: metaphors (lines 6, 11), metonyms (thine azure sister), paradox (unseen presence, destroyer and preserver), anastrophe (leaves dead), comparisons (lines 3, 5, 6), oxymoron (black-pale and pale-red in line 4). These are just some examples.

4) Words from two semantic fields occur systematically: Death and Life. Dead, ghosts, black, pale, hectic, pestilence, dark bed, wintry, seeds that lie cold and low in a grave, corpse, − against: blow her clarion, dreaming (in opposition to dead), buds, feed, living hues and odours.

5) The passivity of 'driven' (line 3) in opposition to the active 'driving' (line 11).

6) Ten lines with 10 syllables (2, 4, 5, 7, 8, 9, 11, 12, 13, 14); stress: eight in the first line (emphasis on first four words), six in line 11, four or five in the others. Conclusion: regular metrical substratum of iambic type, with a slight tendency to the 4 stresses of epic tradition; marking of first line.

7) Syntax: the whole stanza forms one sentence, an invocation with the 'person' invoked at the very beginning, the imperative verb at the very end. All other sentences are imbedded. The lines in which the invocation is renewed, are lines 1, 2, 5 and 13; 'thine' in line 9 also refers to the invoked 'Thou'. Lines 1, 5, 9 and 13 mark the beginnings of the segments of the traditional 4-4-4-2 sonnet.

The formal segmentations of the stanza are: 4 times 3 plus 2 (rhyme-scheme), but not less 4-4-4-2 (syntax, position of 'Thou' and 'thine') or 8-4-2, because of the semantic features (death-Autumn words in the first 8 lines, life-Spring words in the next 4; line 13 is neutral, line 14 brings the two semantic opposites together in a paradox).

The fact last mentioned is most interesting. It means that on the thematic and syntactic level the traditional English model is present. One could also note that the *pointe*-character of the last line is undeniable. Underneath the new model of the *terza rima* type, which is hitting us in the eye, we discover a reassuringly traditional substratum, which helps to confirm the 'sonnetical' character of the first stanza, without weakening the effect of the surface-structure.

The same is true for the other stanzas, but for the time being I must leave the proof of this allegation to the reader. Rather than filling the limited space of this essay with scattered remarks on the four other stanzas, I would like to return to the cycle as a whole.

VII

The first three stanzas deal with the opposition Life-Death in nature, with the emphasis clearly on the conclusion 'Life may spring from 'death'.[25] The perspective (e.g. looking forward to winter and then spring − looking backward to summer) changes from stanza to stanza, but the basic pattern of thought does *not* (the west wind as 'destroyer and preserver', as all-pervading force).

A radical turn in the point of view, however, occurs in stanza IV. Up to this point we have heard about the effects wrought by the West Wind, in nature, in the air, on earth, at sea, all this in a complicated network of cross-references.[26] In stanza IV we are suddenly confronted with the 'narrator', who states that he has been like the West Wind ('tameless, and swift, and proud') and once was his companion. This relation, however, is no longer possible, the 'I' lacks the active force which would make him a confederate of the West Wind. Thus he comes (stanza V) to the point of imploring the 'Spirit' (i.e.

25. This concept of the dialectical relation between life and death probably goes back to Holbach whom Shelley admired. See I. J. Kapstein, o.c.
26. Cf. the Leavis-Fogle discussion.

118

the West Wind) to make him his instrument. At this point we meet with an extremely interesting full turn to the poem itself[27]:

> Drive my dead thoughts over the universe
> Like withered leaves to quicken a new birth!
> And, by the incantation of this verse, etc.

If we read the last eight lines of the cycle again, we realize to what extent we also witness a return to the first stanza. One may well speak of 'cyclic poetry'!

But something has changed too, of course. The first three stanza's could be characterized as an objective picture of the power of the West Wind. The fourth stanza shows the predicament of the poet who has lost his youthful hybris. The fifth stanza confronts us with something like poetics, and a humble kind at that. Only by submitting himself to the creative Spirit which pervades all things in nature[28] (for that is what the West Wind has come to stand for), the poet can make his verse fruitful for mankind. The last line is one full of hope, but doubt is lurking. Hope and doubt both for the poet and for humanity.

Now back from this paraphrasing, which is just an emergency exit, to structural observations: The whole cycle shows once more the model, present in the first stanza, of a dialectical development. Objective power (stanza I-III), subjective weakness (stanza IV), new power to the subject by submitting himself to the objective Spirit (stanza V), or: life, death, life from death. Pointing out this life-from-death theme as a possible summary, is not stretching the parallelism of stanza I with the whole cycle too far. This could be shown by quoting a few lines from the last stanza: 'Drive my dead thoughts over the universe / Like withered leaves to quicken a new birth! '[29]

27. J. Kamerbeek Jr. has repeatedly discussed this type of 'reflexive' utterances in poetry as a sign of 'immanent poetics', which he considers to be one of the characteristic properties of Symbolism. The familiar representation of Shelley as a 'precursor' of Symbolism would find strong support in this hypothesis. I am not certain, however, that Kamerbeek would be very happy with this specific application of his ideas on immanent poetics, since he does not particularly favour 'precursors', 'transition periods' and the like.
28. I need not point out that we have met before with a special relation between the Spirit of the Universe and the sonnet, though in a quite different context!
29. Note the unifying repetition of images from the first stanza (e.g. the dead

And of course I can summon the very last line as my crown witness for the assertion that the 'destroyer and preserver' theme of the first stanza is taken up again at the end as the main theme of the whole cycle: 'O, Wind, if Winter comes, can Spring be far behind?' A repetition indeed, but with ever so much more levels of complicated meaning.

VIII

My conclusion can be brief. By breaking up the first 12 lines of his sonnets into tercets, Shelley did not create one more 'unsonnetic' form with his *Ode to the West Wind,* but, on the contrary, offered a potential solution to an old problem: the reconciliation of the closedness (inner balance) of each separate sonnet with the continuity of the cycle, so that the cycle as a whole repeats on a higher level ('spirally') the process of the first stanza. The emphasis on continuity is reinforced by the *terza rima* scheme. Also, the possible implication of the *terza rima* as a signal for a dialectical development directly points at the thematic structure of the *Ode.* At the same time the links with the traditional English sonnet are very strong, so strong that nothing is lost of its specific potency.

In my opinion Shelley's innovation is not less valuable than the formal variation produced by the Pléiade poets or the one introduced in England in the 16th and 17th Century. After all, not all poems of those sanctified models are great achievements. When we look at it from the point of view of individual result, Shelley's *Ode* can keep company with the high and mighty. Only, from the standpoint of literary history, it did not 'succeed' as a new type. But then, which poet would stand up to a criticism of this kind? Why condemn Shelley for his failure to please the student of literary history, instead of praising him for writing a poem which varies in a personal but highly disciplined way on the strictest genre known in poetry, without hampering its innate potentials?

leaves) but also how these images gain in weight (ambiguity of 'leaves' for instance). A simple natural phenomenon, the west wind, has grown to be the inspiration on which the poet depends. Among other things this is an ethymologization of the word 'spirit'.

It seems quite an achievement to bring together tradition and the individual talent, both with such intensity.[30]

30. It is amazing that Eliot, and with him Leavis and most New Critics, did not discover the *Ode* as a manifesto of 'depersonalization', but could only find condescending and even scornful terms for Shelley as a poet. Fortunately Leavis had an inkling that the *Ode* is superior to almost all the other poems of Shelley, but even in this case he considers him too be overrated.

Bibliography

Fogle, Richard Harter, *The Imagery of Keats and Shelley: a Comparative Study.* Hamden 1962.
Fogle, Richard Harter, 'The Imaginal Design of Shelley's "Ode to the West Wind" '. In: *A Journal of English Literary History* XV,1 (March 1948), pp. 219-227.
Fuller, John, *The Sonnet* (The Critical Idiom 26). London 1972.
Jakobson, Roman and Lawrence G. Jones, *Shakespeare's Verbal Art in 'Th'Expence of Spirit.'* The Hague 1970.
Jost, François, 'Le contexte européen du sonnet'. In: *Zagadnienia Rodzajów Literackich* XIII, 1 (1970), pp. 5-28.
I.J. Kapstein, 'The Symbolism of the Wind and the Leaves in Shelley's "Ode to the West Wind" '. In: *PMLA* LI, 1 (March 1936), pp. 1069-1079.
Kay, George (Ed.), *The Penguin Book of Italian Verse.* Harmondsworth 1958.
Leavis, Frank Raymond, *Revaluation.* Harmondsworth 1964. (First ed. 1936)
Lemaître, Hélène, *Shelley, Poète des éléments.* Caen 1962.
Mönch, Walter, *Das Sonett: Gestalt und Geschichte.* Heidelberg 1955.
Shelley, Percy Bysshe, *Poetical Works.* Ed. by Thomas Hutchinson, a new edition, corrected by G. M. Matthews. London, Oxford, New York 1970.
Spitzer, Leo, 'The Poetic Treatment of a Platonic-Christian Theme'. In: *Romanische Literaturstudien.* Tübingen 1959, pp. 130-159.
Wassermann, Earl R., *Shelley: a Critical Reading.* Baltimore, London 1971.
Wilpert, Gero von, *Sachwörterbuch der Literatur,* Stuttgart, 3rd ed. 1961.

121

ODE TO THE WEST WIND*
[Published with *Prometheus Unbound,* 1820.]

I

O WILD West Wind, thou breath of Autumn's being,
Thou, from whose unseen presence the leaves dead
Are driven, like ghosts from an enchanter fleeing,

Yellow, and black, and pale, and hectic red,
Pestilence-stricken multitudes: O thou,   5
Who chariotest to their dark wintry bed

The wingèd seeds, where they lie cold and low,
Each like a corpse within its grave, until
Thine azure sister of the Spring shall blow

Her clarion o'er the dreaming earth, and fill   10
(Driving sweet buds like flocks to feed in air)
With living hues and odours plain and hill:

Wild Spirit, which art moving everywhere;
Destroyer and preserver; hear, oh, hear!

*This poem was conceived and chiefly written in a wood that skirts the Arno,
near Florence, and on a day when that tempestuous wind, whose temperature is
at once mild and animating, was collecting the vapours which pour down the
autumnal rains. They began, as I foresaw, at sunset with a violent tempest of hail
and rain, attended by that magnificent thunder and lightning peculiar to the
Cisalpine regions.
The phenomenon alluded to at the conclusion of the third stanza is well
known to naturalists. The vegetation at the bottom of the sea, of rivers, and of
lakes, sympathizes with that of the land in the change of seasons, and is consequently influenced by the winds which announce it. — [SHELLEY'S NOTE]

II

Thou on whose stream, mid the steep sky's commotion,   15
Loose clouds like earth's decaying leaves are shed,
Shook from the tangled boughs of Heaven and Ocean,

Angels of rain and lightning: there are spread
On the blue surface of thine aëry surge,
Like the bright hair uplifted from the head   20

Of some fierce Maenad, even from the dim verge
Of the horizon to the zenith's height,
The locks of the approaching storm. Thou dirge

Of the dying year, to which this closing night
Will be the dome of a vast sepulchre,   25
Vaulted with all thy congregated might

Of vapours, from whose solid atmosphere
Black rain, and fire, and hail will burst: oh, hear!

III

Thou who didst waken from his summer dreams
The blue Mediterranean, where he lay,   30
Lulled by the coil of his crystàlline streams,

Beside a pumice isle in Baiae's bay,
And saw in sleep old palaces and towers
Quivering within the wave's intenser day,

All overgrown with azure moss and flowers   35
So sweet, the sense faints picturing them! Thou
For whose path the Atlantic's level powers

Cleave themselves into chasms, while far below
The sea-blooms the oozy woods which wear
The sapless foliage of the ocean, know   40

Thy voice, and suddenly grow gray with fear,
And tremble and despoil themselves: oh, hear!

IV

If I were a dead leaf thou mightest bear;
If I were a swift cloud to fly with thee;
A wave to pant beneath thy power, and share   45

The impulse of thy strength, only less free
Than thou, O uncontrollable! If even
I were as in my boyhood, and could be

The comrade of thy wanderings over Heaven,
As then, when to outstrip thy skiey speed   50
Scarce seemed a vision; I would ne'er have striven

As thus with thee in prayer in my sore need
Oh, lift me as a wave, a leaf, a cloud!
I fall upon the thorns of life! I bleed!

A heavy weight of hours has chained and bowed   55
One too like thee: tameless, and swift, and proud.

V

Make me thy lyre, even as the forest is:
What if my leaves are falling like its own!
The tumult of thy mighty harmonies

Will take from both a deep, autumnal tone,   60
Sweet though in sadness. Be thou, Spirit fierce,
My spirit! Be thou me, impetuous one!

Drive my dead thoughts over the universe
Like withered leaves to quicken a new birth!
And, by the incantation of this verse,   65

Scatter, as from an unextinguished hearth
Ashes and sparks, my words among mankind!
Be through my lips to unawakened earth

The trumpet of a prophecy! O, Wind,
If Winter comes, can Spring be far behind?   70

[Reprinted from: Shelley, *Poetical Works*; edited by Thomas Hutchinson; a new edition, corrected by G. M. Matthews. London, Oxford, New York: Oxford University Press, 1970, pp. 577-579, by kind permission of the Oxford University Press, Oxford.]

NOTES ON "INTERSUBJECTIVITY"
IN LITERARY SCHOLARSHIP

Bernard F. Scholz (Amsterdam)

I

The current discussion about the scientific status of literary scholarship is characterized by a frequent appeal to certain criteria which, it is urged, literary studies have to satisfy if they want to deserve that honorific name of science. Systematicity, falsifiability/ verifiability, and intersubjectivity, to mention the trinity that is most frequently presented as guaranteeing salvation to the literary scholar, have by now acquired the status of shibboleths we have to be able to whisper in order to be admitted into the inner circle. Once there we may hope to come face to face with goddess Empireia, unadorned and free from all subjective fetters both she and us. No longer will it do there to say with that poor unscientific wretch of a poetess, Emily Dickinson, "if I feel physically as if the top of my head were taken off I know this is poetry." Yet we can rest assured of the way already now: "Die Prinzipien der modernen Wissenschaftstheorie gelten für die Literaturwissenschaft insgesamt, wie für jede ihrer Teil-theorien" (Ihwe, 1972, p. 11). "No adequate theory of poetics can be formulated without the basic criteria of general methodology, which will be supposed well-known here" (van Dijk, 1972, p. 174). Characteristically, a discussion – or rather an affirmation – of a decisionistically adopted methodology precedes a discussion of the problems to be thematized, of the aspects of literature to be brought in focus, apparently without there being a clear awareness of the possibility that the methodology one has adopted might preform and distort the problems one wants to attack. Only occasionally is the issue of a "bewußte phänomenologische Stufe in der linguistischen Theoriebildung" (Schmidt, 1973, p. 14) being raised, the demand for an adequate phenomenology of a realm of objects which would, among other things, have to "beschreiben, wie Sprache vorkommt, wozu sie dient, welche Wirkungen sie hervorruft" (Schmidt, 1973, p.

126

13). For literary scholarship, it is obvious, the same demand has to be put forward. Instead, literary scholarship is presented as producing "a set of texts: descriptions, explanations, hypotheses, theories, etc." for which "possible forms" are to be determined by methodology. "Without such a methodological basis", we are being served notice, "it is impossible to know how we must talk about the properties of the literary texts we want to study. And without using this common methodological 'language' or code, our scientific texts will certainly not be understood by other scholars in the discipline" (van Dijk, 1972, p. 168). The 'texts' actually produced in accordance with this view would seem to depend for some of their generic characteristics on the state which methodology happens to have reached at the point of production. As the code evolves, we have to follow its fits and frills, if we want to be understood by our peers, But the assumption appears to be that methodology does not evolve: at least that is the suspicion one gets when one realizes how the essentialism noisily banned from science is creeping back into science under the mask of an essentialist methodology. But if we take it for granted that methodology, like any other human endeavor, has a diachronic as well as a diatopic dimension — how else would it make sense to talk of a 'common methodological code'? — then "not to be understood by other scholars in the discipline" and 'to be understood by other scholars' becomes a grave issue which goes far beyond the confines of the naive hermeneutics of scientific texts we have just glanced at.

It is quite possible that I am placing too much weight on what may well be nothing more than a slip of the methodological tongue; then the code of the work I have been quoting would have to contain a criterion for deciding what is a slip and what is not. As it stands there is no such criterion and we have to give our author the benefit of the doubt. We have before us, we might say, something like a normative poetics of the genre of poetological texts: the code determines the matter and manner of what is to be said. The sanctions against violating the normative poetics of scientifc poetics are exactly what one would expect from such a poetics: we will not be 'understood' by the only people who count.

But in what sense of 'understand' will we not be understood, if the text in which we present our scholarship does not follow certain norms? Certainly it would have been preferable to talk about being 'accepted' — our texts, that is — by our peers, thus making room for the possibility of being understood and yet not being accepted, as is in fact the case whenever we reject somebody else's text on specific grounds, grounds, that is, having to do with the substance of the argument presented to us, and not just with formal niceties of the presentation.

A more adequate hermeneutics of scientific texts in fact cannot but make this distinction. The answer to the question "How can we understand a scientific theory, or improve our understanding of it? " (Popper, 1974, p. 179), Popper has suggested, lies in an attempt to reconstruct a "problem situation" (165) which in turn he defines as a "problem together with its background" (165). On this account "every attempt (except the most trivial) to understand a theory is bound to open up a historical investigation about this theory and its problem, which thus become part of the object of the investigation" (177). This historical investigation terminates in an "idealized reconstruction of the problem situation in which the agent found himself." It attempts to "make the action 'understandable' (or 'rationally understandable'), that is to say, *adequate to his situation as he saw it"* (179; Popper's italics). The weight of this statement can hardly be overestimated: how do we make a description of an action adequate to someone else's situation, not as we see it, but as he saw it? And for whom have we made it 'understandable' if we have done so? And what precisely is involved in the concept of 'situation': is the knowledge somebody has of his situation akin to what Schutz analyzed under the heading of "situational knowledge" (Schutz, 1975, pp. 64ff); and if so, how is this situational knowledge to be made intersubjective?

The component of science which, for lack of a less loaded term, I will call the hermeneutic component, is not an odd feature of the work of the historian of science; it is, still following Popper, an integral part of the progress of science as such: "All growth of knowledge consists in the improvement of existing knowledge which is changed in the hope of approaching nearer the truth" (71). I am not concerned here with Popper's notion of "nearer the truth" which, if it has any meaning in literary studies, would seem to be applicable to the materiality rather than to the phenomenality of the texts. What is important in Popper's position is the fact that we can conclude that since the acquisition of existing knowledge presupposes the reconstruction of a problem situation, i.e. of a problem and its background, growth of knowledge, based as it is on the possession of existing knowledge, also depends on situational analysis. It appears permissible to extrapolate from this a definition of a school subscribing to a specific scientific paradigm as a community of scholars sharing a common situational analysis. This explains why we cannot normally get from every member of a school an explicit situational analysis on which he is founding his conception of the future shape of his discipline: among the members of a school that analysis is itself part of the background which an outsider – both in a diachronic and diatopic sense – has to reconstruct if he wants to understand their theories.

What I earlier called a naive hermeneutics of the scientific text thus has its limited justification: it is a hermeneutics under the conditions of a shared situational analysis. It is naive in the specific sense of lacking a reflection on the situational framework motivating the choice of its particular code, and with it the manner and matter of the scientific text. And it is naive in that it assumes – tacitly, that is – the universal validity of its implicit situational analysis: because of this it appears justified to demand that one should use *the* code in order to be understood, and to confuse the understanding of a scientific text with the acceptance of what it states by one's scholarly peers. In Popper's analysis there is room for conjecturally reconstructing the problem situation in which the agent found himself, and thus understanding it and yet coming to the conclusion that the agent's situational analysis was faulty, on our terms, that is. This is obviously not the same as saying that it is faulty: it amounts to acknowledging that on his terms it was the only possible one.

All this would be very trivial indeed, and would hardly need repeating if we did not see around us signs of a naive dogmatism incapable of realizing that the principles of modern philosophy of science depend for their applicability in literary scholarship on a prior shared situational analysis, too.

We should avoid here a possible a possible confusion in the use of the term situational analysis. The shared – implicit or not – situational analysis characteristic of a school, and the situational analysis we produce to understand that school are not necessarily identical, but I would not, on the other hand, postulate an unbridgeable difference between the two. Popper speaks about "conjecturally" giving an "idealized reconstruction" of the agent's problem situation (179); and his "schema of conjectures and refutations" (168), too, isolates and yet relates the two levels of situational analysis. This schema which, in its simplest form is: $P_1 \rightarrow TT \rightarrow EE \rightarrow P_2$; ($P_1$: initial problem; TT: tentative theory; EE: error elimination; P_2 : problem situation as it emerges from our attempt at solving the problem) (164) involves implicit or explicit situational analyses at both P_1 and P_2. Our attempt at reconstructing P_1 does not amount to making P_1 our own, but to attempting to solve the problem of understanding P_1. Thus "our problem of understanding, P^u, is on a higher level than P_1. That is to say, the problem of understanding is a metaproblem: it is about TT and thus also about P_1. Accordingly, the theory designed to solve the problem of understanding is a *metatheory,* since it is a theory part of whose task it is to discover, in every particular place, what P_1, TT, EE, and P_2 actually consisted of" (176/177).

It would be tempting to see in Popper's schema a partial explication of what Gadamer means by "Horizontverschmelzung" (Gadamer, 1965, p. 289f.). Working this out would require a fullfledged comparative and constrastive analysis of Gadamer's and Popper's hermeneutics, and might bring to light another unsuspected point of convergence in the most recent developments of philosophy of science and hermeneutics.* For us the important point of Popper's analysis of "understanding a theory" lies in his conclusion: "every attempt . . . to understand a theory is bound to open up a historical investigation about this theory and its problem, which thus become part of the *object* of the investigation" (177). Popper does not explicitly state that P_1 already involves a hermeneutic corresponding to that of P^u: but it is clear from his observations on the growth of knowledge that this must indeed be the case.

What then do our stern methodological taskmasters have in mind when they talk about the criterion of intersubjectivity which our scientific texts have to satisfy? Following Popper we must say that we are obviously dealing with two strictly separate meanings of inter-subjectivity which our example of a naive hermeneutics carelessly telescoped into each other. Intersubjectivity$_1$ is the criterion familiar from empiricist philosophy of science: this principle of inter-subjectivity, it hardly needs repeating in an age when the 'basic criteria of general methodology will be supposed well-known', is a sharpening of the principle of verifiability resp. falsifiability: not only must there be a method for verifying resp. falsifying a statement: that method must also be intersubjective, i.e. in principle accessible to any other researcher. This principle of intersubjectivity$_1$, first introduced by the neo-positivists, had, as is well known, the prime goal of branding introspective psychology as meaningless; the underlying assumption was that statements about one's own psychic states could never be verified by another person. Intersubjectivity$_2$ on the other hand refers to P^u, i.e. *our* problem of understanding P_1 and its solution; but it also refers to P_1 as understood by the person whose theory we want to understand, i.e. to his understanding of the problem situation in which he finds himself. Intersubjectivity$_2$ we can tentatively say, provides the framework for intersubjectivity$_1$: since we cannot know from observation what observation is, we have to reach a prior consensus before we know what is to count as an observation and what not.

That this is a difficult point to hold on to becomes clear when we read in an article which Popper wrote in 1971, seven years after the first formulation of his hermeneutics of scientific texts, about "the following somewhat weak form of the principle of empiricism: Only 'experience' can help us to make up our minds about the truth and falsity of factual statements" (12). From Popper's hermeneutics it would seem to follow that the very use of the notion of experience only makes sense in the context of a situational analysis yielding an answer to the question what is to count as experience as far as the level of P^u is concerned, and, for someone trying to reconstruct P_1, as to what counted as experience in the situation under investigation. Popper's own apt definition of data as "adaptive reactions, and therefore interpretations which incorporate theories and prejudices, and which, like theories, are impregnated with conjectural expectations" (145) presupposes the intersubjectivity of a Roycean "community of interpretation" (Royce, 1913, p. 269) as a guarantee for the relative stability of these reactions which is a conditio sine qua non if those data are to function as data.

II

That the problem of intersubjectivity will look different depending on whether we set out from a position which can be characterized as 'methodological solipsism', as 'physicalism' or as 'transcendental idealism' only the most inveterate adherent of the untenable doctrine of the independence of methodology from the philosophy of knowledge will deny. The problem will look different in terms of its systematic importance and subsequently in terms of the urgency with which it requires attention. The eventual choice of a physicalistic instead of a phenomenalistic basis for a "Konstitutionssystem", of a "Basis", that is "die als Grundelemente physische Dinge enthalt und als Grundbegriffe beobachtbare Eigenschaften und Beziehungen solcher Dinge" (Carnap, 1961, p.xi) was for Carnap, among other things, motivated by the fact "daß in bezug auf Eigenschaften und Beziehungen der genannten Art eine größere intersubjektive Übereinstimmung besteht" (xi). The problem of intersubjectivity vanishes, so to speak, as a result of selecting a basis which is believed, rightly of wrongly, to be intersubjective. In the case of the "eigenpsychisch" basis of *Der Logische Aufbau der Welt* that intersubjectivity is not given; it has to be achieved in a process of "Intersubjektivierung" (199).

Behaviorism in psychology and linguistics, it hardly needs repeating, were seen as solving the moot problem of intersubjectivity by promising to operate with a language which could guarantee intersubjectivity due to the fact that the objects which it denotes are intersubjective. In the context of this notion of intersubjectivity belongs Carnap's switch from an "eigenpsychische Basis" to a physicalistic basis; likewise a statement as the following: "Ein Satz über subjektive Erlebnisse ... besitzt bloß eine monologische Bedeutung; er hat nur für das diesen Satz aussprechende Wesen und für kein anderes einen Sinn" (Stegmüller, 1960, p. 395). The "Dingsprache" on the other hand, we are being assured, satisfies the demand for intersubjectivity. That it does so "bedarf keiner näheren Erläuterung" (395). If it is one of the tasks of philosophy to problematize what apparently does not require our special attention then the very selfevidence of the fact that the "Dingsprache" is not in need of further questioning constitutes a problem, and a pressing one at that which requires attention. That it has not received that attention within the positivist tradition, and only now and then outside that tradition, is indeed a scandal of positivism, more serious even than the scandal of philosophy which Alfred Schutz sees in the fact that "so far a satisfactory solution to the problem of our knowledge of other minds and, in connection therewith, of the intersubjectivity of our experience of the natural as well as the socio-cultural world has not been found and that, until rather recent times, this problem has even escaped the attention of philosophers" (Schutz, 1973, p. 57). I call it more serious because in positivism the very condition of the possibility of science is staked on this unquestioned fact. That it can be answered only in the context of an answer to that other scandal is a suggestion which the positivist would reject outright; but the development of Popper's hermeneutics from his empiricist remarks on intersubjectivity in his early *Logic of Scientific Discovery* (1959, original German version 1934, §§ 8, 28) to the position he reached in his *Philosophy of the Objective Mind* (see above) speaks against that bias as does the development of Wittgenstein from his early *Tractatus* to his later philosophy of language games in his *Philosophical Investigations* (cf. Zimmermann, 1975.).

In view of this development of positivism, in which one could even see a sign of convergence with the so-called hermeneutic tradition, it may appear like flogging a dead horse if the following section will turn back to Carnap's *Aufbau* and his discussion of "Intersubjektivierung" in that work. But the "Dingsprache" is far from being dead in social science; it is, in fact, under various disguises, still considered to be one of the ways in which one hopes to secure the honorific title of science to literary studies. I will presently discuss this issue by glancing at N. Groeben's *Literaturpsychologie* (1972) where an attempt is made at laying the foundations of an empirical literary science by coordinating an "Objektivierung der Methodologie" with a "mittelbare 'Subjektivierung' des Gegenstandsbereichs" (Groeben, 1972, p. 170). My argument will be that the in itself laudable intention to supplement the dogma that "die material-objektiven Beschreibungsverfahren" are the "einzige Möglichkeit zur Empirisierung der Literaturwissenschaft" by an empirical literary science taking into account "die sinnhaften Merkmalsräume der literarischen Konkretisation" (183) suffers from the scandal of positivism that the intersubjective nature of even the so-called "subjektiv-individuelle Konkretisation" (168) of a literary work has never received any attention. The suggestion that an empirical literary science could be founded on an "intersubjektive Feststellung und Erfassung" of those subjective and individual concretisations of the reader, I suggest, cannot adequately be carried out within Groeben's philosophical framework. Furthermore, the assumption that in carrying out that program one has fulfilled the fundamental postulate of hermeneutic philosophy of science, "daß die Gegenstands-konstituierung nur durch Verstehen möglich sei" (168) rests on the faulty belief that "Verstehen" is equivalent to that misconceived "Subjektiv-individuelle Konkretisation". In the final section I will suggest that this conception of "Verstehen" is a positivist caricature of the complex act of acquiring and being in possession of life-

133

-worldly knowledge which has to be discarded if literary scholarschip is to reach the status of a social science.

III

Characteristic of the current discussion about the possibility of a truly scientific literary scholarship are programmatic pronouncements like the following one: "Literaturwissenschaft muß sich solche Erkenntnisvorhaben am Forschungsobjekt wählen, die intersubjektive zugänglich und nachweisbar sind" (Schmidt, 1970, p. 50). Making this postulate operational involves for Schmidt a neat separation of two levels of analysis, namely that of a semantic and a semiotic analysis of the meaning of a text. The semantic analysis, carried out by a *homo linguisticus* (O brave new world that has such people in 't!), is not a situation-specific analysis; rather, it is an analysis of "Zeichenwelten, die vom Rezipienten noch nicht durch Deckung an individuellen Korrelatwelten in spezifizierte Bedeutung überführt worden sind" (p. 62). Schmidt's notion of a semiotic analysis on the other hand involves the analysis of the "subjektiv erfüllte Meinung über nichtsprachliche Korrelate in den interpretativen Zuordnungssystemen des Rezipienten". The activity of the reader is – I assume that is what it is supposed to be – rationally reconstructed as follows: on the semiotic level the reader tries "den literarischen Text als Theorie aufzufassen, dem er einen Ausschnitt seiner Erfahrungswirklichkeit als Modell zuordnet" (p. 62). The situation-specificity of semiotic meaning which distinguishes it from semantic meanings involves the doctrine that "semiotische Bedeutungserfüllungen sind nur individuell verifizierbar: Sie sind als solche individuell, spezifisch und historisch punktuell, m.a.w. historische Elemente einer jeweiligen Lebens- und Erfahrungswelt".

Using Alvin W. Gouldner's suggestive concept of domain assumptions (Gouldner, 1971) by which he means background assumptions applied to members of a single domain of research, and constituting, in effect, the metaphysics of a domain, we can describe Schmidt's, and, as evidenced by the abovementioned notion of a subjective-individual concretization of a literary work, also Groeben's positions in terms of a domain assumption about literature involving the notion of a monadic individual encountering a literary work. Whatever that individual states about the literary work he perceives as a reader (not as a "homo linguisticus") is a statement about strictly subjective experiences with only monological meaning. A further aspect of that domain assumption is that of the privacy of the "Lebens- und Erfahrungswelt". Schmidt's characterization of the elements of that world as "individuell, spezifisch und historisch-punktuell" ties in with a global domain assumption which entails a solipsism which is not just methodological as with the early Carnap and with Husserl before he discovered the concept of the lifeworld, but metaphysical. The task of science subsequently becomes, in its heuristic phase, one of finding intersubjectively accessible topics of research, proceeding from the tacit assumption that the only alternative to intersubjectively observable objects of research are introspectively intuitable objects which, as such, do not qualify as research objects. Since those introspectively intuitable objects, about which only monological statements by the person who intuits them are possible, are nevertheless there and cannot summarily be ignored, techniques have to be developed to bring them, too, within reach of science, and to make them, too, amenable to intersubjectively verifiable statements. Hence the exercises in contortionism in literary studies which go under titles such as "Empirisierung" and "intersubjektive Feststellung" (Groeben, 1972). What is never being questioned is the solipsistic domain assumption leading to those impasses.

Now it seems rather ironical that Schmidt, the most prolific producer of pilot programs for a scientistic literary scholarship on the contemporary scene, would take recourse to the concept of a "jeweilige Lebens- und Erfahrungswelt" in order to spell out what I would call the solipsistic fallacy of scientistic literary scholarship: that concept, if it is to have any defined meaning instead of being a fashionable jargon term, belongs in the context of Husserl's lifeworld analyses (cf. Husserl, 1962) where its express purpose is to lead a way out of the dark corner in which "die Gespenster des Solipsismus, oder auch des Psychologismus, des Relativismus spuken" (Husserl, 1929, p. 210), and from which only "philosophische Kinder" (ibid.) run away. "Empirisierung" and "intersubjektive Festellung" are, from the point of view of Husserl's analyses of the structure of the life-world, ways of running away from that corner. The final section of this paper will present a brief discussion of an approach to social science which takes Husserl's analyses as its point of departure: Alfred Schutz' philosophy of social science.

At the moment a few more remarks on intersubjectivity − or rather the avoidance of the problem of intersubjectivity − in the positivist tradition are in place. The genesis of the present dogma of empiricity in Carnap's abandoning of the "eigenpsychische Basis" of his *Aufbau* for a physicalistic basis in his later works is still rather obscure. All we have is Carnap's own somewhat cryptic remark in the preface to the second edition which I already quoted, and which asserts that a basis in "physische Dinge" offers "eine größere inter-subjektive Übereinstimmung" (Carnap, 1961, p.xi.). This reason for abandoning that base has to be contrasted with the principal reason given in the text for selecting the "eigenpsychische Basis" in the first place, in spite of the fact that the conventionalist bent in Carnap's thinking would have allowed for other constitutional systems besides this one: "Die Systemform, die hier dem Entwurf des Konstitutions-systems gegeben werden soll, ist dadurch charakterisiert, daß sie nicht nur, wie jede Systemform, die Ordnung der Gegenstände in bezug auf ihre Zurückführbarkeit zur Darstellung bringen will, son-dern auch die Ordnung in bezug auf die erkenntnismäßige Primarität. Ein Gegenstand . . . heißt 'erkenntmismäßig primär' in bezug auf einen anderen, den 'erkenntnismäßig sekundären', wenn der andere durch die Vermittlung des ersteren erkannt wird und daher zu seiner Erkennung die Erkennung des ersten voraussetzt" (p. 74). The dilem-ma of scientistic literary scholarship with regard to the appearance of the literary work, in Ingarden's terminology: with the concretized aesthetic object (Ingarden, 1968, § 24), can, I believe, be highlighted by the set of alternatives which emerge from a confrontation of these two positions of Carnap: the perceived aesthetic object is primary but not intersubjective, the literary work qua linguistic 'thing' is intersubjective but not primary. Two ways out of this dilemma appear possible, the one chosen by scientistic literary scholarship, which consists in an attempt at intersubjectivizing the primary, non-intersubjective perceived work, the other chosen by adherents of the phenomenological tradition, which consists in an attempt to show that the supposedly non-intersubjective primary aesthetic object is an integral part of an intersubjective social reality, and as such is not in need of an artificial intersubjectivation of the kind proposed by the positivists. Both ways are ways out of the dark corner of solipsism: at least the realization that one has to look for a way is common to both schools.

Carnap believed that the physicalistic constitutional system would be "besonders geeignet für eine rationale Nachkonstruktion der Begriffssysteme der Realwissenschaften" (Carnap, 1961, p. xi). It can be doubted whether this conception of 'Realwissenschaften' is capable of comprising such fields as art history, literary scholarship, sociology, or even economics. It is certain, however, that the switch to a physicalist base left all those 'Realwissenschaften' in the lurch which have to reckon with appearances if they want to fulfil their task, in other words which have, like literary scholarship, to consider the phenomenality of the text besides its materiality. It is therefore not surprising that those aspects of literary study where the materiality of the texts stands in the foreground, were capable of being developed on the basis of a methodology derived from those sciences which exclusively thematize the materiality of the world, in particular physics. The stormy development of a linguistic literary science testifies to this. That there are now calls to be heard from within the positivist camp that "Materialität und Sinnhaftigkeit des literarischen Werks sind zwei aufeinander angewiesene Dimensionen des literarischen Gegenstandes, die in Endeffekt immer in Verschränkung miteinander interpretiert werden sollten" (Groeben, 1972, p. 183) can be taken as a welcome sign that the dimension of appearance which ever since Carnap's switch has been neglected by the positivists is beginning to receive the attention due to it in the social sciences. Those first beginnings, however, are anything but promising: there is no sign that the domain assumption concerning the monadic nature of the phenomenality of the literary work is being questioned. However, it seems to me that this is a *conditio sine qua non* if the literary work is to come in sight as it functions in the social world.

IV.

Having rejected the phenomenalism/physicalism alternative which characterized Carnap's decision to abandon the course he had taken in his *Aufbau,* and which still can be seen to be operative in an argumentation like Groeben's despite the fact that recent developments in philosophy of science have left this position far behind, I want to outline in the final section of this essay the solution which the problem of intersubjectivity in literary studies can be given in the context of a conception of social science as it has been developed in the tradition of Husserl by Alfred Schutz. I hasten to add that in selecting this framework I am not subscribing to a sectarian notion of social science; rather I am placing literary studies in a tradition that can claim Max Weber as one of its founders, and which is currently represented under the name of the humanistic approach to sociology by such outstanding representatives of the discipline as Peter L. Berger and Thomas Luckmann, not to mention Schutz who can be seen as the fountainhead of this school (cf. Berger, 1963; Berger & Luckmann, 1971; Schutz & Luckmann, 1975; Schutz, 1973). The stultifying and anachronistic influence which neopositivism has enjoyed in Europe during the last few years at a time when elsewhere it is falling into deserved oblivion will have to run its course. In the meantime the minority point of view has to be developed.

My starting point is the assumption that the position with respect to intersubjectivity which the later Popper had reached, and which I outlined in the first section of this essay, is one behind which one can fall back only at the risk of becoming an anachronism. At the same time I would suggest that this position is in need of a grounding in what Husserl calls a science of the life world. In other words: Popper's data as "adaptive reactions" are, I believe, not adequately circumscribed as "interpretations which incorporate theories and prejudices, and which, like theories, are impregnated with conjectural expectations" (Popper, p. 145) as long as the fiction is maintained that this impregnating of the 'data' which theories and prejudices occurs for the first time on the level of science.

This fiction is hardly problematic for the natural sciences; as far as the social sciences are concerned, however, it can only be upheld at the expense of the adequacy of one's theories with regard to the realm of objects they are supposed to account for. The community of interpretation referred to earlier is not, as far as the social sciences are concerned, autonomous from the life world; it is, if not embedded in, at least dependent on the commonsense constructs of the life world in the sense that it produces secondary scientific constructs over the primary constructs of the life world. Schutz, in opposition to the logical positivism of Hempel and Nagel, has insisted on the "essential difference in the structure of the thought objects or mental constructs formed by the social sciences and those formed by the natural sciences" (Schutz, 1973, p. 58). The natural scientist *alone* defines, in accordance with the procedural rules of his science, his observational field. His data as adaptive reactions are functions of those procedural rules alone. His observational field is pre-selected and pre-interpreted only by the scientific tradition or paradigm within which he works, and, if we want to give up the romantic fiction that science evolves autonomously rather than at the bidding of the powers that be, his observational field is pre-selected and pre-interpreted, in an age of big science, by grant giving agencies with their own political and economic reasons for letting or not letting evolve. But, and that is the crucial point, unlike the observational field of the social scientist, his facts and data are not pre-interpreted and pre-selected in the sense that the world of nature which the natural scientist explores would " 'mean' anything to molecules, atoms, and electrons" (p. 59). The observational field of the social scientist on the other hand is pre-interpreted and pre-selected in the sense that social reality "has a specific meaning and relevance structure for the human beings living, acting, and thinking within it. By a series of commonsense constructs they have pre-selected and pre-interpreted this world which they experience as the reality of their daily lives" (p. 59). In close agreement with Husserl's conception of "Motivationsgesetzlichkeit" (Husserl, 1950. cf. Scholz, 1975) as the nexus of the social world, Schutz identifies these commonsense constructs as the motivating determinants of human behavior. "The thought objects constructed by the social scientist, in order to grasp this social reality, have to be founded upon the thought objects constructed by the commonsense thinking of men, living their daily life within their social world" (Schutz, 1973, p. 59). This leads Schutz to two postulates for social science which are only too often being ignored by social scientists, and, one might add, by literary scholars frantically trying to prove their scientific respectability by aping as much as possible the methodology of the natural sciences. The first postulate is derived from Max Weber's notoriously misunderstood notion of subjective interpretation: "if the social sciences aim indeed at explaining social reality, then the scientific constructs on the second level, too, must include a reference to the subjective meaning an action has for the actor" (p. 62). And the second postulate — Schutz speaks about the postulate of adequacy which has to accompany the postulate of logical consistency warranting the objective validity of the thought objects constructed by the social scientist — "each term in . . . a model of human action must be constructed in such a way that a human act performed within the real world by an individual actor as indicated by the typical construct would be understandable to the actor himself as well as to his fellow-men in terms of common-sense interpretation of everyday life" (p. 64).

These ideas which have recently gained currency in Habermas' formulations of the various research-guiding interests (cf. Habermas, 1968) but which antedate those formulations by close to two decades, point to the need of a twofold approach to social reality, one practical, one theoretical: apart from applying the postulate of subjective interpretation to the analysis of social reality by studying those primary common-sense constructs in terms of what they mean for their users, and of what their users mean by them, the social scientist has to take the practical step of applying the principle of adequacy to his own secondary constructs. In doing so the presentation of his constructs will allow for communication with the agents of the social world. In the more fashionable terminology of Habermas: his social science will be characterized by a hermeneutic research-guiding interest, and as such, by a potential to serve an emancipatory interest. Only if those primary constructs and their inherent order are made the focal point of social science will it appear possible to avoid the building up of a science characterized by what Habermas has called the technical interest which leads to manipulation of rather than communication with the objects of social science, i.e. man.

Schutz did not sharply distinguish the postulate of adequacy as a principle guiding presentation from the postulate of subjective interpretation as a principle guiding the focus of research. The former, it would seem, guarantees the intersubjectivity of the presentation in the sense of an interpersonal communication between the social scientist and the social agent, e.g. in the form of a literary science *for* the reader; the latter guarantees the focus on the subjectivity and intersubjectivity of the object of research, i.e. on the social world as experienced by the agents of that world, e.g. in the form of a literary science *about* the reader and his literature. That the former is founded upon the latter in the strong sense of being impossible without the latter needs no further demonstration. That the latter seemingly can be conceived of without consideration of the former has been demonstrated by certain abortive attempts at producing a theory about the literary competence of a homunculus called *homo poeticus.* The reason for their failure appears to be this: ignoring the essential difference between the social and the natural sciences outlined above, the text processing analysed by the text grammarians had but little to do with the process of reading of which the reader is aware as an act of constituting for himself the world of the literary work.

This act of constituting the literary work, we can derive from Schutz, an act leading to the production of those life-worldly primary constructs, should form the basis of a literary science seeing itself as a social science.

There apparently has to be a relation between the two postulates in such a way that, whereas the postulate of adequacy can only be carried out if the postulate of subjective interpretations has been followed, the enactment of the postulate of subjective interpretation requires, at least in the heuristic stage of research, an adherence to the postulate of adequacy. Schutz' hesitancy to sharply distinguish the two therefore would seem to be justified: the postulate of adequacy is not only a principle governing the presentation of the secondary constructs to the social agent; it is also a principle securing the appresentation of the agent (cf. p. 125) as a subject experiencing this world by means of primary common-sense constructs. At this point the two postulates shade into each other: the postulate of subjective interpretation focusses precisely on the appresentation of the agent. That they cannot be sharply separated, and that the postulate of adequacy plays a role both in the presentation and the appresentation of the social agent points to an issue of great importance to literary scholarship: the role of dialogue in the social sciences. Consideration of this problem is beyond the scope of this paper.

A few points remain to be made about the nature of those primary constructs, i.e., if we turn to literary studies, about the literary work as read, as perceived, as concretized. The relatively frequent studies of the reading process which take the postulate of subjective interpretation seriously – usually not under that label, though – all tacitly assume the intersubjective nature of those primary constructs; i.e. they assume, at least they do not explicitly deny, that these constructs can be communicated to others. (Examples are to be found in Leibfried, 1970; Iser, 1972; Poulet, 1969). This could be explained by the fact that all of these authors have a greater or lesser affinity with phenomenology. I would personally believe that it is due to the fact that they did not put on neo-positivist blinkers and were thus capable of living up to Weber's postulate of subjective interpretation, and of making sense of the fact that in a life-worldly sense of the term 'intersubjective' we are indeed capable of communicating our concretizations. The rejection of that postulate, it seems, is, when it occurs, motivated by a prior adoption of a philosophy of knowledge allowing only for the phenomenalism/ physicalism alternative. It leads to phenomena such as Groeben's "Empirisierung" of Ingarden's concept of concretization which, in Schutz' words, are due to an adherence to the "basic philosophy of sensationalistic empiricism or logical positivism which identifies experience with sensory observation and which assumes that the only alternative to controllable and, therefore, objective sensory observation is that of subjective and, therefore, uncontrollable and unverifiable introspection"(p. 52).

For Schutz the central issue with which the methodology of the social sciences has to come to grips is an answer to the question: "How is it possible to form objective concepts and an objectively verifiable theory of subjective meaning-structures" (p. 62) It is obvious that those subjective meaning-structures must not be those subjective experiences of our quote from Stegmüller which can only be denoted by statements having "monologische Bedeutung" if that question is to find a positive answer. In other words, Schutz cannot accept the alternatives of sensory observation and unverifiable introspection as covering the whole of experience. His solution lies in the discovery that "my knowledge is not my private affair but from the outset intersubjective or socialized" (p. 11), and is worked out by him by means of an analysis of various aspects of the socialization of life-worldly knowledge, i.e. those primary constructs of the social world. Thus, instead of making "my actual biographically determined situation" (p. 15) the *ineffabile* which haunts both methodological and metaphysical solipsism, he analyses the knowledge of the life world in terms of the "reciprocity of perspectives or the structural socialization of knowledge", in terms of the "social origin of knowledge or the genetic socialization of knowledge" and finally under the heading of the "social distribution of knowledge" (p.10ff.). What emerges from these analyses he sums up in his last work: "meine Lebenswelt [ist] von Anfang an nicht meine Privatwelt, sondern intersubjektiv; die Grundstruktur ihrer Wirklichkeit ist uns gemeinsam" (Schutz, 1975, p.24; cf. also Husserl's analyses of the structure of the life world in Husserl, 1962).

Schutz' analyses of the structure of the knowledge of the life-world have two goals: to dispel the empiricist bias concerning the subjective as being unaccountable and unstatable in intersubjective terms, and to point out that the same empiricism on the other hand takes for granted the social reality which, as experienced by the social agents, should be the express topic of the social sciences.

Empiricism, if applied to the social sciences, he claims, bypasses the subjective-intersubjective structure of social reality and produces scientific constructs which cannot but ignore the primary constructs of that lifeworld. The reason for this is the already mentioned alternative of sensory observation and introspection, leaving out of consideration "the experiential form, by which common-sense thinking in everyday life understands human actions and their outcome in terms of their underlying motives and goals" (Schutz, 1973, p. 65). Schutz employs the traditional term "Verstehen" for that experimental form of knowledge, perhaps a dangerous thing to do in view of the state of petrification which the 'Verstehen-Erklären' dichotomy has by now reached in the minds of opponents and supporters alike. But his use of that term involves anything but a position-taking in that sterile battle: 'Verstehen' for him is "primarily not a method used by the social scientist" (p. 56); i.e. his second degree constructs are not meant to be understood in a way that would differ from the way in which the constructs of the natural scientist are understood, nor are they produced by means of a fundamentally different methodology. Rather, it is an experiential form "in which common-sense thinking takes cognizance of the social cultural world", a result of "processes of learning or acculturation in the same way as the common-sense experience of the so-called natural world" (p. 56). 'Verstehen' is not, as the positivists want to have it, just a useful heuristic crutch on the way to scientific explanation (cf. Abel, 1953), to be discarded once the level of explanation has been reached. Rather, it is the prime *object* of social science if by a social science we mean a science trying to find out "what the actor 'means' in his action, in contrast to the meaning which this action has for the actor's partner or a neutral observer" (p. 57). The life-world is in this sense an understood world which the social scientist attempts to analyse qua understood world. An analogous relation can be specified for a literary science: its task is the analysis of the understood text, an analysis of what the reader means in his reading, in contrast to the meaning which this reading has for a supposedly neutral observer.

It cannot be the task of this paper to work out in detail how such an analysis would proceed. Needless to say that there is still room for the analysis of the materiality of the text, for a physicalistic approach to the text, so to speak, although the life-worldly function of such a literary science has never been made explicit by its proponents.

Only a few hints about areas of literary scholarship can be given here, where the Schutzian approach to social science promises solutions to seemingly unsolvable problems: the distinction drawn between the common-sense knowledge of the lifeworld as a structure on the one hand, and the secondary construct-knowledge of the social sciences which is also structured but along different lines, would seem to allow for a reassessment of the problem of the intersubjectivity of interpretation. This intersubjectivity − or rather the failure of interpretation to live up to the standard of scientific intersubjectivity − is frequently made the touchstone for the decision to deny to interpretation the honorific label of a scientific activity. On the other hand attempts are being made to define 'scientific interpretation' (cf. Oversteegen, 1971) in such a way that the interpretation as a construct fulfills the criteria of methodology. It appears that we have to distinguish a lifeworldly interpretation characterized by a lifeworldly intersubjectivity, which is never a universal one, but one relative to what Husserl calls a "Personenverband" (Husserl, 1962, p. 296 ff.; see also Scholz, 1975) from a scientific one which does indeed strive to fulfill those criteria. If the latter is characterized by the 'if-then' structure of scientific constructs (on the structure of 'scientific' interpretation see Bosse, 1973) the former is characterized by its functional evidence for its users. Whereas lifeworldly interpretation is the systematization of a perceived work of art, grounded in sedimented experience, scientific interpretation is the systematic description of a literary work grounded in a freely chosen theoretical framework.

This admittedly sketchy characterization of the difference between a life-worldly and a scientific interpretation will suffice to suggest that it is unwarranted to apply the standards of scientific interpretation to the constructs of the life-world, and that a literary science will have to carefully study the intrinsic features of those constructs if it wants to catch a glimpse of the manner in which literature functions in the life-world.

Another flogging-boy of scientific literary studies, the socalled essentialism resp. substantialism of traditional literary scholarship likewise needs to be reconsidered. It will then become apparent that the constructs of the life-world *function* as essentialistic constructs, and that *a functionalist science of literature will only have reached its target when it has managed to explain the functional essentialism and substantialism of the life-world.*

Let me conclude with a variation on a comparison sometimes made between "traditional literary scholarship" and astrology, and "modern literary science" and astronomy. For all its methodological shortcomings, I would argue, traditional literary scholarship was close to social reality; what it lacked was the insight that many of its constructs were indeed primary constructs of the lifeworld which should form the basis for the secondary constructs of literary science. What is more, people for better or worse have traditionally ordered their lives in accordance with astrology rather than astronomy. From the point of view of rationality this may be regrettable. On the other hand it was the astrologers who discovered the star of Bethlehem. It would seem to be high time that the astronomers went there, too — by their own method of transportation, of course.

Works Cited:

Abel, Th. "The Operation Called Verstehen", in: H. Feigl and M. Brodbeck, *Readings in the Philosophy of Science.* New York, 1953, pp. 677-688.
Berger, P. L.: *Invitation to Sociology; A Humanistic Perspective.* New York, 1963.
Berger, P. L. and Th. Luckmann: *The Social Construction of Reality.* Harmondsworth, 1971.
Bosse, H.: "Symbolische Makronen; Zum Status der literaturwissenschaftlichen Interpretation (an einem Beispiel aus Ibsens 'Nora')." in: *Lili,* vol. 13 (1973) pp. 7-35.
Carnap, R.: *Der logische Aufbau der Welt,* 2nd. edition. Hamburg, 1961.
van Dijk, T. A.: *Some Aspects of Text Grammars.* The Hague/Paris, 1972.
Gadamer, H.-G.: *Wahrheit und Methode,* 2nd. edition, Tübingen, 1965.
Gouldner, A. W.: *The Coming Crisis of Western Sociology.* London, 1971.
Groeben, N.: *Literaturpsychologie; Literaturwissenschaft zwischen Hermeneutik und Empirie.* Stuttgart, 1972.
Habermas, I.: *Technik und Wissenschaft als 'Ideologie'.* Frankfurt, 1958.
Husserl, E.: "Formale und transzendentale Logik", in: *Jahrbuch für Philosophie und phänomenologische Forschung,* Vol. 10, Halle, 1929, pp. 1-298.
Husserl, E.: *Ideen zu einer reinen Phänomenologie und phänomenologischen Philosophie I.* The Hague, 1950. (Husserliana, vol. 3).
Husserl, E.: *Die Krisis der europäischen Wissenschaften und die transzendentale Phänomenologie.* The Hague, 1962. (Husserliana, vol. 6).
Ihwe, J.: "Ein Modell der Literaturwissenschaft als Wissenschaft", in: S. J. Schmidt, *Zur Grundlegung der Literaturwissenschaft.* München, 1972.

Ingarden, R.: *Vom Erkennen des literarischen Kunstwerks.* Tübingen, 1968.

Iser, W.: "The Reading Process: A Phenomenological Approach", in: *New Literary History,* vol. 3 (1972), pp. 279-299.

Leibfried, E.: *Kritische Wissenschaft vom Text; Manipulation, Reflexion, transparente Poetologie.* Stuttgart, 1970.

Oversteegen, J. J.: "Hermeneutik", in: *Lampas,* vol. 4 (1971), pp. 132-146.

Popper, K. R.: *The Logic of Scientific Discovery.* New York, 1968. (Harper Torchbooks)

Popper, K. R.: *Objective Knowledge; An Evolutionary Approach.* Oxford, 1974.

Poulet, G.: "Phenomenology of Reading", in: *New Literary History,* vol. 1 (1969) pp. 53-68.

Royce, J.: *The Problem of Christianity. Vol. 2: The Real World and the Christian Ideas.* New York, 1913.

Schmidt, S.J.: "Text und Bedeutung — Sprachphilosophische Prolegomena zu einer textsemantischen Literaturwissenschaft", in: Schmidt, ed., *Text, Bedeutung, Aesthetik.* München, 1970.

Schmidt, S. J.: *Texttheorie.* München, 1973.

Scholz, B. F.: "Literatur als Bewußtseinsphänomen: zum Ansatzpunkt phänomenologischer Literaturwissenschaft", in: *Lili, Zeitschrift für Literaturwissenschaft und Linguistik,* vol. 17 (1975) pp. 35-53.

Schutz, A.: *Collected Papers I: The Problem of Social Reality.* The Hague, 1973.

Schutz, A. and Th. Luckmann: *Strukturen der Lebenswelt.* Neuwied/Darmstadt, 1975.

Stegmüller, W.: *Hauptströmungen der Gegenwartsphilosophie,* 2nd. edition. Stuttgart, 1960.

Zimmerli, W.Ch.: " Paradigmawechsel und Streitbehebung. Einheitswissenschaft einmal anders" in: R. Simon—Schäfer/W.Ch. Zimmerli, ed.: *Wissenschaftstheorie der Geisterwissenschaften.* Hamburg, 1975, pp. 340-358.

Zimmermann, J.: *Wittgensteins sprachphilosophische Hermeneutik.* Frankfurt/M., 1975.

EINBILDUNGSKRAFT UND ERKENNTNIS
zu Albert Verweys Auffassung vom Dichtertum

Jan Aler (Amsterdam)

The grandest efforts of poetry are where the imagination is called forth
to produce, not a distinct form, but a strong working of the mind, still
offering what is still repelled and again creating what is again rejected;
the result being what the poet wishes to impress, viz. the substitution
of a sublime feeling of the inimaginable for mere images.

Coleridge

In den neunziger Jahren des vorigen Jahrhunderts vollzog sich eine
wesentliche Wendung im Schaffen des niederländischen Dichters
Albert Verwey. Sein Dichtertum erstieg eine neue Ebene. Den Sinn
dieses Wandels vermittelt uns nicht zuletzt die eifrige, unablässige
Reflexion seines Urhebers selber.

Von jeher freilich kennzeichnete Besonnenheit Verweys Naturell.
In jenen Jahren aber fördert und offenbart sie besonders deutlich
eine grundsätzliche Neuorientierung. In einer denkerischen Anstrengung, zu der Dichter sich nur selten aufraffen, überwindet Verwey da
die Krise seines Schaffens, die sich im Laufe der späten achtziger
Jahre bemerkbar gemacht hatte.

Bei dieser Anstrengung wollen wir einen Augenblick verweilen.
Ihr geistiger Ertrag prägte eine entscheidende Episode in Verweys
Entwicklung: sie machte wahrhaft Epoche. Allein schon aus diesem
Grunde ist sie – beim hohen Rang von Verweys Dichtertum – von
grossem Gewicht.

Darüber hinaus jedoch besitzt das Ergebnis seiner Betrachtung
allgemeine Bedeutsamkeit. Zunächst einmal gilt das von den philosophischen Voraussetzungen, die ins Spielen kamen: metaphysische
und erkenntnistheoretische Gedanken wurden ja in Verweys Doktrin
von der Einbildungskraft kunsttheoretisch wirksam. Durchaus eigen-
ständig knüpfte er da an eine grosse Überlieferung an. In ihrem Raum

wusste Verwey sein Dichtertum zu entfalten, indem er sie seinem schöpferischen Anliegen anverwandelte.

In der Prägung nun, die der Autor diesen Philosophemen verlieh, gewannen sie höchste Aktualität. Sowieso für ihn selber, das dürfte niemanden wundernehmen. Sodann aber auch auf zukünftigere Weise. In Verweys Gedankengängen nämlich bekommt die Einbildungskraft bereits jenes anthropologische Gewicht, das uns inzwischen vertraut geworden ist.

Hier sei nur daran erinnert, wie Martin Heidegger die Einbildung im Zusammenhang mit Kants Grundlegung der Metaphysik als bildende Mitte der ontologischen Erkenntnis freigelegt hat, als den ursprünglichen Quellengrund der beiden Grundquellen, Sinnlichkeit und Verstand. Herbert Marcuses leidenschaftlicher Aufruf zur Erneuerung von Gesellschaft und Kultur ist diesem Vorstoss zutiefst verpflichtet — auch dort, wo sein Appell, den Wahrheitsgehalt der Einbildung anzuerkennen und unser Realitätsprinzip zu revidieren, sich der Denkmittel von Tiefenpsychologie und Marxismus bedient. Hier begegnet sein beschwingtes Ringen um eine Gegenkultur sich nicht nur mit der ästhetischen Erziehung des Menschen, wie Friedrich Schiller sie befürwortete, sondern auch mit Einsichten und Bestrebungen der surrealistischen Bewegung.

Verwey aber hat sich gerade in jenen Jahren, denen wir uns zuwenden wollen, wiederholt mit dem Kantianismus auseinandergesetzt. Die Verwandtschaft seiner Selbsterfahrung mit Auffassungen der Tiefenpsychologie sodann spricht oft aus seinen Reflexionen. Und während er sich immer hartnäckig dagegen wehrte, sein Dichtertum parteipolitisch zu verankern, war seine Auffassung vom Verhältnis zwischen Individuum und Gesellschaft dennoch ausgesprochen sozialistisch. Die brennenden Fragen, die heute in der Diskussion zwischen Marcuse und Norman Brown zur Entscheidung stehen, hätten auch Albert Verwey gefesselt.

Ein Drittes noch ist hier beachtenswert. Verweys Nachdenklichkeit steigerte sich zur Besinnung auf die eigene Reflexion. Dann verweilte sie beim Verhältnis zwischen Denken und Dichten im Dichtertum selbst. Was da erwogen wurde, blieb keine "graue Theorie". Auch bedeutete es keineswegs, dass ein intellektualistischer Hemmschuh dem Fortgang von Verweys Schaffen angelegt wurde. In seiner erstaunlichen Produktivität hat sich vielmehr ein halbes Jahrhundert lang die Symbiose von Intellekt und Einbildungskraft schöpferisch ausgewiesen.

149

Von solchen Dingen darf in der Festschrift für Jan Kamerbeek wohl auch einmal die Rede sein. Generell gehören sie ja in sein Forschungsgebiet. Im vorliegenden Fall indessen ist die Beziehung noch wesentlich enger. Nicht nur bezieht Kamerbeek sich in seinen Schriften verschiedentlich auf Verweys Werk, von Zeit zu Zeit diskutierten wir auch gerne die Betrachtungen des Dichters. Der freundschaftlichen Anteilnahme des heutigen Jubilars an meinem stillen Gespräch mit nachdenklichen Künstlern verdanke ich manche nachhaltige Anregung. Auch die hier folgenden Überlegungen hätten ohne solchen Wink und Zuspruch anders ausgesehen. Deshalb seien sie ihm als Xenion herzlich zugeeignet.

I

Im Verlauf der achtziger Jahre bereitete die Entwicklung des literarischen Lebens Verwey wachsendes Unbehagen. Weder der äussere, sensorielle noch der innere, introspektive Objektivismus entsprachen seinen Bedürfnissen. Diese Unterscheidung allein schon bedeutete ihm Zwiespältigkeit, als ob ein Riss durch die Wirklichkeit ginge, der den Menschen, und a fortiori den Dichter, vereinsamt.

Wie verlief nun der Versuch, dieses Problem zu lösen? Mit den Mitteln philosophischer Reflexion gewann Verwey einen Standort, an dem er aufatmete. Diese Besinnung vollzog sich als fortgesetztes Studium, umfassend und gründlich. Das Krisenbewusstsein veranlasste es nicht, wenn es auch den Einsatz steigerte. Denn der Dichter hielt solche systematische Betrachtung von letzten Dingen für ein Merkmal des Zeitalters und bejahte sie. Er sollte es später einmal dahin formulieren, dass Besonnenheit das eigentlich Moderne sei (*Prosa* VIII,8).

Diesem Grundsatz gemäss handelte er bereits von frühauf. In dem Abschnitt seines Lebens, der uns hier beschäftigt, war es seit dem Ende der achtziger Jahre Spinozalektüre, die in zunehmendem Masse seine Betrachtungsweise bestimmte. Aus diesem Studium ging dann Sommer 1893 der Zyklus *Kosmos* hervor, der später in den Versband *Erde* (1896) aufgenommen wurde. Hier schlägt das zweite Sonett, mit dem Einsatz "Das Leben ist aus der Idee", das Leitmotiv der Wendung in Verweys Schaffen an. Stolz schrieb der Dichter (an Henriette van der Schalk, Anfang August 1893): "Hier ein Sonett, das Spinoza gutgeheissen hätte".

Im ersten Sonett der Reihe (I, 179) hat der Dichter es abgelehnt, weiter noch von Gott zu reden. Auf diesen "toten Namen", der "niemals mehr für unsere Nöte Gnadezeichen" sein könne, verzichte er. Das bildet die Folie zu der Aufforderung, ihm ins "Reich der Bilder" zu folgen. Es ist still, klar, friedlich. Vernunft hat es gestaltet, Geist umschliesst es.

Man beachte den Einsatz: Das Leben ist *aus* der Idee. Die hier gemeinten Bilder sind nicht aus dem Leben, es sind keine *Ab*bilder. Vielmehr hat das Leben – selbst ein Abbild – in ihnen sein *Ur*bild. Der Neuidealismus spricht von jetzt an aus Verweys Werk, und es ist ein objektiver Idealismus, dem das Reich der Ideen die eigentliche Substanz bedeutet. Dem Dichter ist es zugänglich. Er führt dahin.

Leben *aus* der Idee indessen setzt Leben *und* Idee voraus. Soll der Leser solcher Lyrik sich da irgendwelche hinterweltliche Gedanken machen? Die Einleitung für die neue Zweimonatschrift sprach sich über ontologische Verhältnisse deutlicher aus. Verwey entwickelte hier September 1894 Gedanken zur Erneuerung von Kunst, Kultur und Gesellschaft, deren Genealogie er folgendermassen umriss:

> Wir lieben nicht die Griechen, und nicht die Juden... sondern dieses Leben auf dieser Erde... wir glauben, dass wir das Leben darstellen werden, irgends muss es ja sein: unser eigenes Bild vom Leben... De Deo überschrieb Spinoza das erste Buch seiner Ethik – vom Leben. Und seitdem ging Europa ans Werk...

In späteren Aufzeichnungen (die Uyldert S. 55f. veröffentlichte) hat Verwey die Umwälzung, die er damals kommen sah, ausführlich in historischer Perspektive beleuchtet. Hieraus geht deutlich hervor, in welcher philosophischen Optik ihm die Entwicklung des Geisteslebens erschien:

> Dieses Zeitalter war weder renaissancistisch noch christlich. Es war religiös, berief sich aber als solches – wie bereits Lessing und Goethe es getan – auf die Gottesvorstellung von Spinoza. Das Göttliche wurde nicht als stofflich aufgefasst, auch nicht als ausserweltlich. Es war dem Leben immanent. Es war das Leben selbst, das Wesen des Lebens, dasjenige was Spinoza Deus sive Substantia nannte. Überall, so meinte ich, strebte man danach, das göttliche Leben zu kennen, es zu schauen, es darzustellen.

Der Gedichtzyklus *Die Natürliche Erde* (vom November des gleichen Jahres) umkreist gerade in diesem spinozistischen Sinne ständig die Lebensidee. Für seine Vorlesungen, ein drittel Jahrhundert später, erläuterte der Dichter den Sachverhalt mit folgender Aufzeichnung (a.a.O. S. 18):

Gott und die Natur waren für mich beide lebendig. Allein Gott ist das für sich betrachtete, absolute Leben, die Natur dagegen das mannigfaltig bezogene, das relative Leben.

Ich schrak deshalb davor zurück, das Wort Gott zu verwenden. Es lässt sich nicht von christlichen Vorstellungen lösen, und die meinte ich nicht. Ich zog es vor, nur das Wort Leben zu benutzen, und zwar so, dass aus dem Gebrauch selber des Wortes jeweils hervorging, wann ich es absolut und wann relativ auffasste.

Mit diesem Wortgebrauch knüpfte der Autor an die Wendung an, die Johannes van Vloten (1818-1883) dreissig Jahre eher (um Verweys Geburtsjahr) der Spinoza-Interpretation in Holland gegeben hatte. In seinem Sinne war es, dass vermutlich Mitte der Neunziger Jahre Verwey (der 1890 eine der Töchter van Vlotens geheiratet hatte) sich notierte (a.a.O. S. 18):

Mit Spinoza war das Gottesgefühl der älteren Zeit in das Lebensgefühl der Neuzeit übergegangen ... Wer aus Ehrfurcht den Gottesnamen beibehielt, sprach eigentlich von dem, was er auch das Absolute, das Ewige, oder Natur und Leben hätte nennen können.

Van Vlotens Gedanken indessen bewegten sich auf der Linie des atheistischen Positivismus, wie die stürmische Entwicklung der Naturwissenschaften ihn damals gezeitigt hatte. Seinem Szientismus schien nicht nur die theistische Terminologie, sondern auch das ontologische Prinzip Spinozas, die natura naturans, antiquiert zu sein. Verwey dagegen unterschied, wie seine Lyrik es uns vorhin bewies und seine betrachtende Prosa es soeben bestätigt hat, laufend zwischen Wesen und Erscheinung, sowohl anthropologisch wie kosmologisch.

II

Als Verwey denn auch 1895 die Übertragung der *Ethik* durch Herman Gorter zum Anlass nahm, in seiner Zweimonatschrift etwas ausführlicher zu Spinoza Stellung zu nehmen (der Essayband *Stille Turniere* bietet S. 41ff. den Text), da machte er seine Leser mit einem Meister der ... Mystik bekannt. Sechs Jahre zuvor war er mit Gorter, diesem ausgezeichneten Kenner Spinozas, über den Philosophen ins Gespräch gekommen. Da hatte er bereits mit der Idee des Lebens an dessen Ontologie angeknüpft. Jetzt ging er in Wendungen, die bis in Einzelheiten Spinozas Wortgebrauch anklingen lassen, auf das Verhältnis der Substanz zur Erfahrungswelt ein, steckte dementsprechend die Grenzen der diskursiven Erkenntnis ab und erreichte darauf die metaphysische Selbstdeutung des Menschen.

Gleich anfangs erläutert der Autor wieso er *Leben* für *Deus sive Substantia* sage:

> ... weil es mir gerade das zu sein scheint, was ich – vertraut und heilig, wie es mir ist – von Kind an, in dichterischem Traum oder nüchterner Betrachtung, so genannt habe.

Im späten Jugendwerk lässt sich gelegentlich der Ansatz zu einer Verwendung, wie Verwey sie jetzt durchführt, tatsächlich beobachten. Wenn etwa das Leben, wie ein Meer, den Einzelnen als kleine Welle zeitweilig emportreibt (I,77, vom Jahre 1888) – oder wenn das Leben, als das Umgreifende, das den Menschen treibt und befällt, Thema der Lyrik wird (I,81ff.; 1888). Der Ansatz indessen ist als solcher nur im *Rück*blick erkennbar ... Für sich genommen entsprechen die Wendungen dem erweiternden Sprachgebrauch, der 'Leben' ohne weiteres sei es generell, sei es als Kollektivbezeichnung, handhabt. "Vertraut", gewiss, aber "heilig" wäre im Kontext des Jugendwerks eher die Kunst, die Schönheit, die Liebe und – nun ja, natürlich – Gott ...

Im Gedichtzyklus *Cor Cordium* vom Jahre 1886 besitzt die Bezeichnung "Leben" allerdings einen wesenhaften Sinn und erschliesst deutlich eine metaphysische Perspektive. Sie berücksichtigt eben den Lebens-Grund. In Gundolfs Übertragung hebt die Gedichtreihe folgendermassen an:

> Herz meines herzens! Leben das in mir wohnt
> Vielnamiges Geheimnis das ich nenne
> Mein Ich mein Selbst mein Wesen – das dich zeigst
> Allzeit ein anderes und den eignen spruch
> Sprichst ob dir selbst und meinen leib hier machst
> Zum werkzeug deines worts zum instrument
> Auf dem du spielst und tust der erde kund
> Deine gesänge dass sogleich erwacht
> Dies menschtum nah und fern: – dich ruf ich an
> Auf dass du sprichst und mir vom munde fliesst
> Lenz von gesang der über die erde geht
> Und ich nicht mein wort sondern dein wort schreibe.

Hier tut sich die transzendentale Tiefe der Introspektion auf. Darin erfährt der Dichter Heiligstes. Nicht umsonst beginnt das Schlussgedicht von *Cor Cordium*:

> Es lebt kein andrer Gott: Du bist allein.

Verweys Wandel in den neunziger Jahren aber verschafft der Idee des heiligen Lebens erst jene universalistische Spannweite, die den Holismus kennzeichnet. Dann tritt dem Menschen das Selbst aus seinem Gegenüber, aus der Natur nämlich, entgegen. Man vergegenwärtigt sich den hier gemeinten semantischen Wandel des Wortes "Leben" blitzartig, wenn man seine Verwendung in zwei Titeln vergleicht: bei dem Zyklus *Vom Leben* (1888) und bei dem *An das Leben* (1894).

Zurück aber zum Spinoza-Aufsatz! Nachdem der Autor eingangs die notwendige terminologische Erläuterung gegeben hat, vollzieht er sofort den zweiten Schritt, mit dem er die positivistische Spinozadeutung weit hinter sich lässt:

> Dieses Leben, das keinen Anfang und kein Ende kennt, ohne welches nichts ist und ausserhalb dessen nichts sein oder begriffen werden mag, ... dieses Leben ist für Spinoza nur erst die Kern-Idee, das Kern-Wesen, um das herum sich sowohl das kosmische, wie das geistige und sittliche Dasein ordnet.

Dieses philosophische Aperçu erschliesst genau den Zusammenhang, den Verweys Lyrik bereits vor zwei Jahren vorausgesetzt hatte. Denn im Zyklus *Kosmos* hatte ein Sonett die Hoffnung auf eine Bewusstseinserweiterung ausgesprochen (I, 180), in der sich weder Ich noch Welt, sondern "was möglicherweise Ich-und-Welt sei" offenbare. Wie stellte der Dichter solches Hoffen nun dar? Er griff zum Vergleich nach der Mariä Verkündigung: er spreche wie eine, die der Engel besucht habe und die nun guter Hoffnung sei, den *Heiland* zu gebären. Der Aufsatz erhellt nicht nur das Sonett, sondern umgekehrt das Gedicht auch seinerseits die Reflexion. Es beweist nämlich, dass Verweys metaphysische Besinnung − mit Max Scheler gesprochen − ganz und gar nach *Erlösungswissen* strebt.

Erkenntnistheoretisch lässt der Aufsatz sodann nicht den geringsten Zweifel darüber bestehen, wie sich empirisches Wissen zu diesem Urgrund des Seins verhält (S. 42f):

> Weil dieses Leben in allem ist und wir es bald als Seele und bald als Raum erkennen, ist es lehrreich und unserem geringen Verstand auch angenehm, bald dieser Seele, bald jenem Raum im lebendigen All zu folgen... Spinoza lässt von allem, was ist, den Gedanken jeglichen Dinges neben dem Körper jeglichen Dinges bestehen, zwei ewige Scheingestalten unserer Erkenntnis, die notwendig aus dem Wesen folgen. Das Wesen des Daseienden aber sind sie nicht.
>
> Und von dem Gott, der ein denkendes Ding ist, und von dem Gott, der ein ausgedehntes Ding ist, kommen alle Gedanken und alle Körper, und der Gedanke seines eigenen Körpers, das ist der ewiglich in Gott selber wohnende Geist, des Menschen.

Gott als Quell aller Körper und Gott als Quell aller Gedanken, insofern auch des Gedankens unseres eigenen Körpers, der unser Geist
ist: die syntaktische Ambivalenz des Genitivs gestattet es, in einfacher Reihung den Panentheismus zum Ausdruck zu bringen.

Dieser lässt sich weder empirisch, noch diskursiv begründen, er
verlangt eine dritte Gattung der Erkenntnis (S. 47):

> ... die mehr ist als die wechselnde Meinung, mehr auch als das Begreifen
> des Allgemeinen im Besonderen; die ist als die Ausstrahlung des Brennpunkts,
> wo der Geist des Menschen selber ein Feuerkern des Lebens − das brennende
> Leben berührt. Der Mensch, der diese Erkenntnis empfindet, sieht sich selbst
> − nicht seine leibliche Erscheinung des Augenblicks, sondern das Wesen
> dieses Leibes − als ewig und notwendig; und ewig und notwendig weiss er,
> dass er im Leben ist und das Leben in ihm ... und glaubt, dass er mit allen
> Geistern, die einander umgeben und bestimmen, gemeinsam den ewigen und
> unendlichen Geist Gottes bildet.

Auf drei Einzelheiten sei eigens hingewiesen. Eine dritte Gattung der
Erkenntnis: hier bezieht der Autor sich auf den 40. Satz des zweiten
Buches von Spinozas *Ethica*. Dort steht ja nach der "Meinung" und
dem "Begreifen" das "tertium genus cognoscendi" zur Erörterung, −
Erkenntnis, die "empfunden" wird: der Anschluss an Spinoza findet
nicht in einfacher Übersetzung statt. Die *Ethica* spricht bekanntlich
von einer "scientia intuitiva", in der wir "uno intuitu videmus".
Verwey deutet den Sinn dieser dritten Stufe der Erkenntnis. Wenn
sie intuitiv ist, so ist sie unmittelbar einsichtig, nicht-diskursiv. Anschaulichkeit besitzt diese Qualität. Ihr fehlt dann auch nie die Aura
der Gestimmtheit. Der Dichter Verwey hebt durchaus im Sinne
seines Schaffens diesen Aspekt der Unmittelbarkeit hervor. Die
"scientia intuitiva" ist ihm Gefühlserkenntnis. − Sie ist mehr als
Meinen und Begreifen: Spinoza hebt tatsächlich hervor, dass sie
klarer sei. Im weiteren Verlauf wird er sie noch als solche hinsichtlich
ihrer Verwurzelung in unserer Erkenntnis Gottes kennzeichnen: tertium illud cognitionis genus cuius fundamentum est ipsa Dei cognitio
(5. Buch, 20.Satz). Verwey nun setzte für "Gott" den Seinsbegriff des
"Lebens" ein. Unter diesem Blickwinkel entspricht seine dichterische
Praxis durchaus der dritten Gattung Spinozas.

Deutlicher als mit dieser "empfundenen" Erkenntnis kann man
die transrationale Schau des Seins nicht über die wissenschaftliche
Begriffsbildung erheben. Dementsprechend also hiess es in dem
Zyklus *Die natürliche Erde* (I, 236):

Und Schau der Erkenntnis End.

Schau, cognitio intuitiva, das ist die Ebene, auf der sich Wesen erschliesst. Dort vollzieht sich das Rätselhafte, dass der Mensch "sich
selber sieht": die Selbsterfahrung, die den Leser der Gedichtbände
Erde und *Der Neue Garten* als Erscheinung des Wesens in Verlegen-
heit zu bringen pflegt (I, 224):

Du schlossest den äusseren Sinn mir,
Der innere ging mir da auf,

Der sah wie ein Auge durchs Fenster
Mich selbst in schöner Natur.

Bei solcher Transparenz des Daseins erfasste der Dichter die Immanenz des menschlichen Geistes im Göttlichen als Teilhabe am All-
-Leben (I, 226f):

Die Seele von allen Dingen
Ist frei; und lebt allein
Gemeinsam mit Seelen, die singen
Um sie im Kreise herum.

Ihre Stimmen, von der All-Seele
Sind der hörbare Chor.

Alles in allem darf es mithin nicht wunder nehmen, wenn Verwey
gegen Ende seiner Ausführungen zustimmend eine Autorität (Busken
Huet) zitiert. Der Verfasser der klassischen Kulturgeschichte der
Niederlande (*Das Land von Rembrandt*, 1882/84) hatte darauf hingewiesen, wie Spinozas Philosophie manchmal zum Kirchengesang
werde und man nicht aus seiner *Ethik* eine Seite zu lesen glaube,
sondern aus des Thomas von Kempen *Imitatio Christi*. Diese Optik
eben passte dem Dichter vorzüglich.

III

Verweys philosophische Reflexion stand also im Zeichen Spinozas.
Sie bestimmte tiefgehend die Artikulation des Lebensgefühls seiner
Dichtung. Wie verhielt sich nun aber solche intellektuelle Anstrengung zum dichterischen Schaffen? Wie ging der Ertrag dieser
Studien in die Lyrik ein? Solche Fragen müssen noch beantwortet
werden, sonst könnte das Wissen um Verweys Beschäftigung mit
systematischer Philosophie leicht irreführen.

Wie sah Verwey das Verhältnis zwischen Philosophie und Dichtung? Im Jahre 1902 zollte er dem Urteil eines älteren niederländischen Philosophen und Dichters seinen Beifall: "Alle Ergebnisse

der Philosophie sind ihrem Wesen nach poetisch". Uyldert fügt mit
vollem Recht hinzu, das sei einmal ein Satz, der aus Verweys eigenen
Maximen hätte stammen können; denn dieser habe in der Metaphysik
den dichterischen Kern der Philosophie entdeckt (a.a.O.S. 184). Als
Verwey einige Jahre später (1905) seine *Einleitung in die neue
niederländische Dichtung* veröffentlichte, hiess es dementsprechend
dort:

... jeder Philosoph begehrt den Ruhm, dass sein Gedanke das Weltgedicht
ohnegleichen sein wird.

Auch seinen Spinoza betrachtete der Dichter in dieser Optik. Einige
unmissverständliche Zeugnisse vom Jahre 1895 (Von Uyldert
a.a.O.S.278f. veröffentlicht) bestätigen das indirekt. Im Februar lern-
te Verwey nämlich den Philosophen Bolland persönlich kennen. Über
seine Gedanken freilich war der Dichter bereits einigermassen im
Bilde. Denn Bolland hatte sich 1890 an der Zeitschrift *Der neue
Führer* (dessen Schriftleitung Verwey damals noch angehörte) mit
dem Aufsatz *Die Weltanschauung der Zukunft* beteiligt. Hier war
Verwey einer erkenntnistheoretischen und metaphysischen Auffassung begegnet, die seinem eigenen Standpunkt aufs beste ent-
sprach. Bolland hatte dort nämlich "die wissenschaftliche Erkenntnis
der Materie" bloss auf "den äusseren Schein der Weltseele" bezogen.
Er hatte auch menschliche Erkenntnisvorgänge als innere Momente
einer Selbstbesinnung gedeutet, die sich im Busen des All-Geistes
abspiele. Das war dem Dichter also bekannt, und es musste ihm
sympathisch sein, denn beides sollte im kommenden Spinoza-Aufsatz
eine wesentliche Rolle spielen.

Im Februar 1895 machten der Dichter und der Philosoph also
unter so günstigen Vorzeichen Bekanntschaft. Bolland sollte sich bald
als Urheber der Hegel-Renaissance in den Niederlanden auszeichnen.
Verwey hatte sogleich ein tiefschürfendes Gespräch mit ihm, über
letzte Fragen der Erkenntnis. Damit fing ein jahrelange Freundschaft
an. Der Dichter war so tief beeindruckt, dass er einen längeren Bericht verfasste. Von Hegel allerdings ist darin nicht die Rede. Bol-
lands Auffassung schwankte damals noch, und Verwey befasste sich
erst später mit dem deutschen Denker. Da gewann er übrigens nie ein
recht positives Verhältnis zu diesem. Er sah in Hegel letzten Endes
den Erben von Spinoza und Kant, der die Gottesidee des einen mit
der Vernunftidee des anderen verbunden hatte und damit "den Geist
des Menschen zum Wesen alles Erschaffenen vergöttlicht" habe (*Pro-*

sa VIII,179ff., vom Jahre 1905). Von Schelling, dem anderen grossen Denker aus diesem transzendental-spinozistischen Geschlechte, war zwischen Bolland und Verwey (soweit die Dokumente reichen) nie die Rede — merkwürdig genug.

Die Überlegungen indessen, die Bolland gegen Ende des Jahrzehnts dazu veranlassen, *Alte Vernunft* gegen *Neuen Verstand* auszuspielen, beherrschten bereits das Gespräch (so wie der Dichter, von *seiner* Warte aus, es sich aufzeichnete).

Verweys Bericht nun spricht davon, wie Bolland unter einer Einsicht leide, die ihn, Verwey, geradezu beglückte. Was bedrückte den Philosophen damals noch so sehr? Die Machtlosigkeit des Verstandes (a.a.O.S. 278):

> Er sieht ein, da ihm die notwendige Widersprüchlichkeit aller intellektuellen Wahrheit klar geworden, dass er zu seinem Gefühl zurückkehren muss, und als geistiger Mensch zu den Bildern, an denen sein Gefühl hängt, und nun stellt er fest, es sind die alten Termini, höchstens mit einem anderen Gedankengehalt. Er entdeckt, dass man noch kein Mensch-des-neuen-Gefühls ist, wenn man die Unhaltbarkeit der Erscheinungsformen des älteren beweist.

Weshalb sollte die verzweifelte Lage des Philosophen den Dichter nun gerade freuen? Weil dieser ihm indirekt die eigene Auffassung bestätigte. Verwey war längst davon überzeugt, dass der nüchterne Begriff niemals das Leben (in jenem umfassenden und tiefen Sinne, der ihm vertraut war) fassen könne, dass nur Gefühl dazu imstande sei und mithin als unser wichtigstes Organ der Erkenntnis zu gelten habe. Sein Bericht über Bolland drückt es deutlich aus: Gefühl bezieht sich auf Bilder, es hat dann aber auch selbst Bilder zu schaffen. Das führt zur Frage, wie sich Sein und Gefühl, Gefühl und Idee, Idee und Bild zu einander verhalten.

Bereits 1892 notierte Verwey sich, wie die Einbildungskraft aus dunkler Empfindung klare Bilder schaffe (Uyldert, S. 34). Das beleuchtet den Zusammenhang von Gefühl und Bild. Aus dem Frühling 1895 (als er Marx, Kant, Spinoza studierte) überliefert Uyldert (a.a.O.S.72) andrerseits die hier folgende Aufzeichnung. In metaphysischer Perspektive spricht sie von Wirklichkeit und Einbildung:

> Wie herrlich wäre es, wenn ich als die Seele des Alls die Einbildung kennen lernen sollte, denn nur so verstehe ich es... Nur wenn ich das All wie eine grosse Metaphorik betrachte, kann ich glücklich werden.

Das schrieb der Dichter sich also in dem Frühling auf, da er sich an die Spinoza-Interpretation machte, kurz nachdem er sich mit Bolland besprochen hatte... Und an dieser Auffassung hielt er fest. So bemerkt er 1903 in einem Rückblick auf eigene Anfänge (a.a. O.S.197):

> Singendes Bilden hatte räsonnierende Auseinandersetzung abgelöst, und darauf wurden in den Neunziger Jahren die Bilder zu Sinn-Bildern.

Damit wird zwischen anthropologischem und metaphysischem Gesichtspunkt vermittelt: künstlerische Einbildung erschliesst Sinn.

IV

Solche Belege illustrieren, wie durch die Jahre hindurch Verweys Reflexion auf sein Dichtertum den gleichen roten Faden spinnt, der seine Auffassung vom dichterischen Schaffen markiert. Das Primat des Gefühls kennzeichnet sie, sowie die Objektivierung des Gefühlsgehalts im dichterischen Werk. Das Gedicht vermag die Erfahrung vom Leben ins Bild zu setzen. Hierzu bildet Lebensgefühl die notwendige Vorbedingung. Dieses Gefühl ist dabei in zweifacher Weise der Ratio überlegen: letztere leistet solche Erfahrung nicht, auch versagt sie vor deren Objektivierung. Dann kommt der Dichtung ein erkenntnistheoretischer Vorrang vor der Wissenschaft zu und besitzt Philosophie nur als Begriffsdichtung (das Wort sei hier einmal in einem höchst positiven Sinne verwendet!) wahrhaft Geltung.

Verwey huldigte mithin einem ausgesprochenen Antiintellektualismus. Er verkannte dabei indessen keineswegs die wichtige Rolle des analytischen Verstandes in der menschlichen Erkenntnis. Bei seiner transrationalen Besinnung auf die Fülle der Erfahrung bleibt das allerdings eine untergeordnete, wenn auch unersetzliche, Rolle. Der gewandte Dialektiker hatte schon im Bericht über Bolland verzeichnet (a.a.O.S.279), dass diesen gerade sein grosser Verstand dazu gebracht habe, anzuerkennen, wie das Gefühl die höchste Macht in der philosophischen Bewusstwerdung des Menschen ausübe. In dieser Studie braucht mithin die Rolle des Verstandes nicht weiter eigens erörtert zu werden.

An zwei Wendungen in den hier vorgelegten Aussagen Verweys soll vielmehr noch angeknüpft werden, damit wir an Hand der Einbildung einen genaueren Einblick in das Verhältnis zwischen Dichtung und Philosophie gewinnen. Zunächst sei daran erinnert, wie 1903 von einem "singenden Bilden" die Rede war. Diese Bezeichnung wirft Licht auf "de verbeelding", die Einbildung, wie Verwey sie verstand. Als Kategorie der Ästhetik besitzt sie grundlegende Bedeutung. Verwey bestand freilich mit vollem Recht auf ihrer anthropologischen Wichtigkeit überhaupt. Denn allem menschlichen Schaffen ist sie unersetzlich. In unserem Zusammenhang sei sie indessen nur als Prinzip der Dichtung berücksichtigt. Dabei muss dann aber auch dem Umstande Rechnung getragen werden, dass Verwey in diesem Bereich die Anwendung des Wortes "Einbildung" grundsätzlich erweiterte. Diese Dimension soll hier mithin erschlossen werden. Zunächst wenden wir uns ihr zu, unabhängig von Verweys Aussagen. Nach dieser allgemeineren Orientierung knüpft die Darstellung wieder an die Auffassung des Dichters an.

Überblickt man den Bereich des Wortes "Einbildung," so stellt man nicht nur dessen Vieldeutigkeit fest. Man sieht auch, wie die Variabilität seiner Verwendung nicht willkürlich ist. Als Verbalabstrakt bezeichnet das Wort ja zunächst den Akt des Einbildens, sodann einerseits das Ergebnis, das Eingebildete, andrerseits die Voraussetzung: das Vermögen einzubilden, die sogenannte Einbildungskraft. Offensichtlich ist die Aktivität die Quelle dieser Bedeutungsschattierungen. Ihre Dynamik klingt denn auch bei prägnanter Verwendung der Vokabel immer mit.

Das bildnerische Vermögen des Dichters bildet ein, nämlich in ein Medium, in die Sprache hinein. Sprache aber lässt sich sowohl in semantischer als auch in sinnlicher Perspektive bestimmen. Sprache als Bedeutung ermöglicht es dem Dichter, Bilder zu schaffen, den plastischen 'Inhalt' seines Werks. Hierauf beschränkt sich in der Regel die Verwendung von 'Einbildung', 'Einbildungskraft'. Aber einer ganz anderen Plastik muss noch gedacht werden. Man berücksichtigt dann die Sprache als Stoff, als sinnliches Zeichen eben, das Seelisch-Geistiges bezeichnet.

Im Fluss der Rede folgen einander die Sprachlaute. Dieses Phänomen bedingt zwei grundsätzlich neue Aspekte der jetzt gemeinten Plastik. Denn diese lässt sich einerseits unter dem temporalen Gesichtspunkt des Redeverlaufs bestimmen, andrerseits nach dessen klanglicher Beschaffenheit. 'Einbildung' im vollen Sinne des plastischen Ein-Bildens bezieht sich mithin nicht nur auf die inhaltlichen Bilder, sondern gleichursprünglich auf Rhythmus und Klangfarbe des Gedichts. Die Einbildung, als ein Ins-Bild-Setzen, betrifft nicht bloss den Inhalt des Gedichts, sondern das sinnlich-seelische Konkretum in seiner geistigen Bedeutsamkeit überhaupt: das dichterische Ge-Bilde als solches und im ganzen.

Nun mag das sprachliche Gebilde sich zwar unter diesen und anderen Aspekten zergliedern lassen, wenn es aber ein künstlerisches Gebilde ist, ein Kunstwerk eben, so bietet es sich im Kunsterlebnis als die Einheit des Mannigfaltigen dar. Souverän sammelt es zu dieser bedeutsamen Einheit Verschiedenes: die Ein-Bildung als Insbildsetzung ist auch Bildung des Einen, ist In-Eins-Setzung. —

Was bildet aber die dichterische Einbildung dem Medium der Sprache so einheitlich ein? Die Einheit der Lebenserfahrung, antwortet der Dichter. Diese bildet sie der Sprache in der vollen Konkretion des Erlebnisses ein. Im Erlebnis ist der ganze Mensch involviert. Nicht bloss die Sinnesorgane oder der Affekt oder der Verstand bestimmen diese komplexe Einheit. Die Fülle der Erfahrung von Wirklichkeit geht nicht einfach in Sinneseindrücke auf. Sie wird erst erfasst, wenn diese innerlich verarbeitet sind. Nicht der Sinneseindruck oder der Begriff, sondern das Erlebnis entspricht der Lebenswirklichkeit. *Sie* stellt das Kunstwerk dar. Die Einbildung vermittelt im Werk den Gehalt des konkreten Erlebnisses, weil sie mit ihrem Werk den Widerspruch zwischen Innen und Aussen aufhebt. In seiner Einheit stellt das künstlerische Gebilde die ursprüngliche Einheit des Lebens heraus, aus der es hervorgewachsen. Diese Einheit des Lebens liegt *vor* aller Differenzierung in mehrere Erkenntnisvermögen. Ihr entspricht die Synthese, die die Einbildung erzeugt. Was die Einbildung erbildet, ist das wahre Bild der Wirklichkeit. Es ist die Wirklichkeit selbst. Wesenhaft erkennen wir sie erst in ihm. Die Einbildung bringt das Wesen der Dinge ins Bild (vgl. *Prosa* VIII,10).

V

Wir begegneten vorhin dem Leitsatz "Das Leben ist aus der Idee". Er setzt ein Urbild des Seienden im Ganzen voraus. Sodann erklang die Frage: "Ist die Seele des Alls etwa Einbildung?" Sie setzt eine Einbildungskraft voraus, die im Ganzen des Seienden west. Die Verbindung solcher Hinweise bringt eine urbildliche schöpferische Dynamik in den Blick. Passt Verweys Auffassung von der Idee zu solcher Behauptung?

Der Dichter äusserte sich einmal dahin, die Idee sei "eine vorwärtsdrängende Kraft." Als solche sei sie "das Wesen jeglichen Lebens" und werde "nur in dessen Gestalt sichtbar" (*Prosa* III, 187). Spät allerdings (im Jahre 1912) äusserte er sich so prägnant auf ontologischer Ebene. Als er aber 1895 über *Die Idee in der Geschichte*

schrieb (jetzt auch *Stille Turniere,* S. 231ff), drückte er ent-
sprechende Gedanken auf empirischer Ebene aus. Hier fragte er nach
unserer Vorstellung vom Sinn der Geschichte, und er antwortete,
dieser enthülle sich blitzartig (S. 236, S.237) an einer historischen
Tatsache. Die Idee der Emanzipation (um die es dem Autor ging)
leuchte solcherweise aus der Französischen Revolution auf.

Was heisst das? Eine historische Tatsache trifft uns. Sie wird uns
bedeutsam. Sie bewegt uns. Die Gefühlsbewegtheit regt unsere Einbildungskraft an. Sie schafft die Auffassung, die unsere Gedanken
(S.239) über den historischen Sachverhalt, über den Sinn des Ge-
schichtsverlauf überhaupt bestimmt. Da entwickeln wir "ein *Gefühl*
(im Texte kursiviert) für die Tatsache, um die die Geschichte sich
ordnet" (S. 239). Diese Tatsache bildet "die Seele einer solchen Vorstellung vom Lauf der Welt" (S. 237).

Die treffende Charakteristik der Voraussetzungen eines Ge-
schichtsbildes weist also bereits 1895 an einem *Sektor* der Erfahrung
nach, was 1912 knappe Hinweise zum Verhältnis von Erscheinung
und Wesen *generell* zum Ausdruck bringen: die metaphysischen
Grundzüge der Lebenserfahrung überhaupt. Punkt für Punkt ist hierbei der Dichtung recht, was der Historie billig ist.

Überdies ergänzen beide Betrachtungsweisen sich aufs beste. Die
Idee, das Urbild, ist 1912 die innere, prägende Form, die sich jeweils
so zur Gestalt des Lebens verhält, wie die natura naturans zur natura
naturata. Dementsprechend tritt die Idee als forma formans auf. Sie
bildet sich in die Wirklichkeit ein. Sie bildet diese aus. Sie tritt in ihr
in Erscheinung. Sie stellt sich in ihr dar. Solchem Urbild entspricht
menschliche Einbildungskraft. Ihr entspringt (Im Aufsatz vom Jahre
1895) unsere Idee von der Wirklichkeit. Sie spiegelt mit ihrer Einbildung jene Urbildlichkeit.

Bildet diese nun für Verwey eine Ober-, eine Hinterwelt? Keineswegs: "Das Wesen der Dinge ist ihr Wesen, weil es den Dingen niemals entsteigen kann" (Prosa III, 192). Drastischer lässt sich das
Prinzip der Immanenz nicht formulieren. Die Unterscheidung bedeutet keine Trennung.

Dementsprechend untermauert Verwey das Verhältnis zwischen
urbildlicher Einbildung und künstlerischer Insbildsetzung unter metaphysischem Gesichtspunkt (Prosa VIII,34). Dort ist die Rede von der
"Wirklichkeit als einem Ganzen". Davon besitzen wir eine Vorstellung. Diese lässt sich nicht empirisch begründen. In dieser Überlegung
klingt Kants Auffassung von der Idee der Welt als einer Antizipation

der Erfahrung an: sie ist a priori, sie ist eine Vernunftidee. Von all diesen Dingen ist diesmal bei Verwey nicht die Rede. Aber er war gut bewandert in Kants Lehre, und ganz in deren Sinn fasst er diese Vorstellung vom Ganzen als eine Voraussetzung für die Möglichkeit auf, überhaupt von Zusammenhängen in der fragmentarischen Wirklichkeit der Erfahrung zu sprechen.

Diese Vorstellung, heisst es sodann, sei uns "eingeboren". Damit wird an die seit Descartes in der Metaphysik des 17. Jahrhunderts geläufigen Lehre von der "idea innata" angeknüpft. Dann betont der Autor noch einmal den Dualismus von a priori und a posteriori. Da erreicht er den Zusammenhang, der uns hier ständig beschäftigt:

> Aber alle eingeborene Erkenntnis, die äusserlich nicht nachweisbar ist, heisst Einbildung. Ohne Einbildung des Lebens gibt es keine Lebens-Äusserlichkeit.

Im Rahmen transzendentalphilosophischer Begriffsbildung vollzieht dichterische Besinnung auf unsere Erkenntnis hier einen entscheidenden Schritt! Mit schlafwandlerischer Sicherheit wird die theoretische Vernunft der Einbildungskraft zu- und eingeordnet.

Noch unter einem anderen Aspekt indessen ist Verweys Formulierung aufschlussreich. Stellt man nämlich auch noch fest, dass die niederländische Vokabel, die "eingeboren" wiedergibt, ausdrückt, dass das Eingeboren von einer schaffenden Macht ihrem Geschöpf mitgeben wurde (ingeschapen), so hat sich der Kreislauf vollendet. Das dichterische Bild ist ein Eingebildetes. Der Dichter schafft kein Abbild der äusseren Wirklichkeit. Durch diese hindurch vermag er dem urbildlichen Wesen zu entsprechen. Diesem selbst entspringt das Vermögen zu solcher Entsprechung im Dichter. Dann ist die Behauptung auch folgerichtig (*Prosa* III, 192):

> Der höchste Triumph der Einbildung ist erreicht, wenn sie die Aussenwelt als ihre Schöpfung auffasst.

Erst wenn die Umrisse einer Doktrin von der Einbildung aus dem umfangreichen Werk Verweys auftauchen, sieht man auch genauer den Zusammenhang, in dem Überwindung der Lebenskrise möglich wird. Das Selbst ist ergründet. Es hat seinen Grund gefunden. Leben und Werk gestalten sich aus dem schöpferischen Ursprung alles Lebens. Der Dualismus von Ich und Welt ist aufgehoben. Der Mensch kann sich mit der Wirklichkeit als Darstellung der Idee identifizieren. Verwey hebt solche Identifikation als Grundzug der Einbildung hervor (*Prosa* VIII,28). Er verfügt dazu in der niederländischen Sprache über eine einheimische Vokabel: vereenzelviging.

Diese artikuliert mit höchster Plastizität seine Sehnsucht: mit dem anderen *ein* Selbst zu haben, so dass man *es* selber *ist* — im anderen sich wiedererkennen, sich in ihm wiederfinden. Der mystische Grundzug in Verweys Lebensverständnis tritt hier klar zutage.

VI

Die metaphysische Tragweite der Einbildung, die dem Verstand versagt ist, ging schon hervor aus jener Überlegung vom Frühling 1895, sie könne das Wesen der Wirklichkeit sein. Das Prinzip, dass Gleiches nur Gleiches erkenne, fand da — sei es unwillkürlich, sei es bewusst — seine Anwendung. Wie der Dichter sich solche Tragweite in actu dachte, spricht in den gleichen Monaten eine andere Aufzeichnung aus, in der es von der Einbildung heisst (Uyldert, S.72), bei ihr habe der Dichter die Empfindung, er lange mit der einen Hand nach den Dingen, mit der anderen nach dem Unbekannten... In der *Ethica* (2.Buch, 40.Satz) illustrierte Spinoza die dritte Stufe der Erkenntnis, indem er dieses Verhältnis des Bekannten zum Unbekannten heranzog. Es ging ihm um ein Proportionalverhältnis: wenn drei Zahlen gegeben sind, *sieht* man "uno intuitu" die Proportion der beiden ersten und erschliesst an der dritten die vierte Zahl. Und der Künstler? Ihm geht an der Anschauung des Einzelnen der Bezug des Ganzen auf. Am Einzelnen wird "blitzartig" der Sinn des Ganzen sichtbar. Am Verhältnis der Seienden leuchtet das Sein auf. Die Einbildung des Künstlers setzt die ontologische Differenz ins Werk.

VII

In zweierlei Hinsicht kommt der Einbildungskraft ein erkenntnistheoretisches Primat zu: sie bildet der Sprache im Kunstwerk ihre Wahrheit ein — diese verdankt sie ihrer grossen Anschauung von der Wirklichkeit, deren geistigen Gehalt sie erfasst. In der Unmittelbarkeit dieses Erlebens besitzt der schöpferische Vorgang seinen Ansatz. Wie hiess es noch vorhin? "Aus dunkler Empfindung schafft die Einbildung klare Bilder". Das ist der andere Kernsatz, dem wir uns zuwenden müssen.

Dieser stammt, wie gesagt, aus dem Jahre 1892 und wird in der betreffenden Aufzeichnung (Uyldert, S. 34) von einigen aufschlussreichen Bemerkungen begleitet:

Die Einbildung beschäftigt sich also mit dem Dunkelen, dem Ungewussten,

und das versteht sie erst in einem Bild, das sie selber erzeugt, ein neuge-
schaffenes. . . Aus dem Dunkel, das ihn beengt, schafft der Dichter Licht. . .
Immer wieder wendet der Dichter sich dem Dunkel zu, schwer wie es ist vor
Unergründlichkeit.

Einige Jahre später heisst es (*Prosa* VIII,22):

> Was in hellseherischen Augenblicken aus dunklem Strudel emportauchte, das
> habe ich ergriffen.

Der Dichter bringt offensichtlich keine fertigen Gedanken in Verse.
Aus wortloser Versenkung wachsen ihm Sprachformen zu. Wiederholt hat Verwey darauf hingewiesen, dass das Gedicht eine Bewegung, einen Ton besitzt, die sich aus Tiefenschichten des Daseins
erheben — aus dem Lebensgrund eben, der ihm im letzten der Urgrund des Seins ist. Das Geschehen lässt sich mit dem Hervorwachsen
des Traumes aus der Tiefe des Lebens vergleichen, von dem 1902 in
einem dramatischen Gedicht die Rede ist (I,472). Umgekehrt wies
bereits die Aufzeichnung vom Jahre 1892 darauf hin, wie der Ver-
ständige von der Bedrängnis durch die Finsternis nichts wisse — deshalb aber auch nichts von der freudigen Überraschung jener Er-
leuchtung.

Wie ein Leitmotiv spricht auch dieser Grundgedanke aus Verweys
Betrachtungen. Im Jahre 1929 notierte er es sich noch einmal, wie
der Dichter denkend schaffe und wie sich dieser Gedanke als Gedicht
erweist (Hanot, S.159). Oder wie es heisst in einer 1951 posthum
veröffentlichten Selbstdarstellung (Hanot, a.a.O.):

> Der Dichter denkt in Gedichten. Und es sind nicht die Begriffe, es sind die
> Gestalten seiner Einbildung, an denen er sich vergegenwärtigt, was er glaubt.

Verwey hat der Sprache dieses Schaffen der dichterischen Einbildung
aufs eindringlichste eingebildet in Versen des *Neuen Gartens* (1898).
Das Schlussgedicht (I, 247f) des Zyklus, "Neue Neigung", gestaltet
die Phänomenologie der dichterischen Findung. Bald darauf erschloss
mit bewundernswürdiger Fühlsamkeit Friedrich Gundolf das zauber-
hafte Sonett deutschen Lesern:

> Wenn ein wort oft das andre im bewegen
> Sacht sucht bis mehrere zusammenkommen
> Und verse formen die ein unvernommen
> Geheimnis künden — gleichsam späten segen—:
> Dann sizt ders schrieb als wolle das heil nach langen
> Schweigen nicht sprechen (sprachlos nur in träumen)
> Er sucht im süssen fühlsam-zagen schäumen
> Das süsse schöne das schon form empfangen.

Bis voll sein mund von glühenden entzücken
Willenlos formt den klang noch nicht geklärt
Mit staunen seine augen zu berücken.
Im bild das aus ihm für ihn sich erklärt
Erkennt er neu womit sich alle schmücken
Das einer menschheit mitteilt seinen wert.

Hier erfährt der Leser im Duktus der Rede selber, wie Verse sich bilden und einen unerdachten Sinn offenbaren – wie der Dichter dann beglückt über solches Wissen staunt, das ihn befällt. Die eigentümliche Rätselhaftigkeit, die gelegentlich ein Lyrikon Verweys beibehält – wie jenes von der Selbstschau – ist offensichtlich kein Mangel, der aus unzulänglicher Vorbereitung erwuchs, ebensowenig die Folge handwerklicher Fahrlässigkeit (geschweige denn Ungeschick!). Sie haftet dem Gedicht aus solcher Herkunft wesensursprünglich an, sie ist ein Wahrzeichen seiner Authentizität.

Quellenwerke

Literaturnachweise

Albert Verwey, *Oorspronkelijk Dichtwerk,* 2 Bände, Amsterdam-Santpoort 1938.

Albert Verwey, *Proza,* 10 Bände, Amsterdam 1921-1923.

Albert Verwey, *Stille Toernooien,* Amsterdam 1901.

Uebertragungen aus den Werken von Albert Verwey, Stefan George, Friedrich Gundolf, Berlin 1904.

Kunstenaarslevens. De briefwisseling van Albert Verwey met Alphons Diepenbrock enz., hrsg. v. Dr. M. Nijland-Verwey, Amsterdam 1965.

Inedita in:

M. Uyldert, *Uit het leven van Albert Verwey,* Bd. 2: *Dichterlijke Strijdbaarheid,* Amsterdam 1955.

M. Hanot, *De beginselen van Albert Verweys literaire kritiek,* Gent 1957.

***

Zur Einleitung

Martin Heidegger, *Kant und das Problem der Metaphysik* (1929), vierte, erweiterte Auflage, Frankfurt a.M. 1973.

Herbert Marcuse, *Eros and Civilisation,* Boston 1965.

Herbert Marcuse, *Hegels Ontologie und die Grundlegung einer Theorie der Geschichtlichkeit,* Frankfurt a.M. 1932 – vgl. besonders S. 8 in unserem Zusammenhang.

Theodore Roszak, *The Making of a Counter Culture,* New York 1968.

Norman O. Brown, *Life Against Death,* New York 1959.

Ferdinand Alquié, *Philosophie du Surréalisme,* Paris 1955.

DIE PRÄROMANTIK-KONZEPTION UND DIE NIEDERLÄNDISCHE LITERATURGESCHICHTE*

W. van den Berg (Utrecht)

> It became apparent to his students that they would never learn much about
> The Roots of Romanticism but that they would see and hear odd things.
>
> Saul Bellow, *Herzog.*

Der Begriff *Präromantik* und die mit ihm zusammenhängenden Worte *präromantisch* und *Präromantiker* haben, im Gegensatz zu verwandten und ungefähr zur selben Zeit gebildeten Begriffen wie *Prärenaissance* und *Präklassizismus,* in der Literaturgeschichtsschreibung Epoche gemacht. Nicht nur in Frankreich, wo der Ausdruck geprägt wurde, sondern auch in England, Deutschland, Italien und einigen osteuropäischen Ländern, gehören diese Bezeichnungen zu den beliebten Etiketten für die Literatur der zweiten Hälfte des achtzehnten Jahrhunderts. Seit einigen Jahrzehnten hat auch die niederländische Literaturforschung diese Worte entdeckt und angewandt.

Es hat aber den Anschein, dass die Selbstverständlichkeit, mit der man jahrelang diese Termini geführt hat, zu Ende ist. Obleich auch vor dem zweiten Weltkrieg kritische Stimmen vernehmbar wurden, gerät die Präromantik-Konzeption in den letzten Jahren immer mehr in Diskredit. Die niederländischen Literaturhistoriker haben sich bis jetzt kaum an der Debatte beteiligt. Vielmehr hat sich ein Konsensus über die Brauchbarkeit des Wortes gebildet, der eine kritiklose Verwendung fördert und eine kritische Einstellung verhindert. Es fragt sich, ob man sich darüber freuen soll. Schliesslich handelt es sich hier um eine aus dem Ausland übernommene Terminologie, und die anderswo aufgekommenen Bedenken könnten auch für die hiesigen Verhältnisse ihre Gültigkeit haben. Wenn dieser Aufsatz dazu beitragen könnte, dass es hierzulande zu einer Diskussion über die Brauch-

* Aus dem Niederländischen übersetzt von Gerhard Kuipers.

barkeit der Präromantik-Konzeption käme, hätte er sein Ziel erreicht.
Der Literaturhistoriker, der mit dem Terminus Präromantik arbeitet, bekundet mit Hinblick auf die Periodenbegriffe keinen extremen
Nominalismus, sondern er betrachtet sie zumindest als Konzeptionen
"cum fundamento in re."[1] Gesetzt, dass er einen so redlichen Standpunkt wie Wellek vertritt, und eine Periode als "a time section dominated by some system of literary norms"[2] umschreibt, so behält doch
die Bemerkung Guilléns ihre Gültigkeit, dass "literary norms, standards, styles, will tend to form static clusters."[3] Periodenbegriffe
periodisieren nun einmal nicht an erster Stelle Veränderungen. Bei
der Zusammenstellung der vorherrschenden Züge einer Periode "we
subsume change and understress continuity."[4] Auch wenn Wellek die
Einheit einer Periode nicht für absolut hält und er "the survival of a
preceding scheme of norms and also anticipations of a following
scheme"[5] mit in die Betrachtung einbezieht, so sind die statischen
Periodenkonstruktionen in der literaturhistorischen Praxis doch un-
gemein häufig. Nicht zu Unrecht bezeichnet Guillén sie als "instances
of pseudo-diachrony (as they do not render processes of becoming)
and of pseudo-synchrony (insofar as they cover many years at once and
do not really intersect time)."[6] Die Periodenbezeichnungen *Klassizismus* und *Romantik* waren und sind umso eher der Gefahr ausgesetzt,
dass sie zu statischen Konstruktionen reduziert werden, weil die typo-
logische Antithese *klassisch/romantisch* von Anfang an in der literarhistorischen Abgrenzung eine Rolle gespielt hat. Der Literaturhistoriker, der den Übergang vom Klassizismus zur Romantik überzeugend nachweisen will, sieht sich gezwungen, in irgendeiner Weise
die Kluft zwischen den beiden monolithischen Komplexen zu über-

1. H. P. H. Teesing, "Periodisierung". In: *Reallexikon der deutschen Literaturgeschichte,* 1965[2], S. 77.
2. R. Wellek, "The Concept of Baroque in Literary Scholarship". In: *Concepts of Criticism,* New Haven usw. 1964[2], S. 93.
3. Claudio Guillén, "Second Thoughts on Currents and Periods". In: *The
Disciplines of Criticism: Essays in Literary Theory, Interpretation, and History.*
Ed. by Peter Demetz, Thomas Greene, and Lowry Nelson, Jr., New Haven usw.
1968, S. 481.
4. Guillén, S. 492.
5. R. Wellek, "Periods and Movements in Literary History". In: *English
Institute Annual* 1940, New York 1941, S. 91.
6. Guillén, S. 492/493.

brücken. Mit Hilfe einer Präromantik-Konzeption ist er imstande, "die scharf voneinander abgehobenen Bilder der geistesgeschichtlichen Epochen dadurch zu korrigieren, dass man zeigt, wie diese Epochen kontinuierlich miteinander verhaftet sind und wie diese Verhaftungen in einer Reihe von Übergangserscheinungen nachgewiesen werden können."[7] Bestenfalls bekommt die Präromantik so das Gepräge einer Übergangsperiode und der Präromantiker wird zur Übergangsgestalt. Nun ist die Hantierung von Worten wie Übergangszeit, Übergangsperiode und Übergangsgestalt eine heikle Angelegenheit, gegen die Kamerbeek vor einigen Jahren ernstliche Bedenken vorgebracht hat.[8] Soll der Begriff nicht ganz inhaltslos werden, so wird man nicht nur angeben müssen, zwischen welchen Begriffskomplexen der Übergang stattfindet, sondern man wird diese Komplexe auch deutlich definieren müssen. In der Praxis macht das gerade wieder den Weg frei zu weitgehenden Schematisierungen und einfachen Antithesen, die den statischen Charakter der Perioden, zwischen denen der Übergang konstatiert werden soll, noch betonen. Ein Terminus wie Präromantik ruft in dieser Weise die Geister, die er austreiben sollte, mit noch mehr Nachdruck auf. Françoise Gaillard drückt es so aus: "C'est le pont fragile jeté entre les deux grandes discontinuités de l'Histoire littéraire: l'âge classique qui voit régner la raison, et l'âge romantique où domine le coeur."[9] In den meisten Fällen funktioniert der Begriff Präromantik aber kaum als neutrale Bezeichnung einer Übergangsphase, in der das Alte neben dem Neuen in gleichem Masse konstatiert und gewertet wird. Er stellt vielmehr eine exklusive Beziehung zwischen den mit ihm angedeuteten Erscheinungen und der darauf folgenden Romantik her. M.a.W.: *präromantisch* trägt nicht so sehr die mögliche neutrale Bedeutung dessen, was *vorangeht* als vielmehr dessen, was *vorausweist*. Seit der ersten Prägung des Wortes haftet diese Bedeutung dem Begriff an, wie

7. H. Friedrich, "Der Epochebegriff im Lichte der französischen Préromantisme-Forschung". In: *Neue Jahrbücher für Wissenschaft und Jugendbildung* 10 (1934), S. 125.

8. J. Kamerbeek Jr., "Het begrip 'historische overgangsperiode' kritisch bekeken". In: *Forum der letteren* 9 (1968), S. 203/219.

9. Françoise Gaillard, "Le préromantisme constitue-t-il une période? Ou quelques réflexions sur la notion de préromantisme." In: *Le préromantisme. Hypothèque ou hypothèse?* Collection Actes et Colloques 18, ed. Paul Viallaneix, Paris 1975, S. 63.

die jetzt folgende Übersicht der Entwicklung des Terminus in der französischen und komparatistischen Literaturgeschichtsschreibung bezeugt.

Fayolle[10] signaliert den Terminus zum ersten Mal in einem Beitrag Mornets zur *Revue d'histoire littéraire de la France*: "Un 'Préromantique' 'Les soirées de Mélancolie' de Loiasel de Tréogate." Offenbar ist dem Autor sein Neologismus noch so wenig geläufig, dass er es für nötig hält, Anführungszeichen zu verwenden.[11] Obgleich der Begriff in dem Artikel nicht näher umschrieben wird, wird wohl klar, was Mornet damit meint: Loiasel sei eine "âme romantique" (S. 492), "C'est non de raison, mais de sensibilité véhémente qu'elle déborde" (S. 493). Als solcher bilde er eine "preuve nouvelle, que les transformations littéraires ne sont jamais soudaines, que les transitions sont insensibles, que d'innombrables ouvriers y travaillent" (S. 500). Und Mornet schliesst mit den Worten:

Pour les lettres comme pour les moeurs il semble bien qu'il y avait dans quelques âmes françaises, dès 1780, presque tout ce que les romantiques n'ont pas toujours revendiqué comme leur conquête, mais ce que la critique littéraire leur a trop longtemps accordé. (S. 500).

Loiasel de Tréogate ist hier nicht so sehr eine Übergangsgestalt, als vielmehr ein deutlicher Vorläufer der Romantik, der man ihn aufgrund seiner "sensibilité véhémente" eingliedern könne. Mornet mag der erste sein, der einen Vorläufer als *préromantique* bezeichnet, das Manöver, gewisse Gestalten oder Tendenzen aus dem achtzehnten Jahrhundert als Vorausdeutungen auf die Romantik zu betrachten, ist um 1900 keineswegs revolutionär. Der Unterschied ist nur, dass man ehedem, und gelegentlich auch wohl später,[12] eher von einer Romantik des achtzehnten Jahrhunderts als von einer Präromantik sprach. Ich nenne zwei Beispiele aus dem englischen Sprachgebiet: Phelps' *The Beginnings of the English Romantic Mouvement* und

10. Roger Fayolle, "Quand? Où? Et pourquoi la notion de préromantisme est-elle apparue? " In: *Le préromantisme...* S. 48.
11. *Revue d'histoire littéraire de la France* 1909, S. 491/500. Im Jahrgang 1912 fand ich ebenfalls zwischen Anführungszeichen das Wort "préromantisme", 1913 taucht "préromantique" auf, jetzt ohne Anführungszeichen.
12. Man denke z.B. an die Anthologie von Jacques Bousquet, *Le 18e siècle romantique,* Paris 1972.

Beers' *A History of English Romanticism in the Eighteenth Century*.[13] Der Begriff Romantik ist bei Phelps noch sehr wenig umrissen. Auf der einen Seite spricht er von einer ahistorischen Grösse ("the Spirit of Romanticism has never wholly been extinct in English literature"), auf der andern Seite gewahrt er zwischen 1725 und 1765 eine romantische Bewegung, in der "may be found the seeds which sprang to full maturity in Scott and Byron." In ihrer Konstruktion der Romantik des achtzehnten Jahrhunderts bedienen sowohl Phelps als Beers sich eines einfachen Schemas, das auch bei späteren Forschern beliebt ist: zuerst eine kurze, einseitige und negative Skizzierung des Klassizismus, dem sodann die positiv gewerteten losen "romantischen" Elemente gegenübergestellt werden. Auffällig einig sind sich die Autoren in der Etikettierung: man versieht die Wiederentdeckung von Spenser und Milton, den "gothic revival," die Balladendichtung, das neubelebte Interesse für die nordische Mythologie und die Naturpoesie mit diesem Prädikat. Drei Jahre nach seinem Loiasel-Aufsatz betrachtet auch Mornet das achtzehnte Jahrhundert aus romantischer Perspektive. In *Le romantisme en France au XVIIIe siècle*[14] haben sich die früher erwähnten "quelques âmes" zu einer eindrucksvollen Gruppe, deren Spuren sich bis weit vor 1780 verfolgen lassen, herausgebildet:

> Le romantisme de 1830 remonte ainsi jusqu'à des sources lointaines. Par mille issues le XVIIIe siècle a vu jaillir et parfois couler en flots profonds tout ce que les George Sand ou les défenseurs d'*Hernani* revendiqueront comme leur conquête. (S. 261/262)

Mornet kennzeichnet die Romantik des achtzehnten Jahrhunderts als eine Revolte gegen die Vernunft und einen Triumph des Gefühls, der besonders nach 1760 zu vollen Entfaltung gelangt:

> Avant la *Nouvelle Héloïse* les lassitudes et les impatiences se précisent: on se fatigue de l'esprit et de la raison; on rêve des troubles du coeur et des angoisses de la passion; on goûte l'amère volupté des larmes et de l'inquiétude meilleurs que la paix morose. [...] Après 1760, c'est le romantisme tout entier qui conquiert les coeurs. Les âmes sensibles se livrent avec frénésie aux frissons des belles horreurs. (S. 262)

13. W. L. Phelps, *The Beginnings of the English Romantic Mouvement*, Boston 1893; H. A. Beers, *A History of English Romanticism in the Eighteenth Century*, New York 1906.
14. Daniel Mornet, *Le romantisme en France au XVIIIe siècle*, Paris 1912.

Die Romantik des achtzehnten Jahrhunderts lässt sich nach Mornet besonders in den "habitudes sociales," in bestimmten "états d'âme," im "goût profond pour la nature" erkennen, im Interesse für die Romane von Prévost und Richardson, für die Gebirgsnatur, den englischen Garten, die Ruine und das Grabmal. Genaue Angaben über diese Relation zwischen der Romantik des achtzehnten Jahrhunderts als "expression des goûts" und der französischen Romantik von 1830 fehlen jedoch.

Angeregt durch die Anschauungen Mornets, dessen Schrift er 1913 eine lobende Besprechung gewidmet hatte,[15] veröffentlichte Monglond 1930 seine "histoire intérieure" der Präromantik.[16] Als "historien de la vie sentimentale" schätzt er die Präromantik als eine "révolution morale" ein, die das Gefühlsleben erneuere und in dieser Weise die literarische Erneuerung der Romantik vorbereite. Anzeichen eines "préromantisme embryonnaire" ermittelt er schon am Ende des siebzehnten Jahrhunderts, er entdeckt sie in Autobiographien, Reiseberichten, Trivialromanen und "confidences". Präromantisch seien das Naturgefühl, die Pilgerfahrten zum Grab Rousseaus, die Vorliebe für den Herbst, den Abend, die Nacht und das Grabmal. All diese "signes d'une révolution sentimentale" habe Rousseau in ein "tout organique" gestellt, so dass man ihn eher einen Romantiker pur sang als einen Präromantiker nennen dürfe. Wie weit Monglond in seiner Entdeckung von präromantischen Elementen ging, wird klar aus der folgenden Kritik von Kurt Wais:

> Wenn einer *ich* sagt und *confidence* schreibt oder einen Roman oder einmal gegen die Regeln verstösst, wird das schon als *préromantisme* angekreidet und alles Übrige vergessen.[17]

Wenn die eher psychologischen Studien von Mornet und Monglond sich noch darauf beschränken, dass sie den französischen Romantikern zu Ahnen verhelfen wollen, so wandte ein anderer Franzose, Paul van Tieghem, das in seiner Heimat so fruchtbar gewordene Wort zur Bezeichnung literarischer Erscheinungen in ganz Europa an. Durch seine Studien erlangte der Terminus internationale Bekanntheit und konnte sodann wiederum in der nationalen Literatur-

15. *Revue d'histoire littéraire de la France* 1913, S. 204/208.
16. André Monglond, *Le préromantisme français,* 2 tomes, Grenoble 1930.
17. K. Wais, *Das antiphilosophische Weltbild des französischen Sturm und Drang (1760-1789),* Berlin 1934, S. 19.

173

geschichtsschreibung funktionieren. Da auch die niederländische Benennung weitgehend von van Tieghem beeinflusst wurde, empfiehlt es sich, näher ins Auge zu fassen, welche Bedeutung er dem Terminus beimisst.

Van Tieghem, der mit dem Begriff ohne nähere Erklärung in einigen, 1924 von ihm selbst unter dem Titel *Le préromantisme: Études d'histoire littéraire* gesammelten Studien über das achtzehnte Jahrhundert arbeitete, spricht in seinem ein Jahr später erschienenen *Précis d'histoire littéraire de l'Europe depuis la Renaissance*[18] nicht so sehr von Präromantik als von Präromantikern. In seiner Geschichte wird ihnen ein Platz zwischen *La prose classique* und *La poésie romantique* angewiesen. Präromantiker sind nach van Tieghem eine Gruppe von Schriftstellern, besonders von Dichtern, "qui vers la fin de l'âge classique se distinguent de leurs contemporains par des traits qui annoncent le romantisme de l'âge moderne, quoiqu'ils restent classiques à bien des égards." Sie sind Erneuerer in bezug auf ihre "tendances morales, leurs goûts littéraires, leurs sources et leurs modèles." Statt der Vernunft, "qui domine avant eux et autour d'eux," bevorzugen sie "le sentiment et même la sentimentalité." Die Urheimat der Präromantik bildeten die Schweiz und Schottland, ein goldenes Zeitalter erlebte die Präromantik in England (es liessen sich dort sogar zwei Perioden unterscheiden: 1750 bis 1780 und 1780 bis 1800), und in Deutschland. Rousseau wird als der "maître vénéré des préromantiques" angesehen, hervorragende Vertreter sind Klopstock, Herder, der junge Goethe und Schiller. Die niederländischen Repräsentanten sind van Alphen, Bellamy und Bilderdijk. Die Typisierung der Präromantiker als derjenigen, die dadurch, dass sie das Gefühl der Vernunft vorziehen, die Romantik ankündigen, tilgt van Tieghem in einem ausführlicheren Vorbericht zu seinem zweiten Sammelband von Präromantikstudien.[19] Im Gegensatz zu seinen Landsleuten, die "paraissent entendre surtout par *préromantisme* une attitude morale et sentimentale devant la vie, la nature et la société, qui annonce celle de certains romantiques français," möchte er den Terminus ausschliesslich auf die Literatur beschränken:

18. P. van Tieghem, *Précis d'histoire littéraire de l'Europe depuis la Renaissance,* Paris 1925. Dessen *Histoire littéraire de l'Europe et de l'Amérique de la Renaissance à nos jours,* Paris 1946, gibt dasselbe Bild der Präromantik.
19. P. van Tieghem, *Le préromantisme: Etudes d'histoire européenne,* tome 2, Paris 1948[2] (erste Auflage 1929).

Je continue à désigner par ce terme, d'une façon à la fois plus
précise et plus générale, l'expression littéraire de curiosités, de goûts, de
sentiments, d'idées, par lesquels, à l'étranger plus souvent parfois et plus nettement qu'en France, un grand nombre d'écrivains du XVIIIe siècle et des pre-
mières années du XIXe siècle tranchent sur leurs prédécesseurs et leurs contemporains, et sont intermédiaires entre la littérature classique pure et la littérature romantique. (S. V)

Deutlich ist, dass van Tieghem, im Gegensatz zu Mornets "expression de goûts," sich nur mit der "expression littéraire" befassen
will, weniger deutlich, ob diese Präromantik nur ein Sammelname
für eine Anzahl von Werken ist, die irgendwie zu den
vorangehenden oder kontemporänen Konventionen einen Kontrast
bilden, oder aber ob sie als eine historische Periode zu verstehen ist.
Unklar ist schliesslich auch die Andeutung "intermédiaires". Van
Tieghems Ansichten werden etwas deutlicher, wenn er den Begriff
Präromantik gegen die von Farinelli und Baldensperger vorgebrachten
Bedenken verteidigt. Ersterer äusserte die Befürchtung, der Terminus
Präromantik werde "un compartimentage trop rigoureux et artifi-
ciel" auslösen. Van Tieghem beeilt sich, zu erklären, dass eine "tentative d'établir artificiellement des périodes d'histoire littéraire aux
limites nettement tracées" tatsächlich grosse Gefahren in sich trage.
Das ändere aber nichts an der Tatsache, dass man in bestimmten
Zeitaltern "certaines tendances ou idées dominantes" belegen könne,
und in diesem Falle habe der "travailleur, ou le professeur, pour la
commodité de son exposé, [...] le droit de les grouper sous une
appellation commune, claire et utile." Man hat den Eindruck, dass
van Tieghems "tendances ou idées dominantes" sich sehr stark dem
"system of norms" von Wellek nähern, und dass van Tieghem also
ein Periodenbegriff vorschwebt. Soweit möchte er jedoch nicht
gehen. Die Präromantik manifestiere sich zur selben Zeit wie "l'âge
classique" und "la philosophie des lumières"; nicht alle Vorgänger
können als Klassizisten und ebensowenig alle Nachfolger als Romantiker bezeichnet werden. Ein "faisceau de sympathies et de tendances" mache noch keine historische Periode aus.

Es fragt sich, ob der Terminus Präromantik als Andeutung dieser
Erscheinungen wirklich so "claire et utile" ist, wie van Tieghem den
Leser glauben machen will. Durch den Gebrauch, den seine Vorgänger und er selbst in früheren Veröffentlichungen von dem Worte
machten, ist Präromantik keine neutrale Bezeichnung mehr, sondern
eine suggestive Benennung, die die damit angedeuteten Erschei-

nungen mit der Romantik in Zusammenhang bringt. Van Tieghem wünscht diese Verbindung jetzt jedoch nicht herzustellen. Das tritt klar zu Tage aus seiner Selbstverteidigung gegen Baldensperger, der sich gefragt hatte, ob man nicht Opfer einer "illusion d'optique" werde "en étiquetant à part tout ce qui au XVIIIe siècle paraît annoncer le romantisme." Baldensperger habe recht – so van Tieghem – wenn man die Präromantik studieren wollte "avec l'arrière-pensée du romantisme pour chercher dans le passé l'explication de l'avenir:

> Mais on peut très bien l'étudier comme l'expression littéraire de tendances qui ont régné pendant un certain temps, distinctes de celles qui ont suivi comme de celles qui ont précédé. On peut et on doit décrire le préromantisme comme si le romantisme n'avait jamais existé." (S. VII)

Van Tieghem mag noch hinzufügen, dass es übertrieben wäre, jede Verbindung mit Vorgängern und Nachfolgern auszuschliessen; es bleibt jedoch äusserst frappant, dass der Mann, der durch seine Arbeiten der grösste Förderer der Präromantik-Konzeption war, dem Begriff 1929 seine wichtigste Konnotation nimmt. Aufgrund dieser Aussagen braucht es nicht Wunder zu nehmen, dass van Tieghem acht Jahre später eine auffällige Gleichgültigkeit gegen das Wort bekundet. Auf dem zweiten internationalen Kongress für Literaturgeschichte in Amsterdam, der "Les Périodes dans l'histoire littéraire depuis la Renaissance" zum Gegenstand hatte, kennzeichnete Folkierski die Renaissance und die Romantik als "sables mouvants," die in wachsendem Masse die vorangehenden Perioden annektieren.[20] In diesem Zusammenhang widersetzte er sich der Verwendung sowohl des Wortes Prärenaissance als des Wortes Präromantik. In der Diskussion gab van Tieghem die "insuffisante précision" des Wortes zu; "il plaide coupable", soweit es die Verwendung im Titel seiner beiden Sammelbände betrifft. Die noch zu erscheinenden Bände "pourront recevoir un titre quelconque, ils contiendront toujours des études relatives à la même période, qui, à ses yeux, offre des caractères distincts, qu'on l'appelle *préromantisme* ou autrement."[21]

Leider hat van Tieghem dass Bussgewand nicht allzu lange getra-

---

20. W. Folkierski, "Renaissance et Romantisme ou les sables mouvants dans l'histoire littéraire". In: *Bulletin of the International Committee of Historical Sciences,* vol. 9, part III, 1937, S. 325/336.
21. *Bulletin . . .,* S. 336.

gen. Seine 1948 veröffentlichte, einflussreiche Schrift *Le romantisme dans la littérature européenne* enthält einen ersten Teil unter dem Titel *Le préromantisme,* der der Behandlung der europäischen Romantik vorangeht. Die damit nahegelegte enge Verbindung zwischen Präromantik und Romantik wird durch einige Aussagen bestätigt:

On donne depuis quelques dizaines d'années le nom de *préromantisme* au mouvement littéraire qui a précédé le romantisme proprement dit. Comme les termes analogues, et dont les débuts furent à peu près contemporains, de *prérenaissance, préréforme, préclassique,* ce mot a soulevé des objections; mais outre qu'il est désormais entré dans l'usage, il se justifie pleinement si l'on se borne à désigner ainsi l'ensemble des états d'esprit ou de sensibilité, de tendances, de sentiments, d'idées, de formes, d'oeuvres, qui pendant la fin de la période classique offrent des traits qui annoncent le romantisme du XIXe siècle.[22]

Mit der Hilfe einiger Kunstgriffe (der Autor versteckt sich hinter dem objektiver anmutenden *on* und lässt analoge Anwendungen und die "usance" als Argumente gelten) gibt er in unmissverständlicher Weise eine neue Formulierung seiner Präromantik-Konzeption: die zu einem *mouvement* erhobene Präromantik wird von der Perspektive der Romantik her gestaltet. In seiner weiteren Ausführung entkräftet van Tieghem jedoch wieder den "mouvement"-Charakter: im Gegensatz zur Romantik bilde die Präromantik kein "ensemble logique et lié," sondern eine "collection d'efforts isolés." Daher empfehle es sich, nur von *préromantiques* zu sprechen. Auch dann solle man nicht aus den Augen verlieren, dass den ältesten Präromantikern dieser Name nur aufgrund eines einzelnen Aspektes ihres Werkes zukomme. Auch die chronologische und geographische Verbreitung der Präromantik müsse zur Vorsicht mahnen: die ersten Präromantiker manifestierten sich in den dreissiger Jahren in England und Schottland, dann folgten Frankreich und die Schweiz und schliesslich Deutschland. Ab 1760 wachse ihre Anzahl bedeutend, aber in ihrem Streit gegen den Klassizismus und ihrer Vorbereitung auf die Romantik bleiben sie isoliert. Niederländische Präromantiker werden von van Tieghem nicht mehr erwähnt.

Wenn der wichtigste Propagandist des Wortes *préromantique* in verschiedenen Veröffentlichungen solche entgegengesetzten Meinun-

22. Paul van Tieghem, *Le romantisme dans la littérature européenne,* Paris 1948, S. 23.

gen kundgibt und sich selbst wiederholt widerspricht, ist es nicht verwunderlich, dass spätere Literaturhistoriker in ihrer Bezugnahme auf van Tieghem das Wort Präromantik in verschiedenartigem Sinn verwenden konnten. So bekommt die Präromantik in der *Outline of Comparative Literature*, chronologisch zwischen Klassizismus und Aufklärung einerseits und Romantik andrerseits eingebettet, recht deutliche Züge einer spezifischen historischen Periode mit eigenen Dominanten.[23] Andere heben vorzugsweise das Gefühl, das seine Rechte zurückfordert und sich der Vernunft widersetzt, aus dem Komplex von Elementen hervor, die van Tieghem als konstituierend für die Präromantik betrachtete, und sehen darin eine Grundeigenschaft der Präromantik. Ein gutes Beispiel ist in dieser Hinsicht ein Aufsatz von Krejčí aus dem Jahre 1968, in dem als eine Art von gemeinsamem Nenner aller auf van Tieghem zurückgehenden Präromantik-Konzeptionen die "Akzentuierung des Sentiments im Gegensatz zum Rationalismus des Jahrhunderts der Aufklärung" angesehen wird. In diesem Zusammenhang weist der Autor auf die Gewohnheit russischer Gelehrten hin, den Terminus "Sentimentalismus" für Erscheinungen von vergleichbarer Art zu verwenden. Mit beiden Worten sei faktisch dasselbe gemeint: "Die Präromantik ist sentimental in dem gleichen Masse, wie der Sentimentalismus präromantisch ist" (S. 230).[24]

Bezeichnend für die hier angedeuteten Präromantik-Konzeptionen ist, wie bereits gesagt wurde, dass eine Anzahl von Erscheinungen nur

23. Werner P. Friedrich and David Henry Malone, *Outline of Comparative Literature*, Chapel Hill 1954, S. 199/254. Schon 1934 konstatierte H. Friedrich in van Tieghems Präromantik-Konzeption eine gewisse "Verdinglichung": "Der Gradationsbegriff, von dem wir oben sprachen, ist im Grunde hier noch ein Epochenbegriff, dessen Gefahr darin besteht, dass man in seiner Anwendung ein Ordnungsprinzip mit dem geordneten Stoff verwechselt." ("Der Epochebegriff, S. 133).

24. K. Krejčí, "Zur Entwicklung der Präromantik in europäischen Nationalliteraturen des 18. und 19. Jahrhunderts". In: *Aktuelle Probleme der vergleichenden Literaturforschung*, hrsg. von Gerhard Ziegengeist, Berlin 1968, S. 230/249. Diese Meinung wird übrigens nicht von Rudolf Neuhäuser geteilt. In dessen neulich erschienener Schrift *Towards the Romantic Age: Essays on Sentimental and Preromantic Literature in Russia*, The Hague 1974, werden eben die Unterschiede zwischen der empfindsamen und präromantischen Strömung in der russischen Literatur hervorgehoben.

178

aufgrund der Tatsache, dass sie auf die Romantik vorausdeuten, entdeckt, nebeneinander gestellt und gewertet werden. Nur die Retrospektion rechtfertigt ihr Bestehen: "l'aspect romantique du classicisme ne s'est dégagé que par l'effet rétro-actif du romantisme une fois apparu."[25] Mit der Romantik als Geigerzähler tastet der Forscher das achtzehnte Jahrhundert ab, er löst gewisse Elemente aus der Struktur, innerhalb derer sie funktionieren, heraus, und gruppiert sie aufs neue unter dem Nenner Präromantik. Dieses Verfahren widerspiegelt die Ausgangspunkte und die Wertmassstäbe der Literaturgeschichte aus den ersten Jahrzehnten dieses Jahrhunderts. Ursachen, Quellen, Einflüsse und Vorläufer bildeten beliebte Topics einer Literaturgeschichte, die sich noch nicht von einer positivistischen Literaturauffassung und dem Evolutionsmodell des neunzehnten Jahrhunderts losgemacht hatte. Zur selben Zeit steht die Romantikforschung im Mittelpunkt des Interesses. Die Hausse von Romantikstudien war so gross, dass Petersen noch 1926 erklären konnte, dass "die heutige Literaturwissenschaft beinahe mit Romantikforschung gleichgesetzt werden kann."[26] Man braucht noch nicht so weit zu gehen wie die marxistischen Literaturhistoriker, die die Präromantik-These als einen Ausfluss einer bürgerlichen Ideologie entlarven wollen,[27] um ihnen darin beizupflichten, dass die Romantikforschung jener Zeit oft von einer persönlichen Affinität zur romantischen Bewegung aus unternommen wurde. Der heftige Streit zwischen Befürwortern und Gegnern der Romantik in Frankreich liefert einen deutlichen Beweis, wie aktuell die Romantik für viele noch war.[28] Was lag mehr auf der Hand, als dass man, mehr oder

25. Henri Bergson, *La Pensée et le Mouvant*, Paris 1946[22], S. 16.

26. J. Petersen, "Die Wesensbestimmung der deutschen Romantik". In: *Eine Einführung in die moderne Literaturwissenschaft*, Leipzig 1926, S. 2. Angeführt von Winfried Schröder, "Die Präromantiktheorie – eine Etappe in der Geschichte der Literaturwissenschaft? " In: *Weimarer Beiträge* 12 (1966), S. 739.

27. Schröder ist der Meinung, "dass es sich bei der Präromantiktheorie um eine spätbürgerliche Theorie handelt, die mit der Lebensphilosophie engstens verbunden ist und die diese gewissermassen historisch zu legitimieren sucht." ("Die Präromantiktheorie", S. 723/724).

28. Vgl. zu den konservativ antiromantischen und liberal proromantischen Standpunkten in Frankreich um die Jahrhundertwende u.a. Hugo Friedrich, *Das antiromantische Denken im modernen Frankreich*, München 1935; Roger Fayolle, "Quand? Où? Et pourquoi. . . " und Schröder, "Die Prärc ntiktheorie".

weniger in die Defensive gedrängt,[29] dieser hochgeschätzten Romantik zu Ahnen verhelfen wollte und sich zur Annektierung der vorangehenden Periode von romantischer Perspektive her aufmachte?

Jenes günstige Klima für das Zustandekommen und für die Verwendung des Wortes Präromantik ist jetzt kaum noch vorhanden. Von einer strukturalistischen Betrachtungsweise her wird Einspruch erhoben gegen die Loslösung von Themen, Motiven und Elementen aus ihrem Kontext, und fordert man ihr Studium im Rahmen der Systeme, innerhalb derer sie funktionieren. Vereinzelte Ansätze zu dieser Betrachtungsweise rühren übrigens schon aus einer Zeit weit vor dem zweiten Weltkrieg her. So warnte Huizinga schon 1920 vor der gefährlichen Metapher *Vorläufer* aufgrund ähnlicher Erwägungen: "Door iemand tot voorloper te stempelen, licht men hem uit zijn tijd, waaruit hij moet worden verstaan, en ontwricht de historie."[30] Nach ihm haben u.a. Baldensperger, Folkierski und Northrop Frye[31] sich einer Behandlung des achtzehnten Jahrhunderts von einer romantischen Sicht her widersetzt. Ihre Bedenken gegen die "post-festum"-Feststellungen werden in letzter Zeit von u.a. Krauss, Schröder, Jauss, Diaz, Fayolle und Gaillard[32] wiederholt. Welchen Schematisierungen der "discours historique" verfällt, um die "illusion téléologique" gestalten zu können, gibt letztere Schritt für Schritt an. Das retrospektive Urteil geht nach Gaillard von einer

29. Vgl. zu diesem Aspekt besonders Fayolle, "Quand? Où? Et pourquoi. . ."

30. J. Huizinga, "Renaissancestudien I", *De gids* 1920, 4, S. 127.

31. F. Baldensperger, " 'Romantique', ses analogues et ses équivalents." In: *Harvard Studies and Notes in Philology and Literature* 19 (1937), S. 13/105; W. Folkierski, "Renaissance et Romantisme. . ."; Northrop Frye, "Towards Defining an Age of Sensibility". In: *ELH* 1956, S. 144/152.

32. Werner Krauss, "Französische Aufklärung und deutsche Romantik". In: *Perspektiven und Probleme*, Berlin 1965, S. 266/284; Schröder, "Die Präromantiktheorie"; H. R. Jauss, "Schlegels und Schillers Replik auf die 'Querelle des Anciens et des Modernes'." In: *Europäische Aufklärung: Herbert Dieckmann zum 60. Geburtstag*, ed. H. Friedrich und F. Schalk, München 1967, S. 117/140; Jean-Louis Diaz, "Le préromantisme dans le texte: l'exemple de Lanson". In: *Le préromantisme. . . S. 25/37; Fayolle, "Quand? Où? Et pourquoi. . ."; Gaillard, "Le préromantisme constitue-t-il une période? ".*

"évolution vers un stade normatif" aus. Im Falle der Präromantik führe dies zur Konstruktion von zwei Normen: auf der einen Seite entwerfe man die Norm der Aufklärung, der der Rationalismus als Grundeigenschaft angedichtet werde, auf der andern Seite stelle man die Norm der Romantik auf, für die das Gefühl charakteristisch sei. Im Lichte der Norm der Aufklärung manifestiere der sich entfaltende Sentimentalismus sich als ein "élément de désagrégation non registrable sous la même étiquette." Alle abweichenden Elemente werden mit dem Etikett Präromantik versehen, mit ihrer eigenen Norm, der Romantik, konfrontiert und verbunden und als Reaktion gegen die Aufklärung gewertet. Eine derartige Anschauungsweise beruhe auf einer der Analyse vorangehenden dualistischen Konzeption, die den Literaturhistoriker dazu bringe, dass er zwei Kodes hantiert, deren Koexistenz er sich in der zweiten Hälfte des achtzehnten Jahrhunderts nur als Streit und Reaktion denken könne. Innerhalb dieser Konstruktion werde der präromantische Mensch als ein Mensch gezeichnet, der den Widerspruch jener beiden Kodes am eigenen Leibe erfährt. Daher müsse er sich den Umschlag einer rationalistischen Phase in eine Gefühlsphase gefallen lassen, oder aber er werde als ein zwischen Leidenschaft und Vernunft hin und her Gerissener dargestellt (Diderot). Gaillard verwirft dieses Operieren mit den beiden einander ausschliessenden Polen Vernunft und Gefühl als rein intellektuelle Konstruktionen, die der Wirklichkeit nicht gerecht werden. Das Gegenteil ist der Fall: "A un certain niveau d'analyse les deux codes, bien loin d'apparaître contradictoires, se révèlent être les deux manifestations, à des niveaux différents, d'un même système."[33]

Dass diese formellen Bedenken gegen die Verwendung des Wortes Präromantik berechtigt sind, scheint deutlich durch die Ergebnisse der Forschung des achtzehnten Jahrhunderts aus nicht-romantischer Sicht, die mit vielen "fairy tales about 'neoclassicism' and 'romanticism' in the eighteenth century"[34] aufräumt, bestätigt zu werden. Konnte Hazard 1946 noch ein grossartiges Bild dieser Periode konstruieren, in der eine rationalistische erste Hälfte von einer empfind-

33. Gaillard, *"Le préromantisme..." S. 71.*
34. R. S. Crane, *Philological Quarterly* 22 (1943), S. 143.

samen zweiten Hälfte abgelöst wurde,[35] so widersetzen sich heutzu-
tage immer mehr Gelehrte dem Bruchcharakter dieses Jahrhunderts
und befürworten mit triftigen Argumenten die Einheit dieser Periode.[36] In ihrer Beweisführung stützen sie sich u.a. auf Aussagen der
Zeitgenossen selbst, die während des ganzen achtzehnten Jahrhunderts sich deutlich bewusst waren, dass sie in einer aufgeklärten
Zeit lebten.[37] Werner Krauss legt mit Recht dar, dass in dieser Hinsicht das achtzehnte Jahrhundert im Vergleich mit vorangehenden
Jahrhunderten einzigartig sei, weil jetzt zum ersten Mal der Mensch
sich des spezifischen Charakters seiner Zeit bewusst sei. Der Literaturhistoriker müsse sich bei der Konstruktion von Perioden-
Konzeptionen in starkem Masse von Kriterien, die im Bewusstsein einer
solchen Periode verankert sind, leiten lassen.

Die Einheit des achtzehnten Jahrhunderts wird von den Forschern, die dieses Zeitalter als eine Periode sui generis betrachten,
meistens unter das Banner der Aufklärung gestellt.[38] Dies konnte
umso leichter stattfinden, weil die Forschungsresultate ein viel weniger starres Aufklärungskonzept als das bis dahin konstruierte ergaben. Man leugnet den rationellen Aspekt der Aufklärung nicht,
aber man gelangte zur Einsicht, dass die Vernunft viel weniger
"intransigeant, dédaigneux de l'expérience"[39] sei, als man immer behauptet hatte. Das achtzehnte Jahrhundert wird vom Empirismus ge-
nährt, der die Leidenschaften rehabilitiert und dem Gefühl einen
wichtigen Platz einräumt. Mauzi sagt dazu: der Aufklärungsmensch
"impose sa forme à l'univers. Dans cette reconstruction du monde,

35. P. Hazard, *La pensée européenne au XVIIIe siècle,* Paris 1946.
36. Aus dem wachsenden Strom von Veröffentlichungen nenne ich nur den
epochalen Aufsatz des belgischen Komparatisten Roland Mortier, "Unité ou
scission du siècle des lumières?" In: *Studies on Voltaire and the Eighteenth
Century* 26 (1963), S. 1207/1221.
37. Vgl. z.B. Werner Krauss, "Zur Periodisierung der Aufklärung". In:
Grundpositionen der französischen Aufklärung, Berlin 1955, S. VI/XVI.
38. Die Diskussion über die Präromantik-Konzeption wird dadurch kompliziert, dass die Verteidiger meistens von einer Opposition Klassizismus-
Romantik ausgehen, während die Gegner mit den Begriffen Aufklärung und
Romantik arbeiten.
39. Mortier, "Unité ou scission..." S. 1211.

tout est mis en oeuvre simultanément: la raison, la sensibilité, l'imagination, le sens aussi."[40]

Diese neue Prägung des Aufklärungsbegriffs hat dazu geführt, dass man die herrschende Konstruktion einer vorwiegend rationalistischen ersten Hälfte des Jahrhunderts, der eine Periode, in der das Gefühl seine Rechte zurückfordert, folgt, als unbefriedigend abweist. Dem Schema des "Nacheinander," in dem sich Vernunft und Gefühl wie These und Antithese verhalten, stellt man das Schema des "Nebeneinander," in dem Vernunft und Gefühl sich die Waage halten, gegenüber. Entwicklungen innerhalb der Aufklärung werden übrigens nicht geleugnet. So spricht Krauss von einer Frühaufklärung, einer Aufklärung und einer Spätaufklärung,[41] und unterscheidet Mortier eine "phase ascendante," eine "phase triomphante" und eine "phase du reflux."[42] Von dieser Konzeption her erhebt man selbstverständlich Einspruch gegen die Amputation des achtzehnten Jahrhunderts von seiten der Präromantik-These. Damit ist nicht gesagt, dass man die Erscheinungen, die unter dem Nenner Präromantik zusammengebracht wurden, an sich leugnet, aber man widersetzt sich einer allzu leichtfertigen Einverleibung in die Romantik. Wie Krauss bemerkt: "sie widersprechen nicht nur nicht den herrschenden Tendenzen der Aufklärung, sondern sind in ihrem innersten Lebenskern zutiefst verwurzelt."[43] Krauss vertauscht die Rollen: die Annektierung von der Romantik her soll der Aufmerksamkeit für das Eindringen der Aufklärung in die Romantik weichen:

Wir fragen nicht mehr danach, was der Romantik an Vorläuferschaft und an vorbereitenden Tendenzen vorausgeht, sondern wir fragen zuvörderst nach den Elementen, die, aus der vorausgegangenen Aufklärung stammend, ihre Wirksamkeit auf die Romantik nicht verloren: Motive der Aufklärung, die von der Romantik gewahrt und im Sinne der Weiterbildung oder auch einer Verbildung verwandelt wurden.[44]

40. Robert Mauzi, *L'idée du bonheur au XVIIIe siècle.* Paris 1969[4], S. 12/13.

41. W. Krauss, "Der Jahrhundertbegriff im 18. Jahrhundert." In: *Studien zur deutschen und französischen Aufklärung,* Berlin 1963, S. 9/40.

42. Mortier, "Unité ou scission...", S. 1221.

43. Krauss, "Französische Aufklärung und deutsche Romantik", S. 268.

Die Gefahr ist natürlich nicht undenkbar, dass man bei der Entlarvung der Präromantik-These sich zum Gegenteil hinreissen lässt und jetzt der Aufklärung denselben dominierenden Platz, den die Romantik in früheren Untersuchungen einnahm, einräumen möchte. In diesem Zusammenhang ist es schon bezeichnend, dass es gerade die marxistische Literaturwissenschaft gewesen ist, die in der Neubewertung des achtzehnten Jahrhunderts als des Zeitalters der Aufklärung vorangegangen war.[45] Die Tatsache bleibt aber, dass dem achtzehnten Jahrhundert als einer Periode sui generis aus dieser neuen Sicht mehr Recht geschieht als ehedem.[46]

In den letzten Jahrzehnten werden auf diese Weise mehrere von der Romantik annektierte Erscheinungen der Aufklärung "zurückerstattet." Dies trifft z.B. für das Ruinenthema zu, das, wie Mortier[47] nachgewiesen hat, nicht a priori mit präromantischer Empfindsamkeit identifiziert werden darf. Es trifft auch zu für eine Bewegung wie Sturm und Drang, die in der Vergangenheit oft als eine deutsche Variante der europäischen Präromantik bezeichnet wurde.[48] In sehr hohem Masse trifft es zu für den Eckstein der Präromantik-Konzeption: der Manifestation des Gefühls und der Gefühls-

44. A.a.O., S. 268. Vgl. auch István Sötér: "The theory of pre-romanticism simply separated from the enlightenment those new eighteenth century phenomena which survived in nineteenth century romanticism". (István Sötér, "Romanticism-Pre-History and Periodization". In: *The Dilemma of Literary Science*, Budapest 1973, S. 128/129.)

45. Für eine historische Übersicht siehe Schröder, "Die Präromantiktheorie", S. 746/751.

46. Bezeichnend für den Wandel des Interesses ist es, dass auf dem 8. Kongress der I.C.L.A. zu Budapest (1976) nicht die Romantik, sondern die Aufklärung neben der Renaissance und dem frühen zwanzigsten Jahrhundert als eine der "three epoch-making changes in the history of literatures in European languages" zur Debatte gestellt wird.

47. Roland Mortier, "Sensibility', 'Neoclassicism', or 'Preromanticism'? " In: *Eighteenth Century Studies: Presented to Arthur M. Wilson*. Ed. P. Gay, Hannover usw. 1972, S. 155/163. Vgl. dazu auch dessen *La poétique des ruines en France*, Genève 1974.

48. Vgl. u.a. Edith Braemer, "Die Legende von der Präromantik des Sturm und Drang". In: *Goethes Prometheus und die Grundpositionen des Sturm und Drang*, Weimar 1963, S. 40/69.

terminologie. Sehr nachdrücklich stellt Sauder in seiner neulich erschienenen eindrucksvollen Studie zur deutschen Empfindsamkeit
diese unter das Banner der Aufklärung. Er vertritt die Meinung, dass
"eine Geschichte der Empfindsamkeit nur im allgemeinen Rahmen
einer Geschichte der Aufklärung geschrieben werden kann." Die
europäische Empfindsamkeit "war keine Tendenz *gegen* die Vernunft, sondern der Versuch, mit Hilfe der Vernunft auch die Empfindungen aufzuklären."[49]

Obgleich das Wort Präromantik in der niederländischen Literaturforschung erst verhältnismässig spät auftaucht, wurde die endgültige
Aufnahme dadurch erleichtert, dass die Charakterisierung der Literatur der zweiten Hälfte des achtzehnten Jahrhunderts in immer
höherem Grade aus romantischer Perspektive stattfand. Die Über-
sichten aus dem neunzehnten Jahrhundert beschränken sich noch
darauf, dass sie eine literarische Erneuerung um die Mitte des achtzehnten Jahrhunderts konstatieren; als wichtigste Vertreter nennt
man die Brüder van Haren, van Alphen, Bellamy, Nieuwland und
Feith. So spricht de Vries[50] 1810 von "een nieuw en beter tijdperk
der Dichtkunst," von "dichters van meer algemeene verheffing, meer
algemeene smaak voor ware, natuurlijke dichtkunst," die sich von
den "eigendunkelijke voorschriften van altijd schavende, en her-
schavende meesters" befreien. Für de Clercq[51] bedeutet diese Erneuerung mit Recht eine Auflebung: die Brüder van Haren geben
Beispiele einer Ursprünglichkeit, "die in Holland *verdwenen* was."
Van Kampen[52] lässt der "veragtering der Nederlandsche Poezij" in

49. Gerhard Sauder, *Empfindsamkeit, Band I: Voraussetzungen und Elemente,* Stuttgart 1974, S. XV. Ähnlich räumt Armand Nivelle im Kapitel "Lite-
raturästhetik" in *Neues Handbuch der Literaturwissenschaft* Tl. 11: *Europäische
Aufklärung,* Frankfurt am Main 1974, S. 15/56, Änderungen im literarischen
Denken, die ehedem als "präromantisch" bezeichnet wurden, einen Platz in der
Entwicklung der Aufklärung ein.
50. Jeronimo de Vries, *Proeve eener geschiedenis der Nederduitsche dicht-
kunde,* Bd. 4, Amsterdam 1836² (erste Auflage 1810).
51. Willem de Clercq, *Verhandeling ter beantwoording der vraag: welken
invloed heeft vreemde letterkunde, . . . , gehad op de Nederlandsche taal- en
letterkunde, . . .* Amsterdam 1824.
52. N. G. van Kampen, *Beknopte geschiedenis der letteren en weten-
schappen in de Nederlanden,* Bd. 2, 's Gravenhage 1822.

der Periode 1713 bis 1780 die "Herleving der Nederlandsche Dichtkunst" folgen. Hofdijk[53] konstatiert im "tijdvak der Herleving" eine
"degelijke verrijzing des geestes," Jonckbloet[54] spricht von einer
"dageraad eener betere toekomst," die sich bei Dichtern kundgebe,
die zurückkehrten "tot natuur en eenvoud" (van Alphen), "waar-
achtig gevoel" (Bellamy) und "eenvoud en natuurlijkheid" (Nieuwland). Ein Zusammenhang zwischen dieser Auflebung und der Romantik wird noch nicht hergestellt. Busken Huet reserviert das Wort
Romantik sogar ausdrücklich für alles Neue "waardoor, sedert Bilder-
dijks overlijden in 1831 tot heden, onze letteren zich onderscheiden
hebben van die der onmiddellijk voorafgegane periode en van alle
vroegere tijdperken te zamen."[55]

Dennoch wird im selben Jahre die früher konstatierte Auflebung
der Literatur sehr nachdrücklich als der Anfang eines Individualismus
in der Kunst, der sich in der "Beweging van tachtig" "als een moetende
konsekwentie" voll entfalten wird, gesehen. Albert Verwey[56] verleiht dieser teleologischen Anschauung Ausdruck, wenn er es als
Sprachrohr der literarischen Jugend versucht, "door een historische
parallel het optreden van de jonge revolutionairen te rechtvaardigen
en te verklaren."[57] Van Alphen ist nun mit seiner Riedel-
Übersetzung aus dem Jahre 1778 zum "voorman van het Individualismus in de Hollandsche Kunst"[58] promoviert, als Dichter vertritt er
mit Bellamy und Feith "de eerste verschijning der individualistische
kunstidees in de praktijk." Der Sentimentalismus bildet den Anfang

53. W. J. Hofdijk, *Geschiedenis der Nederlandsche letterkunde,* Amsterdam
1864[3].

54. W. J. A. Jonckbloet, *Geschiedenis der Nederlandsche letterkunde,* Bd. 5,
Groningen 1883[3].

55. Cd. Busken Huet, "De Romantiek in Nederland". In: *De nieuwe gids*
1886, 2, S. 169. Es ist bedauerlich, dass dieser massgebende Kritiker, der diese
Zeilen einige Stunden vor seinem Tode schrieb, nicht mehr imstande gewesen ist,
seine Ansichten über die niederländische Romantik in einem abgerundeten Aufsatz niederzulegen.

56. Albert Verwey, "Toen de Gids werd opgericht...". In: *De nieuwe gids*
1886, 2, S. 48/80; 171/195; 1887, I, S. 52/90.

57. C. G. N. de Vooys, "Verwey's verdienste voor de Nederlandse literatuur-
studie". In: *De nieuwe taalgids* 29 (1935), S. 195.

58. Verwey schliesst sich in der Wahl des Jahres 1778 als Wendepunkt dem
Aufsatz J. Hartogs, "Uit het leven van een tijdschrift" (*De gids* 1877, 3, S. 1113,
Anmerkung) an.

"van een nieuw gevoel, hoe zwak ook, in onze letteren." *De gids* und *De nieuwe gids* waren "in kiem in het laatste vijfde van de eeuw" vorhanden, dort fängt "de *revolutie* onzer kunst" an.

Mit derartigen Formulierungen legt Verwey die Grundlage für eine Betrachtung der Literatur des achtzehnten Jahrhunderts aus romantischer Perspektive, obgleich er selbst die "Bewegung der achtziger Jahre" noch als Orientierungspunkt nimmt. Wie gross seine Autorität war, erhellt aus der Tatsache, dass Knuvelder in seinem einleitenden Kapitel über die Romantik sich noch auf die Programmschrift jenes Achtzigers stützt.[59]

In einer nächsten Phase wird die Auflebung der Literatur ausdrücklich mit der Romantik in Verbindung gebracht. Ich nenne einige Beispiele. Kalff[60] will das Wort Romantik nicht für die Literatur der ersten Hälfte des neunzehnten Jahrhunderts reservieren, sondern es nach dem Vorgang englischer Beispiele auch auf die zweite Hälfte des achtzehnten Jahrhunderts beziehen. Daher charakterisiert er die Zeit von 1770 bis 1830 als *De verlichting en de opkomst der romantiek,* und unterscheidet sie von *De nieuwe tijd (de zegepraal der romantiek).* Aufklärung und Romantik betrachtet er als Strömungen, die oft gleichzeitig wirken und auch in einem Autor nicht immer getrennt werden können. Distinktivum der Aufklärung sei die Rationalität, das der Romantik des Gefühl. Prinsen[61] bevorzugt den Ausdruck "nieuwe Renaissance," statt Romantik. Er unterscheidet zwei Phasen: eine, die ihren Anfang in der zweiten Hälfte des achtzehnten Jahrhunderts hat, und eine zweite im neunzehnten Jahrhundert. Die beiden Phasen kehren wieder in der Literaturgeschichte von Lecoutere.[62] Die erste, die im letzten Viertel des achtzehnten Jahrhunderts anfange, komme nicht zur vollen Entfaltung:

[. . .] er wordt slechts een eerste stoot gegeven, die geen ommekeer tot gevolg had [. . .]. Dit pogen, waarvan wij de uitingen kunnen nagaan op het einde der

59. Vgl. dazu meine unten folgenden Ausführungen.

60. G. Kalff, *Geschiedenis der Nederlandsche letterkunde,* Bd. 6, Groningen 1910.

61. J. Prinsen J.Lnz., *Handboek tot de Nederlandsche letterkundige geschiedenis,* 's Gravenhage 1916. Auf S. 442 charakterisiert er die Romantik als die "groote West-Europeesche beweging, die omstreeks 't midden der 18e eeuw zich in al zijn volle kracht openbaart."

62. C. Lecoutere, *Schets van den ontwikkelingsgang der Nederlandsche letterkunde,* Brussel 1918.

187

XVIIIe eeuw en in het begin der XIXe, heet men de eerste periode van het romantisme; de tweede, die omstreeks 1830 valt, brengt de zegepraal van de beweging. (S. 92/93)

Als Ursache des "romantisme in de kunst" wird die Auflebung des Gefühls, die man als "tegenwerking tegen het verstandelijke" interpretiert, angewiesen. Auch Staverman[63] sieht zwei romantische Bewegungen: die erste fängt um 1780 an, die zweite um 1830. Der Konflikt zwischen Vernunft und Gefühl bildet die Ursache "van die grote beweging, die we de *Romantiek* noemen." Die detaillierteste Aufgliederung hat de Jager[64] auf dem Gewissen: bei ihm findet man als Übergangswort zwischen Romantik und Präromantik noch das Etikett Frühromantik. Man beachte seine militanten Metaphern:

> In de Vroeg-Romantiek onderneemt de Romantiek een stormaanval op het Rationalisme (1780-1795), daarna doet het Rationalisme een tegenaanval (1795-1815), waarna een periode van rust of evenwicht intreedt (1815-1830). De Hoog-Romantiek vertoont hetzelfde beeld: 2e stormloop van de Romantiek (1830-'50), 2e reactie van het Rationalisme (1850-'70), rust (1870-'80). (S. 106)

Aus dieser summarischen Übersicht kann man zwei Dinge schliessen: a) die von den Literaturhistorikern des neunzehnten Jahrhunderts noch neutral als "Auflebung der Literatur" bezeichnete Periode des ausgehenden achtzehnten Jahrhunderts wird immer nachdrücklicher als eine "erste Phase der Romantik" angesehen, der um 1830 eine zweite Phase folgt. b) Diese Romantik wird besonders als eine Gefühlsreaktion gegen eine als rationalistisch bezeichnete Aufklärung betrachtet. Man brauchte diese erste Phase nur noch mit dem Namen Präromantik zu versehen, um völlig mit dem Ausland Schritt zu halten.

Diese Etikettierung verzögert sich jedoch länger als man erwarten sollte. Vor dem zweiten Weltkrieg kommt das Wort nur vereinzelt vor und da eigentlich auch nur in bezug auf ausländische Literatur.[65]

---

63. W. H. Staverman, *Dichterschap en werkelijkheid,* redigiert von W. L. M. E. van Leeuwen, Utrecht o.J. [1938], Kap. 5 und 6.
64. Th. de Jager, *De ontwikkelingsgang van de taalkunst der Nederlanden,* Rotterdam 1941.
65. Vgl. für einige frühe, ausschliesslich auf die französische Literatur beschränkte Belege, u.a. *De nieuwe taalgids* 14 (1920), S. 24; *Neophilologus* 8 (1923), S. 314/5; 15 (1930) S. 63; 18 (1933) S. 307; 20(1935) S. 62.

188

Schults[66] gibt seiner Rezension der Dissertation von Spoelstra die suggestive Überschrift "Duitse verlichting en preromantiek in Nederland" mit, aber in der ganzen Besprechung kommt das Wort nur einmal in untergeordnetem Zusammenhang vor. Mehr oder weniger ein Plaidoyer für seine Verwendung hält Serrarens[67] in einem Aufsatz über Swaanenburg. Er möchte niederländische Verwandte finden "van die auteurs, die voor Monglond, Trahard, Mornet, Viatte e.a. de wegbereiders waren van het 'preromantisme'." In Frankreich habe man eingesehen, "dat men de scherp gecontrasteerde beelden der geesteshistorie moet herzien, dat de perioden van frans classicisme en romantiek in continuiteit met elkaar verbonden zijn en dat deze verbondenheid in een reeks van overgangsverschijnselen zijn te demonstreren." Wenn die Niederlande um 1780 "reif" für die Romantik sind, werde man dafür eine Erklärung in der Vergangenheit suchen müssen. "Het moet al gegist hebben, er moet al een onvrede met de idealen von Aufklärung en classicisme bestaan hebben." Literaturhistoriker werden aufgefordert, diese Vorläufer ausfindig zu machen; selbst gibt er schon eine Probe: Luyken, Poot, Wellekens und Swaanenburg, ein Mann von "onverdacht romantisch allooi" dürfe man als Präromantiker betrachten. Soviel mir bekannt ist, hat Serrarens' Aufforderung zu diesem Wurzelziehen bis ins frühe achtzehnte Jahrhundert hinein kaum Anklang gefunden.[68]

In zwei Publikationen, die die Periodisierung zum Gegenstand haben, wird die Bezeichnung Präromantik indirekt zur Diskussion gestellt. Gielen[69] opponiert in "Breuk of continuatie" gegen allzu markante Zäsuren in der Literaturgeschichte. Die Tatsachen zwingen den Geschichtsschreiber dazu, in allzu starren Perioden-Konzeptionen wie Mittelalter, Renaissance und Romantik Berichtigungen vorzunehmen. Die Einführung eines Begriffs wie "Übergangszeit" wird begrüsst: "vandaar is men geraakt tot 'voorlopers' en tot 'prerenais-

---

66. U. Schults, "Duitse verlichting en preromantiek in Nederland". In: *De nieuwe taalgids* 27 (1933), S. 109/115.

67. Ed. A. Serrarens, "Willem van Swaanenburg: Een zonderling uit het begin der 18e eeuw". In: *De gids* 1936,4, S.201/223.

68. Eine Ausnahme bildet vielleicht der Versuch von C. M. Geerars, der den Dichter Poot als einen "vroege voorloper van de Romantiek" bezeichnete. (C. M. Geerars, *Hubert Korneliszoon Poot*, Assen 1954.)

69. Jos. J. Gielen, "Breuk of continuatie?". In: *De nieuwe taalgids* 32 (1938), S. 49/73.

sance' en 'preromantiek'." Skeptischer ist de Backer:[70] Die Kontinuität in der Literaturgeschichte werde durch eine künstliche Einteilung nach Zeitaltern ernstlich gefährdet. Man könne zwar versuchen, die Schwierigkeiten zu lösen, indem man neue Bezeichnungen für Übergangsphasen schaffe, wie Prärenaissance und Präromantik. Es bleiben aber theoretische Fiktionen "waarmede slechts aangeduid kan worden, op een gegeven ogenblik, het meest karakteristieke dat zich gelden doet, maar gedurende dat theoretisch tijdperk zelf zijn veel vruchten voorhanden van het doodgewaande verleden en veel kiemen van het blind genegeerde of niet eens ontwaarde, en dat nochtans komen zal" (S. 130).

Erst nach dem zweiten Weltkrieg beginnt die Bezeichnung Präromantik ihren Aufmarsch in der niederländischen Literaturgeschichtsschreibung. Wie mir scheint, hat besonders Knuvelder[71] dazu beigetragen. Er bringt den Begriff heraus im dritten Band seiner massgebenden Literaturgeschichte, deren erste Auflage 1950 erschienen ist.[72] In der zweiten, geänderten Auflage baut er die Präromantik-Konzeption weiter aus. In der fünften Auflage (1973)[73] lässt er das Wort allerdings nahezu fallen, aber dann ist dieses Etikett, nicht an letzter Stelle durch die Autorität seines Werkes, in der niederländischen Literaturgeschichte eingebürgert.

In der ersten Auflage versteckt die Präromantik sich noch grösstenteils hinter der Beschreibung der Romantik. Knuvelder stützt sich auf die Schemata seiner Vorgänger und unterscheidet in der niederländischen Romantik zwei Phasen, die er mit ebenso militanten Metaphern wie die von de Jager benutzen als "Durchbrüche" typi-

---

70. F. de Backer, "Het begrip 'tijdperken' in de literatuurgeschiedenis". In: *Album René Verdeyen,* Bruxelles usw. 1943, S. 127/132.

71. C. Knuvelder, *Handboek tot de geschiedenis der Nederlandse letterkunde,* Bd. 3, 's-Hertogenbosch 1950; die zweite umgearbeitete Auflage des dritten Bandes erschien 1959, die fünfte umgearbeitete Auflage 1973.

72. Zur Vermeidung von Missverständnissen: es ist nicht meine Absicht, Knuvelder Aussagen vorzuwerfen, die er vor 25 Jahren gemacht hat. Das wäre schon deshalb nicht fair, weil der Autor seine Meinung im Laufe der Jahre geändert hat. Die Besprechung der früheren Auflagen erfolgt nur im Rahmen einer historischen Übersicht der Gestaltung der Präromantik-Konzeption in den Niederlanden.

73. D.h. das Wort wird ausgemerzt, die Präromantik-Konzeption behält ihre Rolle, wenn auch in viel geringerem Masse, bei.

siert. Seine Darstellung gewinnt aber erheblich an Suggestivität durch die Ausführlichkeit, mit der er (über 50 Seiten!) über die Romantik spricht und die Stelle, die er dazu auswählt. Pflegten seine Vorgänger Betrachtungen über Wesen und Umfang der Romantik einzuschalten, wenn sie sich der Jahreszahl 1830 genähert hatten, so lokalisiert Knuvelder dagegen seine umfangreiche Einleitung vor seiner Besprechung des "eerste tijdvak van de moderne letterkunde," einen Zeitabschnitt, den er, auf der Spur von Verwey, mit dem Jahre 1778 beginnen lässt. Die Komposition seines Werkes trägt dadurch schon in starkem Masse dazu bei, die Literatur des späten achtzehnten Jahrhunderts in einen romantischen Rahmen zu stellen.

Wenn Knuvelder in einer Gesamtwürdigung die markantesten Züge der Romantik noch einmal zusammenfasst, konstruiert er eine Opposition zwischen einer vernunftmässigen Aufklärung und einer gefühlsmässigen Romantik, die ganz in das von Gaillard gerügte Schema Vernunft contra Gefühl passt. Aufgrund dieser Konstruktion betrachtet er in anderem Zusammenhang die Gefühlselemente des achtzehnten Jahrhunderts als "romantisch verzet tegen de idealen van de Verlichting." Es ist ein Prozess, der während des ganzen achtzehnten Jahrhunderts im Ausland stattfindet, "waardoor de alleenheerschappij der Rede geweld lijdt, tot nà het midden der eeuw overal in Europa de nieuwe stroming de overhand krijgt" (S. 61). In den Niederlanden finde diese Penetration besonders zu Anfang der Periode 1770-1825 statt. An dieser Stelle führt Knuvelder das Wort Präromantik ein:

> Romantische elementen dringen rond 1778 aanvankelijk krachtig de, in het 18e eeuwse Nederland zo uitermate sterk door Verlichtings- en klassicistische tendenzen overheerste, denk- en gevoelswereld binnen, zodat vaak een eigenaardige vermenging van beide ontstaat, die bij iedere figuur weer anders ligt. Naar analogie van de Prae-Renaissance noemt men deze periode die van de Prae-Romantiek, en verstaat daaronder de periode waarin romantische elementen het oude wereldbeeld gaan beïnvloeden. (S. 62)

Knuvelder reserviert den Ausdruck also nicht für eine Anzahl vereinzelter Elemente, die auf die Romantik hindeuten, sondern er bezeichnet damit eine Periode, deren Anfang wenigstens deutlich feststeht.

Wenig glücklich gewählt finde ich in diesem Zusammenhang ein Wort wie "eindringen" [binnendringen], weil damit viel zu nachdrücklich die Existenz einer selbstbewussten romantischen Strömung, die Infiltrationen in das Bollwerk der Aufklärung ausführt, unterstellt wird. Höchstens könnte man sagen, dass sich innerhalb der Aufklärung Tendenzen entwickeln, die in der Romantik vorherrschend werden. Verwirrend ist auch, dass Knuvelder in der Folge den Terminus Präromantik wieder aufgibt und zur früher verwendeten Bezeichnung "de eerste 'doorbraak' van de romantiek" zurückkehrt. Knuvelder stellt in dieser Weise die Anschauungen seiner Vorgänger und der Verfechter der Präromantik-These einfach nebeneinander, ohne diese miteinander zu verbinden.

Das geschieht ebensowenig in der zweiten geänderten Auflage aus dem Jahre 1959, und dies ist umso merkwürdiger, weil Knuvelder seine Präromantik-Konzeption dort erheblich ausweitet: der umgearbeiteten Einleitung über die Romantik geht ein neues Kapitel *Klassicisme en Preromantiek* voraus, während ausserdem die Anfangsgrenze der Präromantik von 1778 auf 1766 verlegt wird. In dieser Einleitung unterscheidet er die Präromantik nachdrücklich von der Romantik (sie umfasse einige isolierte Strömungen, die sich noch nicht, wie in der Romantik, zu einer Bewegung geeinigt haben und die ebensowenig als zusammenhängend erfahren werden — es sei eher die Rede von Evolution als von Revolution), aber wenn Knuvelder zur Behandlung der niederländischen Literatur nach 1766 schreitet, muss das Wort Präromantik wieder der Bezeichnung " 'doorbraak' van de romantiek" Platz machen.

Bei seiner Ausarbeitung der Präromantik-Konzeption stützt Knuvelder sich hauptsächlich auf die komparatistischen Arbeiten von van Tieghem[74] und Brandt Corstius. Die Opposition Aufklärung-(Prä)romantik wird jetzt durch die Antithese Klassizismus-Präromantik ersetzt. Das bedeutet keine grundsätzliche Veränderung, weil Klassizismus grösstenteils mit Rationalismus gleichgeschaltet wird. Die Präromantik, als Reaktion gegen den Klassizismus aufgefasst, wird denn auch vornehmlich als eine Reaktion gesehen "in de sfeer van het gevoelsleven." Die Empfindsamkeit, ein anders erfahrenes Naturerlebnis, das Ablehnen des normativen Einflusses des klassischen Altertums, die Vorliebe für primitive Literaturformen, das Streben nach Ursprünglichkeit und die Verherrlichung des Genies ergeben sich zwangsläufig daraus. Dabei erfährt die Präromantik noch

---

74. Knuvelder richtet sich vornehmlich nach dessen *Le romantisme dans la littérature européenne,* auch was den Aufbau seiner Einführung in die Romantik betrifft.

192

stärker als bei van Tieghem eine "Verdinglichung": Formulierungen
wie "de preromantiek inspireert zich niet langer op de Griekse of
Romeinse oudheid" [. . .] "zij tastte in beginsel [. . .] het klassicisme
in wezen aan" [. . .] "zij vindt haar inspiratie vooral in de Germaanse
landen" setzen eine konkrete, selbstbewusste Strömung voraus und
vertuschen, dass es sich hier nur um eine literarhistorische Konstruktion handelt.

Die Grenzverlegung des Anfangs der niederländischen (Prä)-
romantik von 1778 nach 1766 geschieht nicht aufgrund der Autorität van Tieghems, der, wie schon bemerkt wurde, 1948 keine
niederländischen Präromantiker mehr anzuweisen vermochte, sondern beruht auf der Verarbeitung einiger in den fünfziger Jahren von
Brandt Corstius veröffentlichten Studien. Dieser vertrat darin die
These, dass um die Mitte des achtzehnten Jahrhunderts "de grote
veranderingen in de Westeuropese literatuur beginnen op te treden,
die de romantiek voorbereiden."[75] Damit schliesst er sich den Befürwortern der Präromantik-Konzeption an, obgleich er das Wort selbst
nur vereinzelt verwendet und variiert mit der Bezeichnung "vroege
romantiek". Die von ihm erwähnten "tendenties tot verandering en
vernieuwing, tot tegenstelling, spanning en strijd" betrachtet er an-
fänglich als eine "reactie der irrationalistische, sentimentele prae-
romantici op het klassicistische rationalisme."[76] Obgleich er in späteren Veröffentlichungen die These vertritt, dass um die Mitte des
achtzehnten Jahrhunderts ein Zeitalter endet und ein anderes an-
fängt,[77] hält er ein einfaches Schema von Aktion und Reaktion für
eine Darstellung, die den komplizierten Verhältnissen gerecht wird,
für unzulänglich. Weil berühmte Klassizisten Erneuerer in anti-
klassizistischem Sinne gewesen seien und der Klassizismus sich in
dem Augenblick, da er seine grossen Triumphe feiert, zu untergraben
beginne, sei es besser, den Prozess als einen "innerlijke overgang van

75. J. C. Brandt Corstius, "Betje Wolff is het niet alleen". In: *De nieuwe taalgids* 43 (1950), S. 212.
76. J. C. Brandt Corstius, "Letterkundige Stromingen en – kritiek in Neder-land tijdens de eerste levensjaren van de maatschappij". In: *Jaarboek van de Maatschappij der Nederlandse Letterkunde te Leiden 1950-1951,* Leiden 1952, S. 12.
77. J. C. Brandt Corstius, "Verschijnselen in onze literatuur aan het einde van de 18e eeuw in verband met veranderende opvattingen omtrent geloof en natuur". In: *De nieuwe taalgids* 44 (1951), S.242.

klassicisme naar romantiek"[78] zu beschreiben. An der grossen Veränderung, die sich in ganz Westeuropa vollzieht, sei in den Niederlanden der junge van Goens beteiligt. In seinen Aufsätzen aus den Jahren 1765 bis 1767 vollziehe sich ebenfalls die Entwicklung von Rationalismus "naar het voorspel van een in klassieke idealen gedrenkte romantiek." Die Komplexität des achtzehnten Jahrhunderts ruft bei Brandt Corstius übrigens grosse Reserven gegen "het trekken van ontwikkelingslijnen, het maken van indelingen en groeperingen" hervor.[79] Der beschränkten Gültigkeit simplifizierender Schemata wurde er sich peinlich bewusst, als er in seiner Studie über E. M. Post versuchte, ihre Werke mit Hilfe der üblichen Etikettierung zu typisieren, und dabei zu dem entmutigenden Schluss kam, dass man eine klassizistische, eine präromantische und eine romantische Post unterscheiden könnte.[80] Diese Erfahrung bringt ihn jedoch noch nicht dazu, dass er diese Klassifizierung aufgibt. Allerdings ist es seiner Meinung nach ein Erfordernis, dass der Benutzer eines Terminus jedesmal angibt, welche Vorstellungen er mit den geführten Bezeichnungen verbindet, und empfiehlt er eine Verfeinerung der Terminologie. Wie dicht er sich dabei den Vertretern einer nuancierten Aufklärungs-Konzeption näherte, erhellt aus der Tatsache, dass er in seinem Schlusskapitel dem Werk der Post einen Platz in der Verschiebung von einer rein rationalistischen Phase der Aufklärung zu einer Phase, wo der Mensch, "zijn ziel, zijn taak en zijn bestemming" zentral stehen, einräumt. Es bleibt aber ein fundamentaler Unterschied: bei Brandt Corstius löst die empfindsame Aufklärung die rationalistische ab, während die Vertreter der Aufklärungs-These gerade die Gleichzeitigkeit und das Gleichgewicht von Vernunft und Gefühl benachdrucken.

Knuvelder lässt Brandt Corstius in seiner Einleitung ausgiebig zu Worte kommen. So betont er wiederholt, dass die Präromantik noch lange von den Aufklärungsidealen beherrscht und unterstützt wird, und lehnt er den Bruchcharakter des achtzehnten Jahrhunderts ab.

78. J. C. Brandt Corstius, "De plaats van Rijklof Michael van Goens in de ontwikkeling van de Westeuropese literatuur." In: *De nieuwe taalgids* 44 (1951), S. 194.
79. J. C. Brandt Corstius, a.a.O., S. 192.
80. J. C. Brandt Corstius, *Idylle en realiteit: Het werk van Elisabeth Maria Post in verband met de ontwikkeling van de Europese literatuur in de tweede helft van de achttiende eeuw.* Amsterdam 1955.

Dennoch habe ich den Eindruck, dass es Knuvelder nur zum Teil gelungen ist, die nicht ganz parallel laufenden Auffassungen von van Tieghem (die Präromantik ist primär eine Reaktion auf den Klassizismus) und Brandt Corstius (der Klassizismus höhlt sich selbst aus) miteinander in Einklang zu bringen. Meiner Meinung nach geht Knuvelder in seiner Grenzverlegung der Präromantik auf das Jahr 1766 und darin, dass er van Goens als frühesten Vertreter nennt, auch weiter als Brandt Corstius beabsichtigte.

Über das weitere Schicksal der Präromantik-Konzeption in den Niederlanden kann ich mich kurz fassen. Von den sechziger Jahren an entwickelte das Wort sich zu einem beliebten und vertrauten Etikett, das in Dissertationen, Monographien, Aufsätzen und Textausgaben mit Vorliebe hantiert wird.[81] Grosse Verschiebungen im Vergleich zu Knuvelders Interpretation finden nicht statt. Seine Beschreibung der Präromantik wird als ein sinnvoller Rahmen betrachtet, innerhalb dessen bestimmte Werke und Autoren einen Platz finden können. So entsteht eine gewisse Kanonbildung hinsichtlich "unserer Präromantiker," deren eiserner Bestand die Dichter van Alphen, Feith ("onze voornaamste preromanticus"), Bellamy, Post, Kleyn, van Engelen en Nieuwland bilden. Als Grundmerkmal der Präromantik wird die Manifestation des Gefühls beibehalten. "Preromantische sensibiliteit," "preromantische gevoeligheid," ja sogar, "preromantische maan-gevoeligheid" sind Typisierungen, die mit Vorliebe benutzt werden. In einem Falle hantiert man das zugrunde liegende Schema Vernunft-Gefühl sogar so starr, dass das blosse Vorkommen von Worten wie *aandoeningen* en *teergevoelig* schon hinreicht, um "nieuwe geluiden" zu signalieren und einen Dichter als Übergangsgestalt zu bezeichnen.[82] Darüber, ob die Bezeichnung sinnvoll ist, wird kaum diskutiert, eine kritiklose Verwendung ersetzt oft

81. Statt eine Aufzählung zu geben, wie häufig andere diesen Begriff verwenden, kann ich besser den Vorwurf gegen mich selbst richten und auf einen Aufsatz hinweisen, in dem ich über die "Europäische Präromantik" gesprochen habe. (W. van den Berg, "Gray, Ossian en Van Winter Tromp". In: *De nieuwe taalgids* 61 (1968), *W.A.P. Smit-nummer*, S. 115.)

82. A. N. Paasman, "J. F. Martinet en de literatuur". In: *De nieuwe taalgids* 63 (1970), S. 9; vgl. auch Bert Paasman, *J.F. Martinet: Een Zutphens filosoof in de achttiende eeuw*, Zutphen 1971, S. 57/58.

die Begriffsbestimmung. Man hat den Eindruck, dass die bei Knuvelder bereits festgestellte "Verdinglichung" des Begriffs sich in den letzten Jahrzehnten weiter durchsetzt. Es hat den Anschein, dass das Wort Präromantik oft weniger eine Anzahl Übergangserscheinungen und Übergangsgestalten als eine Periode sui generis charakterisiert, eine Periode mit eigenen dominierenden Zügen, eingebettet zwischen Klassizismus und Romantik. In diesem Zusammenhang halte ich es für bezeichnend, dass man sich oft nicht mit einer vagen zeitlichen Begrenzung begnügt, sondern einen konkreten fixierbaren Anfangspunkt für die Präromantik entdecken will.[83] Man kann sogar Formulierungen finden, die die Vermutung nahelegen, dass der Autor eigentlich auf der Suche nach einer neuen Übergangsphase ist, jetzt zwischen Klassizismus und Präromantik.[84]

Der niederländische Literaturhistoriker pflegt sich als Erforscher einer kleinen Literatur beim Entwurf von historischen Einteilungen in hohem Masse den herrschenden Klassifikationen aus den "grossen" Literaturen anzuschliessen. Diesem Verfahren ist man, wie die obenstehende Übersicht zeigt, auch bei der Charakterisierung der Literatur der zweiten Hälfte des achtzehnten Jahrhunderts gefolgt. Da nun im Ausland, namentlich in dem Land, wo die Benennung geprägt wurde, ernstliche formelle und inhaltliche Bedenken gegen das Konzept vorgebracht werden, ist die Frage berechtigt, ob auch die niederländische Literaturforschung die Präromantik-Konzeption nicht einer Prüfung unterziehen und sie vielleicht durch das, was ich einfachheitshalber die Aufklärungs-Konzeption nennen möchte, ersetzen sollte. Geschieht Gestalten wie van Goens, van Alphen und Feith nicht mehr recht, wenn man sie als niederländische Vertreter der "späten Aufklärung" betrachtet, als wenn man diese Autoren aufgrund der

83. Ich nenne ein Beispiel aus neuester Zeit: P. J. Buijnsters behauptet in bezug auf van Alphens *Klaagzang* (1775): "Maar niet alleen voor Van Alphen zelf doch ook voor de nederlandse letteren betekende de publikatie van dit gedicht een gewichtig keerpunt: de eigenlijke doorbraak van de preromantiek, waartoe R. M. van Goens en anderen omstreeks 1766 al de theoretische grondslagen hadden gelegd." (*Hieronymus van Alphen (1746-1803)*, Assen 1973, S. 75.)
84. So behauptet G. A. Steffens, *Pieter Nieuwland en het evenwicht*, Zwolle o.J., S.292, man könne Nieuwland "tot de groep 'jongeren' die de overgang hebben doorgemaakt van het classicisme naar de préromantiek" rechnen.

anfechtbaren Antithese Vernunft-Gefühl auf das Prädikat Präromantiker festlegt? Man könnte einwenden, dass die Lage in den Niederlanden sich nicht mit der ausländischen vergleichen lässt, weil um 1770/1780 deutliche Veränderungen im Vergleich zur vorangehenden Periode wahrnehmbar sind. Ich leugne diese Veränderungen nicht: mit den Literaturhistorikern des neunzehnten Jahrhunderts kann man sehr wohl von einer Auflebung oder Erneuerung sprechen. Es fragt sich nur, ob diese Veränderungen nun unbedingt unter das Banner der (Prä)romantik gestellt werden müssen. In dieser Periode verliert die niederländische Literatur einen Teil ihres provinzlerischen Charakters, sie holt, sowohl in der Theoriebildung wie in der literarischen Praxis, in kurzer Zeit einen Teil des beträchtlichen Rückstandes, den man im Vergleich zum Ausland erlitten hatte, nach. Ein einigermassen internationales Niveau wird erreicht. Van Goens, sagt Knuvelder nach dem Vorgang Willes, ist der Mann, "die Nederland uit zijn zelfgenoegzaamheid in de stroom van het Europese denken en dichten wist te dwingen."[85] Das scheint mir eine vorzügliche Typisierung, aber ich kann mich nicht mit dem Gedanken anfreunden, dass diese Mündigkeit als Präromantik gedeutet wird. Wenn man die Auflebung als Präromantik bewertet, macht man m.E. einen, übrigens begreiflichen, Taxierungsfehler. Wenn ich recht sehe, ist dieser Taxierungsfehler auf ein gewisses Unbehagen, das der niederländischen Literaturforschung aus der Romantikforschung geblieben ist, zurückzuführen. Knuvelders Einführungen in die Romantik mögen noch so ausführlich sein, die niederländische Romantik macht nach wie vor einen äusserst kläglichen Eindruck — sie hat, wie Brom es ausdrückt, mehr geflattert als sich im Flug erhoben.[86] Ist die Unterstellung zu kühn, dass man, in Ermangelung einer vollwertigen niederländischen Romantik, sich umso eifriger — und darin durch die Annektierungsversuche im Ausland angeregt und unterstützt — auf die Suche nach vermeintlichen Vorläufern im achtzehnten Jahrhundert gemacht hat?

Präromantik oder Spätaufklärung? Es scheint eine rein terminologische Angelegenheit, aber es ist im Grunde eine Wahl zwischen einer Bewertung der zweiten Hälfte des achtzehnten Jahrhunderts ent-

85. G. Knuvelder, *Handboek...* Bd. 3, 's-Hertogenbosch 1959[2], S. 63.
86. Gerard Brom, *Romantiek en katholicisme in Nederland,* Bd. 2, Groningen usw., 1926, S. 367.

weder aus romantischer Sicht oder aus der Sicht des achtzehnten Jahrhunderts selbst. Meiner Meinung nach ist schon viel gewonnen, wenn man einsieht, dass es für jenen so einleuchtenden aber irreführenden Begriff Präromantik eine Alternative gibt.

EINE SEITE JEAN PAUL

J.C. Brandt Corstius (Utrecht)

I

Auf Seite 647 des zweiten Bandes von Jean Pauls Werken (Ed. München 1959) steht die bekannte Stelle aus Nr. 13 des ersten Teils der *Flegeljahre,* in der dargestellt wird, wie der verloren geglaubte Vult seinen Zwillingsbruder Gottwalt auf den Augenblick vorbereitet, da er ihm seinen Namen nennen wird. Über die doppelte Hauptperson des Romans und ihre innere Beziehung ist vieles geschrieben worden. Es ist nicht meine Absicht, dem etwas hinzuzufügen. Herman Meyer hat, meiner Ansicht nach, die befriedigendste Deutung dieses Verhältnisses gegeben.[1] Ich möchte hier lediglich einige Bemerkungen über den abbildenden Charakter der Sprache in einem kleinen Stück Prosa Jean Pauls machen und weiter etwas über den literarhistorischen Kontext der Stelle sagen.

Wenn der Leser auf Seite 647 angelangt ist, hat er schon die Art und Weise kennenlernen können, wie Vult die Regie führt und den Handlungsverlauf inszeniert, der zu seiner Erkennung führen wird. Völlig der Berechnung seines Bruders entsprechend hat Gottwalt an der Tür desselben Wirtshauses angeklopft, in dem der ihm noch unbekannte nächste Verwandte schon eingekehrt war, und um Unterkunft für die Nacht gebeten. Vult schlägt vor, zusammen das Abendessen einzunehmen, aber vorher noch zum Friedhof zu gehen und dort zu spazieren, wo die aus der Emigration zurückgekehrten Herrnhutter begraben liegen; der Friedhof befindet sich ein wenig höher ausserhalb ihres Geburtsortes. Dort wird er bei Sonnenuntergang etwas auf

Dieser Aufsatz wurde aus dem Niederländischen übersetzt von J. Verbaas.
1. 'Vor allem scheint es uns abwegig, Vult als eine blosse Komplementärbildung zu Walt aufzufassen, wie sehr die Entstehungsgeschichte des Romans auch dafür zu sprachen scheint'. – 'Sind die Brüder einander polar zugeordnet, so bilden sie andererseits zusammen einen Doppelpol der verknöcherten und hartherzigen 'Wirklichkeit' der Philister gegenüber'. Herman Meyer, *Zarte Empirie, Studien zur Literaturgeschichte,* Stuttgart, 1963, S. 71.

seiner Flöte spielen (und so die einer brüderlichen Umarmung ange-
messene Atmosphäre hervorrufen). Gottwalt nimmt diesen Vorschlag
dankbar an. Sommerabend auf dem Lande und Flötenmusik – die
Rührung füllt schon im voraus sein Gemüt. Aufs neue werden in
dieser Weise die Jean Paulschen Ingredienzen, die eine erhabene Stimmung heraufbeschwören müssen, gesammelt: die landschaftliche
Natur, der erhöhte Standpunkt des Betrachters, ein tiefbewegtes
Herz und die Töne einer Flöte.

Der Erzähler von Vults Aktivitäten, denen sich Gottwalt in freudi-
ger Bereitschaft anschliessen will, ist selber als Sprachschöpfer nicht
weniger eifrig damit beschäftigt, die Regie zu führen und zu inszenie-
ren, um den gleichen Zweck zu erreichen. Er ist bestrebt, die Situationen und Begebenheiten seiner Erzählung sprachlich derart zu
gestalten, dass der Leser Verbindungen legt, die ihn auf Begriffe
verweisen, die sich, sei es positiv oder negativ, auf das Phänomen
Zwilling beziehen. Die Verbindung von zwei Wörtern oder Wortgruppen durch das beiordnende 'und' ist ihres häufigen Vorkommens
wegen in diesem Zwillingsroman eine 'normale' Stilform. Ihr abbil-
dender Wert bleibt nichtsdestoweniger gültig wie das Bildnis auf einer
Münze. Etwas ungewöhnlicher ist die Tatsache, dass der Erzähler in
dem Teil von Nr. 13, welcher der Stelle auf Seite 647 vorangeht, die
Anzahl dieser 'Sprachzwillinge' hoch hinauftreibt und sie des öfteren
durch Alliteration, gleiche Silbenzahl und Endreim akzentuiert. Diese
gesteigerte Frequenz einer viel vorkommenden Verbindung bildet
den Hintergrund, vor welchem in diesem vorangehenden Teil Einzelheiten der Erzählung und ihre Kombination durch ihren sprachlichen
Aspekt die Aufmerksamkeit lenken auf gegenseitige Beziehungen,
Gleichheit, Verdopplung, Identität, Teil und Gegenteil, Einheit und
Zweiheit, Separat und Zusammen.

Die Gaststube des Wirtshauses, in dem Gottwalt einkehrt und
Vult auf seine Ankunft gewartet hat, wird 'Korrelationssaal und
Simultanzimmer der Gäste' genannt. Gottwalt tritt ein und bittet
sofort um ein Einzelzimmer, 'eine einmännige Stube'. Einen Augenblick später erscheint Vult und sagt, dass er sich 'des gemeinschaftli-
chen Übernachtens' erfreue. Gottwalt hat nicht nur um ein Einzelzimmer gebeten, sondern auch eine 'dergleichen Abendmahlzeit'
bestellt. Vult schlägt ihm aber vor, zusammen zu soupieren. Das
einzige Zimmer, das der Wirt noch für Gottwalt verfügbar hat, sieht
sonderbar aus: es zeigt sich, dass die westliche Aussenwand einge-

201

stürzt ist. Die Trümmer liegen ein Stockwerk tiefer, aber dort liegen auch Steine und Kalk zur Reparatur bereit. Der Erzähler führt darüber folgendermassen das Wort: '...war die Abendwand nicht sowohl ganz zerstört — denn sie lag ein Stockwerk tiefer unten in ziemlichen Stücken — als wahrhaft verdoppelt — denn die neue lag als Stein und Kalk unten darneben —.' In Vults Interpretation wird der Planet Venus sofort 'Hesper und Luzifer'. Der phantasievolle Gottwalt sieht in dem ihm noch unbekannten anderen Gast einen vornehmen Herrn und deshalb wird (mit einem Worte im Geiste Morgensterns) der grüne Hut seines neues Bekannten ein 'Gegenhut', nämlich der 'eines Bischofs, der einen nur innen grünen und aussen schwarzen trägt'. Der Wirt kommt mit einer Schiefertafel und einem anhängenden Griffel herangelaufen, damit seine Gäste ihre Namen eintragen können. Die materielle Gleichheit beider Instrumente soll betont werden: Vult schreibt einen Namen 'auf den Schiefer mit Schiefer', es ist nicht der seinige, sondern derjenige seines Bruders. Sogar die Tautologie wird nicht gescheut: Vult nennt die Querflöte 'Die wahre Mondachse des innern Monds''. Und sobald sie auf dem Friedhof angekommen sind, werden die Zwillingsbrüder mittels einer auktorialen Bemerkung ohne Umwege in 'Reim' verwandelt: 'Hätte Vult zehn Meilen umher nach einem schönen Postamente für eine Gruppe Zwillings-brüderlicher Erkennung gesucht, ein besseres hätt' er schwerlich aufgetrieben, als der Herrnhuter Totengarten war mit seinen flachen Beeten, worin Gärtner aus Amerika, Asia und Barby gesäet waren, die sich alle aufeinander mit dem schönen Lebens-*Endreim* 'heimgegangen' reimten'.

Nachdem nun der Leser mittels des ungetrennten Wie und Was der Erzählung über die Vorbereitungen des 'moment suprême' der Erkennung unterrichtet worden ist, beginnt die letzte Phase und zwar diejenige, in der das Gemüt Gottwalts sowohl durch die Szene (abendliche Landschaft) wie die Regie (Flötenmusik) mächtig ergriffen wird. Aber auch Vult ist doch so sehr an der Situation und an dem, was geschehen wird, beteiligt, dass er nur einfache Melodien mit hineingestreuten Echos spielen kann. Er hofft, dass sie seinem Bruder angenehm in den Ohren klingen werden. Dies ist tatsächlich der Fall.

'Sie tatens auch. Immer langsamer ging Gottwalt, mit einem langen Kirschzweige in der Hand, zwischen der Morgen- und Abend-Gegend auf und nieder. Seliger als nie in seinem trocknen Leben war er, als er auf die liebäugelnde Rosen-Sonne losging und über ein breites goldgrünes Land mit Turmspitzen in Obstwäldern und in das glatte weisse Mutterdorf der schlafenden stummen Kolonisten hineinsah, und wenn dann die Zephyre der Melodien die duftige Landschaft wehend aufzublättern und zu bewegen schienen. Kehrt' er sich um, mit gefärbtem Blick, nach dem Osthimmel und sah die Ebene voll grüner auf- und ablaufender Hügel wie Landhäuser und Rotunden stehen und den Schwung der Laubholzwälder auf den fernen Bergen und den Himmel in ihre Windungen eingesenkt: so lagen und spielten die Töne wieder drüben auf den roten Höhen und zuckten in den vergoldeten Vögeln, die wie Aurorens Flocken umherschwammen, und weckten an einer düstern schlafenden Morgenwolke die lebendigen Blicke aufgehender Blitze auf. Vom Gewitter wandt' er sich wieder gegen das vielfarbige Sonnenland — ein Wehen von Osten trug die Töne — schwamm mit ihnen an die Sonne — auf den blühenden Abendwolken sang das kleine Echo, das liebliche Kind, die Spiele leise nach. — Die Lieder der Lerchen flogen gaukelnd dazwischen und störten nichts. —

Jetzt brannte und zitterte in zartem Umriss eine Obstallee durchsichtig und riesenhaft in der Abendglut — schwer und schlummernd schwamm die Sonne auf ihrem Meer — es zog sie hinunter — ihr goldner Heiligenschein glühte fort im leeren Blau — und die Echotöne schwebten und starben auf dem Glanz: Da kehrte sich jetzt Vult, mit der Flöte am Munde, nach dem Bruder um und sah es, wie er hinter ihm stand, von den Scharlachflügeln der Abendröte und der gerührten Entzückung überdeckt und mit blödem stillen Weinen im blauen Auge. — Die heilige Musik zeigt den Menschen eine Vergangenheit und eine Zukunft, die sie nie erleben.'

An dieser Stelle bewegt sich der Roman auf dem Stilniveau, das Herman Meyer als 'Hochebene' bezeichnet hat in seiner Betrachtung des Themas von *Flegeljahre* als Sprachdynamik, die auf dem Kontrast zwischen zwei Stilniveaus beruht.[2] Er stellt fest, dass diese stilistische Hochebene vorzugsweise das Gebiet ist, in dem das Erleben der landschaftlichen Natur und das ekstatisch bewegte Gemütsleben dargestellt werden; dies geschieht meistens zusammen, weil in der Darstellung der einen sich das andere widerspiegelt.[3] Musik, die dabei gewöhnlich nicht fehlt, verleiht diesem Erleben einen besonderen Charakter. Sie dient nämlich nicht als Umrahmung einer Situation zur Intensivierung dieses gefühlvollen Zustandes, wie man etwa geglaubt hat,[4] sondern ist Katalysator in dem sich in diesem Erleben vollzie-

2. a.a.O., S. 63.
3. a.a.O., S. 73f.
4. 'Es entspricht nun wieder der musikalischen Konzeption Jean Pauls, dass er die ergreifende Erkennungsszene zwischen den beiden Zwillingsbrüdern musikalisch umrahmt'. Johannes Mittenzwei, *Das Musikalische in der Literatur, ein Überblick von Gottfried von Strassburg bis Brecht,* Halle (Saale), 1962, S. 101.

henden Prozess, worin die zeit-räumlichen Grenzen verschwimmen. Die Gegenwart löst sich in Vergangenheit und Zukunft auf, und die Umrisse der Landschaft geraten in eine Wellenbewegung.

Der erhabene Stil ist im angeführten Textfragment mit viel inhaltlicher Information verbunden durch die Art und Weise, wie die Darstellung von Gottwalts äusseren und inneren Bewegungen Sprache ist. Die grammatische Form eines jeden Satzes ist einfach, und genauso ist es um das gegenseitige Verhältnis der Sätze in grammatischer Hinsicht bestellt. Es werden oft die gleichen formalen Verbindungen gelegt, die durch ihre Wiederholung innerhalb der Übersichtlichkeit der Konstruktionen in ihrem abbilden Wert überaus wirksam sind.

II

Jean Paul schrieb *Flegeljahre* und *Vorschule der Aesthetik* in derselben Zeit; er schob die ästhetisch-theoretische Schrift, Niederschlag langjährigen Denkens und Notierens, zwischen den dritten und vierten Teil des Romans. Und beide Werke sind nicht unabhängig voneinander.

In mehreren Paragraphen der *Vorschule* formuliert Jean Paul seine Gedanken über die Sprache, und dies tut er nicht auf eine abstrakte Weise. Er fängt mit seiner Grammatik an: Verben — intransitive und transitive , ihre Präfixe, ihre Zusammenfügung mit Adverbien — Substantive und Kombinationen von Substantiven, Adjektive, Adverbien, Präpositionen, Kasus usw. Die einfachsten Sprachelemente ('Ja geht nicht alles so ins Kleinste. . .? ')[5] erhalten seine ehrerbietige wie scharfsinnige Aufmerksamkeit, denn sie 'winden. . . die tiefste Welt der Gefühle aus dem Herzen empor'.[6]

Der Romanschriftsteller Jean Paul ist bemüht, die literarische Wirklichkeit, die er schafft, so konkret darzustellen, dass sie gleichsam sinnlich erlebt werden kann. Stil ist seiner Meinung nach Präsentation. Die Möglichkeiten dieser Konkretisierung sieht er in der Sprache selber vorhanden, der Dichter solle sie nur ausfindig machen. Jean Paul illustriert seine Erörterung über diesen Gegenstand mit einer Anzahl Beispielen von 'Sinnlichkeit des Stils', und die Art und Weise, wie er dies tut, ist selber musterhaft.[7] Seine Betrachtung ist

5. *Vorschule der Ästhetik, Werke V,* ed. München, 1963, S. 282.
6. a.a.O., S. 283.
7. Siehe die Paragraphen 77 und 78, a.a.O., S. 278-283.

vor allem aus diesem Grunde interessant; seine Exempla sind grammatischer Natur: er empfiehlt, Abstrakta so viel wie möglich zu vermeiden, das Aktivum zu gebrauchen, das 'participium praesentis' vorzuziehen und Wörter sowie Umschreibungen zu wählen, die eine Handlung und Bewegung ausdrücken und die Vorstellungen scharf umreissen und abrunden.

Mit seinen Bemerkungen über die grammatischen Aspekte des literarischen Textes, welche der Sinnlichkeit der Präsentation dienen sollen, bleibt Jean Paul in der Tradition der Sprachwissenschaft des achtzehnten Jahrhunderts, die sich namentlich den Wortarten zuwandte, oftmals von etymologischem Gesichtspunkt aus. Aber er wäre Jean Paul nicht gewesen, wenn er auch in dieser Tradition nicht auf qualitativ hohem Niveau gestanden hätte, wie aus seinem feinen Sinn für Wortwerte und der Überzeugungskraft und dem Humor seiner Beispiele erhellt.

Bemerkungen über die Syntax macht er nur, wenn er über Wortzusammensetzungen schreibt. Eine Ausnahme bildet eine Stelle — mit Beispielen — über die Präpositionen, die im Deutschen sowohl den dritten als den vierten Kasus regieren und im letzteren Fall seiner Ansicht nach den räumlichen Aspekt der Bewegung vor Augen führen.[8] Im übrigen aber bleiben Verbindungen von Wortgruppen und Sätzen ausser Betracht, was sehr merkwürdig für einen Schriftsteller ist, der, ebenso wie Sterne, wegen der Form seiner Sätze berühmt war und ist. Über den Satz schreibt Jean Paul kaum. Einmal sagt er, dass der Schriftsteller aus Achtung vor seinem Leser einen langen Satz zwanzig kurzen Sätzen vorziehen solle, um diesem die Mühe der Rekonstruktion zu ersparen.[9] Ein anderes Mal schreibt er, dass der Gegenstand die andauernde Abwechslung der Satzlänge und der Stellung der Wörter bestimme.[10]

In seiner Monographie über Jean Paul unterscheidet Max Kommerell im Werke dieses Dichters zwischen zwei Grundformen des Satzbaus: dem Satz, dessen erstes Glied aus einer Reihe einleitender Sätze besteht, die alle auf den letzten Teil der Periode verweisen, und dem Satz, der sich aus mehreren durch Bindestriche getrennten Hauptsätzen zusammensetzt. Beide Formen stehen nach Kommerell

8. a.a.O., S. 281.
9. a.a.O., S. 319.
10. a.a.O., S. 485.

unter dem Primat der Idee der Gleichheit von Seele und Natur. Er spricht in diesem Zusammenhang über die 'Grammatik als eine Ordnung der Kräfte und einen Zustand der Seele', und über grammatische Spannung als den Zustand, in dem Seele und Natur voneinander getrennt sind.[11] Diese Spannung herrscht namentlich im ersten Satztypus, in dem ein jeder der beiden Teile der Periode sowohl die Seele wie die Natur repräsentieren kann. Sie bilden diese Begriffe nicht ab, sondern haben sie — gegenseitig austauschbar — zum Inhalt. Von dieser geisteshistorischen Betrachtung von Jean Pauls Syntax ist die Idee, dass Ausdruck und Inhalt einander wechselseitig bestimmen, weit entfernt; mit anderen Worten: die informative Funktion der grammatischen Form lag ausserhalb ihres Blickfeldes.

Vier Satzperioden bilden zusammen nahezu das ganze angeführte Textfragment. Davon gehören zwei zum ersten Kommerell-Typus, eine zum zweiten, und die Periode, die dann übrig bleibt, kombiniert die Verbindungen durch Bindestriche und die so entstandenen Verbindungen ihrerseits durch Konjunktionen. Letzteres trifft jedenfalls zu, wenn man den Doppelpunkt hinter 'Glanz' trotz des grossen Anfangs-Buchstabens von 'Da' nicht als das Ende des Satzes auffasst. Tut man dies doch, so haben wir es mit fünf langen Sätzen zu tun, von denen drei den zuerstgenannten Typus vertreten und zwei die Bindestriche enthalten.

Der zweite und dritte Satz des Textfragments (die mit 'Seliger als nie...' bzw. 'Kehrt' er sich um...' beginnen) nehmen zusammen gut vierzig Prozent von allen Wörtern des Textes ein. Dieses Paar weist in seiner inneren Beziehung eine Umkehrung der Reihenfolge Hauptsatz (— sätze) — Nebensatz (— sätze) auf. Seine aufeinanderfolgenden Nebensätze werden durch 'und' beiordnend verbunden. Das gleiche gilt für die Aufeinanderfolge der Hauptsätze im dritten Satz. Die vorherrschende Nebenordnung in beiden Sätzen ist also in den Rahmen einer in sich entgegengesetzten Unterordnung gestellt.

Nebenordnung liegt späterhin in uneingeschränktem Masse in den zwei (eventuell drei) übrigen Sätzen vor und wird zudem grösstenteils durch Bindestriche visuell akzentuiert.

Der häufige Gebrauch der Konjunktion 'und' ist, wie schon bemerkt wurde, ein stilistisches Merkmal von *Flegeljahre*. Die Tatsache, dass Gleichheit und Unterschied — der Zwilling als Sprachform —

---

11. Max Kommerell, *Jean Paul,* Frankfurt am Main, 1957[3] (1933[1]), S. 38f.

durch Nebenordnung miteinander verbunden sind, beherrscht die Präsentation bis in die Einzelheiten, zuweilen so überschwenglich, dass dann eine gewisse Eintönigkeit auftritt. Im zitierten Textfragment hat 'und' gleichfalls das Übergewicht über die anderen Verbindungen. Ausser der obenerwähnten satzkonstruktiven Funktion hat es die weitere Funktion, für eine paarweise Wortgruppierung zu sorgen. Dies geschieht in auffälliger Weise bei den Prädikaten mit demselben Subjekt: 'losging . . . und hineinsah', 'aufzublättern und zu bewegen schienen', 'kehrt' er sich um . . . und sah', 'lagen und spielten', '. . . und zuckten . . . und weckten', 'flogen . . . und störten', 'brannte und zitterte', 'kehrte sich . . . und sah', 'schwebten und starben'. Sie nehmen gut fünfzig Prozent von den Prädikaten im Text ein. Eine paarweise Gruppierung mittels 'und' finden wir auch bei den Substantiven: 'Morgen- und Abend-Gegend', 'Landhäuser und Rotunden', '. . . der Abendröte und der Entzückung', 'eine Vergangenheit und eine Zukunft'; ebenfalls bei Adjektiven: 'auf- und ablaufender Hügel', 'durchsichtig und riesenhaft'; und bei Adverbien: 'auf und nieder', 'schwer und schlummernd'.

Auch andere Verbindungen als 'und' bilden Paare; das Asyndeton bei attributiven Adjektiven: 'breites goldgrünes Land', 'in das glatte weisse Mutterdorf', 'schlafenden stummen Kolonisten', 'grüner auf- und ablaufender Hügel', 'düstern schlafenden Morgenwolke', 'blödem stillen Weinen'; Genitivkonstruktionen: 'Mutterdorf der . . . Kolonisten', 'Zephyre der Melodien', 'Schwung der Laubholzwälder', 'Aurorens Flocken', 'Blicke aufgehender Blitze', 'Lieder der Lerchen', 'Scharlachflügeln der Abendröte und der gerührten Entzückung'; ferner die vielen aus zwei Substantiven zusammengesetzten Hauptwörter. Auch die präpositionalen Bestimmungen haben die Funktion, Paare zu bilden. Die Anzahl dieser Wortgruppen ist gross (vierunddreissig) und beträgt vierzig Prozent von allen Wörtern der diesbezüglichen Sätze. Viel mehr als die Hälfte steht in Paaren. Einige Beispiele: 'mit einem langen Kirschzweige in der Hand', 'in Obstwäldern und in das glatte weisse Mutterdorf', 'mit gefärbtem Blick, nach dem Osthimmel', 'Vom Gewitter . . . gegen das vielfarbige Sonnenland', 'in zartem Umriss. . . in der Abendglut'.

Aus diesen Beispielen von Verbindungen im Textfragment zeigt sich der informative Wert dieser syntagmatischen Elemente. Der syntaktische Unterschied, der zwischen dem zweiten und dritten Satz besteht, bildet eine Anzahl räumlich inversiver Bewegungen ab: den hin und her gehenden Gottwalt, die Umkehrung seiner Blickrichtung (nach unten, nach oben) und die Umkehrung des Ortes (westlich, östlich) und des Niveaus (nieder, hoch) der Melodie-Aktivität. Die Verbindungen von Wörtern und Wortgruppen zu Paaren bilden eine Verbundenheit als Paar in Gleichwertigkeit wie im Gegensatz ab, das heisst sowohl das gegenseitige Verhältnis der Zwillingsbrüder Gottwalt und Vult als auch das Echo.

Der zweite und dritte Satz des Textfragments weisen in bezug auf ihre innere Gliederung zwei parallele Satzpaare auf, in denen semantische Äquivalenz vorliegt, die einen abbildenden Wert hat: 1) 'als er auf die liebäugelnde Rosen-Sonne losging'/'Kehrt' er sich um, mit gefärbtem Blick, nach dem Osthimmel'; 2) 'und über ein breites goldgrünes Land mit Turmspitzen in Obstwäldern und in das glatte weisse Mutterdorf der schlafenden stummen Kolonisten im Garten hineinsah'/'und sah die Ebene voll grüner auf- und ablaufender Hügel wie Landhäuser und Rotunden stehen und den Schwung der Laubholzwälder auf den fernen Bergen und den Himmel in ihre Windungen eingesenkt'.

Im ersten Paar korrespondieren 'die liebäugelnde Rosen-Sonne' und 'gefärbtem Blick' mit den Äquivalenten 'Auge' und 'Blick', 'Rosen' und 'gefärbtem'. Es ist eine Korrespondenz der Rückstrahlung. Das zweite Paar hat die Gruppen 'ein breites goldgrünes Land' und 'die Ebene voll grüner. . .'; 'Turmspitzen, Mutterdorf' und 'Landhäuser und Rotunden'; 'Obstwäldern' und 'Laubholzwälder'. Sie deuten auf Übereinstimmung hin und bilden zugleich, vielfach in Kombination der Paare, Gegenparteien. Im Fall 'Turmspitzen, Mutterdorf' und 'Landhäuser und Rotunden' haben wir es mit Wörtern für Bauten zu tun, die mit den Wörtern für Naturobjekte in denselben Sätzen kontrastieren (etwas vom Gegensatz: künstlich-natürlich finden wir auch in 'Obstwäldern/Laubholzwälder'). Von einer Verbindung zwischen Kultur und Natur ist ausserdem die Rede im Vergleich 'auf- und ablaufender Hügel wie Landhäuser und Rotunden'. Eine ähnliche Verbindung lässt sich im letzten Satz des Teils vor dem neuen Absatz ('Die Lieder der Lerchen') nachweisen. Ferner stehen die semantisch aufeinander bezogenen finiten Verbalformen 'hineinsah' und 'sah' in den entsprechenden Sätzen in Opposition (Satzende, Satzanfang), genauso wie die dadurch bezeichnete Blickrichtung (nach unten, nach oben) und die Grössenordnung der angeschauten Objekte. Rückstrahlung, Gegenüberstellung und Zusammengehörigkeit, Umkehrung der Richtung, Gegenpartei: Echo.

Auch zwischen dem dritten Satz des Textfragments und dem Satz (oder dem zweiten Teil des Satzes) im neuen Absatz, der mit 'Da' beginnt, bestehen Übereinstimmungen, die als solche informativ sind. Es betrifft die syntaktisch identische Reihe: 'kehrte sich um – mit – nach – und sah', und die Reihe semantischer Äquivalente: 'roten Höhen, zuckten, vergoldeten Vögeln, Blicke, Blitze/Scharlachflügeln, Abendröte, Entzückung, Auge'. Beide Brüder bewegen sich auf gleiche Weise und in der gleichen Richtung, und es stellt sich heraus, dass, was jeder dann sieht, dank der gemeinsamen Tätigkeit des Auges des einen und des Mundes des andern, verwandt ist. Gottwalt und Vult gleichen einander, und Gottwalt und die Welt, die ihn umringt, sind eins, da beide durch die Abendröte gefärbt und durch die Töne von Vults Flöte gerührt werden. Aber die Wendung 'kehrte sich um', die dazu beiträgt, den zwei Brüdern das Gepräge der Gleichheit zu geben, macht sie auch verschieden. In bezug auf Gottwalt bezeichnen diese Worte eine Bewegung, die wiederholt wird und dabei seinem gerührten Erlebnis der durch die Musik bewegten Landschaft untergeordnet ist (Satzzusammenhang). Dieselben Wörte beziehen sich auf eine gleiche Bewegung von Vult, die er jedoch nur einmal, aber dann auch entschlossen macht, und die einigermassen dezisiv ist ('Da', durch 'jetzt' verstärkt) in Übereinstimmung mit dem 'Jetzt', womit der neue Absatz einsetzt: es wird etwas geschehen, das das Vorhergehende zu seiner Verwirklichung führt. Der Unterschied wird darauf explizite durch die Gruppe 'mit gefärbtem Blick/ mit der Flöte am Munde' ausgedrückt: der eine erfährt es, der andere aber handelt.

III

Auf Vults Vorschlag hin ist ein Friedhof das Ziel ihres Spaziergangs vor der Mahlzeit. Die Begräbnisstätte als ein Ort gefühlvoller Erholung hat um 1800 schon ein langes und reiches Leben in der empfindsamen Literatur des achtzehnten Jahrhunderts hinter sich. In jener Zeit hatte diese Literatur, wenn es sich um das Grab und den Friedhof handelte, die Beziehungen zu nichtfiktiven Texten über diese Gegenstände – auch wenn die Beziehungen immer lockerer wurden – aufrechterhalten: das christliche Traktat und die Predigt über Sterben und Tod, Vergänglichkeit und ewiges Leben, Sünde und Erlösung. Der literarische Spaziergang zwischen den Gräbern war der Umgang mit dem steinernen Lese- und Bilderbuch der Embleme des Todes. Dies galt in gleichem Masse dem Spaziergänger, der von seiten

des Erzählers die Erlaubnis bekam, seinen dabei ausgelösten Gemüts-
erregungen ihren freien Lauf zu lassen, wie seinem Gefährten, der in
dieser Hinsicht die vererbten Reserven wahren musste. Denn ersterem
wurde ja oft genug die Neigung zugewiesen, die landschaftliche
Natur mit emblematischen Aufschriften und architektonischen Konstruktionen zu versehen, die Gedanken und Gefühle hervorrufen sollten. Schliesslich bekommen in der empfindsamen Literatur der Friedhof und der Friedhofsspaziergang eine Aufgabe in der Darstellung der
Gemütsverfassung eines lyrischen Ichs oder eines Romanhelden zuge-
teilt. Das klassische Beispiel dieser Funktion ist der Dezember-Kirch-
hof von Wahlheim in Goethes *Werther*. Mit einer deutlichen Anspie-
lung auf diesen Briefroman — 'Leiden des jungen Walts', so lautet teil-
weise der Titel von Nr. 55 — manipuliert Jean Paul dreissig Jahre später
in der gleichen Weise mit der letzten Ruhestätte der Herrnhuter. Wenn
gegen Ende der *Flegeljahre* Gottwalt sich von Vult verlassen fühlt, ist
der Platz, wo einmal 'die Sonne unter- und der Bruder aufging' an
einem dunklen Nachmittag im November ein düsterer Ort geworden:
'. . .die Bäume waren, anstatt begrabne Gerippe laubig zu bedecken,
selber steilrechte geworden — dabei schneiete es regnerisch — mehr
das Gewölke als die Sonne ging unter — und Abend und Nacht waren
schwer zu sondern' (S. 967).

Das nach S. 647 zitierte Textfragment stellt einen stark ergriffe-
nen Gottwalt dar, der das Romantische im Sinne Jean Pauls erlebt:
das Schöne ohne Begrenzung. Himmel und Erde, Morgen und Abend
gehen ineinander über und verschmelzen in eins. Der Himmel liegt
zwischen den Bergen versunken, der Morgen ist finster und voller
Schlaf, der Abend ein farbig blühendes Sonnenland. In dieser durch
die Musik bewegten Welt ist der Friedhof ein Garten — 'der schlafenden stummen Kolonisten im Garten.' Und der Leser weiss es, denn
auf der vorangehenden Seite hat der Erzähler, indem er mit dem
Wort 'Gottesacker' spielte, die Begräbnisstätte der Herrnhuter bei
ihm eingeführt als einen Garten, in dessen Beete gesäet worden ist,
wo das Leben keimt — 'der Herrnhuter Totengarten mit seinen flachen Beeten' und 'Um jedes stille Beet mit seinem Saat-Herzen lebten
treue Bäume, und die ganze lebende Natur sah mit ihrem jungen
Angesicht herein' (S. 646). Gottwalt und Vult befinden sich an
einem Ort, wo Leben und Tod, Anfang und Ende, Vergangenheit und
Zukunft untrennbar sind. Das Friedhof-Motiv hat auch hier seine alte
Funktion aus der Zeit der empfindsamen Literatur behalten. Es ist

wirksam in der Darstellung des seelischen Empfindens eines der beiden Romanhelden.

Aber dasselbe Motiv erhält hier gleichzeitig eine neue Funktion. Der Friedhof ist nicht nur Begräbnisstätte, er ist auch der Ort, wo die Echotöne sterben, wie es im Text heisst. Somit der Ort der romantischen Poesie: 'So ist z.B. die Musik romantische Poesie durch das Ohr. Diese als das Schöne ohne Begrenzung wird weniger von dem Auge vorgespiegelt, dessen Grenzen sich nicht so unbestimmbar wie die eines sterbenden Tons verlieren'.[12] Und das gleiche bezieht sich in einer anderen und gleichsam direkteren Weise auf Gottwalt: 'Es ist noch ähnlicher als ein Gleichnis, wenn man das Romantische das wogende Aussummen einer Saite oder Glocke nennt, in welchem die Tonwoge wie in immer fernerer Weiten verschwimmt und endlich sich verliert in uns selber und, obwohl aussen schon still, noch immer lautet'.[13] Da steht also der zu Tränen gerührte Gottwalt. In dieser Verbindung mit dem Romantischen erfahren die herkömmlichen christlichen Elemente des Friedhof-Motivs eine Metamorphose: sie werden zu den von der Musik aufgefangenen Signalen aus Jean Pauls ferner, idealer Welt: 'O Musik! Nachklang aus einer entlegnen harmonischen Welt! Seufzer des Engels in uns!'.[14] Und auch an die Musik gerichtet: 'Ja, deine Laute sind Echo, welche Engel den Freudentönen der zweiten Welt abnehmen...'[15]

Aus der empfindsamen Literatur rührt auch das Gewitter auf dem sommerabendlichen Friedhof her. Anders als zwischen Lotte und Werther fällt zwischen den Brüdern noch gerade nicht der Name Klopstock, aber dieser Dichter ist wohl zugegen. Einige Zeilen nach dem hier angeführten Textfragment fallen Gottwalt und Vult einander weinend in die Arme, nachdem der Flötenspieler seinen Namen genannt hat. 'Es donnerte sanft im Morgen. "Höre unsern guten Allgütigen!" sagte Walt' (S. 648). Gottwalt ist in frommer Stimmung. Vult reagiert nicht auf seinen Ausruf, der ein bisschen einem Gemeinplatz ähnlich sieht, sicher nach der Sprachvirtuosität, womit der Erzähler auch den Blitz handhabt, um Gottwalts erhabene Gefühle darzustellen. Eine finstere schlafende Wolke im Osten wird zum Leben erweckt. Der Leser ist schon etwas eher diesem Worte 'schla-

---

12. *Vorschule*, S. 466.
13. a.a.O., S. 88.
14. *Die unsichtbare Loge, Werke I,* ed. München, 1960, S. 60.
15. *Hesperus oder 45 Hundposttage, Werke I,* ed. München, 1960, S. 950.

fenden' in einer Kombination von zwei attributiven Adjektiven begegnet: 'schlafenden stummen Kolonisten – düstern schlafenden Morgenwolke'. Tod und Auferweckung. Aufs neue finden wir Leben und Tod zusammen, eng verbunden durch Rhythmus und Klang, infolge der Bevorzugung von Satzteilen von dreizehn und vierzehn Silben, die in diesem Textfragment viel vorkommen, und durch Alliteration: 'und weckten an einer düstern schlafenden Morgenwolke die lebendigen Blicke aufgehender Blitze auf'. Zum Leben erweckt aus dem Tode. In der sprachlichen Formgebung eines wahren Daseins, das Gottwalt in diesem Moment erlebt, liegen die Musik und das Göttliche nahe beieinander.

Flegeljahre führt noch eine andere Tradition der empfindsamen Literatur fort. Die Darstellung der landschaftlichen Natur und die Gemütsverfassung des Romanhelden werden immer zueinander in Beziehung gesetzt. Aber auch in diesem Punkte ist bei Jean Paul sowohl von Tradition als von Erneuerung die Rede.

In empfindsamen Texten des achtzehnten Jahrhunderts lag der Relation zwischen Natur und individueller Stimmung oft die Idee zugrunde, dass Sympathie die Kraft sei, die alle Dinge im Weltall wechselseitig zusammenhalte und so verhindere, dass die Welt aus einer unübersichtlichen Menge einzelner Entitäten bestehen würde. Die aussermenschliche Natur teile die Gefühle des Menschen, der deshalb seine Emotionen den Dingen zuweisen könne. Auf diese Weise wurden sie zu Bundesgenossen des Gefühls, miterlebenden Zeugen der Ekstase oder des Untergangs. In der Literatur kommt diese Idee zum Ausdruck in der Gestaltung der landschaftlichen Natur: man glaubte, dass bestimmte Formen, Bewegungen und Beschaffenheiten von Naturobjekten mit bestimmten Gefühlen korrespondierten. Der Friedhof der Herrnhuter, wo Gottwalt durch Flötenspiel bei Sonnenuntergang an einem schönen Abend im Juli gerührt wird, ist, wie wir gesehen haben, anders als derselbe Ort im November, wenn Gottwalt diesen in niedergeschlagener Stimmung noch einmal besuchen wird.

Aber der Zusammenhang zwischen der landschaftlichen Natur und der Gemütsverfassung des Helden ist für Jean Paul auch noch aus einem anderen Grunde wichtig, nämlich der Realisierung der literarischen Landschaft wegen. Dieses strukturelle Sprachproblem beschäftigt ihn. Er behandelt es im vierzehnten Programm der *Vorschule* (Titel: 'Über den Stil oder die Darstellung'), Paragraph 80 'Poetische

Landschaftmalerei'. Nach seiner Auffassung strukturiert das Gefühl der Hauptperson die literarische Landschaft. Es macht dasjenige, was sonst in der Aufeinanderfolge der Dinge eine Reihe einzelner Entitäten geblieben wäre, zu einem zusammenhängendem Ganzen: '. . .aber der poetischen Landschaft, welche nur Einzelnes nach Einzelnem aufbreitet, würde das steigende Ganze völlig mangeln und jede Einzelnheit unbegleitet und nackt dastehen, wenn nicht ein inneres poetisches Ganzes der Empfindung das äussere erstattete und so jedem kleinen Zuge seine Mitgewalt anwiese und gäbe' (S. 289f).

Es geht Jean Paul hier also nicht um die ausserliterarische Korrelation zwischen Gefühl und Natur. Und es ist auch klar, weshalb er den Wert ihrer Beziehung für die literarische Gestaltung besonders beachtet. Er ist der Darsteller des romantischen Gefühls. Und für ihn ist dies eines der Gefühle, die nur auf dem Umwege der sprachlichen Darstellung der Natur, in der sie entstanden sind, in Worte gefasst werden können. 'Es gibt Gefühle der Menschenbrust, welche unaussprechlich bleiben, bis man die ganze körperliche Nachbarschaft der Natur, worin sie wie Düfte entstanden, als Wörter zu ihrer Beschreibung gebraucht' (S. 290). Das hier zitierte Textfragment ist ein Beispiel dieses Prozesses der sprachlichen Gestaltung.

Sobald die zwei Spaziergänger auf dem Friedhof angekommen sind, lässt der Erzähler Gottwalt ein wenig hin und her gehen, während Vult, der sich gegen den Stamm eines Kirschbaumes lehnt, auf seiner Flöte spielt. Gottwalt richtet den Blick abwechselnd auf das Schauspiel des Sonnenuntergangs und auf die dunkel werdende Landschaft im Osten. Die Erzählung kondensiert diese sich wiederholende Handlung Gottwalts zu drei Bewegungen: westwärts, ostwärts, westwärts. Über den Sonnenuntergang bei Flötenmusik wird am meisten erzählt, nicht nur, weil die dreiteilige Komposition von Gottwalts Schlendern ihn zweimal zur Sonne und nur einmal nach Osten schauen lässt, sondern auch, weil es sich im neuen Absatz ausschliesslich um dasjenige, was am westlichen Himmel vor sich geht und dessen Widerschein handelt.

In diesem Konzept der Erzählung spielt die Sonne also eine grosse Rolle. Während ihres Untergangs ändern sich ihre Sprachgestalten. Das erste Mal erscheint sie als 'die liebäugelnde Rosen-Sonne', das zweite Mal als 'die Sonne', die die Landschaft 'vielfarbig' macht und die Wolken 'blühend'; und das dritte, letzte Mal als eine schwere Sonne, schon halb schlafend, schwimmend auf ihrer Glut. Nach ihrem Sinken ist sie heilig. Eine Verwandlung von einer leichten und lieblichen Spielerei über allerhand Aktivitäten in frommen Ernst.

Die Töne von Vults Flöte begleiten den Sonnenuntergang. Sie sind zuerst Zephyre, welche die duftende Landschaft, die unter der 'liebäugelnden Rosen-Sonne' liegt, gleichsam luftig aufwärts bewegen. Danach, im Osten, liegen und spielen sie auf den Hügeln und Bergen in der Abendröte. Die Wendung 'lagen und spielten' hat einen personifizierenden Wert, die Töne der Flöte sind leichte, spielende Geschöpfchen, die Licht und Duft in eine sanfte Wellenbewegung versetzen und die Finsternis funkelnd und flackernd beleben. Aber dann lassen sie sich ihrerseits vom Winde zur Sonne tragen. Danach ist nur noch die Rede vom kleinen Echo, lieblichem Kinde, das leise ihr Spiel wiederholt. Schliesslich verklingt, während die Sonne sinkt, die Musik, ihr Echo schwebt auf einem immer mehr schwindenden Leuchten.

In dieser musikalischen Landschaft geht Gottwalt hin und her. Musikalisch ist hier in zweierlei Sinne zu verstehen, denn Jean Paul teilt einer literarischen Landschaft diese Eigenschaft zu, wenn diese eine Gemütsstimmung darstellt (S. 291). Pendelnd geht das willige Opfer von Vults Arrangements durch die Musik, 'diese Poesie der Luft',[16] eine Formulierung, die in diesem Falle auch zwei Bedeutungen hat, weil die Flöte geblasen wird. Und der 'Äther der Tonkunst' (*Flegeljahre* 1024), in dem alles 'fliegen und kreisen' kann, 'die schwerste Erde, das leichteste Licht, ohne zu begegnen und anzustossen' (id.), ist hier ein liebliches, anmutiges Universum. Die Darstellung weist Elemente der Idylle auf: Rosen, Zephyre, spielende Kinder, Schäfchen, ein anmutiges Liebäugeln, einfache auf der Flöte gespielte Melodien, schwebende Düfte und Klänge.

Es wird aber auch implizite auf diese literarische Gattung verwiesen. Das zwölfte Programm der *Vorschule* ('Über den Roman') enthält im Paragraph 73 Jean Pauls bekannte Betrachtung über die Idylle. Darin stellt er u.a. die Frage, was denn eigentlich den Leser an dieser Gattung Freude erleben lasse. In seiner Antwort sind die Momente Kind und Kinderspiel wichtig. Die Freude, die das Lesen einer Idylle einem bereitet, lässt sich, sagt er, mit dem unschuldigen Vergnügen vergleichen, das einer empfindet, wenn er sich auf einer Schaukel leicht auf und nieder bewegt, 'ohne Stösse Luft vor euch

16. *Die unsichtbare Loge*, S. 59.

mit Luft hinter euch tauschend' (S. 260). Nach Jean Paul stellt die
Idylle ein Glück dar, woran nichts fehlt und das der Abglanz einer
glücklichen Kinderzeit ist und deshalb eine liebliche Erinnerung sein
kann. Auch Gottwalt geht vollkommen glücklich durch die Poesie der
Luft 'auf und nieder' (er muss sich dabei aber wohl umdrehen!).

Aber Jean Paul hat die Idylle ausserhalb der grossen Begeisterung
angesiedelt. Er definiert die Gattung als die epische Repräsentation
des vollkommenen kleinen Glücks ('Vollglück in der Beschränkung',
auch wohl 'Vollglück der Beschränkung' genannt), und fügt hinzu,
dass die höhere seelische Entzückung in die Lyrik und die Romantik
gehört. Dennoch steht Gottwalt 'der gerührten Entzückung überdeckt' und zu Tränen gerührt da: Die Elemente der Idylle mögen
zwar in dem Teil des Textes, der dem neuen Absatz vorangeht, verarbeitet sein, aber Gottwalts romantisches Erleben, seine verzückten
Gefühle werden nicht in dem Augenblick, da die Sonne hinter dem
Horizont verschwindet, erregt. Das Textfragment als Ganzes stellt
seine unaussprechliche Gemütsstimmung dar. Das 'Schöne ohne Begrenzung' wird zum Teil mit Hilfe von Bildmaterial aus der Gattung
der 'Beschränkung' evoziert. Jean Paul entnimmt der Idylle eine
Anzahl Elemente, die er auf höherem Niveau anwendet. Die Szene
auf dem Herrnhuter Friedhof ist eine Jean Paulsche Idylle in höherem Sinne. Renate Böschenstein hat darauf hingewiesen, wie bei diesem Dichter die Vorliebe für die Idylle ihr Gegenstück in einer Sehnsucht nach der Ewigkeit findet.[17] Vielleicht wurde es deshalb doch
nötig, Gottwalts inneren Prozess noch einmal in einer Sentenz darzustellen: dem Schlusssatz des Textfragments, worüber hier einiges bemerkt wurde.

Begegnen wir auf einer Seite der *Flegeljahre* einigen Motiven, die
für eine literarhistorische Strömung bezeichnend sind, und einigen
Elementen einer literarischen Gattung, mit der dieser Text sich verwandt zeigt, so wird ersichtlich, wie jene, nach der Auffassung von
Jean Paul, in der Romantik mit einem anderen Inhalt und in einer
anderen Funktion auf einem anderen Niveau vorhanden sind. Wenn
die Wahl dieser Seite einer stärkeren Begründung bedarf als der einer
subjektiven Präferenz, so ist es diese: in ihrer Verbindung mit der
romantischen Poesie Jean Pauls erlangen literarische Traditionen eine
neue und hohe Qualität.

17. Renate Böschenstein, *Idylle*, Stuttgart, 1967, S. 91.

TEXTSTRUKTUR UND REZEPTIONSPROZESS AM BEISPIEL VON NIETZSCHES 'ZARATHUSTRA'.

Elrud Kunne-Ibsch (Amsterdam)

Unter der Textstruktur verstehen wir die internen Beziehungen der Textelemente; die Aktivität des Forschers, der diese Beziehungen aufdeckt, möchten wir mit dem Begriff der Strukturanalyse bezeichnen. Unter der Rezeption verstehen wir die Aktualisierung von Bedeutung, d.h. die Dominantsetzung von Textelementen oder Kombinationen von Elementen. Mit der Opposition von "Struktur" und "Prozess" möchten wir der Erscheinung Rechnung tragen, dass bei einer relativen Stabilität oder Neutralität der Daten in der Relevanznahme der Daten die Veränderlichkeit liegt. *Relativ* stabil nennen wir die Daten, da die Möglichkeit ihrer Aufschlüsselung unter anderem vom Forschungsstand einer Disziplin abhängig ist. Die Dominantsetzung von Textelementen geschieht durch die Projektion des Leserhintergrundes auf den Text in seiner fixierten sprachlichen Anordnung.[1] Die Veränderlichkeit liegt denn auch im Leserhintergrund, im "Sinnsystem", wie Wolfgang Iser es nennt.[2] Ohne dass der geringste Eingriff in die Anordnung der Sprachzeichen in z.B. Voltaires *Candide* nötig wäre, ist das Sinnsystem des heutigen Lesers ein anderes als das des Zeitgenossen, der durch Voltaires Werk zum ersten Mal mit der Kritik an der Leibniz/Wolffschen Präsentation der Schöpfung konfrontiert wurde. Die heutige Aktualisierung von Bedeutung wird darum abweichen von der zeitgenössischen. Bedeutungskonstituie-

---

Die Nietzsche-Zitate sind der Ausgabe: Friedrich Nietzsche, *Werke in drei Bänden,* hrsg. von Karl Schlechta (München: Hanser, 2. durchgesehene Auflage 1960) entnommen und erscheinen im Text unter der römischen Ziffer des Bandes und der Seitenzahl.

    1. Jan Mukařovský, "Ästhetische Funktion, Norm und ästhetischer Wert als soziale Fakten". In: *Kapitel aus der Ästhetik,* Frankfurt a.M.: Suhrkamp, 1970.

    2. Wolfgang Iser, "Die Wirklichkeit der Fiktion — Elemente eines funktionsgeschichtlichen Textmodells". In: Rainer Warning (Hrsg.), *Rezeptionsästhetik; Theorie und Praxis,* München: Fink, 1975, S. 301.

rung liegt im Schnittpunkt von Text und Lesersystem. Eine denkbare
Willkür findet ihre Begrenzung einerseits im Lesersystem, das über-
individuell ist, andrerseits im Text, der — als Repräsentant des
Sprachsystems einer Gemeinschaft — ebenfalls überindividuell ist.
Dieser überindividuelle Charakter ist dem Text sowohl in der Phase
der Kodierung, als auch in der der Dekodierung eigen.

Es lassen sich bei der Herstellung von Bedeutung drei Bedeutungs-
schichten denken: die lexikalische, die textinterne Bedeutung, die
eine Variation der lexikalischen bewirken kann (z.B. kann sich das
Adjektiv "bedeutend" in einer spezifischen textlichen Umgebung als
ironisch herausstellen, eine Bedeutungsnuance, die im Lexikon nicht
verantwortet wird) und die situationelle Bedeutung. Letztere umfasst
die Weltkenntnis des Lesers, die vor allem bei grösserem historischen
Abstand Veränderungen unterliegt: Der Leser des *Zauberberg*, dem
der Ausgang beider Weltkriege gegenwärtig ist, fügt der lexikalischen
und textinternen Bedeutungsschicht eine weitere hinzu, die auf
einem Zuwachs an Kenntnis historischen Materials beruht.[3]

Die Problematik der Unterscheidung zwischen Textstruktur und
Rezeption soll keineswegs geleugnet werden. Namentlich wird das
Eindringen des Leserhintergrundes in die Beschreibung der Anord-
nung von Sprachzeichen nicht immer zu vermeiden sein, wodurch
Relevanzgesichtspunkte bereits auf dem Niveau der angenommenen
Neutralität eine Rolle zu spielen beginnen. Dennoch wird es aufgrund
dieser Unterscheidung eher möglich sein, Interferenzen zu erkennen
und zur Diskussion zu stellen.

Das Mitspielen des Leserhintergrundes bei der Bedeutungskonstituierung in literarischen Texten ist eine Folge des nicht notwendigerweise denotierenden Charakters dieser Texte, ihrer mittlerweile allgemein angenommenen Offenheit, oder — um Isers Begriff zu verwenden — Adaptionsfähigkeit.

Wenn wir zunächst Nietzsches *Zarathustra* als Textstruktur
beschreiben wollen, so geschieht das, um die im Text vorhandenen
Elemente sichtbar werden zu lassen, die jeweilige Rezeptionsansätze
ermöglicht haben. Der zweite Abschnitt dieses Aufsatzes soll dann

3. Nicolas Ruwet, "Synecdoques et métonymies". In: *Poétique* 1975, nr. 23,
S. 372, unterscheidet für die "interprétation des énoncés" fünf Schichten: eine
lexikalisch/syntaktische, eine Referenztheorie, eine Sprechakttheorie, eine
Kontext/Situationstheorie und eine Enzyklopädie, "rendant compte de la con-
naissance du monde".

mit einigen repräsentativen Beispielen die Schnittpunkte von Text und Sinnsystemen angeben, wobei wir in unserem Falle auf schriftlich festgelegte Reaktionen innerhalb des literarischen Systems angewiesen sind (damit ist eine experimentelle Leserbefragung ausgeschlossen, aber auch die Rezeption des *Zarathustra* in Philosophie, Theologie, bildender Kunst, Musik, Psychologie).

Die Anordnung der Sprachzeichen im Zarathustra

Zunächst stellt sich die Frage nach der Gattungszugehörigkeit dieses Werkes. Aufgrund der heute verfügbaren Zuordnungskriteria dürfte sich die Entscheidung, *Zarathustra* zur epischen Gattung zu rechnen, kaum bestreiten lassen. Grundlage dieser Zuordnung ist dabei die Unterscheidung von Personen- und Erzählerrede, so wie sie — von der klassisch-antiken Poetik tradiert — von der modernen Forschung wieder aufgenommen wurde. Für die epische Gattung ist der Wechsel zwischen den beiden prinzipiell möglichen Redeformen konstitutiv. Dass der Wechsel von Erzähler- und Personenrede eine Skala von Möglichkeiten bietet, auf der die Dichotomie beider Redeformen an dem einen Pol angesiedelt ist und ihre Assimilation am andern Pol, hat namentlich Doležel aufgezeigt und auch in eine historische Perspektive gestellt.[4] *Zarathustra* zeigt eine deutliche Trennungslinie zwischen dem *discours du narrateur* und dem *discours des caractères*. Angezeigte direkte Rede, eingeleitet durch Verben des Sagens, ist die einzig vorkommende Redeform der Personen. Es fehlen die nicht angezeigte direkte Rede, die indirekte Rede, der innere Monolog und die erlebte Rede. Damit ist ein stark archaisierendes Redemodell gewählt, das sein Vorbild u.a. in der Bibel findet und das sich von den epischen Verfahren im 19. Jahrhundert eben als archaisierendes Modell unterscheidet. In den Erzählertext-Abschnitten im *Zarathustra* werden bestimmte Erzählerfunktionen in hohem Masse reduziert. Nehmen wir an, dass die Erzählerrede die folgenden Funktionen an sich binden kann: die redeeinleitend/redegliedernde, die handlungsantreibende, die beschreibend/bewertende und schliesslich die mit dem Leser kommunizierende Funktion, so können wir für Nietzsches *Zarathustra* eine Dominanz der redeeinleitenden/redegliedernden Funktion konstatieren; in geringem Masse

---

4. Lubomír Doležel, *Narrative Modes in Czech Literature,* Toronto: University of Toronto Press, 1973.

tritt die beschreibende Funktion hervor, die handlungstragende und
die bewertende treten nur äusserst reduziert auf, der Kontakt zum
Leser ist sporadisch. Die beiden letztgenannten Funktionen – die
Bewertung und der Leserkontakt – werden dagegen in vollem Um-
fang vom Personentext übernommen, der quantitativ denn auch über-
wiegt. Die Besonderheit des Personentextes im *Zarathustra* ist, dass
dieser Text nicht auf Rede und Gegenrede verteilt ist, sondern in der
Hauptsache in einem einzigen Sprecher – Zarathustra selbst – repräsentiert wird. Damit entfällt eine wichtige Funktion der Rede und
Gegenrede, des Dialogs, nämlich durch die Kommunikation der
Personen die Handlung in Bewegung zu bringen. Es sind Zarathustras
Worte, die gesprochen werden und wenn – im dritten und vierten
Teil – neben den Reden und Monologen eine geringfügige Dialogisie-
rung festgestellt werden kann, so ändert sich im Grunde genommen
noch nichts. Die Menschen und Tiere, die Zarathustras Gesprächs-
partner sind, sprechen dieselbe Sprache, Zarathustras Sprache. Auf
diese Weise bleibt die Kommunikationssituation, die Zarathustra mit
anderen Personen unterhält, ohne Einfluss auf ihn, sie zwingt ihn
nicht, sich von anderen Meinungen abzusetzen oder seine eigene zu
revidieren. Dieter Janiks[5] dritte Kommunikationsebene (Romanper-
sonen untereinander) ist damit beträchtlich reduziert, eine Reduktion, die, wie wir bereits erwähnt haben, auch für die zweite Ebene
(Erzähler – impliziter Leser) gilt. Charakteristisch für die Erzählsitua-
tion des *Zarathustra* ist, dass die Hauptperson selbständig Kontakt
mit dem intendierten Leser unterhält, ein erzähltechnischer Umstand,
der nicht ohne Einfluss auf die Rezeption bleiben kann. Dem Leser
wird eine Lehre angeboten, der fiktionale Charakter des Werkes wird
abgeschwächt, eine mögliche Unterscheidung der verschiedenen
Sprecher bleibt wirkungslos, eine Spannung zwischen Erzähler und
Person, die einen relativierenden Effekt zeitigen könnte, fehlt.

Die handlungskonstituierende Funktion des Erzählertextes ist
gering, kurze Abschnitte bilden den epischen "Rahmen". Es werden
vor allem die Bewegungen Zarathustras durch den Raum wiedergege-
ben: "Viele Länder sah Zarathustra und viele Völker" (II, 322);
"Hierauf ging Zarathustra wieder zurück in das Gebirge" (II, 341);
"Als Zarathustra von der Stadt Abschied genommen hatte [. . .] folgten ihm viele" (II, 336).

5. Dieter Janik, *Die Kommunikationsstruktur des Erzählwerks. Ein semiologisches Modell,* Bebenhausen: Lothar Rotsch, 1973.

Die redeeinleitende Funktion des Erzählertextes bildet im gesamten Werk ein konstantes und bindendes Element; diese Funktion tritt auch bei der Personenrede innerhalb der Personenrede (also auf der zweiten Redeebene) noch deutlich zutage ("Die stillste Stunde", II, 399f.). Jeder Sprecherwechsel wird – der dichotomischen Struktur entsprechend – markiert.

Die redegliedernde Funktion manifestiert sich – komplementär zur redeeinleitenden – vor allem in dem regelmässig wiederkehrenden "Also sprach Zarathustra" am Ende eines Redeabschnittes; in den Fällen, die diese Variation erfordern, heisst es auch wohl: "Also sang Zarathustra".

Auch die Selbstgespräche Zarathustras werden eingeleitet und graphisch angezeigt: "Und damals redete Zarathustra also zu seinem frohlockenden Gewissen" (II, 411). Ganz besonders tritt dieses Merkmal in dem leitmotivischen Gebrauch in "Zarathustras Vorrede" in Erscheinung, wo es heisst: "Zarathustra sagte zu seinem Herzen" und als Abschluss der Rede: "Dies hatte Zarathustra zu seinem Herzen gesprochen" oder: "Als er dies zu seinem Herzen gesagt hatte".

Der Erzähler, der bewertet und dabei Kontakt mit dem intendierten Leser aufnimmt, macht von diesen Funktionen einen sehr geringen und dezenten Gebrauch. Dies geschieht etwa auf folgende Weise: "Da verlief sich das Volk, denn selbst Neugierde und Schrecken werden müde" (II, 286). An einer anderen Stelle (II, 341) wird in der Bewertung des Erzählers eine leichte Assimilation an den Personentext spürbar, so dass hier die Dichotomie inzidentell in Richtung auf die erlebte Rede hin durchbrochen wird: "Seine Seele aber wurde voll von Ungeduld und Begierde nach denen, welche er liebte: denn er hatte ihnen noch viel zu geben. Dies nämlich ist das Schwerste, aus Liebe die offne Hand schliessen und als Schenkender die Scham bewahren". Der Erzähler konstatiert an verschiedenen Stellen, dass Zarathustra "traurig" wird (z.B. II, 366) oder "wund am Herzen", "müde geworden und sehnsüchtiger noch als zuvor" (II, 404f.). Auch hierin können wir die bewertende Funktion des Erzählertextes erkennen, ohne dass jedoch ein Kontakt mit dem Leser vorhanden wäre. Ein zurückhaltender Kontakt tritt zutage in der Wendung: "Und sie liebten ihn, wie das Volk liebt: also dass zu gleichen Teilen Liebe und Scheu beisammen sind" (II, 385), und einem offenen Kontakt begegneten wir an einer einzigen Stelle, wo der Erzähler fragt: "Und was glaubt ihr wohl, dass sich damals zutrug? " (II, 552).

Die Kommunikation des Erzählers mit dem Leser nimmt also nur sehr geringen Raum ein und findet sich nicht an den Schwerpunkten des Textes. Die erwähnte Traurigkeit Zarathustras zum Beispiel kann dadurch nicht mit der Lautstärke seiner Verkündigung konkurrieren und darum als relativierender Wirkungsfaktor kaum Gewicht in die Waagschale werfen.

In den beiden ersten Teilen verkündet Zarathustra seine Lehren. Das Volk, zu dem er spricht, ist namenlos und ohne räumliche und zeitliche Fixierung; denotative Elemente, die einen historischen Rahmen ermöglichen, fehlen. Die Dominantsetzung dieses Struktur-elementes, eines "Minus-Verfahrens", wurde ein wichtiger Wirkungs-faktor. Das Volk reagiert auch kaum auf Zarathustra, wodurch die Mindestanforderung, die man an ein *récit* stellen kann, nämlich: A reagiert auf B und umgekehrt, nicht erfüllt wird. Das Kommunika-tionsspiel zwischen den Personen verlagert sich auf die Kommunika-tion zwischen der Hauptperson und dem Leser. Die angeredeten "Ihr" und "Euch" werden die Leser selbst, und in den langen Reden Zarathustras prävaliert denn auch die appellative Funktion der Sprache. Wenn Zarathustra einen Rede-Abschnitt beginnt mit: "Den Verächtern des Leibes will ich mein Wort sagen" (II, 300), so richtet er sich hiermit an seinen intendierten Leser, nicht an den sich zufällig in der Menge befindenden Leibesverächter. Fragen, Ausrufe, die zahl-reichen "Ihr sollt", "Du sollst", die Lehren und Behauptungen, die mit dem biblischen: "Wahrlich [ich sage Euch]" eingeleitet werden und den thetischen Charakter der Aussage akzentuieren, bilden eine Kommunikationsstruktur, die darauf angelegt ist, direkt auf den Leser einzuwirken. Die Vorlage der Bibel entspricht dieser Intention denn auch in hohem Masse. Dass der Religionsstifter aus Persien gewählt wurde, ist einerseits unwichtig, da ja der historische Kontext nicht respektiert wird, andrerseits spielt er jedoch als Anti-Jesus mit, dem Werk den Charakter einer Bibel-Parodie zu verleihen.

Der imperativische Ton der beiden ersten Teile überstimmt die ebenfalls in diesen Teilen vorhandenen Aphorismen. Die Grundstruk-tur des Nietzsche-Aphorismus: Setzung einer allgemeinen Meinung im ersten Teil (oft als Antithese präsentiert) und ihre Relativierung oder Auflösung im zweiten Teil, erweist sich am wirksamsten, je subtiler sich der zweite Teil hinsichtlich der phonologischen, syn-taktischen und semantischen Kombinationen zum ersten verhält, je geringfügiger und damit überraschender die Variation ist. Ein Beispiel unter vielen ist das folgende: "Schaffende waren erst Völker, und spät erst Einzelne; wahrlich, der Einzelne selber ist noch die jüngste Schöpfung" (II, 323).

Ein Aphorismus ist keine Lehre, sondern ein intellektuelles In-Frage-Stellen fixierter Meinungen und steht in deutlicher Opposition zum Setzen *einer* bestimmten Meinung im "Du sollst" der Zara-thustra-Lehre. Die Opposition Lehre/Aphorismus sollte denn auch ein entscheidender Faktor in der Zarathustra-Rezeption werden.

Vom Thematischen her gesehen sind die beiden ersten Teile des *Zarathustra* für eine aphoristische Struktur vorzüglich geeignet. Handelt es sich doch um Kritik an überkommenen Werten, so wie Nietzsche sie auch in *Menschliches, Allzumenschliches* und in *Die fröhliche Wissenschaft* geäussert hat. Der erste Teil behandelt vor allem menschliche Handlungen und Institutionen (Freuden- und Leidenschaften, Lesen und Schreiben, Krieg, Staat, Freundschaft, Nächstenliebe, Ehe, Tod), der zweite Teil Menschentypen (Mitleidi-ge, Priester, Tugendhafte, Gesindel, Weise, Gelehrte, Dichter). Das wertekritisierende Grundthema wird einerseits intellektuell/spiele-risch (als Aphorismus), andrerseits visionär/prophetisch (als Lehre) präsentiert. In der zweiten Präsentationsform klingt thematisch das Konzept vom Übermenschen an, dessen Aufgabe es letzten Endes sein soll, den Gedanken der ewigen Wiederkehr mit dem vom Willen zur Macht zu versöhnen: "Alles 'Es war' ist ein Bruchstück, ein Rätsel, ein grauser Zufall — bis der schaffende Wille dazu sagt: 'aber so wollte ich es!' " (II, 395).

Der dritte Teil ist stark monologisch. Das meiste, was Zarathustra nun sagt, spricht er zu seinem Herzen; er ist traurig, müde und sehn-süchtig, lacht und weint in seiner Einsamkeit, zu der er nach dem zentralen Abschnitt in der Mitte des Buches, überschrieben: "Die stillste Stunde", verpflichtet ist. Zwischen alten, zerbrochenen Tafeln und neuen, halb beschriebenen wartet Zarathustra auf seine Stunde: "Inzwischen rede ich als einer, der Zeit hat, zu mir selber" (II, 443). Doch kann er auch nun nicht nachlassen, hin und wieder seine "Brüder" anzureden. Im allgemeinen aber gilt: Mit seinem Verzicht auf die offizielle Lehrer-Rolle bekommt Zarathustras Sprechstil im dritten Teil eine grössere Variationsbreite. Lyrisch-visionäres Spre-chen findet sich neben Witz und Schelten und gelegentlichem Selbst-spott. Populäre Nietzsche-"Bon" mots finden in diesem Teil ihren Ursprung. Als kleine Probe dieser Geschmacklosigkeit zwei Zitate:

" 'Dem Reinen ist alles rein' – so spricht das Volk. Ich aber sage euch: den Schweinen ist alles Schwein!" (II, 451); "So will ich Mann und Weib: kriegstüchtig den einen, gebärtüchtig das andre, beide aber tanztüchtig mit Kopf und Beinen" (II, 457). Gerade derartige Scherze haben die Neigung, sich schnell aus ihrer textlichen Umgebung zu lösen und sich in der erworbenen Selbständigkeit als äusserst geschichtsresistent zu erweisen.

Zarathustras Erzfeind, der "Geist der Schwere", den zu bekämpfen hauptsächlich den beiden ersten Teilen vorbehalten war, hatte "Zwang, Satzung, Not und Folge und Zweck und Wille und Gut und Böse" geschaffen (II, 445). Dies sind die "alten Tafeln". Gegen die Konkretisierungen dieser zentralen Begriffe hatte Zarathustra in den verschiedensten semantischen Kontexten polemisiert (menschliche Typen, Handlungen, Institutionen). Seinem Übermenschen aus dem dritten Teil fehlen diese konkreten Situationen. Sein semantischer Kontext wird eingeschränkter; es dominieren die Begriffe "neu" und "Zukunft": neue Morgenröten, neue Sterne, neue Nächte, Zukunft, eine neue Tafel, ein neuer Adel, der Tauwind, Sterne und Zukunft, Sämänner der Zukunft (II, 445 ff.). Diese zukünftigen Werte sind unbekannt und können nicht in konkrete Situationen hineingestellt werden. Da sie Künftiges andeuten, fehlt ihnen noch jeder Zusammenstoss mit einer historischen Begebenheit. Sie bleiben vage und einem traditionellen semantischen Bereich verhaftet.

In der zweiten Hälfte des dritten Teiles wird in dem Abschnitt "Der Genesende" abgerundet, was an Handlungselementen im *Zarathustra* enthalten war. Zu Zarathustras Lehre gehört, wie schon erwähnt, der Gedanke der ewigen Wiederkehr des Gleichen, den auszusprechen er sich in "Die stillste Stunde" geweigert hatte. Diese Weigerung verfolgt ihn ("Vom Gesicht und Rätsel") und wird nach einem siebentägigen Schlaf überwunden. Wie bei der Gestalt des biblischen Jesus gehört zu der Aufgabe zu lehren die Verpflichtung, auch das Schwerste zu akzeptieren. Hierin liegt denn auch ein Minimum an Handlung: in beiden Fällen nämlich der Versuch, sich der Aufgabe zu entziehen, und schliesslich doch die Überwindung dieser Schwäche. Zarathustra muss aussprechen, was er lieber verschwiegen hätte: 'Allzuklein der Grösste! – das war mein Überdruss am Menschen! Und ewige Wiederkunft auch des Kleinsten! – das war mein Überdruss an allem Dasein!" (II, 465). Zeugen dieser Überwindung sind nicht Menschen, sondern die Zarathustra umringenden Tiere. Der dritte Teil

223

endet in hymnischen Liedern, deren bekanntestes das "Ja- und Amen-Lied" ist mit seinem Refrain "Denn ich liebe Dich, o Ewigkeit" nach allen Strophen und den auffallenden syntaktischen Äquivalenzrelationen der Strophen 2, 3, 4, 5 und mit leichter Variation der Strophen 6 und 7.

Der vierte Teil beginnt mit einer Raffung der erzählten Zeit ("Und wieder liefen Monde und Jahre über Zarathustras Seele [...] sein Haar aber wurde weiss" (II, 477)) und mit Rede und Gegenrede (Dialog mit den Tieren). Zarathustra spricht mit einer Reihe von "höheren Menschen", die ihn mit ihrem Notschrei (Leitmotiv dieses Teiles) verfolgen: Wahrsager, Könige, ein getretener Mensch, Zauberer, Papst, der hässlichste Mensch, der freiwillige Bettler. Diese höheren Menschen haben die alten Werte hinter sich gelassen. Aus dieser Sicht gehören sie zu Zarathustra. Sie haben aber noch nicht das Stadium des Übermenschen − Zarathustras Stadium − erreicht. Er kann sie nur als Brücke zum Übermenschen akzeptieren. Die Gespräche mit ihnen handeln von ihrem Werteverlust und von dem Vakuum, das dadurch entstanden ist. Am Ende dieser Begegnungen und Gespräche trifft Zarathustra seinen eigenen Schatten, der sich in derselben Situation wie die höheren Menschen befindet. Später versammeln sich die höheren Menschen in Zarathustras Höhle und feiern ihr "Abendmahl" − ein Eselsfest und deutliche Bibelparodie: "Dies aber war der Anfang von jener langen Mahlzeit, welche 'das Abendmahl' in den Historien-Büchern genannt wird" (II, 522). Zarathustra hält bei dieser Gelegenheit wieder Reden, und Zauberer und Wanderer singen ihre Lieder (die Dionysos-Dithyramben, die nicht Zarathustra in den Mund gelegt werden). Erst im "trunkenen Lied", das in einen Rundgesang mündet, ist Zarathustra der Vorsänger.

Der vierte Teil endet mit Zarathustras Aufbruch aus seiner Höhle: "Also sprach Zarathustra und verliess seine Höhle, glühend und stark, wie eine Morgensonne, die aus dunklen Bergen kommt" (II, 561). Dieser Aufbruch in unbestimmte Regionen, der zusammen mit der kurz zuvor ausgesprochenen Bemerkung über die Zeit: "Dies alles dauerte eine lange Zeit, oder eine kurze Zeit: denn, recht gesprochen, gibt es für dergleichen Dinge auf Erden *keine* Zeit" (II, 560) den Schluss des Werkes bildet, fasst noch einmal deutlich den zeit- und raumlosen − damit also zutiefst ungeschichtlichen − Charakter von Nietzsches neuem Menschenbild zusammen.

Die thematische Ebene von *Also sprach Zarathustra* besteht aus

zwei Hauptelementen: der Kritik an den alten Werten, die historisch
festgelegt und der Setzung der neuen Werte, die auf eine zeitlose
Zukunft hin konzipiert sind. Das Thema der Kritik wird sprachlich
auf zwei Arten realisiert: einerseits im Aphorismus, der dem Leser
die Freiheit der Reaktion belässt und andrerseits in der Form der
Lehre, die dem Leser Verpflichtungen auferlegt. Die neuen Werte
erscheinen vorzugsweise als lyrisches Bild. Diese tragenden Strukturelemente treten jedoch nicht im Nacheinander auf, etwa als eine
Entwicklung hin zu einem neuen Zustand, sondern in bunter Folge
durcheinander, so dass das lyrische Bild oftmals abrupt in einer kritischen Bemerkung endet. Wo parodiert wird, ist der Bezug auf die
geschichtliche Vorlage (vor allem die Bibel, aber auch Goethe) erkennbar.

Die Textstruktur des *Zarathustra* zeigt auf dem Gebiete der Er-
zähler- und Personenrede — also auf makrostruktureller Ebene — und
auf syntaktischem Niveau nur eine geringe Variationsbreite. Für
Nietzsche ist die jüdisch-christliche Kultur — Form geworden in der
Bibel — *der* Repräsentant der alten Werte. Er übernimmt ihre Form,
namentlich ihre Syntax. Die "Synfunktion" (Tynjanov) dieser archai-
schen Syntax ist parodistisch. Die Monotonie von Syntax und Redeformen wird einigermassen ausgeglichen durch eine relativ grosse
Selektionsfreiheit im Bereich des lexikalischen Kode. Die verschiedenen menschlich-gesellschaftlichen Situationen, über die Zarathustra
handelt, die semantischen Variationen, die der Aphorismus zulässt,
der hymnische Ton der Dithyramben legen Nietzsche wenig Be-
schränkungen auf.[6]

Anders als in der Bibel ist der Raum im *Zarathustra* ein wichtiges
Element. Es ist die stereotype Landschaft der Berge, Meere, Wüsten,
des Schnees und der Sonne, die den Stimmungen Zarathustras ange-
passt werden. Gelegentlich tritt die Person Zarathustras für einen
Augenblick aus der Landschaftsbeschreibung zurück und verselbständigt sich diese. Dann ist das Resultat ein Jugendstil-Tableau:
"Seht doch hin, wie sie [die Sonne] ungeduldig über das Meer
kommt! Fühlt ihr den Durst und den heissen Atem der Liebe nicht?
Am Meere will sie saugen und seine Tiefe zu sich in die Höhe trinken:
da hebt sich die Begierde des Meeres mit tausend Brüsten. Geküsst

6. Für Einzelheiten des Stils siehe: Pieter Pütz, *Friedrich Nietzsche,* Stuttgart:
Metzler, 1967.

und gesaugt *will* es sein vom Durste der Sonne; Luft *will* es werden
und Höhe und Fusspfad des Lichts und selber Licht!" (II, 380).[7]
Zarathustra tritt im folgenden Satz aber bereits wieder auf: "Wahr-
lich der Sonne gleich liebe ich das Leben und alle tiefen Meere".
Bemerkenswert in dieser Beschreibung ist das kursivgesetzte "will".
Es bringt ein stark anthropologisches Element in die Naturdarstellung
und ist analog zu der Sprechweise der Lehrreden.[8]
   In den Zusammenhang der Beschreibung von Textelementen im
Zarathustra gehört eine Eigenart von Nietzsches Metaphernbildung.
Es wiederholt sich hierbei der Prozess des Aphorismus, auf den wir
bereits hinwiesen. So geschieht es, dass eine konventionelle Metapher
aufgebaut, auf einen antithetischen Höhepunkt geführt und im Aphorismus aufgelöst wird. Am Beispiel der letzten Strophe aus dem "Ja-
und Amen-Lied" sei dieser Prozess illustriert. Durch den semantischen Rahmen: "Himmel, Flügel, Licht-Fernen, schwimmen, Freiheit" wird die Metapher, in der Zarathustra als ein Vogel erscheint,
vorbereitet. Zugleich wird damit das semantische Merkmal der schwe-
relosen Bewegung stark akzentuiert. Eine Mensch/Tier-Metaphorisie-
rung gehört zum traditionellen Metaphernbestand und bietet auch
kein Verständnishindernis. Komplizierter wird die Metapher jedoch
in dem Moment, wo der Begriff "Vogel" nicht als solcher, sondern in
der Zusammensetzung "Vogel-Weisheit" erscheint. Das akzentuierte
Merkmal "Bewegung" wird aus seiner Vorrangstellung durch die Einführung des auf der Hierarchie der semantischen Merkmale bereits
abgeschatteten "+denken" (für den Menschen) vertrieben; damit
wird erreicht, dass die Merkmal-Übertragung, die bisher vom Vogel
auf den Menschen stattfand ("+schwerelose Bewegung") in umge-
kehrter Richtung — vom Menschen auf den Vogel — geschieht. Auf
dem antithetischen Höhepunkt dieser Umkehrung angelangt wird das
ikonische Prinzip auf der phonologischen Ebene eingesetzt und wie-

   7. Durch das Genus im Deutschen stellt sich bei diesem Bilde eine kleine
Unebenheit ein, die das Französische zum Beispiel nicht kennt: *le* soleil und *la*
mer fügen sich leichter in Nietzsches Bild. In diesen und ähnlichen Fällen liegt
denn auch eine Spannung vor zwischen dem ikonischen Prinzip, das die Literatur
kennzeichnet, und dem arbiträren grammatischen Geschlecht.
   8. Für den Anteil des Willens in der Strömung des literarischen Jugendstils
siehe: Elrud Kunne-Ibsch, "Der Wille zum schönen Leben. Enthistorisierung als
Verfahren in der Erzählung des Jugendstils". In: *Neophilologus* 57 (1973), S.
217-231 und S. 317-329.

derum die Bewegung aktualisiert: "Singe! Sprich nicht mehr!" Aphoristisch ist der Schluss: "sind alle Worte nicht für die Schweren gemacht? Lügen dem Leichten nicht alle Worte? " (II, 476). An dieser Stelle wird der Begriff der Weisheit aus der sich normalerweise einstellenden Verbindung mit dem Wort gelöst und der Verbindung mit der Bewegung zugeführt. Die Relation der beiden Glieder: Vogel und Weisheit, wird durch den Begriff der Freiheit hergestellt, der zunächst auf die Bewegungsfreiheit des Vogels zielt, dann aber auch die Assoziation "geistige Freiheit" nahegelegt.

Ähnliche Prozesse der Metaphorisierung und Antithesenbildung lassen sich im *Zarathustra* wiederholt nachweisen. Es sind dies die aus dem Frühwerk Nietzsches bekannten aphoristischen Verfahren, die bei einer Lektüre, die auf das semantische Mikroniveau gerichtet ist, aktualisiert werden und die Monotonie der Redeform durchbrechen können.

Wir haben eine in keiner Weise erschöpfende Analyse des Werkes vorgenommen, um die verschiedenen Dominantsetzungen begründen zu können, um Anschlussstellen für Rezeptionsweisen in der Werkstruktur zu rechtfertigen.

Rezeptionsweisen von "Also sprach Zarathustra".

Als Nietzsches Zarathustra zu wirken begann, war es die antinaturalistische Form und Bedeutung, die Aufmerksamkeit erregte und Zustimmung erntete. Ein frühes Zeugnis (1891) dafür ist bei Leo Berg zu finden, der von Nietzsche sagt, er lasse alles in neuen Farben erscheinen, "Fernsichten eröffnend und jäh in das ferne unbekannte Land weisend [. . .]. Seit ihm datiert die Abkehr vom Naturalismus".[9] Grottewitz (1890) spricht von dem Todesstoss, den Nietzsche dem "Realismus samt seiner Herdenmoral" gegeben habe;[10] Landsberg von einer Kultur, "in der Schönheit, Grösse und Macht dem höher entwickelten Menschen eine fruchtbare Stätte des Wirkens und Handelns gewähren".[11]

Im Jahre 1895 erschien der erste Jahrgang der Zeitschrift *Pan,* eine exklusive Zeitschrift, die zur wahren Kunst erziehen, nicht aber

9. In: Gotthart Wunberg, *Die Literarische Moderne. Dokumente zum Selbstverständnis der Literatur um die Jahrhundertwende,* Frankfurt a.M.: Athenäum, 1971, S. 79.
10. a.a.O., S. 61.
11. a.a.O., S. 166.

sich den Wünschen des Publikums beugen wollte. Die beiden ersten Jahrgänge enthalten Fragmente aus *Zarathustra*. Frei in seiner Wahl hat man Abschnitte aufgenommen, die Aristokratie und Exklusivität und ein Sich-Lösen aus (historischen) Bezügen erkennen lassen. Einige Beispiele mögen diese Feststellung erhärten:

"Auf Höhen bin ich heimisch, nach Höhen verlangt mich nicht. Ich hebe die Augen nicht empor; ein Niederschauender bin ich, einer der segnen muss; alle Segnenden schauen nieder".

"Noch rauscht die Wetterwolke: aber schon hängt glitzernd, still, schwer Zarathustras Reichtum über die Felder hin.

"Wirf dein Schweres in die Tiefe, Mensch vergiss! Göttlich ist des Vergessens Kunst! Willst du fliegen, willst du in Höhen heimisch sein: wirf dein Schwerstes in's Meer! Hier ist das Meer, wirf dich in's Meer! Göttlich ist des Vergessens Kunst!"

Ein Rezeptionsstrang, der den *Zarathustra* zur Reaktion gegen den Naturalismus zählt, findet seine Begründung in den folgenden Elementen der Textstruktur: das namenlose Volk, die fehlende räumliche und zeitliche Fixierung, der geringe Anteil von handlungsauslösenden Momenten, die Abwesenheit einer multilateralen Kommunikation, in der A auf B reagiert. Der Zarathustra-Raum ist nicht die Grossstadt des Naturalismus, es ist nicht ein Raum, der Einfluss auf die Personen ausübt, sondern ein Raum, mit dem der Prophet sich umgibt, Dekor, Staffage.

Ein solches Mass an Enthistorisierung erreicht Nietzsche nicht eher als im *Zarathustra*. In seinen frühen Schriften, ganz besonders in der *Unzeitgemässen Betrachtung* über David Strauss, nimmt er Stellung zu kulturgeschichtlichen Fragen, die sich aus historisch fest umrissenen Ereignissen herleiten: der deutsch-französische Krieg mit der deutschen Siegesstimmung. Im *Zarathustra* ist dieser historische Bezug als Hintergrund der dort vollzogenen Entwertungen anwesend; er wird indessen nicht explizit, und die "Stimmung wie Windesstille in einer Bergluft, die so leicht, so ätherrein ist, dass keine Ansteckungsstoffe in ihr vorhanden sind",[12] tritt bei entsprechendem Sinnsystem der Rezipienten in den Vordergrund. Wie sehr ein solches Sinnsystem sich seit der Jahrhundertwende etabliert hatte, können

12. Georg Brandes, "Friedrich Nietzsche. Eine Abhandlung ueber aristokratischen Radicalismus" (1888). In: *Menschen und Werke. Essays,* Frankfurt a.M.: Rütten und Loening, ²1895, S. 191.

wir dem programmatischen Vorwort Karl Wolfskehls zum Jahrgang 1911 des *Jahrbuch für die geistige Bewegung*[13] entnehmen (der George-Kreis ist hier am Wort). In Wolfskehls "Weltanschauung des Jahrbuchs" wird ein Selbstverständnis des neuen Jahrhunderts gegenüber dem alten ausgedrückt, bei dem gerade der Gegensatz zwischen dem Historischen und dem Zeitlos-Gültigen die entscheidende Rolle spielt: "Dass dies möglich wurde sezte eine völlig andere stellung voraus als sie die denker des vorigen jahrhunderts einnahmen: während sie aus dem historischen, logischen oder sozialen gegensatz, aus der ablehnung des vorhandenen, also aus der negation, ihre forderungen, bis zum 'übermenschen' stellten, können jetzt aus der selbstdarstellung eines neuen und doch zeitlos gültigen, aus der anerkennung einer lebendigen geistigen welt, also aus der position die richtmaasse genommen und neue werte nicht gefordert sondern gesezt werden". Wolfskehl betrachtet Nietzsche offensichtlich als den End- und Wendepunkt des vorangehenden Jahrhunderts. Sein Übermensch repräsentiert die neuen Werte; diese aber entstammen noch nicht der Position, sondern der Negation, sie werden noch nicht gesetzt, sondern postuliert. Ein weniger scharfsichtiger Kritiker als Wolfskehl wird den "historischen, logischen oder sozialen Gegensatz", die "Ablehnung des Vorhandenen" in Nietzsches Werk vom Übermenschen, in seinem *Zarathustra,* nicht mehr sehen.

Als 1908 Henry van de Velde den Einband für die Ausgabe des *Zarathustra* im Inselverlag entworfen hatte, wurde die Jugendstil-Rezeption des Lesers visuell vorbereitet und alle Aufmerksamkeit auf den feierlich-zelebrierenden Stil dieses Werkes gelenkt. Der *Zarathustra,* Nietzsches "fünftes Evangelium", passte sich dem neuen säkularisierten Messianismus ausgezeichnet an. Das in der Redeform auffällig häufige "Ich will", "Du sollst", das als fragendes Korrelat nur noch die rhetorische Frage zulässt, setzt neue Werte, wägt aber nicht mehr relativierend die alten Werte gegen die neuen ab. In der *Fröhlichen Wissenschaft* dagegen hatte Nietzsche die Hypothese, den vorläufigen Versuchs-Standpunkt gepriesen (II, 206).

Interessant in diesem Zusammenhange ist ein Aufsatz von Paul Fechter aus dem Jahre 1935. Von *Zarathustra* sagt Fechter, dass der Gedanke der ewigen Wiederkehr "ein ganzes Buch mit seinem *von keiner Vergangenheit mehr getrübten,* neuen Glanz erfüllen konnte".

13. hrsg. von Friedrich Gundolf und Friedrich Wolters, S. 9.

"Der Moment, die Wahrheit und Erkenntnis allein des Moments, ist das Beglückende, weil sie im Augenblick als Rausch und Gipfel des Augenblicks *ohne alle Kontrolle an den benachbarten Momenten* aufblitzt".[14] Nietzsche wird in die Reihe derer aufgenommen (Klinger, Dehmel, Van de Velde), die *"unter verneinendem Verzicht auf jede Beziehung nach rückwärts* eine neue traditionslose Welt der Formen und des Stils" schaffen.[15] [Hervorhebungen von E.K.-I.]

Die Gestalt des Zarathustra in Nietzsches Werk ist ohne Vergangenheit. Seine ersten dreissig und weiteren zehn Lebensjahre werden nicht erzählt. Der Umschlag vom 40jährigen Schweigen zum Lehren und Reden geschieht mit Hilfe des Satzes: "Endlich aber verwandelte sich sein Herz" (II, 277), ohne dass eine wie auch immer beschriebene Ursache diese Verwandlung erklärt. Die Zarathustra-Gestalt also legt die von Fechter angegebene Rezeptionsweise nahe. Ein "Verzicht auf jede Beziehung nach rückwärts" liegt allerdings nicht vor, wenn wir an die Bibel als Vorlage denken und an die Entwertungen, die Nietzsche ja nur aufgrund einer bestehenden kulturgeschichtlichen Situation vornehmen konnte. Dieses Element in der Textstruktur sollte jedoch erst später ans Licht treten.

Interessant in diesem Zusammenhange ist eine Nietzsche-Rezeption in Frankreich, die in dem Buch von Geneviève Bianquis erwähnt wird. Es handelt sich um das Urteil der Dichterin Comtesse de Noailles, von der Bianquis sagt: "Ainsi, par un piquant détour, c'est une femme poète qui a le mieux recueilli en France l'inspiration dionysiaque de Nietzsche, cette 'félicité azurée' qui gonfle de soleil et d'air embaumé certains chapitres du Zarathoustra. Les aspects tragiques, les aspects critiques, les aspects constructifs de la doctrine lui échappent totalement".[16] Aus den Worten Geneviève Bianquis' geht hervor, dass sie in Nietzsches *Zarathustra* kritische Elemente zu entdecken weiss. Im allgemeinen stand die französische kritisch-intellektualistische Szene einer Rezeption *Zarathustras* im Wege. Auch auf André Gide konnte *Zarathustra* schliesslich nur als ein Werk unter anderen – ihn mehr ansprechenden – Nietzsche-Schriften wirken.

14. Paul Fechter, "Nietzsches Bildwelt und der Jugendstil". In: Jost Hermand (Hrsg.), *Jugendstil*, Darmstadt: Wissenschaftliche Buchgesellschaft, 1971, S. 352.

15. Paul Fechter, a.a.O., S. 356.

16. Geneviève Bianquis, *Nietzsche en France; l'influence de Nietzsche sur la pensée française,* Paris: Félix Alcan, 1929, S. 78.

Innerhalb des literarischen Systems erscheint *Zarathustra* in seiner ersten Wirkungsphase als anti-naturalistisches Dokument und wird bei der Ausbreitung anti-naturalistischer Tendenzen in der Literatur auch als solches gewertet. Die Textstruktur rechtfertigt diese Stelle im System vollauf. Die besondere anti-naturalistische Strömung, die der Jugendstil darstellt, konnte dieses Werk für sich in Anspruch nehmen aufgrund der im vorangehenden beschriebenen Dominantsetzungen. Als solche waren zu nennen: das Herauslösen aus den Bezügen zur Vergangenheit, die Unbestimmtheit der neuen Werte, das Vertrauen in einen elitären Menschentypus, der sich einen traditionslosen glanzvollen Augenblick notfalls erzwingen kann.

Der Vorgang der Zarathustra-Rezeption im Expressionismus ist etwas komplizierterer Art. Zu der textlichen Grundlage und dem Leser-Sinnsystem des Expressionismus kommt ein Faktor, der für die Wirkung verantwortlich ist, hinzu, nämlich die im Jugendstil erfolgte Relevanznahme. Diese wird vom Expressionismus her nicht angefochten; es findet also nicht der in der Geschichte der Literatur bisweilen zu beobachtende "Rekurs auf den Text selber" statt, der das Ziel hat, von der Last möglicher "angeschwemmter" Bedeutungen zu befreien und der dann zu einem völlig neuen Rezeptionsansatz führen kann. Über Nietzsches Wirkung im Expressionismus liegt ein wertvoller, instruktiver Aufsatz von Gunter Martens vor, auf den wir uns in mancher Hinsicht denn auch gern beziehen wollen.[17]

Zunächst fällt als Stütze für die behauptete Stabilität der Rezeption in Jugendstil und Expressionismus auf, dass *Zarathustra* als Wirkungsfaktor auch im Expressionismus erhalten bleibt und sich das Interesse an Nietzsche keineswegs auf andere Schriften verlagert. Die erkenntniskritischen Schriften entziehen sich weiterhin der Rezeption.

Wenn wir die Dynamisierung, die Auflösung des zeitlichen Stillstandes sowie des räumlichen Tableaus als das Hauptelement in der Systemablösung von Jugendstil und Expressionismus sehen, so wird die Veränderung in dem "Foregrounding" von Texteigenschaften auf folgende Weise sichtbar: Die expressionistische Sinngebung richtet sich auf den dynamischen Aspekt des Aufbruchs zu dem neuen Men-

17. Gunter Martens, "Im Aufbruch das Ziel. Nietzsches Wirkung im Expressionismus". In: Hans Steffen (Hrsg.), *Nietzsche – Werk und Wirkungen,* Göttingen: Vandenhoeck, 1974, S. 115-166.

schentypus, findet Anschluss an jene Teile der Lehrreden Zarathustras, in denen dieser Aufbruch, die Zertrümmerung der alten Tafeln, thematisiert wird. Die Loslösung wird damit zum Selbstzweck. Weder die alte Position, noch das neue Ziel werden angegeben. Letzteres ist eine Erscheinung, die von der Jugendstil-Rezeption her bekannt ist — allein war im Jugendstil nicht der Aufbruch, sondern der — statische — *moment suprême* (vor oder nach dem Aufbruch zu situieren) der wichtigste Faktor. In dem folgenden Satz von Georg Heym kommt die Rezeptionsrichtung des Expressionismus zum Ausdruck: "Ferner und ferner sehen zu lernen, sich wegwenden vom Augenblick und dem Übermenschen zu leben, lehrt uns Zarathustra".[18]

Zeitlose Ferne, die Lösung aus dem Augenblick und die Lehre eines unbestimmten Zukunftsideals sind die Anschlussstellen, die expressionistische Dichter — von denen Heym ein Vertreter ist — im *Zarathustra* finden. Weder das Wohin noch das Woher der Bewegung sind historisch fixiert: "Die vitalistische Aufbruchssituation war es somit, die aus den Schriften des Lebensphilosophen in die Dichtung des beginnenden 20. Jahrhunderts übernommen wurde".[19] In dieser "geschichtslosen" Aneignung des *Zarathustra* bleibt die Verbindung zum Jugendstil erhalten.

Martens betont diese Kontinuität: "Zwar haben die Expressionisten den Jugendstil-Nietzsche nicht vorbehaltlos übernommen [. . .], aber ihr eigenes Nietzsche-Bild ist in dieser Tradition vorherbestimmt. Das zeigt nicht nur die Vorliebe für 'Also sprach Zarathustra', sondern auch die weitgehende Verkennung der sprach- und erkenntniskritischen Perspektiven in den Schriften dieses Philosophen".[20]

In der Nietzsche-Rezeption spielt eine Erscheinung eine Rolle, die nicht gemeinhin für Rezeptionen anderer Schriftsteller und Werke und sicher nicht in gleichem Masse gilt. Dies ist die Wirkung, die eintritt, ohne dass der Text selber gelesen wäre, eine Wirkung, die aufgrund der heftigen Diskussion der Persönlichkeit des Philosophen stattfin-

18. Georg Heym, *Dichtungen und Schriften,* hrsg. von K. L. Schneider, Band 3: *Tagebücher, Träume, Briefe,* Hamburg und München: Ellermann, 1960, S. 44.
19. Gunter Martens, *Vitalismus und Expressionismus. Ein Beitrag zur Genese und Deutung expressionistischer Stilstrukturen und Motive,* Stuttgart usw.: Kohlhammer, 1971, S. 54.
20. Gunter Martens, "Im Aufbruch das Ziel", a.a.O., S. 130; diese Feststellung gilt insbesondere für den Dramatiker Reinhard Johannes Sorge.

det und aufgrund der Isolierung der Lehre aus der textlichen Umgebung. Wie oben gezeigt, ermöglichen die Strukturmerkmale der Dichotomie von Erzählertext und Personentext und die Zentralisierung der Personenrede auf die Hauptgestalt eine solche Isolierung. Martens führt für die Wirkung ohne den Basistext noch ein weiteres Argument an, nämlich die bei Nietzsche in hohem Masse vorhandene Wirkung über Drittautoren.[21]

Wurden in *Pan* Fragmente aus *Zarathustra* aufgenommen, so steht die *Aktion* in dieser Hinsicht nicht nach. Im Jahre 1912 erscheint in der Spalte 230 ein Fragment aus dem Abschnitt *Von alten und neuen Tafeln* (in der Nietzsche-Ausgabe: II, 443ff.), unter dem Titel: "Tauwind". Der Tauwind ist ein "wütender Stier, ein Zerstörer, der mit zornigen Hörnern Eis bricht". Bewegung und Kampf durchbrechen die Stille: " 'Im Grunde steht alles still' — das ist eine rechte Winter-Lehre, ein gut Ding für unfruchtbare Zeiten [. . .]. 'Im Grund steht alles still' —: dagegen aber predigt der Tauwind" (II, 448). Nietzsches Tauwind predigt also nicht gegen bestimmte Missstände, sondern gegen den Stillstand, die Bewegungslosigkeit schlechthin.

Martens geht in diesem Zusammenhange auf die nachweisbare Wirkung von Nietzsches *Zarathustra* auf den expressionistischen Dichter Ernst Stadler ein, für den die "fundamentale Qualität des Lebens die zweckfreie und ziellose Bewegung"[22] ist: "Du Sturm, du Schrei, aufreissend Hornsignal zum Kampf, du trägst auf weissen Rossen mich zu Tat und Tag".[23]

Untersuchen wir den Abschnitt *Von alten und neuen Tafeln*, dem "Der Tauwind" entstammt, näher, so stellt sich heraus, dass die dreissig Unterabschnitte zahlreiche Aphorismen enthalten, z.B.: "Genuss und Unschuld nämlich sind die schamhaftesten Dinge: Beide wollen nicht gesucht sein. Man soll sie *haben* —, aber man soll eher noch nach Schuld und Schmerzen *suchen!* —" (II, 446). Der Aufbau des Abschnittes verläuft im ganzen etwa folgendermassen: Auf eine Reihe allgemeiner, aphoristischer Behauptungen folgen hymnische Verse, welche die eher abstrakten Gedankengänge auflösen, um nach kurzer Zeit wieder zum Gedanklichen zurückzufinden: "Es gibt einen alten Wahn der heisst Gut und Böse" (II, 448).

21. a.a.O., S. 130.
22. a.a.O., S. 143.
23. Ernst Stadler, "Meer". In: *Dichtungen*, hrsg. von K. L. Schneider, Bd. 1, Hamburg: Ellermann, o.J., S. 169.

Für die Rezeption im Expressionismus spielen die Aphorismen als Anknüpfungspunkte jedoch ebenso wenig eine Rolle wie für die Jugendstil-Rezeption. Dagegen findet die expressionistische Rezeption vor allem Anschluss an Metaphern, deren semantische Merkmale Aufbruch, Bewegung, Kampf sind, und auch an Wortzusammenfügungen, die noch nicht den statischen Zustand der akzeptierten Zusammensetzung erreicht haben, ihn auch nicht erreichen wollen, und in denen der Bindestrich den noch unvollendeten beweglichen Aspekt angibt ("Fluss-Tierbändiger", "Krämer-Gold"). Dergleichen Zusammensetzungen finden wir bei Gottfried Benn im Gedicht "Schnellzug" (*Söhne,* 1913): "Hügelgram", "Hügelglück", "Abgrundglück". Benn nimmt insofern eine besondere Stellung unter den Expressionisten ein, als er über eine integrative Kenntnis der Nietzscheschen Schriften verfügt. Obwohl *Zarathustra* ihm vertraut war (die Bewegung des Tanzes ist z.B. wichtig), nimmt dieses Werk keineswegs einen exklusiven Platz ein.[23a]

Wenn Thomas Mann im Jahre 1947 sein vernichtendes Urteil über Nietzsches *Zarathustra* fällt, so findet das nicht allein seine Ursache in dem historischen Ereignis des zweiten Weltkrieges, sondern ist zugleich eine Fortsetzung der veränderten Zarathustra-Rezeption im Modernismus, einer Strömung, zu der Thomas Mann zu rechnen ist. Thomas Manns Verdikt lautet: "Dieser gesicht- und gestaltlose Unhold und Flügelmann Zarathustra mit der Rosenkrone des Lachens auf dem unkenntlichen Haupt, seinem 'Werdet hart' und seinen Tänzerbeinen ist keine Schöpfung, er ist Rhetorik, erregter Wortwitz, gequälte Stimme und zweifelhafte Prophetie, ein Schemen von hilfloser Grandezza, oft rührend und allermeist peinlich – eine an der Grenze des Lächerlichen schwankende Unfigur".[24]

Manns Bewertung steht in krassem Gegensatz zu der von Nietzsche selbst, der folgendes über seinen *Zarathustra* an Overbeck schreibt: "Dies Buch, von dem ich Dir schrieb, eine Sache von zehn

23a. Siehe auch Friedrich Wilhelm Wodtke, "Gottfried Benn". In: Wolfgang Rothe (Hrsg.), *Expressionismus als Literatur. Gesammelte Studien,* Bern und München: Francke, 1969, S. 309-332. In diesem Sammelband ist auch der Aufsatz von Hans Schumacher über Reinhard Johannes Sorge von Interesse.

24. Thomas Mann, "Nietzsche's Philosophie im Lichte unserer Erfahrung". In: *Schriften und Reden zur Literatur, Kunst und Philosophie,* Bd. 3, Frankfurt a.M. und Hamburg: Fischer, 1968, S. 27.

Tagen, kommt mir jetzt wie mein Testament vor. Es enthält in der grössten Schärfe ein Bild meines Wesens, wie es ist, *sobald* ich einmal meine ganze Last abgeworfen habe. Es ist eine Dichtung und keine Aphorismen-Sammlung" (III, 1200).

In der Reaktion der Modernisten auf Nietzsche findet eine wichtige Veränderung im Verlauf des bisherigen Rezeptionsprozesses statt. *Zarathustra* nämlich – der bis dahin grösste Wirkungsfaktor – wird aus seiner Vorrangstellung vertrieben und aus dem Nietzsche-Bild weitgehend verdrängt. Wieder lassen wir Thomas Mann das Wort führen: "Nietzsche war vor allem ein grosser Kritiker und Kultur-Philosoph, ein aus der Schule Schopenhauers kommender europäischer Prosaist und Essayist obersten Ranges, dessen Genie zur Zeit von 'Jenseits von Gut und Böse' und der 'Genealogie der Moral' auf seinen Scheitelpunkt kam. Ein Dichter mag weniger sein als solch ein Kritiker, aber zu diesem Weniger reichte es nicht [. . .]".[25]

Als Prosaist und Essayist mit erkenntniskritischer, relativierender Perspektive wird Nietzsche zu einem Kronzeugen modernistischer Autoren. Aus seinen Schriften der früheren und mittleren Periode wird zitiert, die späten Schriften bedeckt man vorzugsweise mit dem Mantel des mitleidigen Verständnisses (man verbindet seine dort etalierte Selbstüberschätzung mit seiner Biographie). *Zarathustra* gegenüber ist man verlegen. Das Werk ist zu sehr eine Einheit, als dass man auch hier auf die Krankheit rekurrieren könnte. Thomas Manns Aufzählungen: "Rhetorik, erregter Wortwitz, gequälte Stimme, zweifelhafte Prophetie" enthalten ungefähr alle Tabus des modernistischen Kode. Der prophetische Gestus der Lehrreden, der eindringende und zugleich aufdringliche "Ich will – du sollst!" – Imperativ sind ein Affront für den detachierten und distanzierten "Es könnte so sein, dass . . ." – Vorschlag gerade dieser literarischen Strömung. Geht es den Modernisten doch nicht darum, irgendeine Heilslehre, einen Übermenschen mit unbestimmtem Ziel zu schaffen, sondern darum, Fragen zu stellen an alles, was sie angeht, kritische Fragen vor allem an alles, was ihnen nahesteht. Gerade diese Fähigkeit "über alles ihm Ehrwürdige" zu sprechen (über Wagner, das Deutschtum, das Christentum) bewundert Mann an Nietzsche. Ein solcher Kritiker und Kulturphilosoph aber kann nicht dem historischen Fixpunkt entfliehen, er muss die "alten Tafeln" benennen, bevor er sie zerbricht.

25. a.a.O., S. 26f.

Und das nun ist Nietzsches Bemühen in all seinen Schriften, die über Wagner, über die Romantik, über deutsche Schriftsteller und französische, über die antike Kultur und die moderne, über die Bildungsanstalten und die Erziehung, über das Christentum und die Moral, über den Fortschrittsglauben, den Darwinismus und Bismarcks deutsches Reich handeln.

Wie aber — da sie den *Zarathustra* schwerlich aus dem Oeuvre Nietzsches eliminieren können — rezipieren die Modernisten dieses ihnen so fremde Werk? Hierbei ergibt sich die folgende Konstellation: Konnte *Zarathustra* bisher als selbständiger Wirkungsfaktor funktionieren, so muss man diese Selbständigkeit im Modernismus als beendet betrachten. Von nun an ist eine Wirkung *Zarathustras* nur noch über die Kenntnis der kritischen Schriften Nietzsches möglich, und zwar indem man eine Kontinuität der kritischen Intention im *Zarathustra* voraussetzt. Nietzsche war "von Anfang an ganz da, war immer derselbe [. . .]. Was sich ändert, ist allein die Akzentuierung, die immer frenetischer, die Stimmlage, die immer schriller, die Gebärde, die immer grotesker und fürchterlicher wird [. . .]. Nicht genug aber ist die vollkommene Einheitlichkeit und Geschlossenheit von Nietzsche's Lebenswerk zu betonen".[26] Aus dieser Einbettung des *Zarathustra* in die erkenntniskritische Nietzsche-Wirkung im Modernismus erfolgt bei einer Reihe von Autoren eine durch die spezifische Relevanznahme bedingte Umgruppierung der Strukturelemente dieses Werkes. Man entdeckt aphoristische Elemente, historische Bezüge; der Messianismus wird zur Bibel-Parodie, und der lehrhafte Ton erhält höchstironische Potenz und wird als bewusster Kontrast zum intellektualistischen Spiel eingesetzt. Mit diesem Kontrast arbeitet Musil zum Beispiel, wenn er in *Der Mann ohne Eigenschaften* den prophetischen Gestus Nietzsches von Ulrich fernhält, Clarissa dagegen hiermit ausstattet.

Die modernistische Rezeption Nietzsches — und damit auch die seines *Zarathustra* — wurde in Deutschland sehr einflussreich, und vielleicht dürfte man sogar soweit gehen zu behaupten, dass sie noch stets nicht beendet ist. Die Dominantsetzung der kritischen Position Nietzsches geschieht in der Philosophie und im Bereiche der Literatur. Beda Allemann sieht im *Zarathustra* die Parodie: "Er parodiert inzwischen einen biblisch-hymnisch-feierlichen Sprechstil".[27] Peter

26. a.a.O., S. 28.
27. Beda Allemann, *Ironie und Dichtung,* Pfullingen: Neske, 1956, S. 48.

Pütz lobt den Aphoristiker: "Das Buch ist sehr viel heller, als man vermutet hat, und Witz und Verstand herrschen über das Dunkle".[28] Karl Schlechta ist es ebenfalls darum zu tun, Zarathustra aus der vermeintlichen Sonderstellung zu befreien: "Aber das ist es ja gerade: zieht man vom Zarathustra ab, was daran alttestamentarischer Prophetenton ist, entkleidet man ihn der neutestamentlichen Entlehnungen, Anspielungen, Inversionen und Perversionen – d.h. nimmt man ihn vom Piedestal des echten 'Buchs der Bücher' herunter, so steht er fast unauffällig inmitten der obligaten Thematik. Sogar dasjenige, was dann als spezifischer Zarathustra-Ton übrig zu bleiben scheint – gewisse Bilder, Situationen, Stimmungen –, ist keineswegs neu: Man findet es schon in 'Menschliches, Allzumenschliches' ".[29]

Im Jahre 1944 erschien im zweiten Jahrgang der Zeitschrift *Trivium* ein Aufsatz von Michael Landmann: "Zum Stil des 'Zarathustra' ". Dieser Aufsatz ist exemplarisch für die modernistische Rezeption. Ausgangspunkt ist wiederum die Einheitlichkeit des Nietzscheschen Oeuvres: "Auch die Formenwelt der übrigen Werke ist in ihm [*Zarathustra*] unverloren".[30] Der Aphorismus als wichtiges Element des Nietzsche-Stils wird im *Zarathustra* in gesteigerter Form wiedergefunden: "Und das genuine Instrument eines solchen Fortissimo, der Aphorismus mit seiner Kunst der Pointe, der Hintergründigkeit und Doppeldeutigkeit – ist er im *Zarathustra* nicht nur noch ausgelassener und übermütiger geworden? ".[31] Der hypothetische, versuchsweise Charakter des modernistischen Verhältnisses von Signifikant und Signifikat kommt in Landmanns folgender Äusserung über Nietzsches Wortgebrauch zum Ausdruck: "Durch geschickte Ummodelung lässt sich auf diese Weise fast jedes Wort aus einem früheren Zusammenhang wieder aufgreifen und einem neuen Zusammenhang einverleiben. Wie in der modernen Chemie kann aus allem alles werden".[32] Nietzsches häufiger Gebrauch der Stilfigur des Zeugmas hat nicht die Funktion, "das Anschauliche zu heben, sondern sogar umgekehrt es zu durchqueren".[33] In Nietzsches Welt des Werdens steht

28. Peter Pütz, a.a.O., S. 46.
29. Karl Schlechta, *Der Fall Nietzsche. Aufsätze und Vorträge,* München: Hanser, 1958, S. 18.
30. Michael Landmann, a.a.O., S. 280.
31. a.a.O., S. 280.
32. a.a.O., S. 287f.
33. a.a.O., S. 296.

jede Möglichkeit offen und ist folglich keine vorauszusehen. Dies gilt jedoch nur dann — und hiermit wendet ein modernistischer Rezipient sich gegen den expressionistischen —, wenn "das Werden nicht seinerseits einer Norm untersteht".[34]

Etwa in die gleiche Zeit wie die modernistische Rezeption — aber im prinzipiellen Gegensatz zu ihr — fällt ein Rezeptionsstrang, der nicht eigentlich eine literarische Periode darstellt, sondern der eine ideologisch-politische Unterströmung repräsentiert. Es ist dies der nationalsozialistische Wirkungsstrang. Er musste wiederum die kritischen Schriften Nietzsches zurückdrängen und den *Zarathustra* in den Mittelpunkt stellen. Die kritischen Schriften mit ihrer expliziten Angabe mancher historischen Daten und dabei namentlich mit ihrer Kritik an allem, was sich als deutsch und tief und kulturtragend stets wieder überschätzt, und mit der gleichzeitigen Aufwertung romanischer Kultur verbieten von vornherein den Anschluss an das Interpretationssystem des zukünftigen Dritten Reiches. *Zarathustra* dagegen lässt ja alle historischen Beziehungen offen und lädt zur eigenen Auffüllung ein. Leo Berg formulierte bereits im Jahre 1897 hinsichtlich des Übermenschen, der im Nationalsozialismus wichtig wurde: "Nietzsche sagt nicht, wer und was der Übermensch ist, denn dieser schwebt vollständig in der Luft und ist nur mit wenigen Strichen ins Blaue gezeichnet. Er ist ein Wort, ein Ideal, ein Gedanke, ein Traum, ein Wunsch, eine Sehnsucht, oder wenn man will: die Quintessenz seines neuen Adels [. . .]".[35]

Es war dann ein Leichtes, vom nationalsozialistischen Denksystem aus zur Auffüllung der im *Zarathustra* präsenten "Unbestimmtheitsstellen" gerade in Bezug auf das Konzept des Übermenschen überzugehen und eine Gleichsetzung dieses Konzeptes mit dem deutschen Herrenmenschen vorzunehmen. Hinzukommt dann die Annahme einer natürlichen, gegebenen Vorrangstellung dieses Menschentypus; eine etwaige in der Textstruktur des *Zarathustra* verankerte Selbstüberwindung moralischer, intellektualistischer Art (der Gedanke der ewigen Wiederkehr) wird nicht wahrgenommen. Das "vivere periculosamente" — immer mehr verselbständigt und aus seiner textlichen Umgebung gelöst — beginnt seinen Siegeszug: " 'Leben überhaupt

34. a.a.O., S. 298.
35. Leo Berg, *Der Übermensch in der modernen Literatur. Ein Kapitel zur Geistesgeschichte des 19. Jahrhunderts,* Paris, usw.: Albert Langen, 1897, S. 71f.

heisst in Gefahr sein'. Das ist Nietzsche. Ich sage nicht, dass der lyrisch-musikalische Bacchant, der ekstatische Schwärmer, nicht auch echter Nietzsche sei. Aber dieser von der Zeitstimmung ungebührlich in den Vordergrund gedrängte lyrische Ekstatiker ist nur die eine Seite [. . .]. Diese Tatseite des Nietzscheschen Wesens hat sich in einer Entdeckung ersten Ranges fruchtbar erwiesen: in der Entdeckung des Agons und seiner Bedeutung für die griechische Kultur".[36] In diesem Zitat polemisiert Bäumler gegen die Rezeption im Jugendstil und Expressionismus und stellt zugleich die Kontinuität von Nietzsches Spätschriften mit den Frühschriften her, indem er Nietzsches Sicht auf das Griechentum auf den Wettstreit-Aspekt festlegt und reduziert.

Der nationalsozialistische Rezeptionsansatz mit seinem Volumen und der Ausstrahlungskraft, die Slogans eigen ist, übertönte die modernistische Aufnahme Nietzsches. Letztere, die auf Unterscheidungen und Nuancen angewiesen ist und die Kenntnis des Details voraussetzt, bleibt eher dem Spezialisten vorbehalten. Eine Wirkung in die Breite erreicht sie damit kaum, und dies nun war gerade der Erfolg der nationalsozialistischen Rezeption.

Seit dem Ende der fünfziger Jahre ist es denn auch stiller um *Zarathustra* geworden. Mit Michael Landmann sind wir geneigt, diese Stille als wohltätig, als Befreiung von einer Faszination zu bewerten. Landmann hatte mit seiner Stilanalyse eine solche Befreiung erstrebt und die Lockerung einer Bindung, "die ohnedies zu stark ist, als dass sie je zerreissen könnte".[37] Desto überraschender zeichnen sich zwei neue Rezeptionsansätze ab, einer – vorläufig noch als Einzelfall – in Deutschland, ein anderer – grösseren Ausmasses – in Frankreich.

Anke Bennholdt-Thomsen kündigt in dem Untertitel ihrer Studie einen Neuansatz im Rezeptionsprozess des *Zarathustra* an, indem sie ihre Arbeit als *Eine Revision* bezeichnet.[38] Die für die Problemstellung dieser Studie bestimmende Vorentscheidung liegt in dem Interesse am Kommunikationsaspekt von Sprache. Im Gegensatz zu der verbreiteten Auffassung der Forschung, derzufolge *Zarathustra*

36. Alfred Bäumler, *Bachofen und Nietzsche,* Zürich: Verlag der neuen Schweizer Rundschau, 1929, S. 36f.
37. Michael Landmann, a.a.O., S. 302.
38. Anke Bennholdt-Thomsen, *Nietzsches 'Also sprach Zarathustra' als literarisches Phänomen. Eine Revision,* Frankfurt a.M.: Athenäum, 1974.

eine Mischung aus verschiedensten Elementen darstellt, sieht Bennholdt-Thomsen aus der Perspektive der Kommunikationstheorie deutlich durchstrukturierte Kapitel, motivierte Argumentation, konsequente Aufeinanderfolge der Reden.[39] Der wissenschaftliche Hintergrund der Autorin ist das Modell der Rhetorik und auch die Konzeption des russischen Formalismus. In ihrer Umschreibung der poetischen Funktion nimmt sie unter Berufung auf Jakobson, aber unter Verwendung rhetorischer Terminologie an, dass die Darstellung (verba) neben dem Auszusagenden (res) eine entscheidende Bedeutung hat und dass sich daher Nietzsches *Zarathustra* vom Philosophischen abheben und dem Literarischen zuordnen lässt. Die Einheitlichkeit des gesamten Werkes erblickt sie in der Entwicklung und Konsequenz der dort behandelten Sprachproblematik, die ihrer Meinung nach für Zarathustras Weg bestimmend ist. Zunehmende Erkenntnis geht Hand in Hand mit zunehmendem Sprachvermögen, das Zarathustra in dem Augenblick erreicht, wo er die Lehre von der ewigen Wiederkunft nicht mehr verdrängt, sondern sie artikulieren kann.[40]

Zarathustra weist kein Innenleben auf, das ausserhalb seiner Worte fassbar wäre; diese Feststellung bringt Bennholdt-Thomsen zu dem Ausspruch: "Das Subjekt des Sprechens ist nichts anderes als sein Kommunizieren".[41] Unsere Analyse der Textstruktur weist ebenfalls in diese Richtung, obwohl die Autorin unserer Meinung nach mit etwas zu grosser Entschiedenheit das berichtete Innenleben ausschliesst. Diese Beobachtung trifft nämlich nicht für die Fälle zu, wo der Erzähler von Zarathustra sagt, er sei traurig in seinem Herzen oder einsam und müde. Im grossen und ganzen ist Bennholdt-Thomsen in dieser Frage jedoch zuzustimmen.

Das Sinnsystem der Rezipientin, das auf das Werk projiziert wird, ist in diesem Rezeptionsansatz das sprach- und kommunikationstheoretische Interesse, das in der Gegenwart im wissenschaftlichen Bereich herrscht. Das thematische Material und die kompositorischen Mittel, die diesen Ansatz stützen, sind in den Abschnitten zu suchen, in denen Zarathustra den Gedanken der ewigen Wiederkehr bewältigt, nämlich in drei Phasen: ihn erfährt, verschweigt und schliesslich ausspricht. Die Passagen ungehemmter Redseligkeit werden dabei

39. a.a.O., S. 147.
40. a.a.O., S. 189.
41. a.a.O., S. 196.

zwangsläufig abgeschattet. Gerade jedoch aufgrund dieser Passagen hatte die auf die Sprachkritik Nietzsches gerichtete Forschung *Zarathustra* ausgeklammert. Das Schweigen hatte man in diesem Text bislang nicht gesehen, und man hätte höchstens tiefenpsychologisch die Redseligkeit als Schweigen interpretieren können.

Ein neuer Wirkungsschwerpunkt für das Werk Nietzsches bereitet sich seit einigen Jahren in Frankreich vor. Die intellektualistische französische Ambiance hatte — von Einzelfällen abgesehen (wie die erwähnte Mme de Noailles) — keinen Anlass gesehen, den *Zarathustra* als besonders kongeniales Werk in ihrer Mitte aufzunehmen. Darum darf man die kürzlich erfolgte Dramatisierung dieses Werkes ein bemerkenswertes Ereignis nennen. Jean-Louis Barrault verantwortet diese Dramatisierung auf folgende Weise: " 'Ainsi parlait Zarathoustra' est de fait, et par-dessus tout, un immense poème: un hymne à la vie".[42] Marx und Freud haben ihre Zeit gehabt, jetzt, wo das Leben selbst zum ersten Male wirklich in Gefahr ist, hat Nietzsches Stunde geschlagen. Der kritische Nietzsche hat seine Verdienste, aber, so fährt Barrault fort, "j'apprécie encore plus les envolées positives de son Esprit. C'est sous ce second angle qu'il me paraît le plus original".[43] Es folgt eine Beschreibung der Elemente, die als grösste Stimulanz wirken, eine Beschreibung, die sich unmittelbar in die deutsche Jugendstil-Rezeption der Jahrhundertwende einfügen könnte: "Mais surtout quand il sème pour des moissons futures, quand il invoque le soleil, quand il se sent lumière, quand son coeur déborde de miel, quand il veut tout donner, quand il est léger, dansant, plein d'une 'joyeuse méchanceté' ".[44] So verwunderlich ist es allerdings nicht, in unserer Zeit mit ihrem Interesse für Art Nouveau eine Zarathustra-Rezeption in diesem Sinne vorzufinden, zumal für Frankreich dieser Rezeptionsansatz ja nicht eine Wiederholung, sondern eine Entdeckung ist.

Ein Beweis für die in Frankreich herrschende Disposition, Nietzsche zu rezipieren, dürfte das im Jahre 1972 in Cerisy-la-Salle gehaltene Kolloquium sein, dessen Ergebnisse der Öffentlichkeit in der Publikation *Nietzsche aujourd'hui?* zugänglich gemacht

42. Jean-Louis Barrault u.a., *Nietzsche: A propos de 'Ainsi parlait Zarathoustra'*, Paris: Gallimard, 1974, S. 10.
43. a.a.O., S. 28.
44. a.a.O., S. 29.

wurden.[45] Das Paradigma, die Forschungskonvention französischer Geisteswissenschaftler unserer Jahre könnte man global als eine Kombination von Sprachphilosophie und Psychologie bezeichnen (Lacan ist ein Hauptvertreter dieser Richtung). Diese Kombination ist denn auch das Sinnsystem, das die Rezeption des *Zarathustra* bestimmt. Bernard Pautrat kann als Repräsentant dieser Richtung in Cerisy gelten. Aus der sprachlichen Struktur des *Zarathustra* schliesst Pautrat, dass der Hauptgedanke (la tête), die ewige Wiederkunft, sich der Formulierung widersetzt hat, dass *Zarathustra* eine "contradiction entre la nécessité de l'énonciation et l'impossibilité de l'énoncé" darstellt.[46] Die auf diese Weise entstandenen textuellen Leerstellen "mettent l'éternel retour en position de trou".[47] "Trou dans le texte, autour duquel tout s'organise".[48] Da es gerade der Hauptgedanke (la tête) ist, der diese Leerstelle bildet (hier kommt noch das "Medusenhaupt", das Nietzsche in den Vorarbeiten zu *Zarathustra* erwähnt, ins Spiel), spricht Pautrat von einem "texte proprement décapité".[49] Eine philosophische Auffüllung der Leerstellen, eine Weiterentwicklung des Wiederkunftgedankens im Sinne von beispielsweise Löwith oder Fink lehnt Pautrat in der Diskussion, die sich seinem Vortrage anschliesst, ab, da es sich im *Zarathustra* nicht um einen philosophischen Text handele: "Je me refuse à dissocier arbitrairement ce que philosophiquement on prétend que cela veut dire et la façon dont cela se dit".[50]

Der sprachliche Befund, "le trou textuel", ist für Pautrat Anlass, das Interpretationssystem der Symbolik Freuds auf *Zarathustra* zu projizieren und darin Fetischismus und Kastration als wichtige Bedeutungsfelder zu entdecken. Den Vorwurf, er benutze den Nietzsche-Text nur als "prétexte", nimmt Pautrat gelassen hin; der Philosoph und Mensch Nietzsche, so sagt er, "me laisse d'une certaine manière tout à fait indifférent".[51] Eine sichere Basis für seine Bedeutungskonstituierung erstrebt er nicht: "Alors, que tout ce que je dis se situe à un niveau de très grande fragilité, c'est mon plus cher espoir".[52]

45. Paris: Union Générale d'Editions, 1973, zwei Bände.
46. a.a.O., Bd. 1, S. 19.
47. a.a.O., S. 21.
48. a.a.O., S. 18.
49. a.a.O., S. 19.
50. a.a.O., S. 34f.
51. a.a.O., S. 42.
52. a.a.O., S. 47.

Das Interesse an der Formulierung des Hauptgedankens manifestiert sich, wie wir gesehen haben, auch im kommunikationstheoretischen Ansatz Bennholdt-Thomsens. Diese Autorin allerdings sieht in Nietzsches *Zarathustra* eine Entwicklung, die über das Verschweigen zum Aussprechen des Gedankens führt. Pautrat, dem es auch nicht entgehen kann, dass in der Tat etwas über den Gedanken ausgesagt wird, stellt die Frage, wer den Gedanken ausspricht und in welcher Situation das geschieht. Die Antwort muss dann sein: im Traum und als Rätsel, und ausserdem wird er den Tieren in den Mund gelegt – also bleibt er eine Leerstelle. Bis zu dieser Feststellung sind die Rezeptionsansätze von Bennholdt-Thomsen und Pautrat vergleichbar und diskutierbar. Beide repräsentieren sie das Interesse der heutigen Literaturwissenschaft an der Sprache als Medium der Kommunikation. Der weitere Schritt, *Zarathustra* als "prétexte", ist eine spezifisch französische Variante. Roland Barthes hat den Gedanken, dass ein literarischer Text für den Leser ein "prétexte" zu einem neuen, eigenen Text sein kann, mit Vehemenz verteidigt.

Die Stille um *Zarathustra* ist wieder gewichen. Diese seltsame Mischung aus Ekstase, Scherz und Kritik bietet offenbar einer jeden Generation Möglichkeiten zur Aufnahme in den lebendigen literarischen Bestand. Um Persönliches nicht zu verbergen: Mit viel Überzeugung möchte ich eine Empfehlung von Karl Schlechta weitergeben: "Daher ist es auch im Grunde gleichgültig, mit welchem Werk man die Lektüre beginnt; nur mit dem 'Zarathustra' und mit den letzten Schriften des Jahres 1888 sollte man nicht anfangen: man macht es sich dann aus Geschmacksgründen unnötig schwer, in den unbezweifelbaren Ernst des Gesamtwerkes einzudringen".[53]

53. Karl Schlechta, *Der Fall Nietzsche,* S. 21.

DAS "THETISCHE" DEMONSTRATIVPRONOMEN

Frank C. Maatje (Utrecht)

Ein Brief an Jan Kamerbeek

Lieber Herr Kamerbeek! Eine Fortsetzung unserer Diskussion, die sich jetzt bereits über ein Jahrzehnt hinzieht — einer Diskussion, welche wir bald mündlich und à front, bald in Briefform miteinander über das in der Überschrift dieses meines Beitrags angedeutete Thema geführt haben, erschien mir eine geeignete Beglückwünschung zu Ihrem Geburtstag. Mit der g e d r u c k t e n Form dieser Fortsetzung (erstmalig in der Geschichte zumindest u n s e r e r Auseinandersetzung!) möchte ich jedoch beileibe nicht behaupten, daß ich die betreffenden Fragen, in deren Bann wir beide schon so lange stehen, endgültig gelöst zu haben meine! Wohl aber veranlaßt mich diese Form dazu, die Mitleser dieses Briefes zunächst einmal in unsere Geheimsprache einzuweihen, sie über die Bedeutung des in der Überschrift figurierenden geheimnisvollen Adjektivs aufzuklären, damit wir sie zum Mitüberdenken unseres Problems auffordern können. Zu diesem Zweck schicke ich also eine kurze " E x p o s i - t i o n " voraus.

Im Jahre 1952 haben Sie in einem niederländischen Interpretationsaufsatz über das Gedicht "ΟΙΝΟΥ ΕΝΑ ΣΤΑΛΑΓΜΟΝ..." des Lyrikers J. H. Leopold[1] m.W. als erster auf eine besondere Funktion des Demonstrativpronomens *deze/dit* (dt. *dieser/diese/dieses*[2]) hinge-

---

1. J. Kamerbeek Jr., "Leopold's 'Eén druppel wijn'. Ontwerp voor een interpretatie". In: *De nieuwe taalgids* 45 (1952), S. 129-136, insbes. S. 129-130.
2. Das Niederländische hat beim Demonstrativpronomen ein Zweiklassensystem: *deze/dit* neben *die/dat,* ebenso wie das Englische (*this*/Mz. *these, that*/Mz. *those,* nur daß die niederl. *deze-* und *die*-Formen sowohl vor den sog. "*de*-Wörtern" in der Einzahl, wie vor den sog. "*het*-Wörtern" und "*de*-Wörtern" in der Mehrzahl stehen; der Gebrauch von *dit* und *dat* beschränkt sich auf die "*het*-Wörter" in der Einzahl). Ähnlich wie im Englischen spielt die materielle oder geistige "Entfernung" vom Sprechenden (*deze/dit* bezieht sich "von Haus aus"

wiesen. Diese Funktion bezeichneten Sie als "r e f l e x i v " in genau bestimmbaren Fällen; von einer grammatischen Kategorie war damals noch nicht die Rede (und auch später eigentlich nur implizite). Hierbei war "reflexiv" nicht gemeint im Sinne des gewöhnlichen rückbezüglichen Fürworts, sondern im Sinne einer sich a u f s i c h   s e l b s t beziehenden Sprachform. Diese Sprachform s e t z t (poniert), zumeist mit Pathos, ihre eigene Existenz, und − so muß man wohl ergänzen − die Existenz des im dazugehörigen Substantiv ausgedrückten Begriffsinhalts. In unseren späteren Gesprächen über diese Erscheinung bezeichnete ich das Pronomen denn auch als ein *"deze/dit* ponens"; Sie selber schlugen einmal als kennzeichnendes Adjektiv den Terminus "t h e t i s c h " vor. Ich glaube, terminologisch kommt das auf dasselbe hinaus; wir wollen aber über die bloße Terminologie hinausgehen und nach den poetologischen und linguistischen Implikationen fragen, denn auf diese − insbesondere auf erstere − kommt es, wie ich ganz sicher weiß, auch Ihnen an.

Als Beispiel für die Mitleser dieses Briefes gebe ich, statt Leopolds auch in anderer Hinsicht äußerst schwieriges Gedicht zu bemühen, das von Ihnen selbst angeführte Vondelwort:

Wanneer dit tijtlijk leven endt,/   *Sobald dies der Zeit verhaftete Leben endet,/*
Begint het endelooze leven.[3]   *beginnt das Leben ohne Ende.*

Neben die anaphorische und die deiktische Funktion des Fürworts trete Ihrer Meinung nach hier, wie auch in Leopolds Gedicht und in vielen anderen Fällen, eine "reflexive": *Dit tijtlijk leven, dieses der Zeit verhaftete Leben,* sei eben vom Dichter mittels des Fürworts als *tijtlijk,* als *der Zeit verhaftet,* g e s e t z t . Ich interpretiere, wie Sie

auf Näheres, *die/dat* auf Ferneres) im allgemeinen eine recht untergeordnete Rolle: Die Formen sind also meistens ohne weiteres austauschbar. Es gibt jedoch Fälle, in denen ausschließlich *deze/dit* am Platze ist. Zu diesen Fällen gehört die hier zu behandelnde "thetische" Verwendung. In der deutschen Sprache, mit ihrem Dreiklassensystem (betontes *der/die/das* neben *dieser/diese/dieses* und *jener/jene/jenes*), fehlt die genaue Entsprechung der niederländischen Gegenüberstellung, da ja sowohl niederl. *deze/dit* wie *die/dat* mit *dieser/diese/dieses* übersetzt werden kann. Aus dem Grunde lassen sich Substitutionsproben (das "thetische" *deze/dit* kann eben nicht durch *die/dat* ersetzt werden) im Deutschen leider nicht durchführen.

3. "Leopold's 'Eén druppel wijn' ", S. 129.

sehen, diesen Ihren bemerkenswerten Gedanken bereits ein wenig in
m e i n e m   Sinne, fasse ihn aber gerade deshalb auf so tautologische
Weise zusammen, damit zum Ausdruck gebracht wird, daß nach Ihrer
Ansicht von Anaphora oder Deixis nicht die Rede sein könne, weil
weder auf Vorangegangenes noch auf in der außersprachlichen Welt
sich Befindendes hingewiesen werde, sondern eben nur auf in der und
durch die Sprache E n t s t e h e n d e s .

Sie zeigten sodann, wie diese pronominale Funktion für die Struktur des betreffenden Leopoldschen Gedichtes von größter Bedeutung
sei. Denn gerade in der dritten Strophe dieses längeren Gedichtes, in
der das Pronomen figuriere, werde das Entstehen des ganzen Gedichtes selbst beschrieben: Das Gedicht beschreibe, in Ihren eigenen
Worten, sich selbst in ebendieser dritten Strophe. So habe das Pronomen seinen Anteil an der immanenten Poetik des Gedichtes[4]. –
Aber, allgemeiner gesprochen: Bei Vondel wie bei Leopold sei dieses
deze/dit ein Mittel, ein gewisses P a t h o s zum Ausdruck zu bringen; bei jenem handle es sich um das Pathos der Sterblichkeit, bei
diesem um ein Pathos der "Individuation", der Vereinzelung also[5].

Etwa ein Jahrzehnt später lenkten Sie in einem Aufsatz über den
niederländischen Lyriker J. C. Bloem erneut die Aufmerksamkeit auf
die besondere Funktion des Pronomens: (ich übersetze) "Im Normal-
fall liegen das bezeichnende Wort und die bezeichnete Sache (im
weitesten Sinne) auf völlig verschiedenen Ebenen. Wenn aber das
Demonstrativpronomen *deze/dit* (bzw. dessen Äquivalent in einer
anderen Sprache) nicht auf die außersprachliche Wirklichkeit verweist und ebensowenig auf bereits Gesagtes, bleibt nur eine einzige
Zeigerichtung als Möglichkeit übrig, nämlich, auf sich selbst. Man
könnte auch sagen: In diesem Fall ist das am nächsten Liegende, auf
das das Fürwort ja im allgemeinen [wenigstens im Niederländischen[6]]
verweist, eben das Wort *dit/deze* selbst. Es bedeutet sich selbst, es ist
was es bedeutet. Das bezeichnende Wort und die bezeichnete Sache
verschmelzen. Und diese Verschmelzung kann als ein privilegierter
Fall der Einheit von Form und Inhalt gelten. Das 'reflexive' Demon-

4. a.a.O., S. 130, 133-134.
5. a.a.O., S. 130. Daß ein prinzipieller Unterschied zwischen diesen beiden
Arten des Pathos festzustellen ist, zeigt die unten zu besprechende Austausch-
probe mit *unser(e)*; vgl. auch Anm. 17.
6. "Im allgemeinen" ist hier zugleich zu betonen und einzuschränken, vgl.
Anm. 2.

strativum läßt sich außerordentlich gut in der Lyrik verwenden. Wörter, die von Natur (was die Griechen φύσει nannten) sich selbst bedeuten, haben gleichsam magischen Charakter, sie sind dünn gesät. Dichter sollen sie in Ehren halten!"[7].

Sprach ich oben von einer "Exposition", so ist es jetzt wohl auch am Platze, von gewissen "e r r e g e n d e n M o m e n t e n " unseres kleinen Dramas in der Geschichte der niederländischen Lyriktheorie zu sprechen, die sich anläßlich der Veröffentlichung Ihres Bloem-Aufsatzes ergaben. Der Amsterdamer Kritiker Jessurun d'Oliveira, Mitherausgeber der Zeitschrift der damaligen literaturkritischen Avantgarde, *Merlyn,* brach eine für Außenstehende äußerst amüsante, wenn auch nicht sonderlich fruchtbare Polemik vom Zaune[8]. Was nun seine Bedenken gegen Ihre theoretischen und interpretativen Erörtertungen anbelangt, so kann ich mich kurz fassen, da dasjenige, was ihm Hauptsache war, mir Nebensache ist, und umgekehrt. Ihre Beobachtungen rekapitulierte er – m.E. an sich vollkommen sinngemäß – folgendermaßen: Eine auffällige Erscheinung in Bloems Lyrik sei die sog. R e d u k t i o n , d.h. die Erscheinung, daß umfassendere Begriffe zu einem einzigen Aspekt reduziert, gewissermaßen zusammengezogen würden, der dann als wesentlich oder kennzeichnend anzusehen sei. Als Beispiel entlieh er Ihrem Aufsatz den Bloemschen Satz (aus dem Gedicht *Ademen (Atmen)*):

Leven is niet veel meer dan adem-   Zu leben, heißt kaum mehr als Atem
halen[9].   zu holen.

Nur gleichsam nebenbei erwähnte d'Oliveira Ihre Beobachtung, daß diese Reduktion häufig von einem "auf sich selbst verweisenden" Demonstrativum eingeleitet werde, wie z.B. in *In memoriam*:

7. J. Kamerbeek Jr., "Vijf gedichten van J. C. Bloem". In: *Forum der letteren* 4 (1963), S. 176-190, das übersetzte Zitat auf S. 178; ebenfalls in: J. Kamerbeek Jr., *De poezie van J. C. Bloem in Europees perspectief.* Amsterdam 1967, S. 5.
8. H. U. Jessurun d'Oliveira, " ' "Dit dal" *is* een dal' ". In: *Merlyn* 2 (1963/64), Heft 1, S. 45-51. Siehe für die bibliographischen Daten bezüglich der Fortsetzung dieser Diskussion: *De poezie van J. C. Bloem in Europees perspectief* (vgl. Anm. 7), S. 1, Fußnote *.
9. H. U. Jessurun d'Oliveira, " ' "Dit dal" *is* een dal' ", S. 45-46. Verwiesen sei hier weiter auf die neue, mit der Rechtschreibungsreform des Jahres 1954 in Einklang gebrachte Fassung letzter Hand des Bloemschen lyrischen Gesamtwerkes: J. C. Bloem, *Verzamelde gedichten.* Amsterdam ³1968, die sämtlichen Zitaten und Übersetzungen in meinem Beitrag zugrundeliegt.

247

Wat blijft ons over van dit lange derven,/ *Was bleibt uns denn von dieser*
                                               langen Dürftigkeit,/
Dat leven is? [10]   *die Leben heißt?*

Nicht jedoch auf diese Reduktion spitzte sich d'Oliveiras Kritik zu,
und erst gar nicht auf die besondere Funktion, die dem "reflexiven"
Pronomen dabei häufig zufällt, sondern auf eine andere von Ihnen
beobachtete Erscheinung: Kraft der Position, die ein Wort in einem
Gedicht einnimmt, würden oft bestimmte Bedeutungsaspekte des
betreffenden Wortes hervorgehoben. So werde in den auf obiges Zitat
aus *Ademen* folgenden Zeilen:

Maar dat is: in de diepten van dit   *Das aber heißt* [nämlich: dieses "Atem-
dal/   holen"]: *In den Tiefen dieses*
                                           Tales/
De oneind'ge ruimte tot zich in   *den unendlichen Raum in sich einzu-*
te leiden   *führen*

durch die vom Gedicht selbst aufgezwungene Stimmführung *dit dal*
(dieses Tal) tatsächlich zu einem T a l , zu einer melodischen
Senkung, was der Bedeutung des Wortes entspreche. D'Oliveira über-
schrieb seinen Aufsatz denn auch mit Ihrem eigenen Wort: "Dieses
Tal *ist* ein Tal", Ihrer Meinung nach infolge seiner Stellung am Ende
der Zeile[11].

Der Mißverständnisse aufseiten d'Oliveiras in dieser Polemik
waren viele. Wir wollen aber die Diskussion über diesen zweiten
Punkt nicht weiter verfolgen. Er ist in unserem Zusammenhang nur
insofern interessant, als sich auch in dem von Ihnen postulierten
"Positionswert" (so möchte ich mich ausdrücken) eines Wortes
dieselbe Erscheinung feststellen läßt, die Sie als charakteristisch für
das "reflexive" Demonstrativum erachteten: Das Wort "bedeute" —
positionis causa — "sich selbst".

Zu den " e r r e g e n d e n   M o m e n t e n " gehörte drei Jahre
später auch die Besprechung Ihres Manuskriptes einer Aufsatzsamm-
lung über die Lyrik J. C. Bloems[12] im Kreise unseres Utrechter
Institutes für Allgemeine Literaturwissenschaft, — einer Besprechung,

10. H. U. Jessurun d'Oliveira, " ' "Dit dal" *is* een dal' ", S. 45.
11. a.a.O., S. 46-47; vgl. weiter den in Anm. 7 aufgeführten Aufsatz Kamer-
beeks, S. 179-181, und *De poëzie van J. C. Bloem in Europees perspectief* (vgl.
Anm. 7), S. 6-9.
12. *De poëzie van J. C. Bloem in Europees perspectief*: s. Anm. 7.

die mich nicht unbeteiligt ließ . . . Eine leicht revidierte Fassung Ihres früheren Bloem-Aufsatzes[13] sollte den Auftakt zu einer Betrachtung der Bloemschen Lyrik aus europäischer Perspektive bilden. Nach der Diskussion faßte ich 1966 in einem Brief an Sie meine Reflexionen zum Thema des "reflexiven" hinweisenden Fürworts noch einmal zusammen: (ich übersetze aus einer undatierten Abschrift) "Das Demonstrativum spezifiziert das durch das dazugehörige Substantiv Bezeichnete und reduziert letzteres entweder auf (a) etwas in der Sprechsituation materiell Vorhandenes, oder auf (b) etwas, das in dieser Sprechsituation gedacht werden kann. Die sog. 'deiktische' Anwendung des Demonstrativums bezieht sich auf (a) wie (b). Zu der Kategorie (b) gehört selbstverständlich auch das ganze vorangehende Informationsangebot, auf das verwiesen werden kann, da es ja in die Sprechsituation eingegangen ist und mithin als etwas Spezifisches vom Sprechenden und Hörenden gedacht werden kann. Es ist letztere Verwendung, die man als 'anaphorisch' zu bezeichnen pflegt. Im Grunde handelt es sich aber einfach um eine 'deiktische' Verwendung, die sich auf eine frühere 'Eingabe' des Sprechenden bezieht. 'Deixis' und 'Anaphora' sind also keine gleichwertigen Kategorien — die Anaphora ist allenfalls eine Untergattung der Deixis." Ich möchte heute noch hinzufügen (unterbreche also meinen Brief aus dem Jahre 1966): Zu der Kategorie (b) gehört auch das sog. Determinativum, das wir beide, Sieselbst sowie ich, damals unberücksichtigt gelassen haben. Auch das Determinativum verweist auf eine Eingabe des Sprechenden, nicht jedoch "rückwärts," sondern "vorwärts", es kündigt diese an, als ein vom Sprechenden wie Hörenden zu Denken-des. — "Was Sie nun als 'reflexiv' bezeichnen", so fuhr mein Brief fort, "ist 'deiktisch' außerhalb der gewöhnlichen Sprech- bzw. Schreibsituation. Im literarischen Werk ist ja erstens keine Sprechsituation da, in der auf materiell Vorhandenes verwiesen werden kann: Alles ist eben 'gedacht'."

Nun, letzteres gilt allerdings nicht nur für das literarische Werk, sondern für jede Art der schriftlichen Kommunikation, in der der Schreibende und der Lesende in Entfernung miteinander "sprechen". Im Fall eines literarischen Werkes kommt aber noch etwas hinzu: A l l e s , was auf Grund der Eingaben des Schreibenden vom Lesenden gedacht werden soll, gehört exklusiv zu der im Werk aufgestell-

13. s. Anm. 7.

ten Welt. Der "Inhalt", das Ganze der Wortbedeutungen und sonstiger semantischer Bezüge des Werkes, entwirft ja keinen A u s s c h n i t t aus der außersprachlichen Wirklichkeit, wie es z.B. eine Zeitungsnachricht tut. — "Erscheint nun [ich zitiere wieder aus meinem Brief] das Demonstrativum in dieser nicht normal denotierenden Art der Sprachverwendung eines dichterischen Werkes, ohne daß es anaphorischen [oder determinativen] Wert hat, so wird die Bedeutung des dazugehörigen Substantivs [inklusive etwaiger Adjektive und Bestimmungen] als spezifisch für die im Werk aufgestellte Welt g e s e t z t . Es wird auf etwas verwiesen, das es anderweit nicht gibt, und damit ist das Bezeichnete vorhanden. Freilich, letzteres gilt gewissermaßen, wie bereits angedeutet, für die ganze 'fiktionale' Sprachverwendung: Es ließen sich hier leicht Parallelen zu Roman Ingardens Theorie der 'Quasi-Urteile' aufdecken[14]. Das Eigentümliche des auf nicht Vorhandenes verweisenden Demonstrativums jedoch ist es, das es das Gesetzte s p e z i f i z i e r t , d.h. als spezifisch für das betreffende Gedicht hinstellt [wie ich am Schluß zeigen werde]. Es läßt sich wohl kaum leugnen, daß diese Verwendung des deiktischen Demonstrativums — sozusagen an einer Stelle, an der es dem Anschein nach keine Funktion haben kann, da im Grunde die Möglichkeit, auf etwas zu verweisen fehlt — mit dem psychischen Prozeß zu tun hat, der m.E. die letzthinnige Erklärung für des Lesers Interesse an literarischen Werken enthält: dem Prozeß nämlich der Identifikation des Lesers mit dem Autor." Ich füge jetzt deutlichkeitshalber hinzu: ". . . mit dem Autor", insofern dieser in der literarischen Aussage das Wort führt, also nicht mit der biographischen Persönlichkeit, sondern mit dem implizierten Sprechenden. Darin liegt m.E. die Funktion der Dichtung im allgemeinen und die der Lyrik im besonderen; es ist hier aber nicht der Platz, diesen Gedanken weiter auszuführen.

Nach anfänglicher Ablehnung Ihres Konzeptes der "Reflexivität" des hinweisenden Fürworts (dem T e r m i n u s stehe ich auch

14. Vgl. Roman Ingarden, *Das literarische Kunstwerk*. Tübingen [4] 1972, S. 169-196. Es sei nebenbei bemerkt, daß der Terminus "fiktional" hier nicht den engen Sinn hat, den ihm Käte Hamburger beimißt (s. u.a. ihre *Logik der Dichtung*. Stuttgart [2] 1968, S. 153-186). Hamburger schließt ja gerade die Lyrik, wie auch die Ich-Erzählung, aus dem Bereich des Fiktionalen aus (a.a.O., S. 187-232 u. 245-268). Der hier von mir gehandhabte Begriff stimmt überein mit dem ausführlich in meinem Grundlagenbuch *Literatuurwetenschap. Grondslagen van een theorie van het literaire werk*. Utrecht [3] 1974, erörterten.

heute noch skeptisch gegenüber!) führte die Verbindung Ihrer Ausführungen über das in Frage stehende Phänomen einerseits mit
meinen eigenen Gedanken über den ontologischen Status des dichterischen (fiktionalen) Werkes andererseits, die in den darauffolgenden
Jahren in meinem einführenden Handbuch zur Literaturtheorie[15]
ihren Niederschlag fanden, für mich die "P e r i p e t i e " herbei!
Daß ich mich jedoch noch nicht getraute, die Erscheinung des ponie-
renden Demonstrativs in meiner Theorie aufzunehmen, erklärt sich
aus einer gewissen Unsicherheit, die sich kurz nach unserem Gedankenaustausch des Jahres 1966 einstellte. Immer mehr drängte sich
mir die Frage auf: Sprechen wir eigentlich noch über dasselbe? Handelt es sich im Grunde nicht um ganz verschiedene Phänomene bei
dem, was Herr Kamerbeek und ich ins Auge fassen?

Eine kleine Bestandsaufnahme Ihrer Beispiele im ersten Kapitel
der Bloem-Studie schien diese Annahme, diese Furcht, zu bestätigen.
Ich zitiere daraus in diesem Zusammenhang nur die von Ihnen selbst
als exemplarisch angeführten englischen Textstellen[16]:

von Wordsworth (aus *The Prelude*):
> [. . .] ere we learn to live
> In reconcilement with our stinted powers;
> To endure *this* state of meagre vassalage, [. . .];

von Coleridge (aus *Love*):
> All thoughts, all passions, all delights,
> Whatever stirs *this* mortal frame,
> All are but ministers of Love,
> And feed his sacred flame.

Und von Shakespeare (aus *The Merchant of Venice,* Lorenzo spricht
zu Jessica):
> Such harmony is in immortal souls;
> But whilst *this* muddy vesture of decay
> Doth grossly close it in, we cannot hear it.

Die verhältnismäßig zentrale Stelle, die Beispiele gerade dieser Art in
Ihren Ausführungen — auch vorher schon: vgl. das oben angeführte
Vondelwort aus Ihrem Leopold-Aufsatz — einnahmen, und die Kom-

15. s. Anm. 14.
16. "Vijf gedichten van J. C. Bloem" (vgl. Anm. 7), S. 177-178, und *De poëzie van J. C. Bloem in Europees perspectief* (vgl. Anm. 7), S. 4.

251

bination mit anderen Beispielen, in denen das Demonstrativpronomen einen doch etwas anderen ontologischen Status zu haben schien, bildeten für mich "r e t a r d i e r e n d e   M o m e n t e " im Handlungs- und Gedankenablauf unseres kleinen lyriktheoretischen Dramas. Sollte ich Beispiele von der Art der eben angeführten Textstellen mit einem kennzeichnenden Adjektiv versehen, so würde ich nicht zögern, sie als "metaphysisch" zu bezeichnen. *Dit tijtlijk leven, this state of meagre vassalage, this mortal frame, this muddy vesture of decay*: Es handelt sich in allen diesen Fällen um den Versuch, die Essenz des Daseins sub specie aeternitatis in Worten zu fassen. "Des Daseins", – nicht speziell des Daseins so wie es in der Dichtung gestaltet wird, sondern des Daseins schlechthin. Der Ursprung der Verwendung des Demonstrativs in diesem Kontext liegt denn auch wohl in der Theologie. Vom systematischen Standpunkt gesehen mag das gemeinsame Thema der Beispiele: die Vergänglichkeit, Memento mori, rein zufällig sein, entwicklungsgeschichtlich betrachtet ist es das keineswegs. Es spricht hier der Dichter als Pfarrer; der Gläubige, der am Sonntag in der Kirche die Predigt belauscht, wird mit dieser Art der Verwendung des hinweisenden Fürworts völlig vertraut sein. Zugegeben: oben erwähnte Identifizierung durch den Hörenden mit dem Sprechenden, die Auffassung der Situation des Sprechenden als eine den Hörenden unmittelbar angehende, trifft auch hier zu. Das Demonstrativ läßt sich ohne weiteres durch das Personalpronomen ersetzen: *Dieses der Zeit verhaftete Leben* ist *mein/Dein/unser Leben, this mortal frame* ist *my/your/our body,* usw.[17]. Der Gebrauch beschränkt sich also nicht auf die Dichtung, das ihm innewohnende Pathos ist nicht spezifisch literarisch[18]. Selbstverständlich

17. Ganz im Gegensatz also zum *deze/dit* der "Individuation" bei Leopold, vgl. "Leopold's 'Eén druppel wijn' " (s. Anm. 1), S. 130.
18. Ich weise beiläufig darauf hin, daß diese theologische Verwendung auch außerhalb des religiösen Bereichs produktiv geworden ist, und daß sie besonders in der politischen Sprache ein gleichsam säkularisiertes Pendant bekommen hat. (Auch das spricht dafür, die erwähnte thematische Gemeinsamkeit der literarischen wie theologischen beispiele als vom s y t e m a t i s c h e n Standpunkt rein zufällig zu betrachten.)
In politischen Reden begegnen in den letzten Jahren häufig Wendungen wie *dieses Land, dieser Staat,* wo einfach "unser Land", "unser Staat" gemeint ist. Ein Redner auf einer Parteiversammlung "weitet" die Zuhörerschaft, die ja nicht die ganze Partei umfaßt, gerne leicht "aus", indem er von *dieser Partei* spricht, und damit eigentlich "unsere Partei" meint. Ein niederländischer General sprach

führt die Substitution des hinweisenden Fürworts durch das persönliche einen gewissen stilistischen Verlust herbei. Aber der Kern der Sache, der "Informationswert", sozusagen, bleibt dabei unangetastet.

Letzteres scheint mir jedoch in den Fällen, die ich vorläufig nur negativ, nämlich als "nicht-metaphysisch" bezeichnen kann, nicht der Fall zu sein. Es wären demnach zwei Arten des im lyrischen fiktionalen Werk vorkommenden Demonstrativums zu unterscheiden: solche, die auch in nicht-fiktionaler Sprache vorkommen, und solche, die die besondere Funktion haben, eine Welt im dichterischen Werk zu erstellen.

Die "L ö s u n g d e s K n o t e n s"?   D i e hier Ihnen – gerade Ihnen! – anbieten zu wollen wäre wohl etwas vermessen. Einen Vorschlag möchte ich Ihnen aber nicht vorenthalten. Sehen wir uns noch einmal das Gedicht von J. C. Bloem an, das Sie vor allem im Hinblick auf das Demonstrativ *deze/dit* interpretiert haben[19]. Ich gebe dem niederländischen Gedichttext eine deutsche Übersetzung bei, in der ich auf die an einigen Stellen sehr naheliegende wortwörtliche Übertragung absichtlich verzichtet und vielmehr versucht habe, den lyrischen Ton des Originals im Deutschen wiederzugeben:

Het baanwachtershuisje
Het kleine huis, dat aan de spoorbaan staat,   (1)
Waarlangs de koorts van 't reizen komt gevlogen,
– De bonte was hangt aan de lijn te drogen –
Wie weet, hoe zacht daarbinnen 't leven gaat?

En deze jonge moeder met het kind –   (5)
Haar dromen drijven op haar zuivre zinnen
Naar de verliefdheid van het eerst beminnen
Bij de oude omhelzing van de zomerwind.

neuerdings in einem Interview – u.zw. ausdrücklich: nicht anaphorisch! – sogar von *dit leger* ("dieses Heer"), während er doch in der betreffenden Sprechsituation selber der einzige Vertreter "dieses Heeres" war. Soviel ich sehe kommt amerikanischen Politikern das Urheberrecht dieses säkularisierten "thetischen" Demonstrativs zu. So verwendete Präsident L. B. Johnson mit Vorliebe Wendungen wie *this nation* in seinen Fernsehansprachen, indem er mit vor Emotion zitterndem Finger auf "this very soil" von "God's own country" zeigte. (Damit wäre der Kreis freilich wieder geschlossen!)

19. "Vijf gedichten van J. C. Bloem" (vgl. Anm. 7), S. 186-188, und *De poëzie van J. C. Bloem in Europees perspectief* (vgl. Anm. 7), S. 17-20.

Maar zelfs al was dit onuitzegbre mijn,
Nog zou het diepst verlangen niet verdwijnen   (10)
Om na dit derven en dit lange schijnen
Eindlijk te zijn.

Das Bahnwärterhaus
Das kleine Haus, das an das Bahngleis stößt,   (1)
an dem vorüberrast des Reisens Fieber,
— die bunte Wäsche trocknet an der Leine —
wer weiß, wie sanft dadrin das Leben fließt?

Und diese junge Mutter mit dem Kind —   (5)
auf ihren reinen Sinnen schwimmen ihre Träume
zum Taumel hin der ersten jungen Liebe
in der alten Umarmung durch den Sommerwind.

Und wär jedoch dies Unsägliche mein,
noch verschwände nicht die tiefe Sehnsucht,   (10)
am Ende dieser dürft'gen Existenz und dieses Scheins
zuletzt zu *sein.*

Viermal begegnet hier das Demonstrativ *deze/dit*: Z. 5, 9, und 11. Viermal "zeigt" das sprechende lyrische Subjekt. Auf was zeigt es? Um diese Frage zu beantworten, ist es in diesem Fall unbedingt notwendig, zuerst festzustellen, aus welcher r ä u m l i c h e n Perspektive es spricht. Das Gedicht nimmt ja eindeutig seinen Ausgangspunkt in einer ausdrücklich als räumlich gesetzten Welt: Darauf deutet bereits der Titel hin. In Ihrer Interpretation fällt auf, daß Sie auf die Perspektivenfrage nicht eingehen. Vielleicht hielten Sie die Lösung dieser Frage im vorliegenden Fall für so naheliegend, daß Sie eine Erörterung für überflüssig erachteten. Um Mißverständnissen zuvorzukommen möchte ich jedoch klarstellen, daß es m.E. keinem Zweifel unterliegen kann, daß der "point of view" des lyrischen Subjekts, daß der "Stand"ort, aus dem die lyrische Welt in diesem Gedicht vorgeführt wird, in dem (nicht explizit erwähnten, aber implizit angedeuteten) Z u g (wahrscheinlich sogar: D-Zug oder Eilzug) zu lokalisieren ist. Das Bild, das aus dem Zugfenster "aufgenommen" wird: das kleine Haus, unmittelbar am Gleis, die Wäscheleine, die junge Frau mit dem Kind auf dem Arm, ist eine mit sehr wenigen aber wesentlichen Komponenten versehene Momentaufnahme. Gleich darauf ist der Zug vorbei, und das lyrische Subjekt, das implizierte Ich (vgl. *mijn/mein* in Z. 9), wieder auf sich selbst, auf die eigene Situation zurückgeworfen. Soweit ich mich dessen aus früheren Gesprächen mit Ihnen über dieses Gedicht entsinne, stimmen Sie dieser Auffassung der Perspektive bei. – Zwei Welten begegnen sich hier also in dem Gedicht: die Welt des Subjekts, die durch *des Reisens Fieber* vertreten wird, eine Welt des *Scheins,* eine *dürftige Existenz,* einerseits, und, andererseits, hart am Rande, eine andere Welt, eine *"unsägliche",* eine Welt des häuslichen Glücks, des Fortlebens glückseliger Erinnerungen. Das Fazit, das aus dieser Gegenüberstellung gezogen wird, ist aber durchaus un-biedermeierhaft: Auch ein Anteil an diesem *"Unsäglichen"* würde nicht ausreichen, das Dasein auf die Ebene des *Seins* (Z. 12) zu erheben. Das Leben bliebe *dürftig,* der *Schein* würde nicht aufgehoben. Dasein ist Abglanz.

Man braucht dieser Philosophie von der Unzulänglichkeit menschlichen Lebens nicht zuzustimmen (ich persönlich tue es nicht!), um einzusehen, daß in ihrem Ausdruck dem Fürwort *deze/dit* eine ganz besondere Funktion zufällt. Am "gewöhnlichsten" ist noch diese Funktion in *dit onuitzegbre/dies Unsägliche* von Z. 9. Es handelt sich hier zunächst um einfache Anaphora, um die Zurückverweisung auf das in den beiden ersten Strophen Geschaute[20]. Andererseits kann man sich fragen, ob nicht eine gewisse Verallgemeinerung vorliegt: Das Bild des Bahnwärterhauslebens steht ja stellvertretend für eine ganze Welt schlichten Glücks, die für das lyrische Ich verschlossen ist. Das Pronomen hat auf diese Weise auch eine zugleich zusammenfassende und verallgemeinernde Funktion, welche verlorenginge, wenn man es durch *dat* ersetzte. Dennoch, richtig "thetisch" ist es nicht, denn dasjenige, worauf es verweist, ist durch die vorherige "Eingabe" des Sprechenden bereits sprachlich vorhanden. Richtige "thetische", "reflexive" Pronomina ("reflexiv" in Ihrem Sinne), das steht wohl außer Zweifel, finden sich in der 11. Zeile: *dit derven/ diese dürftige Existenz, dit lange schijnen/dieser Schein* (nebenbei: niederl. *lang* läßt sich hier kaum adäquat in die deutsche Übersetzung einfügen). *Derven* und *schijnen* sind – ich übersetze Ihre eigenen Worte – "mit existenziellem Pathos und existenzieller Spannung aufgeladen", und werden mittels des Fürworts *dit* – wie Sie sich ausdrücken (ich übersetze wieder) – "geschärft"[21]. Das Pronomen trägt

---

20. Vgl. auch: *De poëzie van J. C. Bloem in Europees perspectief,* S. 49.
21. "Vijf gedichten van J. C. Bloem", S. 187, und *De poëzie van J. C. Bloem in Europees perspectief,* S. 19 bzw. 18.

dazu bei, *derven* und *schijnen* als kennzeichnend für die menschliche Existenz als solche hinzustellen, und es handelt sich bei Bloem, wie Sie ebenfalls selbst gezeigt haben, um eine Lyrik, welche die "condition humaine" zum Hauptthema hat[22].

Bleibt also das erste *deze/diese,* auf Z. 5. Ebensowenig wie *dit* in *dit derven en dit lange schijnen* durch *dat* ersetzt werden kann, läßt sich für *deze* in *deze jonge moeder* die (niederländische) Form *die* substituieren. D i e *jonge moeder* wäre nicht in dem Maße "gegenwärtig", wie sie es jetzt ist. In Ihrem Interpretationsaufsatz und in Ihrer Bloem-Studie schweigen Sie sich über dieses *deze* aus. Sie wissen aber bereits aus unserem letzten Gedankenaustausch und Briefwechsel (1973) über das "thetische" Demonstrativpronomen und insbes. über dieses Gedicht, daß ich ebendieses Fürwort das interessanteste der Vierzahl finde. Mit diesem *deze* beschwört Bloem eine ganze Welt herauf: *deze jonge moeder/diese junge Mutter* ist dadurch da, daß sie genannt wird. Es handelt sich, soweit ich sehe, um einen typisch lyrischen Zug: In der Epik, z.B. im Roman, habe ich diese Verwendung des hinweisenden Fürworts vergebens gesucht. Wenn ausnahmsweise einmal in einem Romananfang eine Entität (Person oder Sache), unvermittelt durch ein Demonstrativ "gezeigt", eingeführt wird, z.B. im stream of consciousness einer Gestalt, folgt immer eine nähere Bestimmung ihrer Identität, so daß "auf längere Sicht" doch eine Art "Determinativ" vorliegt. Und im Drama, das ja auf die Bühnenaufführung angelegt ist, sind Entitäten räumlich veranschaulicht, so daß ein Ponieren mittels des hinweisenden Fürworts entbehrlich ist. – So wie das P r ä t e r i t u m in der Epik ein Merkmal der Fiktionalität des E r z ä h l e n s darstellt, so dürfte das "t h e t i s c h e " D e m o n s t r a t i v ein Indiz für das fiktionale

22. a.a.O., S. 181, bzw. *De poëzie van J. C. Bloem,* usw., S. 10 und passim; vgl. weiter: Jan Kamerbeek Jr., *Albert Verwey en het Nieuwe Classicisme. "De richting van de hedendaagsche poëzie" (1913) in zijn internationale context.* Groningen 1966, S. 8.

l y r i s c h e S p r e c h e n sein[23]. Wäre damit nicht ein Kriterium für die Gattungspoetik gewonnen?

Ergebenst
Ihr
Frank C. Maatje

Utrecht, im Herbst 1975

23. Weiteres Beispielmaterial aus der Geschichte der europäischen Lyrik seit Baudelaire, das diese Hypothese unterstützen soll, ist bereits dankenswerterweise von Fräulein A. M. C. J. Geurts gesammelt worden; ich muß es aber hier aus Raumgründen unterdrücken. Besagtes Material werde ich zu gelegener Zeit einer Einzeluntersuchung zum Problem bestimmter Wortarten in der Lyrik zugrundelegen. – Auch die Beantwortung der Frage, inwiefern das "thetische" Demonstrativpronomen oder eine der hier unterschiedenen Untergattungen dieses Pronomens eine g r a m m a t i s c h e Kategorie darstellt, möchte ich einstweilen aufschieben. Ich beschränke mich hier auf die allgemeine, aber prinzipielle Feststellung, daß die Literaturtheorie, in unserem Fall die Gattungs- bzw. die Lyriktheorie, sprachwissenschaftlich gesehen eine P e r f o r m a n z theorie bildet. Gerade der Verlauf der Diskussion über das erwähnte "fiktionale Präteritum" sollte uns zur Vorsicht mahnen.

DER EITLE HOF IN BUKOLISCHER SICHT

Herman Meyer (Amsterdam)

Das Vorliegende ist ein Kapitel aus dem Bereich meiner noch unabgeschlossenen Untersuchungen zum Thema der motivischen und topischen Antithese von Hütte und Palast, vom Altertum bis in die jüngste Neuzeit. Ich lege diese Kostprobe unserm verehrten Jubilar mit umso mehr Freude auf den Geburtstagstisch, weil er in Gespräch und Diskussion sowohl für das Thema wie für die Behandlungsart lebhaftes Interesse gezeigt hat.

Die Kritik am eitlen Hofleben im Zeitalter des Humanismus soll im folgenden greifbare Gestalt gewinnen, indem wir uns mit einigen an und für sich recht heterogenen Texten befassen und diese in einen gewissen thematischen und auch kausalen Zusammenhang miteinander bringen. Es handelt sich um zwei Briefe des berühmten Humanisten Enea Silvio Piccolomini, um eine Ekloge des zu seiner Zeit kaum weniger berühmten Dichters Baptista Mantuanus, und schliesslich um die sehr freie Übertragung dieser Texte ins Englische in einigen Eklogen von Alexander Barclay.[1] Von diesen drei Autoren ist Barclay gewiss der weniger bedeutende, aber sein Werk beansprucht unsere besondere Aufmerksamkeit, weil in diesen Bearbeitungen Hofkritik und Bukolik so reizvoll konvergieren; oder anders gesagt: der Palast wird hier in einer bisher ungekannten Eindringlichkeit von der Hirtenhütte aus gesichtet.

Im November 1444 greift in Österreich die Pest um sich. Im Umkreis der Reichskanzlei Kaiser Friedrichs III. in Wiener Neustadt werden Todesfälle gemeldet. Der Kaiser verordnet daraufhin, dass die

1. Zitiert wird nach folgenden Ausgaben: *Der Briefwechsel des Eneas Silvius Piccolomini,* hrsg. von Rudolf Wolkan, 1. Abt., 1. Bd., Wien 1909; Enea Silvio Piccolomini, *Briefe,* übersetzt und eingeleitet von Max Mell, Jena 1911; Baptista Mantuanus, *The Eclogues,* hrsg. v. Wilfred P. Mustard, Baltimore 1911; Alexander Barclay, *The Eclogues,* hrsg. von Beatrice White, London 1928.

Kanzlei zeitweilig in das Landstädtchen Bruck an der Mur verlegt
wird. Als Kanzleisekretär amtiert seit einigen Jahren Enea Silvio Piccolomini, der übrigens schon im nächsten Jahr in den geistlichen
Stand eintreten und 1458 als Papst Pius II. auf den Stuhl Petri berufen werden sollte. Aus einem hohen aber völlig verarmten Adels-
geschlecht in Mittelitalien gebürtig hatte Enea Silvio, nach dürftiger
und harter Jugend auf dem Lande, als geschickter Diplomat und
Hofmann, und nicht weniger als humanistischer Gelehrter und Poet
schon eine erfolgreiche Laufbahn hinter sich; vor zwei Jahren hatte
der Kaiser ihn zum Poeta laureatus gekrönt.[2] Im ländlichen refugium
schreibt Enea Silvio nun 1444 die beiden Briefe, die uns angehen. In
dem ersteren von beiden spricht er – nach einem kurzen und gerade
durch seine nüchterne Sachlichkeit erschütternden Bericht über die
Pestseuche in Wiener Neustadt und in wirkungsvoller Entgegen-
setzung zu demselben – von seinem jetzigen Glücksgefühl in der
freien Natur, worauf er in allgemeinerem Sinne das Lob des Landlebens anstimmt:

> nunc illud te volo scire beatum mihi videri, qui vitam ab negotiis procul
> publicis sibi delegit sicut prisca gens mortalium consuevit. quis enim non
> felicem illum dicat, qui nullo fenore aut ere alieno obligatus rura suis bobus
> exercet.[3]
>
> Nun weisst du, wo ich bin und was ich treibe. Und ich möchte dir jetzt erklären,
> wie selig mir der erscheint, der von Stadtgeschäften fern lebt wie einst der Men-
> schen erst Geschlecht zu leben pflegte! Denn wer wird den nicht glücklich
> nennen, der, von allem Zins und allen Schulden frei, die Väterflur mit seinen
> eigenen Rindern pflügt.

Schon bei den ersten Worten horchen wir auf: Das ist ja, von einem
Wort zum anderen, eine prosaische Umsetzung des Eingangs von Hora-
zens 2. Epode:

> Beatus ille qui procul negotiis,
>   Ut prisca gens mortalium,
> Paterna rura bobus exercet suis
>   Solutus omni faenore. . .

> Dem Manne Heil, der fern von der geschäftgen Welt,
>   Dem Urgeschlecht der Menschen gleich,

2. Zum Biographischen vgl. Georg Voigt, *Enea Silvio de' Piccolomini als
Papst Pius der Zweite, und sein Zeitalter,* 3 Bde, Berlin 1856-1863; R. J.
Mitchell, *The Laurels and the Tiara, Pope Pius II.,* London 1962.
3. Wolkan, S. 447.

Das väterliche Feld mit eignen Stieren baut
Und nichts von Zinsgeschäften weiss, . . .

So geht es weiter, eine ganze Seite lang wird die 2. Epode von Vers
zu Vers umgeschrieben. Es wäre der Mühe wert, die Art der Para-
phrase genau zu analysieren. Hinsichtlich der sachlichen Aussage erweisen sich die Änderungen — sowohl Auslassungen wie Hinzu-
fügungen — als geringfügig und wenig relevant. Weil der Schein entstehen soll, dass gänzlich vom Heute aus gesprochen wird, hat der
Briefschreiber keine Verwendung für römische Mythologica (Priapus,
Silvanus, Jupiter tonans u. ä.), die die Gegenwartsillusion zerstört
hätten. Umgekehrt gesellen sich zu den ländlichen Sabinerinnen und
den sonnverbrannten Frauen Apuliens im Brieftext die alttestament-
lichen Gestalten Sara, Rebecca und Rachel. Zur neuzeitlichen
Aktualisierung dient weiter eine kleine Änderung, die uns besonders
angeht, nämlich wo, anders als bei Horaz, das behagliche Landleben
ausdrücklich vom Leben bei Hof abgegrenzt wird. Während bei Horaz
der Landmann nicht als Bittsteller im Vorgemach mächtiger Bürger
(superba civium/ potentiorum limina) zu antichambrieren braucht,
schiebt Enea Silvio hier das Schreckbild der Bittstellerei an hoch-
fahrenden Hofhaltungen ein: "non fastidiosis curialibus est sup-
plex."[4]

Fesselnder ist die formale Änderung: die Umsetzung der me-
trischen Verse in wohlklingende ciceronianische Prosa ist ein stilistisches Bravourstück ersten Ranges. Sollen die Entlehnungen als
Plagiat unbemerkt bleiben, oder soll der Briefempfänger den Zitat-
charakter erkennen und die montierte Prosa als literarischen Lecker-
bissen goutieren? Wie dem auch sei, der Text wirkt wie ein Hut mit
doppeltem Boden: was einerseits als frische und unbelastete Wirklichkeitsdarstellung erscheint, erweist sich unter anderem Gesichtswinkel
als eine kostbare Probe literarisch-bildungsmässiger Bastelei, als
kunstvolle Einlegearbeit. Wir halten diese doppelte Beschaffenheit im
Hinblick auf folgendes in Gedanken fest:

Das Lob des Landlebens im Brief an Johann Lauterbach bildet ein
Gegenstück zu dem ungefähr gleichzeitigen, ungleich längeren Brief
über das Elend der Hofleute, der den Umfang und den Charakter einer
Abhandlung hat und denn auch als selbständiges Traktat "De miseriis

4. Ebenda.

curialium" weite Verbreitung gefunden hat.[5] Der Verfasser weiss, worüber er redet, hat er ja schon lange mit den Hofhunden (inter aulicos canes)[6] gebellt. Überhaupt zeigt er die sachliche Einstellung eines Menschen, der sich schon in harter Jugend einen klaren Blick für die weniger schönen Realia des täglichen Lebens zu eigen gemacht hat. So ist Enea Silvios Traktat der beachtenswerte Auftakt einer Reihe von Hofkritiken, deren Höhepunkte dann Antonio de Guevara, "Menosprecio de Corte y Alabanza de Aldea" (1539) und das Kapitel "De la cour" in la Bruyères "Les caractères" (1688) bilden.

Unsere Aufmerksamkeit wird gebannt durch das Zusammengehen von humanistischer Formgebung und populärem, drastischem Realismus. Ohne uns auf eine eingehende Analyse einzulassen, können wir die Dosierung von beiden doch an Hand von Beispielen andeuten. Der Aufbau des Traktats ist sehr übersichtlich. Der Autor stellt seine Gedanken und Beobachtungen gleich im ersten Satz, ja durch dessen erstes Wort unter den oberen Leitbegriff der stultitia, der Torheit derjenigen, die sich ohne zwingende Notwendigkeit dem Fürstendienst widmen und dadurch ein unglückliches Leben führen.

> Stultos esse, qui regibus serviunt, vitamque tum infelicem tum miserrimam ducere curiales, vereor, ne qui me arguant mihique maledicant, si hac epistola, quam tibi sum scripturus, ostendero.[7]

> Dass die von Sinnen sind, welche den Königen dienen; dass die Hofleute ein unglückliches, ganz elendes Leben führen — ich fürchte, sie werden es mir übel nehmen und mich beschimpfen, wenn ich das in meinem Briefe darlege.

Nach einer kurzen, durch eine reizende Anekdote gewürzten Nebenbetrachtung über das existentielle Gegenteil, das zurückgezogene Landleben ("apud privatos viros") wird das Hauptthema der stultitia in klarer Gliederung aufgefächert: Alle Hofleute handeln entweder aus Ehrgeiz und Ruhmsucht (sie suchen honores und famam seculi), oder sie suchen Macht (potentiam), Reichtum (divitias) oder Vergnügungen (voluptates); eines ist ebenso töricht wie das andere. Diese Rubrizierung liegt dann zugleich der vierteiligen Disposition der Abhandlung zugrunde.

Schon in den ersten drei Teilen finden sich messerscharfe Invekti-

5. Georg Voigt, a.a.O., 2. Bd., S. 288 zählt die Abhandlung zu Eneas beliebtesten und verbreitetsten Schriften.
6. Wolkan, S. 455.
7. Ebenda, S. 453.

ven. Etwa unter den Stichworten "honores" und "fama seculi":
Wenn Fürsten Personen niederen Standes am Hofe emporkommen
lassen, so geschieht das nicht wegen deren Verdienste, sondern bloss
um den unmoralischen Absichten der Fürsten zu nützen. Er sucht
sich nur solche aus, die seine Laster (avaritia, luxuria, crapula, cru-
delitas) teilen:

sic est sane. placet avaro regi, qui pecunias undecunque refert. gratus est
luxurioso, qui virgines adque maritas sibi conciliet. carus est ebrio, qui com-
bibit. crudeli jocundus est, qui sanguinem quam multum effundit humanum.
nemo acceptus est nemoque ex parvo statu prefertur aliis, nisi magno aliquo
facinore sese principi conciliaverit.[8]

So ist es: einem geizigen König gefällt ein Mensch, der von überall Geld
zusammenscharrt. Einem üppigen ist der willkommen, der ihm Mädchen und
Frauen geil macht. Willkommen ist dem Säufer, wer trinkt. Dem Grausamen
ist lieb, wer möglichst viel Menschenblut vergiesst. Keiner ist ihnen recht und
keiner wird aus niederem Stande erhoben, der die Fürsten nicht mit irgendeiner Schändlichkeit zu gewinnen weiss.

In noch schrillerem Tone schildert der Autor unter "divitias" die
ständige Lebensgefahr, in der Hofleute durch die Kriminalität der
Fürsten schweben. Diese bereichern manchmal Leute, wie wir die
Schweine mästen; sind sie fett, so werden sie abgestochen.[9] Als Beispiel dient der Tod Senecas auf Neros Geheiss. Zu gleicher Zeit ist die
humanistische Rede geschmückt mit erlesenen Zitaten aus der Bibel,
den Kirchenvätern und den römischen Autoren, vor allem aus Juvenal.

Saftiger und deftiger wird die Redeweise naturgemäss in der Ru-
brik "voluptates", die in sich nach den fünf Sinnen gegliedert ist, und
natürlich ganz besonders dort, wo der Geruch und der Geschmack
(sensus odorandi et gustandi) fällig werden. Hier zieht der Autor alle
Register, um das Ekelhafte der Mahlzeiten, mit denen die Höflinge
vorlieb nehmen müssen, ja recht fühlbar zu machen. Er kann den
schmutzigen Holzbecher, aus dem der Hofmann den miserablen Wein
zu trinken kriegt, so drastisch veranschaulichen, dass einem sensiblen
Leser die Lust zu trinken auf Wochen vergehen könnte. Um die
Beschreibung der Speisen steht es nicht anders. Während dem ge-
frässigen Fürsten herrliche Fische aus den entlegensten Teilen des
Mittelmeers vorgesetzt werden, bekommt der Hofmann nur Fische zu

8. Ebenda, S. 459.
9. Ebenda, S. 463.

essen, die nach dem Dreck stinken, in dem sie gelegen haben, oder solche, die sich in den Kloaken der Städte ernährt haben. Bei Beschreibungen von so ungeheuerer Unappetitlichkeit pflegt der Leser bekanntermassen, die Nachprüfungen bestätigen es, zunächst an "echten" Realismus zu glauben, an Darstellung des direkt und spontan aus der "Wirklichkeit" Aufgegriffenen. Die stinkenden Fische haben aber die ganze Würde literarischer Überlieferung, die Kloake ist römisch und stammt aus Juvenals V. Satire:

> vos anguilla manet longae cognata colubrae,
> (aut glacie aspersus maculis Tiberinus et ipse)
> vernula riparum, pinguis torrente cloaca
> et solitus mediae cryptam penetrare Suburae (V. 103-106)

> Euer wartet ein Aal, ein Verwandter der mageren Schlange,
> oder ein Tiberfisch, vom Frost ganz fleckig, auch er ein
> Bürger des Ufers, im Strom der Kloake gemästet, gewohnt durch
> Abzugkanäle ins Zentrum zu schwimmen entlang der Subura.[10]

Dieser Sachverhalt ist symptomatisch. Gerade die Beschreibungen der niederen Bereiche, des Schmutzigen und Hässlichen sind gespickt mit Juvenal-Zitaten, die aber zum grössten Teil (etwa drei Viertel) kaschiert sind und den Eindruck eines unentwegten Realismus hervorrufen sollen.

Das Verwischen der literarischen Spuren ist deutlich funktional bedingt, in einem Sinne, der uns direkt angeht. Enea Silvios Satire betrifft ein neuzeitliches Phänomen, den Hof und die Hofleute. Um dieses sichtbar zu machen, benutzt er ein fernes Analogon, das Elend der die reichen Herren umschwänzelnden clientes in spätrömischer Zeit. Durch die Tarnung der Zitate entsteht der Schein, als handle es sich nicht um Analogie, sondern um Identität mit der gegenwärtigen Wirklichkeit.

Ähnliches gilt nun freilich auch, wo unser Pamphletist wohl auf regelrechte Hofkritik aus der Antike zurückgreifen kann. Ich habe als Probe einmal aus dem bekannten Chor der ätolischen Frauen in Senecas "Hercules Oetaeus" (V. 583-705) stichwortartig das Sündenregister der "aula" verzeichnet und es mit Enea Silvios Invektiven verglichen. Kaum ein Stichwort dort, das hier nicht seine genaue Entsprechung gefunden hätte. Hierin zeigt sich deutlich der gelehrt-

---

10. Nach: *Römische Satiren,* übertragen von Otto Weinreich, 2. Aufl., Zürich 1962, S. 227.

literarische Charakter des Realismus oder Scheinrealismus von Enea Silvios Hofsatire. Er wird uns bei der Behandlung von Alexander Barclays Hirtendialogen noch zu schaffen machen.

Vom Hof zur Hütte: wir wechseln hinüber zu Baptista Mantuanus, dessen Eklogensammlung (1498) mit Recht in ganz Europa grosse Popularität genoss und ihm den Ehrennamen eines zweiten Vergil, eines "Christianus Maro" (Erasmus) eintrug. Mantuanus hat wie kein anderer, nach der Vorgängerschaft Petrarcas und Boccaccios, den Charakter der neuzeitlichen Ekloge geprägt: die pastorale Ein-kleidung nicht als Mittel zur Weltflucht, sondern als Vehikel scharfer Satire. Was uns, ähnlich wie an Enea Silvios Traktat, an Mantuanus Eklogen fesseln muss, ist die Modalität seines Realismus, jetzt eines Realismus, der auch die Hütte in die Wirklichkeitsdarstellung hinein-nimmt und ihr in der 6. Ekloge, auf die wir uns beschränken werden, einen zentralen Platz gibt.

Das Bild des Gehöfts, das hier gleich am Anfang der Ekloge entwor-fen wird, im Dialog zwischen Cornix und Fulica, ist von erstaunlicher Griffigkeit und Anschaulichkeit. Mantuanus ist ein Meister des sprechenden Details. Die vom heulenden Boreas gepeitschte, unter der Schneelast zusammengeduckte Hütte wird uns nach diesen allge-meineren Andeutungen noch stärker vergegenwärtigt durch das her-vorspringende Bild des Eiszapfens am Dachfirst. Dann wechseln wir unvermerkt von der Aussensicht ins Innere des Gehöfts hinüber. Die Ochsen stehen angebunden, der Pflüger geniesst seine Ruhe, der Erdboden schläft, der Schafstall ist geschlossen, der Schäfer faulenzt; die Bäuerin Neaera sitzt in Rauch gehüllt an dem Herd und röstet Gerste. Fürwahr ein Genrebild, das sich sehen lassen kann! Es belebt sich dann gleich zur Handlungsszene in der Schilderung des Schweine-schlachtens, bei dem für die ungekämmten und ärmlich gekleideten Bauernkinder ein ländliches Spielzeug abfällt. Die gerade ausge-nommene Schweinsblase wird nämlich mit Bohnen gefüllt und dann aufgeblasen. Bald durch Fusstritte, bald mit Fäusten und Ellenbogen gestossen, fliegt der primitive Fussball laut rasselnd hin und her, wobei es offenbar darauf ankommt, dass er eben in der Luft bleibt und den Boden so wenig wie möglich berührt. So vertreiben die Kinder die eisige Kälte. Wir aber, so sagen sich die beiden Hirten, wollen lieber ins warme Stroh kriechen und mit Geplauder die Zeit kürzen, während die angewärmte Milch zum Käse gerinnt. So ist eine eklogische Gesprächssituation gegeben, der das Gesprächsthema reizvoll entspricht. Ausgangspunkt ist der (wirklich oder scheinbar) krasse Gegensatz zwischen den bitteren Entbehrungen des Landmanns und dem Wohlleben des Städters. Bevor die Disputation richtig in Gang kommt, wird das Genrebild erst noch durch ein unterbrechendes Handlungsmoment bereichert: der ältere Hirt schickt den jüngeren in den Stall, mit genauer Anweisung, dem Vieh Grummet zu geben, die Löcher in den Wänden noch einmal mit Stroh zu stopfen und nach dem Verlassen des Stalls den Riss zwischen Tür und Türschwelle mit Gänsemist zuzuschmieren, weil nichts dem Vieh mehr schade als grosse Kälte. Der Hirt watet bis zu den Knien im Schnee; das Hüttendach kann die Schneelast kaum tragen und auf dem First erhebt sich eine spitze Schneemütze.

Den Inhalt des Gesprächs deuten wir nur kurz an. Fulica, der jüngere Hirt, erzählt die Geschichte von den ungleichen Kindern Evae, um den erwähnten Unterschied zwischen Stadt und Land (discrimina ruris et urbis, V. 53) begreiflich zu machen. Die bekannte Erzählung erscheint hier in anti-dörflicher Tönung: die Landleute stammen eben von Evas minder-wertigen Kindern ab und es ist nur gerecht, dass sie den andern dienstbar (servile genus, V. 104) sind. Der welterfahrenere alte Hirt lehnt dies entschieden ab und prangert seinerseits die Städter unter sozial-ethischem Gesichtspunkt aufs schärfste an. Sein vernichtendes Urteil über die Städter "vi, fraude, dolisque laborant" wird dem Leser durch öftere Wiederholung so richtig eingehämmert.

Während der Inhalt der Disputation uns nur mittelbar angeht — als Gegenbild der Dörflinge erscheinen ja nur Städter und nicht, wie in der auslösenden Erzählung von den ungleichen Kindern Evae, Könige und Herzöge — ist die rahmende Situationsschilderung für unser Thema von kaum zu überschätzender Bedeutung. Wohl nie zuvor war in der Literatur die Hütte und das Hüttenleben so umständlich und farbig veranschaulicht worden. Die Malerei bietet etwa gleichzeitig Entsprechendes. Wir greifen nicht zu hoch, wenn wir Mantuanus' Winterbild sowohl hinsichtlich der Artung wie des künstlerischen Niveaus neben das berühmte früheste Hüttenbild der Malerei stellen: das in seiner liebevollen Detailwiedergabe bezaubernde Februarbild der Brüder aus Limburg in "Les très riches heures du Duc de Berry".[11] Und ebenso werden wir dem Realismus dieser

11. *Les très riches heures du Duc de Berry*, hrsg. von Jean Longnon und

Ekloge nur gerecht, wenn wir das bäuerliche Ballspiel mit Breughels dörflichen Kinderspielen[12] ineinssehen. Die Analogie ist übrigens in soziokultureller Hinsicht interessant genug. Das dörfliche Thema sowohl des Stundenbuchs wie des Breughelschen Gemäldes ist nämlich durchaus auf den höfischen Konsum gerichtet, und dies wirft ein Seitenlicht auf unsere Eklogen hinsichtlich der Frage ihres sozialen Gebrauchswertes. Auch hier haben wir mit adligem Konsum zu rechnen. Als hoher Geistlicher − seit 1483 Generalvikar der Kongregation der Karmeliter zu Mantua, seit 1513 Oberhaupt des ganzen Ordens − war Baptista Mantuanus zu gleicher Zeit in der höfischen Welt zu Hause und genoss dort, wie aus manchen biographischen Einzelheiten hervorgeht, ein überaus hohes Ansehen.[13]

Der englische Geistliche Alexander Barclay (um 1476-1552), der sich durch seine Übertragung von Sebastian Brants "Narrenschiff" schon einen Namen gemacht hatte, führte die Eklogen in England ein, zuerst durch Bearbeitungen nach Mantuanus.[14] Seine 5. Ekloge "Amintas and Faustus, of the disputation of Citizens and men in the Country" entspricht der sechsten seines Vorbildes. Inhaltlich fügt er kaum Neues hinzu. Es ist aber fesselnd zu sehen, dass und wie er Mantuans realistische Innovationen aufgreift und weiter ausbaut. So gibt er in einem dem eigentlichen Dialog vorangehenden "Argument" eine genaue Situationsschilderung: er lässt die beiden Schafhirten in der Hütte von einem der beiden zusammenkommen, worauf dann Angaben über ihr Äusseres und über ihren Lebenslauf folgen. Amintas, der jüngere von beiden, hat lange in London gelebt und hat sich dann, nachdem er sich ohne viel Erfolg in allen möglichen Berufen durchgeschlagen, aufs Land zurückgezogen. Der andere, Faustus, obgleich etwas besser dran, ist auch arm genug:

> Yet nothing he had to comfort him in age,
> Saue a milch cowe and a poore cotage, ... (V. 35f.)

Raymond Cazelles, englische Ausgabe, übersetzt aus dem Französischen von Victoria Benedict, London 1969.

12. Im Kunsthistorischen Museum in Wien.

13. Symptomatisch: 1515, im Jahre vor seinem Tode, übernahm Mantuanus den Auftrag, als Apostolischer Legat Frieden zwischen König Franz I. und dem Herzog von Mailand zu stiften.

14. Barclays Eklogensammlung ist eine Kompilation aus verschiedenen Lebensperioden. Die Datierung ist schwierig, vgl. White a.a.O., S. LIX.

Überhaupt hebt Barclay Armut und Entbehrung noch ausdrücklicher hervor als Mantuan:

> When these two herdes were thus together met,
> Hauing no charges nor labour them to let,
> Their shepe were all sure and closed in a cote,
> Them selues lay in litter pleasauntly and hote.
> For costly was fire in hardest of the yere,
> When men haue moste nede then euery thing is dere,... (V. 45-50)

Das wohlige Liegen im warmen Stroh und Heu, "this litter hote", wird im Laufe des Gesprächs leitmotivisch wiederholt. Auch beim winterlichen Hüttenbild werden die Pinselstriche kräftiger angesetzt:

> The colde snowe reacheth muche higher then my knee,
> Scant may the houses suche burthen well susteyne,
> Lesse hurte is tempest and sodayne storme of rayne,
> On toppe of the chimney there is a heape of snowe
> So hye extending our steple is more lowe,
> The snowe is so white and the sunne so bright,
> That playnly Amintas amased in my sight. (V. 204-210)

Die Mantuan-Bearbeitung bedeutete für Barclay Vorübung zu einer selbständigeren Leistung: Er transponiert Enea Silvios Traktat ins Eklogische und lässt dadurch die Palast- wie die Hüttenthematik in ebenso unerwarteter wie reizvoller Weise konvergieren. Als Rahmenteil schafft er wieder eine bukolische Situation. Diese Situation bildet übrigens nicht bloss einen äusseren Rahmen um den Inhalt des humanistischen Traktats herum, sondern sie verwächst mit diesem zur Einheit: Enea Silvios Worte werden in passender Adaptierung den dialogisierenden Hirten in den Mund gelegt. Wiederum ist der Rahmen weitaus das Eindruckvollste an Barclays Leistung. Besonders das Bild des alten Graukopfs Cornix ist so gelungen, dass wir es in pleno zitieren müssen.

> Two simple shephaeardes met on a certayne day,
> The one well aged and with lockes hore and gray,
> Which after labours and wordly busines
> Concluded to liue in rest and quietnes.
> Yet nought had he kept to finde him cloth nor fode,
> At diuers holes his heare grewe through his hode,
> A stiffe patched felt hanging ouer his eyne,
> His costly clothing was thredebare kendall grene,
> His patched cockers skant reached to his knee,

In the side of his felte there stacke a spone of tree,
A botle his cote on the one side had torne,
For hanging the eare was nere a sunder worne.
In his owne hande alway his pipe he bare,
Whereof the sound him released of his care,
His wallet with bread and chese, so then he stood,
(A hooke in his hande) in the middest of his good.[15]

Wiederum drängt die Übereinstimmung mit Zügen der Bauerndarstellung in der bildenden Kunst von den Brüdern aus Limburg bis zu Breughel, Adriaan Brouwer und Adriaan van Ostade sich auf; die Entsprechungen sind so evident, dass wir sie kaum aufzuzählen brauchen. Die Situation wird schärfer erfasst als in Barclays voriger Ekloge: Das Unwetter hat das Getreide zu Boden geschlagen und auch unter der Herde Schaden gestiftet; der junge Hirt Coridon hat die Mühen und Entbehrungen satt und will in die Stadt ziehen, im Vertrauen, dass er bei Hof schon eine Stellung finden wird. Zur Warnung schildert Cornix ihm das Elend der Hofleute. Dadurch ist eine Situation existentieller Entscheidung geschaffen: Wie wird Coridon reagieren? Er lässt sich überzeugen, aber dazu bedarf es vieler Worte: Barclay wälzt den Text seiner Vorlage so breit aus, dass er nicht weniger als drei Eklogen mit ihm bestreitet.

Im Grunde ist es witzig genug, den Gegensatz zwischen den Sprechern zu bedenken: dort in der Vorlage der gebildete Poeta laureatus mit seinem geschliffenen Humanistenlatein, hier der malerischzerlumpte Hirt. Barclay bemüht sich zwar redlich, die Hirten in natürlicher Weise, "in homely language not passing their degree"[16] sprechen zu lassen, aber er vergisst dieses sinnvolle Vorhaben immer wieder und legt dem Sprecher alle humanistische Gelehrsamkeit in den Mund, die die Vorlage bot, bis zur − typisch humanistischen − kasuistischen Erhärtung des Behaupteten durch die Aufzählung einer langen Reihe berühmter Namen aus dem römischen Altertum.[17] Stärker noch: der alte Hirt nennt nach Humanistenart selbstgefällig seine gelehrte Quelle, die er dabei in den pastoralen Bereich hineinzieht. Um Coridon zu überzeugen von der Wahrheit der Behauptung,

15. Anfang des "Argument" der l. Ekloge; a.a.O., S. 5.
16. Im Prolog, a.a.O., S. 3.
17. 1. Ekloge, V. 680 ff.

dass es unmöglich sei, am Hof in ehrenvoller Weise Karriere zu machen, fügt er hinzu:

These be the wordes of Shepherde Siluius,
Which after was pope and called was Pius.[18]

Und wiederum noch stärker: zusammen mit Enea Silvio kann auch die von diesem angeführte Quelle, gleichsam als Quelle zweiten Grades, angeführt werden. Wir geben ein Beispiel, an dem sich Verschiedenes ablesen lässt. Enea Silvio hatte geschrieben: "Denn so pflegen Fürsten manche Leute zu bereichern, wie wir die Schweine mästen und, wenn sie fett sind, abstechen. So lesen wir über Seneca und Longinus, die nach Juvenals Meinung ihrer Reichtümer wegen getötet wurden," worauf er das betreffende Juvenal-Zitat folgen lässt. Daraus wird bei Barclay:

How many haue be slayne me needeth not expresse
Of such as them erst auaunced to riches.
So princes are wont with riches some to fede,
As we do our swine when we of larde haue nede.
We fede our hogges them after to deuour,
When they be fatted by costes and labour.
In like wise princes promoteth many one,
And when they be riche, they gnaw them to the bone.
Like as Longinus and Seneca doubtlesse,
Which as sayth Codrus were slayne for their riches,
So writeth Pius (whom some Eneas call)
A clause alleaging of famous Iuuenall.[19]

Wir sehen: der *eine* scharfgeschliffene Satz der Vorlage wird vierfach paraphrasiert und um einige populär-drastische Wendungen bereichert; danach wird noch ein bukolischer Gewährsmann eingeschoben, bis schliesslich die wirklichen Quellen korrekt angeführt werden. Das krampfhafte Missverhältnis zwischen realistischer Volkstümlichkeit und humanistischer Gelehrsamkeit, das sich hier einmal grotesk zuspitzt, ist im Grunde charakteristisch für unseren ganzen Text. Wir atmen auf, wo der Dichter im abschliessenden Rahmenteil, nicht mehr an die Vorlage gebunden, seine Hirten einfach kann sprechen lassen, wie ihnen der Schnabel gewachsen ist. Am Schluss der ersten Ekloge heisst es:

18. 1. Ekloge, V. 737 f.
19. 1. Ekloge, V. 1245 ff.

Looke vp mate Cornix, beholde into the west,
These windy cloudes vs threatneth some tempest,
My clothes be thin, my shepe be shorne newe,
Such storme might fall that both might after rewe.
Driue we our flockes vnto our poore cotage,
To morowe of court we may haue more language.[20]

Von Eneo Silvio über Mantuanus und Barclay zu ersterem zurück: der Zirkelgang sollte dazu dienen, einsichtig zu machen, auf wie gespanntem Fuße in der Hofkritik und in der ihr sich zugesellenden Bukolik Realismus und Gelehrsamkeit miteinander verkehren. Für die Vorstellung des Palastes sowie die der Hütte ist dieser Sachverhalt von wesentlicher Bedeutung.

20. 1. Ekloge, V. 1309 ff.

MARCELLUS EMANTS' ROMAN
EEN NAGELATEN BEKENTENIS: ABRECHNUNG MIT ERNST VON FEUCHTERSLEBEN, ERNEUERUNG DES NATURALISTISCHEN ROMANS

A. L. Sötemann (Utrecht)

Hat es jenen Ernst von Feuchtersleben, den "oberflächlichen Philosophen" aus dem Roman *Een nagelaten bekentenis* (Ein hinterlassenes Geständnis) und sein Buch *Gezondheidsleer der ziel* vielleicht wirklich gegeben? * Diese Frage stellte ich mir, als ich Emants' Roman wieder einmal zur Hand nahm. Zwar hat der Autor selbst mitgeteilt, daß ihm bei seinen Romanen immer Personen, die er kannte, als Vorbild dienten, denen er dann hinterher erfundene Namen gab.[1] Aber der ganze Fiktionalisierungsprozeß: die Transformation von Elementen der 'unorganisierten', chaotischen Wirklichkeit in die strukturierte, kohärente, zielgerichtete Vermittlung eines Welt- und Lebensbildes, die ein (guter) Roman darstellt, bringt eine derartig fundamentale Neuordnung jener Wirklichkeitselemente mit sich, daß deren Lokalisierbarkeit minimal wird. Das Suchen nach ihnen hat denn auch in den weitaus meisten Fällen recht wenig Sinn, wie sich auch aus der Tatsache ergibt, daß nach Emants' eigener Aussage die Urbilder seiner Romanfiguren von anderen nicht erkannt wurden.[2] Die Suche nach den Urbildern führt den Leser sogar bei den reinsten Vertretern des realistischen oder naturalistischen Romans nicht zu richtigerem

*Übersetzung: I. Daniels-Benjamin. Eine holländische Fassung dieses Artikels wurde aufgenommen in die *Handelingen der Koninklijke Zuidnederlandse Maatschappij voor Taal- en Letterkunde en Geschiedenis* 29 (1975) — erschienen: 1976 — S. 217-234.

1. E. d'Oliveira Jr.: 'Marcellus Emants'. In: *De mannen van '80 aan het woord, gesprekken met Nederlandsche letterkundigen.* (Die Achtziger am Wort, Gespräche mit holländischen Schriftstellern.) Amsterdam, [1909]. S. 134.

2. "Aber wenn [die Leute] anfangen zu raten: Wen meint er denn eigentlich? , dann hauen sie meistens glatt daneben."

Verständnis, sondern wird ihn eher vom wesentlichen Gehalt des Buches ablenken. Von viel größerer Bedeutung ist darum eine kritisch-analytische Untersuchung der inneren Struktur des Werkes, des ganzen Komplexes von Mitteln, die den Leser dahin bringen sollen, das im Buche zum Ausdruck gebrachte Weltbild als (in der fiktionalen Als-ob Situation) überzeugend, aufzunehmen.

Dies alles schließt jedoch nicht aus, daß es zu einer sinnvollen Problemstellung *im Rahmen des Romans* führen könnte, Näheres über Ernst von Feuchtersleben und sein Buch zu wissen. Der Leser hat es hier nämlich mit etwas grundlegend anderem zu tun, als dort, wo im Roman über das Werk des fiktionalen (eventuell: fiktionalisierten) de Kantere: *Het leger der menschen* (Das Heer der Menschheit) gesprochen wird. Dieser gepflegte, stattliche ehemalige Geistliche, der seine wohlgesetzten, mit klangreicher Stimme vorgetragenen Worte mit ausdrucksvollen Gebärden unterstreicht, der sein kränkliches Töchterchen mit zärtlicher Liebe umhegt, bildet mit seinem Ehrgeiz und seinen in ein rosiges Licht getauchten Lebensanschauungen in jeder Hinsicht einen so deutlichen Gegensatz zu der Ich-Gestalt Termeer, daß kein Zweifel an seiner strukturellen Integration aufkommen kann. Um seine Auffassungen zu erhärten, beruft der ehemalige Pfarrer sich jedoch auf eine Schrift von Feuchterslebens, so, wie eine Romangestalt sich auf einen willkürlichen anderen (wirklichen) Philosophen berufen könnte.

Wäre ich in der österreichischen Literatur des Biedermeier besser bewandert gewesen, hätte ich mir meine Frage wohl gar nicht gestellt. Ich hätte dann gewußt, daß Ernst von Feuchtersleben eine historische Gestalt ist, ein Wiener Arzt, der von 1806 bis 1849 lebte. Er ist unter anderm der Verfasser eines Büchleins, das es zu einer außergewöhnlichen Verbreitung und Beliebtheit brachte: *Zur Diätetik der Seele.* 1838 erstmals erschienen, erlebte es noch siebzig Jahre später, im Jahre 1908, seinen fünfzigsten Druck in den riesigen Auflagen von Reclams 'Universal-Bibliothek'.[3] Es wäre mir dann auch bekannt gewesen, daß die *Diätetik* lange Zeit als der Inbegriff der biedermeierlichen Philosophie gegolten hat, sodaß, wenn de Kantere sich auf dieses Werk bezieht, der Hinweis für Emants' Zeitgenossen deutlich erkennbar gewesen sein muß, zumal, da auch einer hol-

3. Ich zitiere nach: E. von Feuchtersleben: *Zur Diätetik der Seele.* Leipzig o.J., Universal-Bibliothek.

ländischen Übersetzung – die tatsächlich den von de Kantere im Roman erwähnten Titel: *Gezondheidsleer der ziel* trug – ein beträchtlicher Erfolg zuteil geworden war: Im Jahre 1874 erschien eine dritte Auflage, "nach der siebenunddreißigsten deutschen Ausgabe neu für die Niederlande bearbeitet", bei Jan D. Brouwer in Amsterdam.[4]

Wie bereits erwähnt, beruft sich de Kantere, der in physischer, psychischer und weltanschaulicher Hinsicht Termeers genauer Gegenpol ist, wiederholt auf den Österreicher, dessen Name nicht weniger als viermal in dem Roman genannt wird.[5] Diese Tatsache wurde für mich der Anlaß, mich näher mit von Feuchtersleben zu beschäftigen.[6] Ernst von Feuchtersleben ist nicht nur Dichter, Autor von Aphorismen und Verfasser der im doppelten Sinne populären *Diätetik,* sondern zudem, oder besser überdies, ein Gelehrter von Format: Ein Psychiater, der im Jahre 1845 seine Vorlesungen an der Wiener Universität als *Lehrbuch der ärztlichen Seelenkunde* erscheinen ließ. Dieses Werk wurde noch vor wenigen Jahren in einer Geschichte der medizinischen Psychologie als epochemachend charakterisiert[7]: "The ideas of [. . .] E. Feuchtersleben (1806-1849) [. . .] certainly signalized a new era in psycho-pathology and a new approach to the study and treatment of mental diseases". Der zentrale Gedanke ist, daß psychologische und physiologische Symptome als Aspekte einer biologischen Totalität gedeutet werden. Hier offenbart sich also eine klare

4. E. von Feuchtersleben: *Gezondheidsleer der ziel.* Bearbeitet von M. Buys. Amsterdam, 1874[3].

5. *Een nagelaten bekentenis.* [3. Auflage.] Amsterdam, 1951. S. 137, 139, 170, 171.

6. Vgl. unter anderen: W. Bietak: *Das Lebensgefühl des "Biedermeier" in der österreichischen Dichtung.* Wien usw., 1931. W. Bietak: 'Grillparzer – Stifter – Feuchtersleben, die Unzeitgemässen des Jahres 1848'. In: *DVJS* 24 (1950). S. 243-268. H. Seidler: 'Ernst Freiherr von Feuchtersleben; seine geistes- und literaturgeschichtliche Stellung in der österreichischen Restaurationszeit.' In: *Anzeiger der Österreichischen Akademie der Wissenschaften.* Phil.-hist. Klasse 106 (1969). S. 235-249. Man vergleiche auch: *Begriffsbestimmung des literarischen Biedermeier.* Hrsg. von E. Neubuhr. Darmstadt, 1974. Wege der Forschung Bd. 318, und selbstverständlich: F. Sengle: *Biedermeierzeit. Deutsche Literatur im Spannungsfeld zwischen Restauration und Revolution, 1815-1848.* Bd. I, II. Stuttgart, 1971-'72. Der dritte Band dieser umfangreichen Studie ist zur Zeit noch nicht erschienen.

7. G. Zilboorg: *A history of medical psychology.* New York, 1967. Das Zitat auf S. 475.

274

Einsicht in die Einheit der menschlichen Persönlichkeit, die, wie Zilboorg feststellt, mit den heutigen Auffassungen über die Natur der Geistes- und Gemütskrankheiten noch immer in wichtigen Punkten übereinstimmt.[8] Feuchtersleben weist in seinem Buch wiederholt auf die eminente Bedeutung erblicher Faktoren und auf den großen Einfluß des Milieus hin.[9] Daß er den Begriff der 'psychischen Freiheit' stark relativiert (§ 56), ist denn auch eine Weiterführung dieser Erwägungen, besonders wenn es sich um pathologische Erscheinungen wie z.B. die Hypochondrie handelt (§ 100 - 102). Die Prognose ist bei dieser Gemütskrankheit ungünstig: "Der Ausgang ist entweder, in seltenen Fällen (sehr langsam), in Genesung, oder (gewöhnlich) gar keiner, d.h. der Zustand bleibt sich bis ans Ende des Lebens gleich, oder in Folgekrankheiten, worunter sogenannte Psychosen bei weitem die häufigsten sind [. . .]."[10]

Es fällt nicht schwer sich vorzustellen, daß die hier nur kurz skizzierten Auffassungen Wasser auf die Mühle eines Naturalisten sind, wenn auch in von Feuchterslebens *Lehrbuch* nicht direkt die Rede ist von Determinismus im Sinne eines säkularisierten calvinistischen Sündenbegriffes, dem man wohl bei vielen Naturalisten begegnet und den Willem Termeer, der Protagonist aus *Een nagelaten bekentenis,* so charakteristisch in Worte faßt: "Ich weiß nicht, wie viele Vorfahren ausschließlich zu ihrem egoistischen Vergnügen gelebt haben müssen, um ein Wesen ans Licht der Welt zu bringen [. . .], das sich, wie ich, seiner unauslöschlichen Jämmerlichkeit bewußt ist und dadurch ihrer aller Schuld sühnt."[11]

Man darf erwarten, daß der populär-wissenschaftlichen *Diätetik* die gleichen Auffassungen zugrunde liegen wie dem *Lehrbuch.* Und wirklich spricht der Verfasser auch hier stets über Geist (Seele) und Körper als Aspekte eines Ganzen, über "mitgeborne Empfänglichkeit" und über "angeerbte [. . .] constitutionelle" Krankheiten.[12] In *diesem* Buch findet sich sogar eine Stelle, die den soeben zitierten Worten Termeers verblüffend ähnelt: "Der Enkel, der verzweifelnd über das Geheimnis seiner Leiden brütet, kann die Lösung in den Sünden der Väter finden."[13] Es ist jedoch zu bemerken, daß er

8. Ebda., S. 477/478.
9. *Lehrbuch der ärztlichen Seelenkunde.* Wien, 1845. Bes. § 52-54.
10. Ebda., S. 243.
11. *Een nagelaten bekentenis.* S. 105.
12. *Diätetik.* Passim, z.B. S. 6-8 und S. 17f. Das Zitat auf S. 29.
13. *Diätetik.* S. 39.

hierüber in seiner *Diätetik* zwar etliche Male, aber doch gleichsam nur beiläufig, spricht; diese Ansichten sind hier einer ganz anderen Per-' spektive untergeordnet. Die *Diätetik* ist nämlich keine medizinische Abhandlung für ein breiteres Publikum, sondern, wie Sengle in seiner *Biedermeierzeit* mit Recht bemerkt, eine "bewußt schlichte, medizinisch-moralische Vollkommenheitslehre", oder noch stärker: "eine volkstümliche Erbauungsschrift", (die, seiner Meinung nach, zur Tradition der Erbauungsliteratur gehört und nur in diesem Rahmen ganz verständlich wird.)[14] Das Büchlein verlegt sich besonders auf die Hypochondrie und es ist bemerkenswert, wie weitgehend die Beschreibung von deren Symptomen, obgleich weniger systematisch geordnet, mit jenen in den schon genannten Paragraphen des *Lehrbuch* geschilderten, übereinstimmt. Aber *ein* wichtiger Unterschied wird gemacht: Der Moralist Feuchtersleben unterscheidet, seinem erbaulichen, stärkenden und läuternden Ziel zuliebe, zwischen einer sozusagen freiwillig gewählten Hypochondrie und "einer anderen [Art], welche der Arzt zu behandeln hat", wobei man allerdings, wie gesagt, keine nennenswerte Verschiedenheit der beschriebenen Erscheinungsformen zu entdecken vermag.[15] Dieser 'Kunstgriff' berechtigt ihn dann zu einer optimistischen Darlegung, die sich durch das Fehlen innerer Folgerichtigkeit auszeichnet. Wie authentisch hypochondrischer Natur die Symptome auch sein mögen, der Moralist versichert uns hier immer wieder: Der Geist hat den Körper in seiner Gewalt und wo ein *Wille* ist, ist auch ein Weg; und "wenn er [der Mensch] die eigene [Energie] aus sich zu erregen nicht vermag, versetze er sich durch einen Ruck in einen Zustand, in welchem er *wollen muß.*"[16] Es wird aber dem aufmerksamen Leser inzwischen nicht entgehen, daß Feuchtersleben selbst nicht selten trüben Stimmungen unterworfen ist — wenn er nicht gar zur Hypochondrie neigt. Ich zitierte nur einen seiner Aphorismen: "Eine Kunst, das Leben zu verlängern? . . . Lehrt den, der es kennen gelernt hat, lieber die Kunst es zu ertragen!"[17] Ohnehin hegte der Verfasser der *Diätetik* eigentlich keine großen Hoffnungen auf Erfolg. Die 'Einleitung' der deutschen Ausgabe schließt mit den Worten: "Ob durch diese wohlgemeinten Reflexionen auch nur Ein Hypochondrist geheilt oder er-

14. F. Sengle: *Biedermeierzeit.* Bd. II, S. 87.
15. *Diätetik.* S. 101.
16. *Diätetik.* S. 34. Vgl. auch z.B. S. 57.
17. Ebda., S. 125.

heitert werden wird? Ich zweifle." In einer Vorbemerkung zur ersten Auflage geht er sogar noch einen Schritt weiter: "Was man selbst nie zu leisten vermöchte [. . .], das wagt man als Philosoph zu lehren."[18] Angesichts der Tatsache, daß Feuchtersleben selbst tatsächlich den Anforderungen seiner Theorie nicht gewachsen war, muß man fast von tragischer Ironie sprechen. Im Jahre 1848 hatte er seine Ernennung zum Unterstaatssekretär im österreichischen Kultusministerium erhalten, aber als er "sein edles Streben fast immer verkannt sah, gab er schon nach vier Monaten seine Entlassung", wie Schmidt in einer biographischen Skizze mitteilt, die in die Reclam-Ausgabe der *Diätetik* aufgenommen wurde.[19] "Er war willens seine Stellung an der Universität wieder aufzunehmen, vermochte es aber wegen seines in Folge der bitteren Erfahrungen in seiner früheren Stellung äußerst geschwächten Gesundheitszustandes, nicht mehr." Im September 1849 starb er im Alter von 43 Jahren.

Die folgenden Betrachtungen sind das Ergebnis der Gegenüberstellung von *Een nagelaten bekentenis* und *Diätetik*.

Es ist kaum zu verwundern, daß Emants mit seinem scharfen Verstand die Ungereimtheiten der *Diätetik der Seele* sofort durchschaute. Es leuchtet ein, daß diese Schrift ihn überaus irritierte, gerade weil er die wissenschaftlichen Erkenntnisse vollkommen überzeugend fand, während der "ethische Überbau", wenn ich ihn so nennen darf, nicht nur völlig aus der Luft gegriffen war, sondern sich durch die ihm angeblich zugrunde liegenden Anschauungen erst recht als Luftspiegelung entpuppte. Erinnert man sich zudem an die außergewöhnliche Verbreitung des Büchleins, so versteht man, daß das Ganze auf Emants den Eindruck eines ungeheuren und gefährlichen Schwindels gemacht haben muß, den es aufzudecken und anzuprangern und gegen den es die Öffentlichkeit zu schützen galt. In *Een nagelaten bekentenis* wird Feuchtersleben ausdrücklich als "jener oberflächliche Philosoph" gebrandmarkt, im Grunde ist jedoch das *ganze* Buch vom Kampf gegen seine Lebensphilosophie erfüllt. Treulich spiegeln sich die Auffassungen des Moralisten von Feuchtersleben in den Worten von Termeers Opponent de Kantere, auch wo dies nicht explizite ausgesprochen wird. Aber noch frappanter ist es, daß die Hauptperson die Eigenschaften und den psychophysiologischen Habitus verkörpert, die der Psychiater Feuchters-

18. Ebda., S. 24, bzw. S. 14.
19. Ebda., S. 10-11.

leben als symptomatisch für den Hypochonder aufzählt. Ohne Er-
barmen ätzt Termeer sein Selbstbildnis: Er ist ein ängstlicher Feig-
ling, ein pathologischer Lügner, der immer nur eine Rolle spielt, er ist
eitel und faul, ein einsamer, verbitterter und eifersüchtiger Egoist, der
vor Taten zurückschrickt und sich in fruchtlose Phantasien verliert,
unfähig, je seine 'Freiheit' zu nutzen; er ist 'klimatischen' Einflüssen
gegenüber überempfindlich, ein Schwächling, der alle Schuld der ihn
umringenden Welt zuschiebt und sich beschreibt als "ein blasses,
schmächtiges, unbedeutendes Männlein, mit glanzlosem Blick und
kraftlosem, offenem Mund – viele werden sagen: dieses Ekel",
immerzu verstrickt in das sterile und deprimierende Nachdenken über
sich und seine Lage. (de Kantere: "Sie zeichnen sich viel zu schwarz
und Sie denken viel zu viel nach"; Feuchtersleben, "eine ehrwürdige
Stimme, als Wieland gestorben war, an einem Sarge" zitierend:
"Wenn der Mensch über sein Körperliches und Sittliches nachdenkt,
findet er sich gewöhnlich krank.")[20] Termeer hält sich denn auch für
"eine Degeneration", erblich belastet mit "den Sünden der Väter".
Es erscheint mir überflüssig, hier zur Bestätigung Zitate anzuführen,
während eine flüchtige Lektüre der *Diätetik* schon ausreicht, um nahezu Stück für Stück denselben negativen Eigenschaften als charakteristisch für den 'eingebildeten' Hypochonder zu begegnen. (Ein
Unterschied von denen der 'echten' Kranken aus dem *Lehrbuch* läßt
sich freilich, wie ich oben schon bemerkte, kaum feststellen.) Ich
habe kaum einen Unterschied in der Darstellung des Krankheitsbildes
zwischen von Feuchtersleben und Emants finden können. Nur sind
die Phantasiegebilde Willem Termeers ausgesprochen sinnlicher
Natur, während dieses Thema von dem Österreicher mit keinem Wort
erwähnt wird; und umgekehrt weist der letztere auf die von den
eigenen Körperfunktionen ausgehende Faszination hin, die wiederum
im *Bekentenis* wenig zur Sprache kommt. Es ist jedoch bemerkenswert, daß *ein* in der *Diätetik* genannter Zug von Termeer ausdrücklich abgelehnt wird: Feuchterleben nennt die an dieser Krankheit leidenden auch "pedantisch": "Es sind besonders drei Gemüths-
lagen, die zu jener [von Feuchtersleben als nicht 'authentisch' charak-
terisierten] Hypochondrie disponiren [...] Sie heißen: Egoismus,
Müßiggang. Pedantismus."[21] Zwei Mal weist Termeer diese (und

20. *Bekentenis.* S. 142; bzw. *Diätetik.* S. 101.
21. *Diätetik.* S. 107. Man hat mich inzwischen darauf aufmerksam gemacht,
daß die Bedeutungen des Wortes "pedantisch" im Holländischen und Deutschen

nur *diese*) Beschuldigung ab. "Weißt du, was du bist? Ein pedantischer Narr!", so fährt sein Vater ihn an. Und gerade über diesen ungerechten Vorwurf weint der Knabe lange und bitterlich. Für ihn ist hierdurch bewiesen, daß seine Eltern ihm weder Liebe noch Verständnis entgegenbringen: "Ich, der ich mich selbst so klein, so unbedeutend, so verachtet, so verstoßen finde . . . pedantisch!" Und als sich später zeigt, daß seine Frau, Anna, die Pedanterie für die Grundlage seines Verhaltens hält, nimmt er sich wegen "dieser maßlosen Ungerechtigkeit" das Recht, künftig ganz zu schweigen.[22]

Es kann meines Erachtens kaum daran gezweifelt werden, daß *Een nagelaten bekentenis* vom wissenschaftlichen Gesichtspunkt aus und von der Lebensanschauung her nichts anderes ist als *eine* große, gegen von Feuchtersleben gerichtete, Polemik.

Selbstverständlich, damit ist noch lange nicht alles gesagt. Schließlich — oder muß ich sagen: an erster Stelle — ist *Een nagelaten bekentenis* keine wissenschaftliche Streitschrift, sondern ein Roman. Ein Roman, allerdings, der, ganz im Sinne der naturalistischen Tradition, wenigstens die Nebenabsicht verfolgt, den Beweis für die These zu liefern, daß es einem erblich belasteten Hypochonder schlechterdings unmöglich ist, sein Schicksal zu überwinden. Es ist ja, wie gesagt, das wesentliche Merkmal eines Romans, wie überhaupt jedes Kunstwerks, daß seine Struktur darauf angelegt ist, den Leser nicht (nur) verstandesmäßig von der Richtigkeit des darin ausgedrückten Welt- und Lebensbildes zu überzeugen, sondern ihn dahin zu bringen, dieses auch gefühlsmäßig als sinnvoll anzunehmen und sogar zu teilen, wenn auch nicht gleich in die Praxis umzusetzen. Emants wählte, um dies zu erreichen, die Form eines Bekenntnisses, in dessen Verlauf Willem Termeer systematisch seine Lebensgeschichte erzählt. Schon gleich auf der ersten Seite erfährt der Leser, daß Termeer seine Frau ermordet hat, wodurch die Aufmerksamkeit ganz auf die Motive konzentriert wird, die zu dieser Tat geführt haben. Nicht, den

nicht identisch sind. Die Bedeutung 'übertrieben genau und ordnungsliebend' hat das Wort auch im Holländischen; aber die 'dummstolze Selbstgefälligkeit' des Holländischen fehlt im Deutschen. Der Übersetzer der *Diätetik* war sich dessen offenbar nicht bewußt (er übersetzt "Pedantismus" einfach mit "pedanterie"), und da Emants, wie der Gebrauch des holländischen Titels beweist, offenbar die Übersetzung benutzt hat, lag das Mißverständnis nahe.

22. *Bekentenis* S. 43 und 45, bzw. S. 119.

Leser bis zum Ende in Spannung zu halten, ist das Anliegen des Buches, sondern Verständnis zu wecken für die Veranlagung und Entwicklung der Hauptperson. Nicht das *Was,* sondern das *Warum* und das *Wie* sollen den Leser fesseln. Der Aufbau zeigt eine geschlossene, zyklische Form: Am Ende schließt sich der Kreis der wenigen Begebenheiten, indem die rhetorische Frage aus dem dritten Satz des Buches: "Ich bin also wieder frei, aber was nützt mir jetzt diese Freiheit?" sich bewahrheitet hat und, in andere Worte gefaßt, wiederholt wird. Der Leser hat dann ja schon zu wiederholten Malen gesehen, daß Termeer – selbstverständlich! – mit seiner Freiheit nichts anzufangen weiß. Weder mit zwanzig Jahren, nach dem Tod seiner Eltern; noch bei der Rückkehr nach Holland von seiner ausgedehnten, aufs Geratewohl unternommenen Auslandsreise; noch auch nachdem er sich von dem Parasiten van Dregten und dessen üblen Freunden losgelöst hat. Die letzten Sätze des Buches bestätigen dies auf makabre Weise. Termeer erwägt, seine gerade erst wiedereroberte Freiheit diesmal auf heillose und definitive Weise aus der Hand zu geben, indem er sich seiner geldgierigen Maitresse Carolien ausliefert: "Wenn ich ihr nun einfach alles gestünde und ihr gleichzeitig das Verfügungsrecht über mein ganzes Vermögen anböte; könnte sie ... wollte sie ... mich dann um dieser Tat ... dieser Missetat willen ... nicht doch ... nicht vielleicht doch ... lieben?" Diese Frage ist überhaupt keine Frage, und Termeer selbst weiß das auch. Der suggestive Titel des Romans legt denn auch die Annahme nahe, daß dieser endgültige Verzicht auf seine Freiheit, oder die Tatsache, daß er sich auch dazu wieder nicht durchringen kann, regelrecht zur allerletzten Befreiung geführt hat: zur Befreiung aus dem Leben.[23]

23. Die Interpretation von "nagelaten" als 'unterblieben' statt 'postum' ist meines Erachtens absolut unhaltbar. (Vgl. J. J. Oversteegen: 'Nagelaten'. In: *Merlyn* 2 (1963/64). Heft 3, S. 83). Oversteegen führt aus, daß Termeer "unmittelbar nach dem Schreiben seiner Beichte" gestorben sein muß, weil im Roman erzählt wird, daß Termeer und seine Frau eine Vorstellung von Emants' Theaterstück *Artiest* besuchen. Dieses Stück erlebte im Jahre 1894 seine Uraufführung, und im gleichen Jahr ist auch der Roman erschienen. (Oversteegen: 'Uit de donkere dagen van voor Freud'. In: *Merlyn* 2 (1963/64). Heft 2, S. 1-22. Die Ausführungen auf S. 8/9.) Diese Argumentation ist jedoch gleichfalls unhaltbar. Laut Mitteilung auf dem Titelblatt von *Artiest* ist das Stück am 13. März 1894 zum ersten Mal aufgeführt worden. In Emants' Roman wird indessen berichtet, daß nach dem Theaterbesuch "lange Zeit verstrich". Danach zeigt sich, daß Anna

Die Einführung der Ich-Gestalt ist so negativ gehalten wie nur denkbar ist: Der Mörder seiner eigenen Frau nennt sich ein "blasses, schmächtiges, unbedeutendes Männlein, mit glanzlosem Blick, kraftlos", er bezeichnet sich als gefühlsarm, ängstlich, einsam, als feige, sterilen Phantasien ergeben, lügenhaft, diebisch, als einen schroffen Egoisten, immer nur mit sich selbst beschäftigt, der ihn umringenden Welt gegenüber gleichgültig und schließlich als faul und verbittert. Kurz, auf zehn Seiten entfaltet sich vor dem Leser ein vollständiges Porträt von Feuchterslebens Standardtyp des Hypochonders, mit all seinen widerwärtigen Zügen. Und nach dieser äußerst negativen Einleitung wird die ganze Psychographie des neurasthenischen Hypochonders sozusagen logisch-kausal abgewickelt, unter Anrufung der naturalistischen Leitgedanken.

In *einer* Hinsicht jedoch weicht dieser Roman grundlegend von der naturalistischen Tradition ab: Es ist ein Ich-Roman. Es ist allgemein bekannt, daß in der zweiten Hälfte des neunzehnten Jahrhunderts in immer steigendem Maße Einwendungen gegen den auktorialen Erzähler, 'der sich in alles einmischt', erhoben wurden. Dichtern wie Flaubert und Turgenjew wurde es als großes Verdienst angerechnet, daß sie so 'objektiv' erzählten. Obgleich sie mit demselben auktorialen, allwissenden Erzähler arbeiteten, wurde doch wenigstens beim Leser der Eindruck vermieden, daß der Erzähler ihm in ihren Romanen auf Schritt und Tritt begegnet, um ihn zu belehren, wie er die Personen und ihre Handlungen zu interpretieren und — dies vor allem — zu bewerten habe. Bekanntlich war es das Ziel der Naturalisten, dem Roman den Charakter eines naturwissenschaftlichen Versuchs zu geben, mit dem man die Hypothesen über die erbliche Determiniertheit des Individuums und den Einfluß von Milieu und Erziehung experimentell nachweisen wollte. (Dieses Ziel ist, infolge des unvermeidlich fiktionalen Charakters jeden Romans,

schwanger ist. Das Kind, das geboren wird, bleibt über anderthalb Jahre am Leben. Und erst nach dem Tod "des Wurms" entwickelt sich die Beziehung zu de Kantere. Der Mord findet erst statt, nachdem dieser ins Ausland verzogen ist. Im Ganzen muß diese Periode doch sicher drei Jahre gedauert haben. Das bedeutet aber, daß das Erscheinungsjahr des Romans –1894 – unmöglich die Deutung von "nagelaten" als 'postum' unterstützen kann. Emants läßt – und das haben auch andere Autoren so gemacht – sein Buch zum Teil nach dem Erscheinungsjahr spielen. Die Interpretation 'postum' ist gleichwohl die einzig mögliche, da der Roman ja tatsächlich das Geständnis enthält; es ist also nicht 'unterblieben'.

per se nicht zu verwirklichen.) Darum ist es jedoch selbstverständlich, daß gerade der naturalistische Autor sich um eine möglichst 'objektive' Erzählweise bemühte; der Leser sollte möglichst wenig einem persönlichen Erzähler begegnen. Und das bedeutete, daß man versuchte, Flauberts diesbezüglichen Vorschriften: *impassibilité* und *impartialité* zu betrachten, so genau wie möglich zu folgen. In diesem Zusammenhang scheint gerade der Ich-Roman die ungeeignetste Form zu sein, die sich denken läßt.

Emants befand sich durch all dies in einer verzwickten Lage. *Een nagelaten bekentenis* beweist deutlich, daß er nicht nur darauf bedacht war, eine 'klinische' Krankengeschichte, einen 'casus', mit *impartialité* und *impassibilité* vorzulegen. Offenbar lag ihm daran, seiner These, Willem Termeers Lebensweg habe in absolut determinierter Richtung verlaufen *müssen,* die größtmögliche Eindringlichkeit und Überzeugungskraft zu verleihen. Um dies zu erreichen, war nun gerade die Darbietung der Geschichte als (scheinbar) eigenes Erlebnis ganz besonders geeignet. Aber noch ein anderer und eigentlich wichtigerer Umstand spielt eine Rolle: Der Roman ist nicht nur ein Geständnis, er ist auch ein Plädoyer und eine Rechtfertigung. Termeer *konnte* nicht anders sein, als er war; er *konnte* kein anderer werden, als derjenige, den erbliche Veranlagung, Erziehung und Milieu ihn zu werden vorbestimmt hatten, und er konnte also auch nicht anders handeln, als er tat. Sollte nun der endgültige Eindruck des Buches tiefer schürfen, nicht nur intellektuelles Einverständnis, sondern eine aus Mitgefühl, aus Sympathie hervorquellende Zustimmung hervorrufen, dann mußte die Möglichkeit einer *gewissen, allmählichen* Identifizierung eingebaut werden, und dazu ist die Ichform gerade hervorragend geeignet.

Von diesem Gesichtspunkt aus betrachtet, erscheint nun auch die so eindringlich negative Einleitung in einem neuen Licht äußersten Raffinements: Sie sorgt dafür, daß der Leser sich anfangs maximal de-solidarisiert: schlimmer kann es gar nicht mehr werden, das Abscheulichste weiß er vom ersten Augenblick an. Hiernach kann nur noch ein Prozeß von wachsendem Verständnis für Termeer in Gang kommen, der auch durch heftige Erschütterungen, von unvorhergesehenen Handlungen hervorgerufen, nicht mehr beeinträchtigt werden kann. Schon auf der zweiten Seite wird der Leser direkt in die Situation hineinbezogen, wo Termeer sich selbst, und also auch dem Leser, die Frage stellt: "Finde ich denn selbst meine Tat [den

Mord] *so* außergewöhnlich, *so* unerhört, *so* furchtbar? " Seine Antwort muß dem Leser in diesem Augenblick absurd vorkommen:
"Ach nein, dafür hat sich alles viel zu allmählich ineinandergefügt."
Gerade durch diese Anordnung wird es dem Leser ermöglicht, sich
schließlich Termeers Blick auf das Ganze weitgehend anzuschließen
und seine Meinung zu teilen. Ein wichtiges Hilfsmittel ist in diesem
Zusammenhang auch die sorgfältig über das ganze Buch verteilte,
ausdrückliche Unterstützung des deterministischen Grundmotivs, das
mit dem Ausspruch: 'Glaubst du, daß auch ich nicht lieber anders
hätte sein wollen, als ich bin', in vielfältig abgewandelter Form, in
Erscheinung tritt. "Nur allzu oft habe ich die Bemerkung machen
hören, daß ein Mensch, der seine Fehler kennt, auch fähig ist, sie
auszurotten. Ach, ach, wie wenig Selbsterkenntnis müssen diejenigen
[Feuchtersleben u.a.!] besitzen, die das sagen!" Mit näherer Erläuterung versehen findet sich diese Bemerkung schon auf der vierten
Seite (S. 19) und erscheint, im Wortlaut variiert, in extenso, an noch
zehn Stellen: auf den Seiten 32, 51, 68/69, 78/80, 105, 122, 136,
140/41, 152 und 198.

Aber als Naturalist konnte Emants sich andererseits natürlich auch
nicht damit zufriedenstellen, nur eine subjektive Lebensgeschichte zu
erzählen: Er brauchte eine objektive Grundlage. Es liegt auf der
Hand, daß der Typ des Hypochonders, den Termeer verkörpert, mit
seiner Neigung zu übermäßiger Introspektion und Selbstreflexion,
dauernd damit beschäftigt ist, sich *rationalisierend* zu rechtfertigen
und zu verteidigen. Gleichzeitig soll es dem Leser klar werden, daß
er, gerade durch seine krankhafte Veranlagung, die Dinge verzerrt
darstellt. Auf diese Weise entsteht ein prinzipieller Konflikt zwischen
der objektiv-vernünftigen Beurteilung von Termeers Handeln und
Denken seitens des Lesers, und seiner eigenen, nur scheinbar vernünf-
tigen Motivierung.

Mit welchen Mitteln hat Emants nun versucht, den Widerspruch
dieser beiden Arten von rationalem Denken zu verdeutlichen? Mit
anderen Worten: Welche Kunstgriffe bieten dem Leser Gelegenheit,
neben oder unter der krankhaft rationalisierten Verzerrung eine sozusagen 'objektiv-rationale' Schicht zu finden?

An erster Stelle hat Emants eine nicht unbeträchtliche Anzahl
wichtiger faktischer Inkonsequenzen in Termeers Bericht verarbeitet.
Die Geschichte von der mißlungenen Beziehung zu der schwedischen
Pianistin ist ein gutes Beispiel. Obwohl ihre Schönheit ihn beein-

druckt, hat er nur ein erotisches Abenteuer im Sinn: "Daß ich absolut nicht in sie verliebt war, bewies mein [schon vorher erwähnter] unleugbarer Widerwille gegen ihre groben Finger, der den Abschiedshanddruck für mich zu einer unangenehmen Berührung werden ließ [. . .] es würde mir vielleicht gelingen, ihre entgegenkommende Haltung auszunutzen, ohne meinen Kopf in die Schlinge zu stecken", und kurz danach ist die Rede von seiner "Rolle eines ernsthaften Bewerbers". Als aber aus der erhofften Liebschaft nichts geworden ist, spricht er von seiner "zertretenen, lebendigen Liebe", und auf der Rückreise ist er wahrhaftig in Träumereien über "ihre zarte Berührung meiner Hand" versunken.[24]

Noch viel stärker kommt dies zum Ausdruck im Bild seiner Frau Anna. Termeer schildert sie als eine Kälte ausstrahlende, gefühlsarme Frau, die nur in der ersten Zeit ihrer Beziehungen mit ihrem "lautlosen Lachen", und weil sie für ihren Verlobten Partei ergreift gegen ihre "Harleveener [philiströsen] Bekannten", noch einen gewissen Reiz auf ihn ausübt. Aber schon bald ist davon nichts mehr übrig, und ist sie "die Frau, die es verschmäht, sich auszusprechen und die nur ehrfurchtsvoll zu ihrer eigenen Vortrefflichkeit aufblickt." Als die Freundschaftsbande zwischen Anna und de Kantere sich in Zuneigung verändern, zeigt sich jedoch deutlich, daß sie die Fähigkeit, warme Gefühle zu hegen, durchaus nicht verloren hat: Es kann kein Zweifel darüber aufkommen, daß sie jetzt unter *de Kanteres* Einfluß steht, ihr "lautloses Lachen" ist wieder da, sie singt wieder, und in ihren Augen sieht Termeer "ein träumerisches Zartgefühl, das sie mir niemals gezeigt hat."[25]

Seine Behauptung: "Unser Verhältnis hätte ein besseres sein können, wenn Anna mir nicht so deutlich und so oft zu verstehen gegeben hätte, daß ich außerstande war, etwas Gutes oder Angenehmes in ihrem Leben zu bedeuten",[26] ist völlig inkonsequent; Annas Haltung gerät in ein schiefes Licht, da Termeer jetzt sein eigenes Verhalten ganz unberücksichtigt läßt.

Zwar bemerkt auch der Ich-Erzähler die widersprüchliche Natur mancher der hier erwähnten (und vieler anderer) Aussagen, bezeichnet sie sogar als solche, aber ihre Zahl und ihr Gewicht ist, wie sich bei genauem Lesen herausstellt, viel größer als Termeer uns vermuten

24. *Bekentenis.* S. 60, 61, 68 und 70.
25. Ebda., S. 88, 97, 111, 162/163, 166, 168, 170/171.
26. Ebda., S. 121.

284

läßt. Und nur auf dem Niveau der Kommunikation zwischen *Autor* und Leser wird ihre Bedeutung ganz offenbar, indem sie enthüllen, daß Termeers Weltbild eine verzerrte Wahnvorstellung ist.

Dieses Phänomen darf man mit einem gewissen Recht Ironie nennen, aber die Ironie spielt bei Emants auch noch eine viel direktere Rolle, und zwar eine so auffallende, daß sie dem Leser kaum entgehen kann. Auf eine ausführliche Auseinandersetzung über die Unmöglichkeit, angeborene psychische Eigenschaften mit Erfolg zu bekämpfen – es handelt sich in diesem Fall um die Feigheit –, und über die Dummheit von Leuten, die glauben, das sei *wohl* möglich, folgt unmittelbar die ungereimte 'Schlußfolgerung': "Mit etwas klug dosiertem Druck hätten meine Eltern meinem unglücklichen Dasein *also* eine andere Wendung geben können." (S. 20, kurs. von mir.) Nur wenige Seiten weiter erzählt Termeer, daß er fühle – "richtiger, wähne" –, alle fänden ihn "unangenehm, lästig, unbedeutend." Er erzählt dann weiter, wie er sich allen Versuchen, ihn in das gesellige Leben einzubeziehen, entzog und beschließt dann diesen Bericht mit den Worten, daß "alles *also* zusammenwirkte, um mir jedes aktive Auftreten immer mehr zuwider zu machen [...]" (S. 38, kurs. von mir). Und das, während seine eigene Darstellung der Umstände mit größter Deutlichkeit beweist, daß die Ursache nur in ihm selbst liegt. Etwas derartiges wiederholt sich viele Male. Noch ein Beispiel möchte ich zitieren: Als sein Schwager, van Swamelen, ein paarmal versucht hat, ihm eine Stellung zu besorgen, er aber jedesmal abgesagt hat, ist seine 'Schlußfolgerung': "Er hätte doch verstehen müssen, daß ich, mir selbst überlassen, mich niemals zu einem solchen Schritt [bei jemand einen Besuch abzustatten] würde aufraffen können! [...] Sollte es möglich sein, daß er den Vorwänden, unter denen ich seine Stellungen abgeschlagen habe, Glauben geschenkt hat? [...] Ein wenig freundschaftlich aufgedrängte Hilfe hätte dem Gefühl [sich zu *nichts* aufraffen zu können] so leicht ein Ende bereitet!"[27] Solche Inkonsequenzen gehören zweifellos zum Krankheitsbild des Hypochonders, aber durch ihren Stellenwert und das dadurch verursachte Überraschungsmoment werden sie zugleich Träger der ironischen Funktion: Sie relativieren Termeers Weltbild.

Indem er die besprochenen Widersprüche und Ironisierungen in den Roman einflicht, gibt der Autor sich heimlich hinter dem Rücken der Ich-Gestalt zu erkennen. Er lenkt die Interpretation und

27. Ebda., S. 114/115.

Evaluation des Lesers in eine Richtung, deren Termeer sich sozusagen 'gar nicht bewußt' ist. Emants hat in *Een nagelaten bekentenis* ganz gewiß einen archimedischen Punkt gestaltet, von dem aus Termeers Erde aus ihrer Bahn gehoben werden kann.[28] Mit anderen Worten: In den subjektiven Ich-Roman hat er die objektive Schicht eingebaut, die der Naturalist nicht entbehren kann. Hiermit hat Emants eine sehr bedeutende Erneuerung der Romantechnik zustande gebracht. Es gab zwar Vorbilder in der älteren Literatur – Batavus Droog-stoppel aus *Max Havelaar,* wenn wir uns auf die niederländische Literatur beschränken[29] –, bei diesen handelte es sich jedoch immer um grelle Ironisierungen, während die Ironisierung uns hier in einem Buch begegnet, das von Anfang bis Ende in tiefernstem Ton gehalten ist. Und im Gegensatz zu Multatuli, der eine prinzipielle De-Solida-risierung des Lesers, Droogstoppel gegenüber, bezweckt, ist Emants gerade daran gelegen, beim Leser Sympathie für Termeer zu er-wecken. Mit unverkennbarem Ernst bemüht sich Termeer um größtmögliche Ehrlichkeit seiner Darstellung (man denke z.B. nur an seine zahllosen Selbst-Berichtigungen). Indem er die Verzerrtheit der Darstellung bloßstellt, beweist der Autor erst recht deutlich, daß der Hypochonder der Gefangene seines Wahnes ist und ihm nie ent-kommen kann.

Noch einen zweiten wichtigen Schluß kann man aus diesen Über-legungen folgern: Nachdem wir feststellen konnten, daß der Autor Termeers Auffassungen des öfteren relativiert, dürfen wir aus dem Fehlen einer solchen Relativierung wohl schließen, daß sie absichtlich weggelassen ist. Das bedeutet also, daß er Termeers Ansichten teilt, wenn das Gegenteil nicht ersichtlich ist. Anderenfalls hätte er an diesen Stellen versagt und wäre es ihm nicht gelungen, die Reaktion des Lesers, seinen Wünschen entsprechend, zu lenken. Das technische Raffinement, das er durchweg entfaltet, macht diese Annahme sehr unwahrscheinlich. Namentlich trifft dies zu, wo die Idee der cha-rakterbestimmenden erblichen Belastung erörtert wird. Immer wieder steht sie im Roman zur Diskussion und nirgends tritt diesbezüglich ein Meinungsunterschied zwischen Autor und Protagonist zutage. De

28. Im Gegensatz zu dem, was Oversteegen darüber sagt. 'Donkere dagen' S. 14.

29. Vgl. A. L. Sötemann: *De structuur van* Max Havelaar*; bijdrage tot het onderzoek naar de interpretatie en evaluatie van de roman.* Utrecht, 1966. 2 Bde. Bd. I S. 38-45 und S. 28-32.

Kantere dagegen, von Feuchterslebens Sprachrohr, zweifelt an der Erblichkeitslehre — freilich in recht geistlosen und unbedeutenden
Worten: "Ja, wenn wir der Erblichkeitslehre ganz gewiß wären . . . ja,
dann . . . aber das ist bei dieser Theorie noch weniger der Fall als bei
anderen. Finden Sie nicht, daß wir vorläufig besser daran tun werden,
der starken Stimme unseres Herzens zu folgen, als den unbewiesenen
Behauptungen einer angefochtenen und anfechtbaren Lehre? "[30]

Ich teile also Oversteegens Auffassung nicht: Emants war, wie sich
aus *Een nagelaten bekentenis* ergibt, auch selbst Anhänger des Glau-
bens an ein sich vererbendes Schicksal. Der Roman ist nicht nur "ein
Buch über einen Mann, der an die Erblichkeit des Schicksals glaubt",
sondern auch ein "Buch über das Wirken [dieses] Schicksals."[31]

Es ist bemerkenswert, daß außer der Ironie des Autors noch eine
zweite Art von Ironie in dem Buch zu finden ist: Termeers eigene.
Man könnte sagen, neben fundamentaler gibt es hier immanente Ironie. Wir sahen schon, daß Termeer sich für eine unglückliche Abnor-
malität, für "eine Degeneration" hält. Obgleich aber der Ton des
Romans durchweg ernst bleibt, weiß er es doch seinem "Leser" besonders gut klarzumachen, daß die vielgepriesene glückliche Normalität, oder besser noch: der angebliche Zustand dauernder Glückselig-
keit des 'normalen Menschen' in der bitteren Wirklichkeit des Lebens
nichts als ein Trugbild ist. Etwa zwanzigmal bringt er diese Auffassung mehr oder weniger ausführlich zur Sprache. Sarkastisch und
ironisch, wie in der folgenden, direkt an den Leser gerichteten An-
sprache: "Verehrter, geschätzter, wohlanständiger, edelgesinnter
Leser, wenn du glaubst, aus freiem Willen so vortrefflich geworden zu
sein, warum bist du dann nicht noch besser? Weil du nicht wolltest,
oder weil du nicht konntest? " Oder: "Wenn ich ihn richtig verstehe,
kennt der wahrhaft normale Mensch die abstumpfende Leblosigkeit
gar nicht und braucht also keine gekünstelten Empfindungen, um
sich zu ermuntern. Ganz von selbst ergreift alles, was schön, großartig
und seines Mitgefühls würdig ist, ihn tief in seiner stets aufnahme-
bereiten Seele." Oder, subtiler: "Wenn auch bei uns die Poesie
fehlte, die den Haushalt anderer junger Ehepaare zu durchdringen
scheint [. . .]", und: "Zufrieden werden zu können, wie — glaubte ich

30. *Bekentenis.* S. 135.
31. Oversteegen: 'Donkere dagen'. S. 20/21.

– die Mehrzahl der Menschen war [. . .]". Gerade solche scheinbar beiläufig hinzugefügte Bemerkungen, wie diese letzten und wie auch zum Beispiel die folgenden: "die Freiheit, die – wie ich glaubte – jedem Menschen zuteil wurde"; "[. . .] zu leben, wie andere Frauen zu leben *schienen*"[32], zeigen dem Leser unmißverständlich, in wie hohem Grade das 'normale Glück', oder sogar die Normalität der 'normalen' Menschen nur Schein ist, – und daß Termeer sich dessen deutlich bewußt ist. Auch diese, vom Protagonisten getragene Ironie soll vom Leser aufgefaßt und *au sérieux* genommen werden. Sie wird übrigens von einer Anzahl unverhüllter Aussagen des gleichen Tenors unterstützt. Ich zitiere einige: "[. . .] gewöhnt mich selbst zu unter-, oder eigentlich andere Leute [. . .] zu überschätzen . . .", und: "Hätte ich damals nur eingesehen, daß die Gleichgültigkeit der Menschen gewöhnlich ihre Strenge sehr mildert." Besonders aber möchte ich aufmerksam machen auf eine wichtige Ausführung über den 'normalen Menschen', seine Selbsttäuschung, seine Hypokrisie der Außenwelt gegenüber und seine Neigung, in anderen zu verurteilen, was er bei sich selbst beschönigt. Die Schlußfolgerung lautet wie folgt: "Da ich jetzt die Zahl der normalen Menschen nicht mehr für so groß und folglich ihre Normalität nicht mehr für so beneidenswert rein erachte, kommt es mir wahrscheinlich vor, daß Selbsterkenntnis immer, Erfahrungen mit anderen aber nur dann pessimistisch machen, wenn man sich selbst und die eigenen Erfahrungen nicht für eine schöne Ausnahme von einer häßlichen Regel hält."[33]

Es scheint auf der Hand zu liegen, daß die Funktion dieses Komplexes von Äußerungen ist, im Geist des Lesers ein Bild Termeers hervorzurufen, das ihn in manchen nicht unwichtigen Hinsichten weniger ungewöhnlich darstellt, als dem ersten Eindruck nach zu erwarten war. Anders ausgedrückt: Dieser Komplex ist ein wesentlicher Bestandteil von Emants' Strategie, um beim Leser den Prozeß einer allmählichen – wenn auch natürlich niemals vollständigen – Identifikation mit der Ich-Gestalt, zu fördern. Es zeigt sich per Saldo, daß Emants' Spiel mit Relativierung und Distanz äußerst kompliziert und fesselnd ist.

Vom Niveau des Autors her bekommt übrigens der negative Blick der Ich-Gestalt auf das 'Glück' der 'normalen' Menschen noch ausdrückliche Unterstützung, da alle anderen Personen des Romans –

32. *Bekentenis.* S. 198, 68, 113, 93, 33 und 166.
33. Ebda., S. 34, 36 und 78/79.

auch wenn man von der 'Verfärbung', die Termeer anbringt, absieht — ebensowenig ein zufriedenes und befriedigendes Leben führen: Annas Eltern und deren Bekanntenkreis, die schwedische Pianistin, van Dregten und natürlich auch de Kantere — der gar kein Geheimnis daraus macht, und dessen nach Termeers Ansicht so beneidenswert 'reine' Beziehung zu Anna schließlich auch auf eine Enttäuschung hinausläuft. Sogar hinsichtlich der 'erfolgreichen' van Swamelens wird dafür gesorgt, daß starke Zweifel aufkommen.

Ich bin mir bewußt, daß die hier vorliegenden Ausführungen bei einem kritischen Leser den Eindruck hervorrufen könnten, daß sie hier und da gefährlich in die Nähe eines Zirkelschlusses kommen. Bei diesem Roman, genau wie bei jedem anderen, kommt es ja eigentlich auf die Verständigung zwischen Autor und Leser an. Mittel zu diesem Zweck ist im Fall von Emants' Roman die äußerst subjektiv erzählte Geschichte eines Menschen, von dem man keineswegs annehmen darf, er leihe nur dem Autor seine Stimme. Die beschriebenen Widersprüchlichkeiten in Termeers Erzählung und die deutliche Ironisierung *eines Teils* seiner Behauptungen beweisen diesen Sachverhalt. Bis dahin braucht man keine Störung der Verständigung zu befürchten. Etwas heikler wird die Sache, wenn ich behaupte, die Ansichten des Autors und des Protagonisten stimmten überein, sofern man das Gegenteil nicht aufzeigen könne. Diese Behauptung ist im streng logischen Sinne unbeweisbar, wenn sie auch einleuchtend ist, aufgrund der Tatsache, daß das Gegenteil an anderen Stellen des Romans unzweideutig zum Ausdruck kommt. Aber wirkliche Schwierigkeiten entstehen da, wo ich behauptet habe, eine gar nicht so geringe Zahl von Aussagen des Protagonisten — gleichgültig, ob sie nun ironisch formuliert sind, oder nicht — sei vom Leser *au sérieux* zu nehmen, im Gegensatz zu anderen, die Symptome seines verzerrten Weltbildes seien. Wo liegt die Grenze zwischen diesen beiden Gruppen und mit Hilfe welchen Kriteriums kann man sie unterscheiden? Zweifellos werden viele Leser anders reagiert haben als ich. Ich fürchte, daß ich mich im Grunde nur auf mein 'sachverständiges' Urteil berufen kann: Die Lektüre von Emants' Werken — Romane und Novellen, Gedichte, Essays, Vorworte, Briefe und Interview — hat mir ein ziemlich gutes Bild, mit vielen Einzelheiten, von seinem Verständnis des menschlichen Daseins verschafft. Das Gleiche gilt für eine Gruppe mit ihm verwandter Schriftsteller. Aufgrund dieser Kenntnisse, verbunden mit der Bereitschaft, mich in diese Auf-

289

fassungen einzuleben, habe ich versucht, mir ein Bild der Leserrolle, die Emants in *Een nagelaten bekentenis* hineingearbeitet hat, zu formen. Das heißt also: ein Bild jenes Komplexes von Reaktionen, die Emants von einem adäquaten Leser erwartet. Die Hypothese muß ihre Überzeugungskraft von der Tatsache herleiten, das keine offenkundigen Widersprüche und Ungereimtheiten zutage kommen, wenn man bei der Lektüre diese Einsichten dem Verständnis zugrunde legt. Eine andere Auffassung müßte eine Interpretation vorführen, die zu einem ebenso kohärenten Kommunikationsprozeß führt, und die auch im gleichen Maße die historische Situation hinsichtlich der weltanschaulichen und literarischen Auffassungen und Konventionen berücksichtigt.

Soweit ich feststellen konnte, ist *Een nagelaten bekentenis* der erste Ich-Roman in der westeuropäischen Literatur, dessen Held negativ und sogar eine pathologische Persönlichkeit ist. Wohl war ihm natürlich Dostojewski mit seinen *Aufzeichnungen aus dem Kellerloch* (1864) geraume Zeit zuvorgekommen, ein Buch, in dem die Ich-Gestalt sich sogar selbst einen "Antihelden" nennt. Und auch er beginnt seine Geschichte mit den Worten: "Ich bin ein kranker Mensch . . . Ich bin ein bösartiger Mensch . . . Ich bin ein abstoßender Mensch." Ich habe nicht ausfindig machen können, ob Emants dieses Buch und auch die Erzählung *Die Sanfte,* in der neben tiefschürfenden Unterschieden auch parallel verlaufende Züge nachweisbar sind, gekannt hat. Es ist jedenfalls sehr gut möglich, daß er sie gekannt hat. Von den *Aufzeichnungen* war im Jahre 1886 eine französische, und 1888 eine holländische Übersetzung erschienen; *Die Sanfte* wurde 1886 sowohl ins Französische wie ins Niederländische übersetzt.[34] Falls Emants diese Werke Dostojewskis tatsächlich gekannt hat, so bleibt es trotzdem wahr, daß *Een nagelaten bekentenis*, das sich so deutlich von ihnen unterscheidet, ein Roman von großer Originalität ist, dessen Wert hierdurch kaum beeinträchtigt wird.

Ich hoffe, hiermit klargelegt zu haben, daß ein Schriftsteller der neunziger Jahre, der seiner Zeit eher voraus war, sehr wohl imstande

34. J. M. Romein: *Dostojewski in de westersche kritiek.* Haarlem, 1924. S. 210, 217, 211 und 217. — Von *Die Sanfte* war übrigens schon 1877 eine französische Übersetzung in Sankt Petersburg erschienen.

war, ja, es als Notwendigkeit betrachten konnte, mit einem Roman gegen einen typischen Vertreter des Biedermeiers wie Feuchtersleben in die Schranken zu treten, gerade weil dieser, auch vom damals vorherrschenden naturalistischen Standpunkt aus, als Wissenschaftler noch vollkommen aktuell war, während gegen ihn, als (noch immer einflußreichen) seicht idealisierenden Moralphilosophen, schärfste Kritik geboten war. Als schöpferischer Künstler hat Emants sich jedoch nicht damit begnügt, sein Plädoyer in der Form eines schon traditionell gewordenen relativ-objektiven Romans zu halten. Mit der Wahl einer scheinbar extrem-subjektiven Erzählhaltung durchbrach er das herrschende System naturalistischer Romankonventionen. Dabei ist es ihm dank äußerstem Raffinement in der Anwendung technischer Mittel gelungen, scheinbare und wirkliche Objektivität auf verschiedenen Niveaus in seinen Roman einzuflechten. Er erreichte dies mit Hilfe der inneren Widersprüche in den Ausführungen des Protagonisten und der Doppelschichtigkeit der Ironie: neben der immanenten Ironie seiner Hauptperson steht die eigene, fundamentale Ironie des Autors. Mit diesem Spiel, das uns sehr subjektiv anmutet, ist es Emants gelungen, sein — von seinem Standpunkt aus objektives — Ziel zu erreichen. Der Gewinn den er hier, im Vergleich zur traditionellen naturalistischen Romantechnik, erzielt, besteht in einer größeren Komplexität und einer intensiveren Anteilnahme des Lesers, ohne daß er auf die vom Naturalismus angestrebte Objektivität als solche zu verzichten braucht.

Emants trat sieben Jahre nach dem *Bekentenis,* im Jahre 1901, noch einmal hervor als Erneuerer des Romans. Das damals veröffentlichte Buch *Inwijding* (Einweihung) ist nämlich der erste konsequent ·personale Roman, ein Roman also, in dem man keiner Erzählerinstanz begegnet, der "sich selbst zu erzählen" scheint, und in dem man nur eine einzige Gestalt von innen her kennenlernt. Dieser Roman erschien zwei Jahre vor *The Ambassadors* von Henry James, dem Roman, der in der internationalen Fachliteratur als das erste Beispiel dieses Verfahrens gilt. Zweifellos haben beide Romanciers unabhängig von einander diese Erneuerung gefunden, die natürlich nur vor dem Hintergrund eines Flaubert, eines Turgenjew und der französischen Naturalisten denkbar ist. Trotzdem stellt sie eine sprunghafte Mutation der Romantechnik dar, die von größter Bedeutung war, da sie den dominanten Romantypus der ersten Hälfte des zwanzigsten Jahrhunderts geprägt hat.[34a]

Ich glaube denn auch keine übertriebene Schlußfolgerung zu ziehen, wenn ich Marcellus Emants einen der wichtigsten Erneuerer des Romans um die Jahrhundertwende nennen möchte. Leider mußten, infolge der geringen Verbreitung seiner Muttersprache, seine Bedeutung und sein Einfluß im internationalen Rahmen sehr beschränkt bleiben.[35]

34a. Erst nachdem dieser Artikel gesetzt war, stellte ich dank einem Hinweis Prof. Dr. W. Schmids fest, daß auch in diesem Fall Dostojewski Emants — und Henry James — weit voraus gewesen ist: *Der Doppelgänger* (1846) ist zwar ein ausgesprochen auktorialer Roman, aber (fast) nur die Hauptperson Goljadkin wird von innen her beleuchtet; und die lange Novelle *Die Wirtin* (1847) weist sogar vollauf alle Merkmale der personalen Erzählung auf.

35. 1906 ist *Een nagelaten bekentenis* in einer deutschen Übersetzung von Rhea Sternberg unter dem Titel: *Bekenntnisse eines Dekadenten* erschienen; 1969 wurde eine französische Übersetzung von S. Margueron: *Une confession posthume* herausgegeben; eine amerikanische Ausgabe ist soeben veröffentlicht worden: *A posthumous confession*, übersetzt von J. M. Coetzee.

VON DER *DOCTRINE* HER GESEHEN.*
DER FRANZÖSISCHE KLASSIZISMUS IN HUYDECOPERS
ACHILLES

S. F. Witstein (Leiden)

In der letzten Auflage seiner Literaturgeschichte schreibt G. Knuvelder über Huydecopers *Achilles* (1719): "Dit stuk geldt bij velen voor het beste achttiende eeuwse Frans-klassieke treurspel. Feit is dat het werk grote opgang gemaakt heeft niet alleen in zijn eigen tijd, maar ook daarna: tot in de 19e eeuw werd het met succes bekroond".[1] (Dieses Stück wird von vielen als das beste französisch-klassizistische Trauerspiel des achtzehnten Jahrhunderts betrachtet. Tatsache ist, dass das Werk grosses Aufsehen erregt hat nicht nur in seiner eigenen Zeit, sondern auch danach: bis ins 19. Jahrhundert wurde es mit Erfolg gekrönt).

Der letzte Herausgeber des *Achilles,* C. C. J. van Schaik, hat in der Einleitung zu seiner 1961 erschienenen Ausgabe des Dramas keinen Versuch zu einer eingehenden Bewertung dieses Trauerspiels, auf dessen Konto gut 100 Jahre lang offenbar gut gefüllte Theatersäle kamen, unternommen. Er begnügt sich damit, dass er aus der 1959 von L. Strengholt besorgten Ausgabe von Rotgans' *Eneas en Turnus* eine Aufzählung von 16 Punkten übernimmt, in der Strengholt die Faustregeln der *doctrine classique* formuliert hatte. Van Schaiks Folgerung in Bezug auf den *Achilles* beschränkt sich auf die Feststellung: "Het zal iedere lezer duidelijk zijn dat Huydecoper zich vrijwel steeds nauwkeurig aan de regels gehouden heeft".[2] (Es wird jedem Leser klar sein, dass Huydecoper die Regeln fast immer genau beobachtet hat). Wenn man nun die Kriterien finden will, die ent-

*Für die Anfertigung der Übersetzung des niederländischen Originals ins Deutsche danke ich Herrn drs. G. Kuipers.

1. G. P. M. Knuvelder, *Handboek tot de geschiedenis der Nederlandse letterkunde.* 's-Hertogenbosch, 1971[5], S. 519.
2. *Achilles,* S. 14.

scheiden, aus welchen Gründen das Stück jahrelang als Bestseller der französisch-klassizistischen Dramatik gegolten hat, so wird man an erster Stelle untersuchen müssen, in welcher Weise Huydecoper in seiner dramatischen Spitzenleistung die Vorschriften der *doctrine classique* realisiert hat. Mit den folgenden Bemerkungen hoffe ich, einen ersten Ansatz zu einer derartigen Untersuchung geben zu können.

Der *Achilles* ist eine *imitatio* der Achillfabel, wie sie in der *Ilias* vorkommt. Eben durch diese Stoffwahl hat Huydecoper sich als ein guter Schüler des Horaz erwiesen und selbstverständlich auch seines Landmanns Andries Pels, der die Lehren des Horaz in französisch-klassizistischem Sinne bearbeitet hatte. Der römische Poet hatte den Theaterdichtern seiner Zeit empfohlen, ihre Dramenstoffe eher der *Ilias* zu entnehmen als aus eigener Erfindung zu schöpfen,[3] – ein Ratschlag, den Pels in seiner Schrift *Gebruik en misbruik des tooneels*[4] wiederholte. Horaz widersetzte sich jedoch jeder Änderung der traditionellen Charakterzeichnung.[5] Tatsächlich hat Huydecoper, abgesehen von höfischen Zügen, mit denen er Achill und Briseis in ihrem gegenseitigen Betragen ausgeschmückt hat, die hergebrachte Typisierung nicht geändert: Achill ehrgeizig und störrisch in seiner Gekränktheit,[6] Agamemnon voller Bereitschaft, den verübten Fehltritt zu begleichen. Nur Briseis, bei Homer nicht mehr als ein Name, ist zu einer deutlicher umrissenen Gestalt herausgearbeitet worden.[7] Die Ereignisse wurden aber genau eingehalten, obgleich in der Zeitfolge einige auffällige Änderungen vorgenommen wurden.

Die Bühnenhandlung verläuft wie folgt: Achill, der von dem Heerführer Agamemnon durch den Raub seiner geliebten Gefangenen Briseis tödlich in seiner Ehre verletzt war, weigert sich während der vier ersten Akte, noch länger an den Kämpfen um Troja teilzunehmen. Die Lage der Griechen mag noch so heikel sein: trotz aller

---

3. *The art of poetry* in Horace, *Satires, Epistles, Ars Poetica.* With an English translation (London usw., 1961, The Loeb Classical Library), S. 460-461, Vss. 128-130.

4. Der von mir benutzte Text befindet sich in *Q. H. Flaccus dichtkunst op onse tyden en séden gepast* (Amst., 1677, sign. U.B. Utrecht, Z.qu.127[1]), S. 39.

5. *The art of poetry*, Vss. 121-124.

6. Vgl. A. Pels, *Q. Horatius Flaccus dichtkunst op onze tijden en zeden gepast.* Ed. M. A. Schenkeveld-Van der Dussen (Assen, 1973), S. 69,*ann. ad.* Vs. 289.

7. Siehe "Voorrede", ed. Van Schaik, S. 23-24.

Bitten, die Waffen wieder aufzunehmen und trotz der prächtigsten Versöhnungsgeschenke, die Agamemnon ihm anbieten lässt, bleibt der Held unerbittlich. Inzwischen gelingt es den Trojanern, unter der Führung Hektors, in einem Teil der griechischen Flotte Feuer anzulegen. Erst wenn im letzten Auftritt des vieten Aktes Ulysses mit der Unheilsnachricht erscheint, dass Patroklos im Kampf gegen Hektor gefallen sei, ergreift Achill die Waffen, aber ausschliesslich, um seinen Herzensfreund zu rächen. Es ist sein Vorsatz, falls er den trojanischen Prinzen erschlagen sollte, danach ebenfalls Agamemnon zu töten, den man ja den Urheber des Streites, die prima causa des Unheils, das Patroklos widerfahren ist, nennen konnte. Im fünften Akt erzählt der alte Phenix Briseis, die abermals als neue Geste der Versöhnung von Agamemnon nach Achills Zelt geschickt wurde, wie Achill, um Hektor zu bekämpfen, bei den Schiffen angekommen war, dort den leichtverwundeten Agamemnon vorgefunden hatte und diesen auf der Stelle hatte töten wollen. Als Ulysses sich aber vor den Heerführer gestellt und den Helden angeredet hatte, sei Achill zwar davongeeilt, auf Hektor zu, jedoch mit dem Ausruf, er werde Agamemnon auf jeden Fall umbringen, falls der Trojaner seiner Hand entrinnen sollte. Darauf erscheint ein Bote, der erzählt, wie Achill Hektor das Leben genommen hat. Als Achill darauf ins griechische Lager zurückkehrt, ist er offenbar noch immer nicht zur Versöhnung mit Agamemnon bereit, trotz der Lobreden, die dieser ihm spendet. Erst als Ulysses ihn ausdrücklich ermahnt, Vernunft anzunehmen "eer de haat der Goden hun gedult verwint", fallen ihm die Schuppen von den Augen. Er erkennt, dass Patroklos durch seinen Starrsinn den Tod gefunden hat und bietet Agamemnon ewige Freundschaft an. Die Griechen haben ihren gewaltigen Schutzherrn zurückgewonnen, und ihre Notlage hat ein Ende genommen.

In der *Ilias* jedoch findet die Versöhnung mit Agamemnon nicht nach dem Zweikampf Achills mit dem trojanischen Prinzen statt, sondern davor. In seiner Trauer um Patroklos beschuldigt der Held sich letzten Endes, dass er in seinem Groll über die ihm zugefügte Beleidigung müssig bei den Schiffen gesessen habe, ohne dass er seinem Herzensfreund oder seinen anderen Genossen irgendwie von Nutzen gewesen wäre. Diese neue Erkenntnis seines Starrsinns führt eine plötzliche Änderung seines Verhaltens herbei. Er verwünscht seinen Zorn und den Streit und schlichtet die Streitigkeit mit Agamemnon.[8] Darauf wird von den Griechen ein Massenangriff geführt, in dem Achill zahlreichen Trojanern den Tod gibt und schliesslich auch Hektor in einem greulichen Zweikampf tödlich trifft.

Das Anziehende der homerischen Fabel lag m.E. für Huydecoper als französisch-klassizistischen Dramatiker hauptsächlich in der "Bekehrung" des Achill, in der Erkenntnis, dass durch sein Betragen die Griechen in eine so heikle Lage geraten waren. Nach dem Vorgang des Aristoteles unterschied der Klassizismus nämlich zwei Arten dramatischer Handlung, *simplex* bzw. *complex*. Letztere Art, die für die eleganteste galt, verband die Schicksalsänderung der Helden mit sehr bestimmten Bedingungen, der *peripeteia* und der *agnitio*. Unter *peripeteia* verstand man einen "changement de fortune [qui] modifie, non pas seulement la situation matérielle des héros, mais leur situation psychologique".[9] Es kommt noch ein Element hinzu, das der hier angeführte Scherer nicht beachtet, nämlich, dass dieser "changement de fortune" vollständig sein muss, so dass der Held in eine Lage gerät, die dem von ihm angestrebten Zustand oder dem Zustand, den er bisher als unwandelbar akzeptiert hatte, diametral entgegengesetzt ist.[10] Die *agnitio* ist eine plötzliche, überraschende Entdeckung der Wahrheit, die man in aristotelischem Sinne umschreiben könnte als "a change from ignorance to knowledge".[11] Für den Helden, in dem sich ein derartiger Wechsel vollzieht, ändert sich zugleich die Perspektive, so dass eine entweder psychische oder eine sowohl psychische als materielle Umkehr (*peripeteia*) die Fortsetzung der *agnitio* darstellt. Diese beiden Ornamente der Bühnenhandlung dienen dazu, dass der Knoten, die Intrige, in überraschender Weise gelöst werden kann und der Handlungsverlauf auf ein vom Dichter gestecktes Endziel hin gelenkt wird.

Im homerischen Epos ist eben der Prototyp einer *agnitio* da, wo Achill plötzlich zur Einsicht gelangt, dass seine Unversöhnlichkeit ein heilloses Ausmass angenommen hat, wofür Patroklos und soviele andere mit dem Leben büssen mussten. Eines der Ornamente der Bühnenhandlung fand Huydecoper also offenbar in seiner Quelle vor.

8. *Ilias,* XVIII, Vss. 101-113.
9. J. Scherer, *La dramaturgie classique en France* (Paris 1964), S. 86.
10. Vgl. Aristotle, *The poetics* in *The poetics;* "Longinus", *On the sublime;* Demetrius, *On style* (London usw. 1960, The Loeb Classical Library), Kap. XI, S. 40-41.
11. *Ibid.*

Er brauchte die Worte des epischen Achill nur dem Geschmack seiner
Zeit gemäss zu amplifizieren, und sein Drama war mit einem eindrucksvollen "change from ignorance to knowledge" versehen. Und
so verfährt Huydecoper auch tatsächlich. Gegen Ende des fünften
Aufzugs, nach der dringenden Ermahnung des Ulysses, entfliessen
dem zur Einsicht gebrachten Helden auf einmal die Worte der Reue
in reichlicher Fülle:

> Goôn die my eindlyk geeft mijn blind gezigt te ontsluiten
>
> . . . .
>
> Ik ben gestraft; en zie dat myne schuld, ô smart!
> Patroclus, u het staal van Hector dreef in 't hart
> (Vss. 1827 . . . 1830).

Aus dieser veränderten Perspektive führt der Dichter nun auch in
Achills psychischer Lage, ganz den Regeln gemäss, einen totalen Um-
schwung herbei, denn seine wütende Mordgier gegen Agamemnon
schlägt um in eine hochgestimmte Freundschaft:

> 'k Omhels u, als mijn vriend, en zweer by 't hoofd der Goden
> Dat ik na dezen, meer als eertyts uw' geboden
> Betrachten zal. Laat ons een' vriendschap maaken, die
> Geen jaar, geen eeuw, na deze oit weêr gebroken zie
>
> (Vss. 1839-1842).

Eine *agnitio* hat eine rein rhetorische Funktion. Sie kommt zustande
durch die Steigerung der Erwartung in eine Richtung, die dem end-
gültigen Ausschlag der Ereignisse entgegengesetzt ist, so dass ihr Wert
völlig von dem Grad der Überraschung bestimmt wird, die sie den
Zuschauern zu bereiten weiss. Huydecoper hat die delektativen und
emotionellen Möglichkeiten der *agnitio* möglichst gut auszunutzen
versucht. Bis ans Äusserste hält er die prekäre Situation der Gegenüberstellung eines tollwütigen Achill und eines reuevollen Agamemnon aufrecht. Noch keine 50 Verse, bevor der Held im fünften
Aufzug sich von einem "Blinden" in einen plötzlich Sehenden verwandelt, hat der als Besieger Hektors zurückkehrende Achill den
Heerführer noch mit Schmachworten überhäuft und dessen Ge-
schenke erneut abgewiesen. Wenn aber die *agnitio* schliesslich erreicht, die Feindschaft abgeschworen und das Volk aus der Not erlöst
ist, m.a.W. wenn die Überraschung aufgetischt und das Spannungs-
element aufgehoben ist, dann wird das Spiel auch schnell zu Ende
geführt.

Dadurch, dass die Versöhnung bis ans Ende des Spiels auf-
geschoben wird, wurde auch die Finalität des Dramas eine andere als
die im Epos. In der *Ilias* bewegen sich die Ereignisse, von Patroklos'
Tod über die Beendung des Konflikts mit Agamemnon, auf die Ver-
geltungsaktion hin, die Achill entbrennen lässt und als deren Klimax
der Zweikampf mit Hektor vorgeführt wird. Im Drama dagegen ist
das Endziel nicht die grossartige Racheaktion, sondern die Wieder-
herstellung der Beziehungen zwischen dem besten Streiter und seinem General, die die Rettung des Griechentums bedeutet. Die Ethik
der Tragödie fusst denn auch auf der falschen Einstellung Achills,
dem der verletzte Stolz so schwer wiegt, dass er das Volk vom Feind
bis an den Rand des Abgrunds treiben lässt. Die starre Unbeugsam-
keit eines Einzelnen, für die die andern büssen müssen, bildet denn
auch das Hauptthema der Dialoge, während im "Opdragt aan . . . Mr.
Willem vander Muelen" die Folgen von Achills Zorn gedeutet werden
als exemplarisch für das Elend, das unbeherrschte Machthaber über
ihre Völker zu bringen pflegen.[12] Diese Lehre lässt Huydecoper ausserdem als Motto auf dem Schutzblatt anbringen – wobei er einen
Satz aus Horaz' *Epistula* 2 (Lib. I) benutzt: *Quicquid delirant Reges,
plectuntur Achivi* (toutes les folies des rois, les Achéens en portent la
peine).[13]
Man fragt sich jedoch, ob es tatsächlich unvermeidlich war,
zwecks dieser anderen Zielsetzung und Moral die Zeitfolge der Ereignisse der *Ilias* so eingreifend abzuändern. Ist es doch leicht denkbar, dem Publikum die von Huydecoper vertretene Lehre unter Beibehaltung der *agnitio* im von Homer überlieferten Augenblick ange-
deihen zu lassen, nämlich als Reaktion auf den Tod des Patroklos,
d.h. in der letzten Szene des vierten Aktes. Der Dichter hätte dann
den ganzen fünften Akt der Besiegelung von Achills erneuter Identifikation mit der griechischen Sache widmen können, wie sie jetzt (als
Botenbericht) in der Besiegung Hektors und in der Wiederkehr des
mit überschwenglichen Lobreden von Agamemnon und den übrigen
Fürsten gefeierten Siegers ins Lager zum Ausdruck kommt. Nun hat
Huydecoper eine derartige Möglichkeit in seiner "Voorrede" ausdrücklich abgewiesen. Das Argument, das er dazu vorbringt, entnimmt er
einer fingierten Reaktion des Publikums; es ist also rhetorischer Art.

12. Ed. van Schaik, S. 20, Vss. 11-20.
13. Horace, *Epitres.* Texte établi et traduit par F. Villeneuve. Paris 1964, S.
[45].

299

Die Lösung des Konflikts in einem früheren Stadium sei unmöglich, weil die Zuschauer kein Interesse mehr am fünften Akt mit "de dood van Hector, en het geene daaromtrent meer verhaald wordt" (dem Tod Hektors und mit allem, was da umhin erzählt wird) hätten, wenn die Versöhnung zwischen Achill und Agamemnon schon im vorigen Akt zustande gekommen wäre.[14] Aber warum hat denn Huydecoper den Zweikampf zwischen den beiden Koryphäen nicht völlig getilgt und durch eine selbsterfundene Fiktion, die ganz zum Streit zwischen Achill und Agamemnon passte, ersetzt? Dies war jedoch ausgeschlossen, weil bei der allgemeinen Bekanntheit der homerischen Achillfabel jeder Ersatz für den berühmten Kampf nach Patroklos' Tod der Glaubwürdigkeit, die ja eine der Grundprinzipien der *doctrine classique* war,[15] zuwider gewesen wäre. Aber auch Huydecopers "Glaube" in Hinsicht auf den Geschmack des Publikums und der darauf beruhende Aufschub der *agnitio* bis zu den letzten 60 Versen des Schlussaktes sind auf eine französisch-klassizistische Auffassung und auf ein literarisches Gesetz zurückzuführen, dessen Ursprung sich − selbstverständlich − in der *ars poetica* des Aristoteles findet.

Aristoteles beschreibt das Drama, und namentlich die Tragödie, als die Darstellung einer *vollständigen Handlung*, d.h. einer Handlung mit Anfang, Mitte und Ende. Nachdem er diese Termini definiert und das Ende umschrieben hat als das Resultat von etwas anderem, dem nichts anderes mehr folgt, gibt der Stagyrit als seine Meinung zu erkennen, dass wohlkonstruierte Plots denn auch nicht aufs Geratewohl, sondern nach den soeben von ihm gelieferten Formeln anfangen und enden sollten.[16]

Die Vorschrift der Vollständigkeit der Handlung hat für die französisch-klassizistische Theaterpraxis weitreichende Folgen gehabt. Corneille, dessen Theorien grossen Einfluss auf die Bildung der *doctrine* im Punkte der Einheit der Handlung gehabt haben,[17] verbindet in seinem *Discours du poëme tragique* mit dieser Vorschrift die Konsequenz, dass Handlungen momentaner Art − bei denen einer der die volständige Handlung konstituierenden Teile fehlt − verpönt

14. Ed. Van Schaik, S. 26.
15. R. Bray, *La formation de la doctrine classique en France* (Paris 1957), S. 210-211.
16. *The poetics*, S. 30-31, Kap. VII, 2-8.
17. Scherer, *La dramaturgie*, S. 104.

sind.[18] In diese Kategorie gehören z. B. Handlungen mit einem anderen Objekt als das bisher dargestellte. So soll nach dem Urteil Corneilles die Freude zweier Liebenden, die nach vielen Missgeschicken endlich zusammengeführt sind, kurz sein, und er kritisiert Sophokles' *Ajax*, wo, nach dem Tode des Protagonisten im vierten Akt, im nächsten Aufzug gar der Streit zwischen Menelaos und Teuker vorgeführt wird.[19] Sowohl in diesem Streit als in der Freude des wiedervereinigten Liebespaares, richtet die Handlung sich auf ein anderes Objekt als das der vorangehenden Akte. Im ersten Beispiel sind es nicht länger die Enttäuschungen des Ajax, auf die sich die Handlung richtet, im zweiten Fall sind es nicht mehr die Missgeschicke, denen die Liebenden die Stirn zu bieten haben. Sowohl in der fingierten Komödie als im Drama des Sophokles fängt mit dem neuen Handlungsobjekt eigentlich auch eine neue Handlung an, die aber die obligate Dreiteilung nicht verwirklichen kann. Wenn man sich diesem rein rationellen Handlungsmodell anschliesst, so ist die Folge, dass immer ein genaues Zusammenfallen der Lösung der Intrigue, die ja die Handlung zu ihrem logischen Ende führt, mit dem konkreten Ende des Dramas beachtet werden muss. Die aristotelische Logik, die vorschreibt, dass nur dann von einem Handlungs*ende* die Rede sein kann, wenn die Aufführung tatsächlich nicht fortgesetzt wird, benutzt Corneille nur implizit. Explizit verteidigt er jedoch die *Vollständigkeit der Handlung* nicht mit einem logischen, sondern mit einem rhetorischen Argument, nämlich mit der Notwendigkeit, das *taedium* zu vermeiden,[20] damit die delektative Funktion, die das Drama als solches besitzt, nicht gefährdet werde. "Comme il est nécessaire que l'action soit complète, il faut aussi n'ajouter rien au delà, parce que quand l'effet est arrivée, l'auditeur ne souhaite plus rien et s'ennuie de tout le reste". [21] Da *taedium* eine Kollektivbezeichnung ist für eine unbegrenzte Anzahl von Faktoren, die die literarische Kommunikation beeinträchtigen, kann ein Kritiker nach Belieben jede literarische Konstruktion als von diesem Übel angesteckt betrachten. Im französischen Klassizismus traf dieser Vorwurf diejenigen Handlungen, die z.B. der Forderung der *Vollständigkeit* nicht

18. *Théâtre complet,* ed. P. Lièvre (Paris 1957, 2 tomes), t. I, S. 71.
19. *Ibid.,* S. 70.
20. H. Lausberg, *Handbuch der literarischen Rhetorik* (München 1960), § 1244 (S. 823), besonders §§ 268, 538.
21. *Théâtre complet,* t. I, S. 70.

gerecht wurden und das Spiel über die Grenze der Lösung der Intrigue hinausdehnten.

Ähnliche Auffassungen vertrat auch Pels in seiner Schrift *Gebruik en misbruik des tooneels.* Auch er nimmt den Standpunkt ein, dass die Lösung des Knotens und der Dramenschluss zusammenfallen sollen. Dabei bezieht er neben dem logischen Prinzip ("sluiten") ebenfalls das rhetorische Passepartout – die Gefährdung der *delectatio* ("behaaglyk zyn") – in die Betrachtung ein:

Geen Spél ter waereld kan behaaglyk zyn, nóch sluiten,
. . . .
. . . . . zo zy [sic] na de ontwarring wordt gehoord
(*Gebruik,* S. 44).

Er tadelt es denn auch, dass Hooft in seinem *Geeraerdt van Velsen* den Flussgott De Vecht noch auftreten lässt "na Graaf Floris néêrlaag" (nach der Niederlage des Grafen Floris), so dass die Langeweile seines Erachtens den Zuschauer erfasst.[22]

Kommt nun, wie im *Achilles,* eine Intrige zur Lösung durch eine *agnitio,* so wird das Drama darin sein Ende finden müssen. Da Horaz für die Gliederung der Dramenhandlung fünf Akte fordert, ist die Konsequenz, dass im vorliegenden Fall die *agnitio* erst im fünften Akt stattfinden kann. Wenn Huydecoper also die Möglichkeit einer Versöhnung zwischen Achill und Agamemnon im vorletzten Akt unter Berufung auf das Desinteresse des Publikums an dem, was noch während eines ganzen Aktes vorgeführt werden sollte, verwirft, so folgt er genau der Spur von Corneille-Pels. Da die Vollständigkeit der Handlung verletzt wird, wenn ihr eine Handlung mit andersartigem Objekt hinzugefügt wird, schliesst die Beachtung der Vollständigkeit zugleich die Beachtung der Einheit der Handlung mit ein.

Der Aufschub der *agnitio* bis zum allerletzten Moment brachte für Huydecoper die Notwendigkeit mit sich, weitere Änderungen in der homerischen Fabel vorzunehmen, und er wählte dazu die von Achill geäusserten Drohungen, er werde nach der Konfrontation mit Hektor Agamemnon des Lebens berauben. Diese Drohungen haben in der Dramenhandlung eine einheitsfördernde Funktion. Durch dieses Vorhaben konnte der Dichter ja in der Erwartung der Zuschauer eine Verbindung zwischen dem bevorstehenden Zweikampf mit dem Trojaner und dem Ausgang des Streites mit dem Heerführer zustande

22. *Gebruik,* S. 45.

bringen, und zwar derart, dass eine kausale Verbindung entsteht, wobei die Ausführung von Achills Absicht, Agamemnon zu erstechen, durch den Ausgang des Kampfes mit Hektor bedingt ist. Damit ist der Zweikampf eine unentbehrliche Phase im Austrag des Streites zwischen Achill und Agamemnon geworden.

Die Weise, wie der Zweikampf sorgfältig in die Konflikthandlung verwoben ist, liefert ein Beispiel einer Stoffbehandlung, die sowohl auf die Verwirklichung von *Vollständigkeit* als von *Einheit* der Handlung gerichtet ist. Dazu wurde das Prinzip der kausal fortschreitenden Handlung angewendet, ein Prinzip, das Corneille ausdrücklich vorschreibt. In seinem *Discours des trois unités* sagt er, indem er seine Argumente mit zwei aristotelischen Sätzen belegt, dass alle Handlungen eine derartige Verkettung haben sollen, "que les dernières soient produites par celles qui les précèdent".[23] Alle Handlungen, die nicht kausal verbunden sind, werden als künstlerisch minderwertig verurteilt, wobei er sich nicht scheut, auch sein eigenes Werk als lehrreiches negatives Beispiel anzuführen. So schreibt er: "Les Maures viennent dans *le Cid* après la mort du Comte, et non pas à cause de la mort du Comte; et le pêcheur vient dans *Don Sanche* après qu'on soupçonne Carlos d'être le prince d'Aragon, et non pas à cause qu'on l'en soupçonne; ainsi tous les deux sont condamnables".[24] Eine derartige rügenswerte Aufeinanderfolge der Handlung wäre im *Achilles* ohne die beiden an Agamemnon gerichteten Drohungen entstanden. In der jetzt zustande gebrachten Konstruktion erwarten die Zuschauer den Tod Agamemnons nicht nach dem Sieg Achills über Hektor, sondern aufgrund dieses Sieges — also nicht "après", sondern "à cause de" — (erste Drohung), und später aufgrund ("à cause de") der Annahme, dass Hektor der Rachegier des unbändigen Achills entrinnen würde (zweite Drohung).

Da nun aufgrund der Handlungsvollständigkeit die Gesamthandlung sich nach der Lösung des Knotens vollzogen haben muss, ist es letzten Endes diese Lösung, die alle kausal verbundenen Handlungen regiert. Man könnte von einer schrittweisen Ästhetik als pragmatischer Konsequenz der Regel der Handlungseinheit sprechen, da jedes Handlungsmoment die Lösung der Intrige näherbringt und auf diese Weise das Drama seinem Ende zuführt. Wo Handlungen

---

23. *Théâtre complet,* t. I, S. 121.
24. *Ibid.*

dargeboten werden, die keine Phase auf dem Weg zur Lösung, bzw.
zum Ende darstellen, wäre von der *doctrine* her gesehen nur die Rede
von Handlungswucherung, von einem nicht-funktionellen Surplus, das
der Vereinheitlichung schadet.
Dass diese Auffassungen theoretisches Gemeingut waren, beweist
Pels. Klar formuliert er das Prinzip der Einheit der Handlung als eine
durchaus lineare Lenkung auf das Ende hin, wobei Abschweifungen
vom rechten Weg nicht gestattet sind; letzteres selbstverständlich,
weil sonst der delektative Charakter des Dramas beeinträchtigt wird:

> Geen Spél ter waereld kan behaaglyk zyn . . . .
> . . . . zo zy [sic] buiten
> De stóf blyft, én niet klaar verstaanelyk dringt voort
> Na 't einde . . . .
> *(Gebruik, S. 44).*

Zur Unterstützung seiner Behauptung nennt er Hooft und Vondel die
als Bühnendichter versagt haben:

> Mét all' hunn' taal, én kunst . . . . . .
> Alleen omdat ze niet gestaâg na 't énde jaagen
> *(Gebruik, S. 44).*

Er weist auf die Priesterin Zegemond in Hoofts *Baeto* und auf
Potifars Gespräch mit Joseph über das Apisfest in Vondels *Joseph in
Egypten* hin zur Exemplifizierung dessen, was ich als Handlungswucherung und nicht-funktionelles Surplus bezeichnet habe. Dagegen
wird auch hier wieder das französisch-klassizistische Dogma in struc-
turalibus durch das rhetorische Argument der Notwendigkeit, das
taedium zu vermeiden, sicher gestellt. Was Zegemond alles auftischt,
und wie wissenswert Potifars religionshistorische Ausführungen sein
mögen, nach Pels langweile es den Zuschauer, weil dieser nur am
Schicksal Baetos bzw. Josephs interessiert sei.

> Ja, schoon het geen ze zégt geheel verstaanlyk was,
> Het komt tót voortgang van de handel niet te pas.
> Men haakt te weeten, hoe 't . . . .
> Mét Bato . . . . zal énden.
>   't Gesprék, dat Potifar ook voert mét Jozéf in
> Egipte wégens 't feest van Apis
> . . . .
> . . . . 't is leerzaam, ik beken 't;
> Maar 't stoort de kyker, die, verlangende na 't énd
> . . . .

Mét weêrzin aanhoort al het zéggen, hoe vol pit,
. . . . dat niet récht toegaat op dat wit
(*Gebruik, S. 44-45*).

Huydecoper hat bei seiner Strategie, die Zweikampfhandlung in die Konflikthandlung zu integrieren, auf jeden Fall dafür Sorge getragen, dass sein Publikum nicht "met weêrzin aanhoort al het zéggen" (mit Unwillen alles Gerede anhört), denn jede der von Achill an Agamemnon gerichteten Drohungen ist darauf angelegt, dass die Handlung "klaar verstaanelyk dringt voort na 't einde" (klar verständlich aufs Ende hindrängt). Denn wenn Achill auszieht, Hektor zu bekämpfen und Agamemnon bei den Schiffen vorfindet, wodurch er die Gelegenheit bekommt, seinen Beleidiger schon jetzt herauszufordern statt, wie er vorhatte, nach dem Zweikampf, stellt es sich heraus, dass der Heerführer leicht verwundet ist.[25] Dadurch ist eine unheilvolle Konfrontation unmöglich geworden, und ist die erste Phase auf dem Wege zu einer glücklichen Lösung abgeschlossen. Achill ist zu einer Alternative genötigt, und er entscheidet sich dafür, den Versehrten einfach hinzumorden, falls es Hektor gelingt, ihm zu entrinnen. Da dies Hektor nicht gelingt, konstituiert offenbar die Bedingung, mit der Achill die Tötung Agamemnons verbunden hatte, die nächste Phase im "gestaâg na 't énde jaagen" (unentwegt dem Ende zujagen). Weil Achill als Sieger zurückkehrt, muss notwendigerweise Mord als Mittel, den Streit zum Austrag bringen, eliminiert werden. Dadurch entsteht dann endlich der Raum für die *agnitio* als Lösung der Intrige und als letzte Handlungsphase.

Trotz der Intelligenz, die auf die Integration der beiden Handlungen, des Konflikts mit Agamemnon und des Kampfes mit Hektor, verwendet wurde, wodurch in der *agnitio* eine vollständige Überraschung geboten werden kann, hat eine Lösung, wie Huydecoper sie hier entwirft, nach dem orthodoxen Klassizismus künstlerisch-technisch nur geringen Wert. Corneille meint in seinem *Discours du poëme dramatique,* dass eine Lösung, die nicht auf einem konkreten äusseren Anlass basiert, nicht eben von "grand artifice" zeuge.[26] Und später schreibt er in seinem *Discours des trois unités* aufgrund des Prinzips, dass Handlungen sich kausal auseinander entwickeln sollen: "Dans le dénouement je trouve . . . à éviter, le simple change-

---

25. Dies stimmt überein mit der ersten Begegnung des homerischen Achill mit Agamemnon nach dem Tode des Patroklos. Siehe *Ilias* XIX, Vss. 51-53.

26. *Théâtre complet,* t. I, S. 70.

ment de volonté".[27] Achills Bekehrung beruht letzten Endes auf
nichts anderem als auf einer einfachen Willensänderung, nicht, wie
Corneille es vorschreibt, auf einer äusseren Tatsache, wie sie in der
Ilias mit dem Tode des Patroklos gegeben ist.

Wenn auch die strenge *doctrine* Huydecopers Manipulationen mit
dem Stoff deutliche literarische Qualität abspricht, so war es doch
eben der Eingriff im letzten Akt, wodurch der Dichter der Forderung
entgegenkam, die Pels dem horazischen Rat, vorzugsweise home-
rische Stoffe zu dramatisieren, hinzugefügt hatte. Pels hält das Resultat erst dann für befriedigend

> Wén gy die stoffen zo kunt kneeden, draaijen, wénden
> Dat zy nooit eveneens [*op dezelfde wijze,* SFW] beginnen, loopen, énden
> (*Gebruik,* S. 39).

Die hier formulierte Forderung einer freien Nachahmung, *imitatio
ingenua,*[28] hat Huydecoper deutlich erfüllt. Er hat es verstanden, den
homerischen Stoff so zu "kneten" und zu "drehen" (kneeden,
draaijen), dass er unter Beibehaltung der bekannten Ereignisse aus
der Achillfabel einen anderen dramatischen Verlauf geschaffen hat,
einen Verlauf, der den Vorschriften der *doctrine* über die Vollständigkeit und Einheit der Handlung gemäss war.

Erfindungsgabe hat er übrigens auch schon gezeigt, indem er den
Stoff um die Gestalt von Briseis bereichert hat. Aber wie Huydecoper
selbst schon in seiner "Voorrede" bemerkt hatte, bedeutet das anmuti-
ge Frauenzimmer, das das Liebeselement vertritt, hauptsächlich eine
Konzession an das Publikum; ihre Anwesenheit bildet ja genau genommen eine flagrante Verletzung der Handlungseinheit. Vom strukturellen Standpunkt her gesehen ist sie nicht mehr als eine zweite
Zegemond und "taugt sie nicht zum Fortschreiten der Handlung"
(komt tot voortgang van de handel niet te pas). Ihre Rolle ist keine
Phase auf dem Weg zum Spielende, was Huydecoper auch gern ein-
gesteht, wenn er in der "Voorrede" feststellt, dass ihre Person "te
veel is, dewyl hy zelve niets tot de ontknooping van 't geheel
doet"[29] (zuviel ist, weil sie selbst nichts zur Lösung des Ganzen
beiträgt). Achills Geliebte steht jedoch in ihrer überflüssigen

27. *Théâtre complet,* t. I, S. 124.
28. G. J. Vossius, *Opera,* t. III (Amstelodami 1647), *De imitatione,* Kap. IV,
§§ 2-3, S. 177; vgl. M. Fuhrmann, *Einführung in die antike Dichtungstheorie*
(Darmstadt 1973), S. 122-124.
29. Ed. Van Schaik, S. 24.

Anwesenheit nicht allein. Sie teilt dieses Odium mit Ajax, der nach dem ersten Aufzug nicht mehr auf der Bühne erscheint, mit Phenix, wofern er nicht als Augenzeuge auftritt, und sogar mit Ulysses, bevor dieser im fünften Akt auf die Endlösung hin handelt. Ebenso wie Briseis beschränken diese Gestalten sich in ihren Dialogen mit Achill darauf, dass sie eitle Versuche anwenden, den Unerbittlichen aufs Schlachtfeld zu treiben.

Da sie ausserdem fast alle kummervoll auf die äusseren Kriegsereignisse reagieren, die sich ja so überaus ungünstig für die Griechen gestalten, hat ein beträchtlicher Teil der Dialogführung den Charakter einer *expolitio,* einer variierenden Wiederholung derselben Thematik.[30] So lässt sich Ulysses in den Versen 173-192 des ersten Aktes wie folgt hören:

> . . . . Waar, waar zullen uwe vrinden,
> O onverbidlyke, dan eene schuilplaats vinden?
> Wie zal het bange volk, in dien bedroefden stand,
> Verlosschen konnen van des Overwinnaars hand?
>
> . . . .
> . . . . Ach! laat u toch beweegen;
> En denk om 't naberouw . . . .
>
> . . . .
> Geef, geef ons 't leven weer, en toon, in deezen staat,
> Dat de eer uws Vaderlands u noch ter harte gaat
> (S. 38-39).

Und Phenix variiert in den Versen 1313-1320 des vierten Aktes mit:

> De Goden, langsaam in hun straffen, toonen klaar
> Door duizend tek'nen, in wat schrikkelyk gevaar
> Ge ons en u zelven stort . . . .
>
> . . . .
> Neem deez' vermaaningen dan eindlyk wel in acht.
> Zo gy uw pligt tot heil van 't vaderland, betracht,
>
> . . . .
> . . . .
> 'k Verzeker u, uw' hand alleen kan ons bevryden
> (S. 83).

Diese Ästhetik der Variation, des Kopiösen, die so kennzeichnend für das 16. und angehende 17. Jahrhundert ist,[31] vertritt eine ältere

30. Lausberg, *Handbuch,* §§ 830-842.
31. M. Doran, *Endeavors of art* (Madison 1954), Kap. 2 "Eloquence and copy", S. 24-52.

Stufe im Vergleich zur Ästhetik des französischen Klassizismus, in der eben, wie wir gesehen haben, jedes Surplus als nicht-funktionell angesehen wurde. Obgleich Huydecoper theoretisch die gebräuchliche Ästhetik der *doctrine classique* unterschreibt und auch bekundet, dass er bestimmte Eingriffe, die von der *doctrine* her gesehen für notwendig gehalten werden, durchführen kann, fühlt er sich offenbar noch gut heimisch in der künstlerischen Praxis, die zu einer Theorie der Vergangenheit gehört.

Wenn man den Erfolg betrachtet, dessen sich der *Achilles* jahrelang hat erfreuen dürfen, scheint es, dass das Theaterpublikum eine solche konservative Stellungnahme sehr wohl zu schätzen wusste.

TABULA GRATULATORIA

J.C.van Aart, Muiderberg
Academische Boekhandel,
   Amsterdam
W.J.Aerts, Groningen
W.van den Akker, Utrecht
J.M.M.Aler, Amsterdam
Allert de Lange, boekhandel,
   Amsterdam
G.E.Alvarez, Groenekan
Ton Anbeek, Amsterdam
Atheneum Bibliotheek, Deventer
Hans Bakker, Amersfoort
W.F.Bakker, Driebergen
Mieke Bal, Utrecht
W.van den Berg, Utrecht
Bibliotheek Arnhem
Bibliotheek der Rijksuniversiteit
   Leiden
Bibliotheek der Rijksuniversiteit
   Utrecht
Bibliotheek van de Technische
   Hogeschool Eindhoven
Bibliotheek van de Universiteit van die
   Oranje-Vrijstaat, Bloemfontein,
   Zuid-Afrika
Bibliotheek van de Vrije Universi-
   teit, Amsterdam
Elisabeth J.Bik, Tilburg
D.A.M.Binnendijk, Amsterdam
T.A.Birrell, Nijmegen
Wilhelmina J.Bladergroen, Glimmen
G.H.Blanken, Voorschoten
W.Blok, Groningen
R.Boele, Deventer
Books Import Export S.A., Fri-
   bourg, Zwitserland
A.V.N.von Bormann, Bussum
J.Bosch, Amstelveen

Bouvier Universitätsbuchhandlung,
   Bonn, BRD
J.C.Brandt Corstius, Odijk
M.C.Brands, Amsterdam
J.M.Bremer, Castricum
W.J.M.Bronzwaer, Nijmegen
O.M.Brouwer-van Velthooven,
   Haarlem
C.C.de Bruin, Leiden
Boudewijn Maria Ignatius Büch,
   Leiden
M.Buning, Amsterdam
P.P.J.van Caspel, Groningen
H.P.Colmjon, Lunteren
H.A.Combé, Castricum
I.Daniëls-Benjamin, Amsterdam
L.E.D.Das, Nijmegen
A.F.Dekker, Den Haag
Dekker en Nordemann's Wetenschap-
   pelijke Boekhandel, Amsterdam
Department of Comparative Litera-
   ture of the University of Alberta,
   Edmonton, Canada
Jean Deroy, Heemstede
C.de Deugd, Utrecht
K.A.Deurloo, Amsterdam
R.J.J.Doeve, Heemstede
S.Dresden, Leiden
A.M.Duinhoven, Amsterdam
H.Duits, Amsterdam
Duits Seminarium, Amsterdam
H.Edzes Jr., boekhandel, Groningen
A.W.G.Eijgendaal, Leiden
Frits Ekkel, Laren (Gld)
Enno Endt, Amsterdam
J.van der Eng, Amsterdam
Engels Seminarium, Amsterdam
Erasmus boekhandel, Amsterdam

B.H.Erné, Amersfoort
E.M.Evers, Utrecht
M.Evers, Amsterdam
Sjoerd van Faassen, Den Haag
L.Faverey-Zečković, Amsterdam
K.Fens, Zandvoort
D.W.Fokkema, Utrecht
H.de la Fontaine Verwey, Amster-
dam
Frans en Occitaans Instituut,
Utrecht
M.F.Fresco, Leiden
H.Furstner, Amsterdam
E.G.A.Galama, Hilversum
A.F.van Gemert, Amsterdam
Mia I.Gerhardt, Utrecht
W.P.Gerritsen, Utrecht
M.Gerritsen-de Beus, Maarn
J.L.Goedegebuure, Zoeterwoude
B.M.Groen, Vianen
Maria de Groot, Scheveningen
E.K.Grootes, Haarlem
R.R.A.van Gruting, Utrecht
M.Grygar, Amsterdam
J.D.F.van Halsema, Amsterdam
J.T.Harskamp, Londen, Engeland
John Ralston Haynes, Cambridge,
Ma., USA
W.Hellinga, Amsterdam
Toke van Helmond, Amsterdam
R.C.Hoogland-Willeumier, Utrecht
W.J.van Hoogstraten, boekhandel,
Den Haag
B.L.Hijmans Jr., Eelde
Instituut voor Algemene Literatuur-
wetenschap,Groningen
Instituut voor Algemene Literatuur-
wetenschap, Leuven, België
Instituut voor Algemene Literatuur-
wetenschap, Nijmegen
Instituut voor Algemene Literatuur-
wetenschap, Vrije Universiteit,
Amsterdam
Instituut voor Engelse Taal- en Let-
terkunde, Utrecht
Instituut voor Neerlandistiek,
Amsterdam

Instituut voor Romanistiek, Afd.
Frans-Roemeens, Amsterdam
Instituut voor Vergelijkende Litera-
tuurwetenschap, Utrecht
Instituut De Vooys voor Nederlandse
Taal- en Letterkunde, Utrecht
P.A.Jacobs, Naarden
F.Jansonius, Assen
E.M.Janssen, Rotterdam
Hanns Janssen, Buchhandlung,
Bochum, BRD
Astrid Jensen, Veenendaal
H.U.Jessurun d'Oliveira, Schermer-
horn
Danielle Johnson-Cousin, Urbana,
Ill., USA
Martien J.G.de Jong, Namen, België
P.J.Kaaij, Lelystad
Jan Kal, Amsterdam
E.Kamerbeek, Rotterdam
J.C.Kamerbeek, Santpoort
E.L.Kerkhoff, Amsterdam
F.Ketner, Utrecht
J.J.Kloek, Nieuw-Loosdrecht
W.G.Klooster, Amsterdam
Jeannette Klusman, Amsterdam
P.J.Koets, Ellemeet
S.Kooi, Amsterdam
J.G.Kooij, Amsterdam
K.J.J.Korevaart, Leiderdorp
E.Korthals Altes, Utrecht
F.de Kruijf-Toppen, St.Oedenrode
J.M.J.W.Kuin, Amsterdam
G.Kuipers, Utrecht
Elrud Kunne-Ibsch, Amsterdam
Gerd Labroisse, Amsterdam
Chr.van der Leeuw-Moltzer, Amster-
dam
H.H.J.de Leeuwe, Utrecht
H.R.P.Leferink, Peize
S.J.Lenselink, Dordrecht
W.U.S.van Lessen Kloeke,
Amsterdam
F.P.Ligthart, Amsterdam
M.A.Lindenburg, Delft
F.M.Lorda Alaiz, Landsmeer
B.Luger, Amsterdam

F.Lulofs, Amsterdam
J.J.H.van Luxemburg, Haarlem
W.van Maanen, Utrecht
F.C.Maatje, Utrecht
J.A.Mak, Amsterdam
W.Maschmeijer, Amsterdam
K.Meeuwesse, Nijmegen
Meulenhoff-Bruna B.V., Amsterdam
Herman Meyer, Amsterdam
J.M.Meijer, Amsterdam
P.W.M.de Meijer, Amsterdam
C.Minis, Amsterdam
J.J.A.Mooij, Groningen
Ulla Musarra-Schrøder, Nijmegen
M.S.G.K.van Nierop, Amsterdam
F.R.Noske, Amstelveen
Nutsacademie Rotterdam
Martinus Nijhoff B.V.,
    Den Haag
J.W.Oerlemans, Rotterdam
S.P.Olivier, Durban, Zuid-Afrika
H.A.van Oort, Amsterdam
A.J.van Oosten, Amstelveen
Osiandersche Buchhandlung,
    Tübingen, BRD
C.Ouboter, Rotterdam
J.J.Oversteegen, Amsterdam
A.N.Paasman, Putten
Claude Pichois, Nashville, Tenn.,
    USA
J.Plessen, Bilthoven
J.B.W.Polak, Amsterdam
Hannemieke Postma, Leiden
Harry G.M.Prick, Delft
Provinciale Bibliotheek Zeeland,
    Middelburg
G.F.Pijper, Amsterdam
A.Quak, Amsterdam
H.E.Reeser, Bilthoven
M.H.van Rens, Groningen
Karel Reijnders, Overasselt
G.van der Rhee, Bloemendaal
Francine van Rhijn, Velp
L.C.Roosenschoon, Amsterdam
L.Ross, Diemen
André-Michel Rousseau, Aix en
    Provence, Frankrijk

C.J.Ruijgh, Amsterdam
Margaretha Schenkeveld, Amsterdam
Maria A.Schenkeveld-van der Dussen,
    Heemstede
P.J.Schermer, Enkhuizen
P.F.Schmitz, Oegstgeest
J.Schneider, Den Haag
Bernhard F.Scholz, Amstelveen
P.H.Schrijvers, Castricum
M.T.M.Segers, Amsterdam
Seminarie voor Vergelijkend Litera-
    tuuronderzoek, Gent, België
Slatner & Starkmann, booksellers,
    Londen, Engeland
Slavisch Instituut, Utrecht
E.H.Smeets, Utrecht
Jacob Smit, Camberwell,
    Australië
W.A.P.Smit, Utrecht
A.L.Sötemann, Utrecht
Spaans Seminarium, Amsterdam
J.H.van Straten, Oosterhout
J.N.Swallow, Amsterdam
Swets Book Services, Lisse
J.A.G.Tans, Haren
J.V.Terpstra, Roden
Jacqueline Thibault-Schaefer, Sewaneé
    Tenn., USA
R.J.A.Twiest, Groningen
Universiteits-Bibliotheek, Amsterdam
Universiteitsbibliotheek, Katholieke
    Universiteit Leuven, België
S.A.Varga, Amstelveen
J.Verbaas, Ermelo
P.E.L.Verkuyl, Haren
G.J.Vis, Schoorl
H.de Visser, Amsterdam
A.L.Vos, Amsterdam
K.de Vreese, Baarn
G.J.de Vries, Wolfheze
J.P.Vijn, Amsterdam
H.A.Wage, Den Haag
A.H.van der Weel, Amsterdam
H.C.Weiland, Utrecht

Westfälische Wilhelms-Universität,
 Niederländisches Seminar,
 Münster, BRD
P.de Wispelaere, Maldegem, België
S.F.Witstein, Leiden
C.A.Zaalberg, Leiden
E.C.Zeijlstra, Amsterdam
A.J.A.van Zoest, Amsterdam
Peter van Zonneveld, Amsterdam